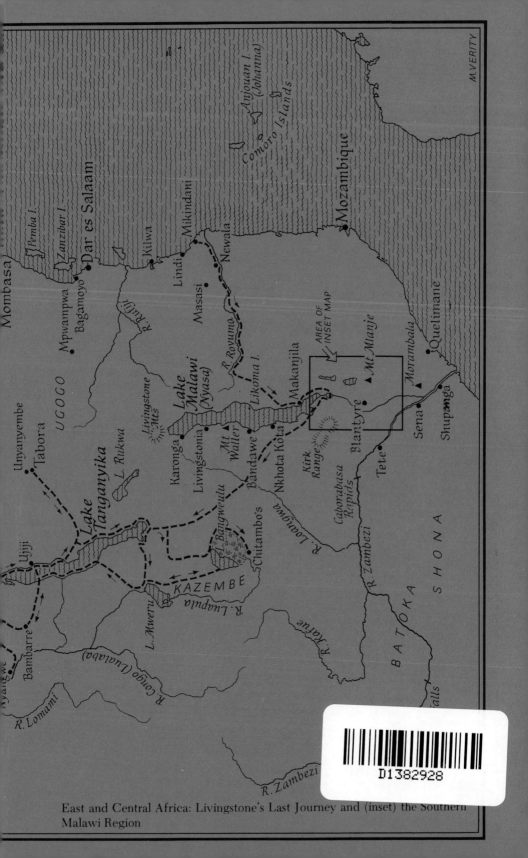

M.VERITY

Mombasa

Pemba I.
Zanzibar I.
Dar es Salaam
Mpwampwa
Bagamoyo

R. Rufiji

UGOGO

Kilwa

Lindi
Mikindani

Masasi

Newala

R. Rovuma

Anjouan I. (Johanna)

Comoro Islands

Mozambique

Quelimane

Livingstone Mts

Lake Malawi (Nyasa)

Likoma I.

Makanjila

AREA OF INSET MAP

Mt. Mlanje

Morambala

Sena

Shupanga

Unyanyembe
Tabora

Lake Tanganyika

L. Rukwa

Karonga
Livingstonia

Mt Waller

Bandawe

Nkhota Kota

Kirk Range

Blantyre

Tete

R. Zambezi

Ujiji

L. Bangweulu

Chitambo's

R. Loangwa

Caborabasa Rapids

BATOKA

SHONA

Bambarre

R. Congo (Lualaba)

L. Mweru

KAZEMBE

R. Luapula

R. Kafue

R. Lomami

R. Zambezi

Falls

D1382928

East and Central Africa: Livingstone's Last Journey and (inset) the Southern Malawi Region

LIVINGSTONE'S LEGACY

BROUGHT BY FAITHFUL HANDS
OVER LAND AND SEA
HERE RESTS
DAVID LIVINGSTONE,
MISSIONARY,
TRAVELLER,
PHILANTHROPIST,
BORN MARCH 19.1813,
AT BLANTYRE, LANARKSHIRE,
DIED MAY 1.1873,
AT CHITAMBO'S VILLAGE, ULALA.

FOR 30 YEARS HIS LIFE WAS SPENT
IN AN UNWEARIED EFFORT
TO EVANGELIZE THE NATIVE RACES,
TO EXPLORE THE UNDISCOVERED SECRETS,
TO ABOLISH THE DESOLATING SLAVE TRADE,
OF CENTRAL AFRICA,
WHERE WITH HIS LAST WORDS HE WROTE,
"ALL I CAN ADD IN MY SOLITUDE, IS,
MAY HEAVEN'S RICH BLESSING COME DOWN
ON EVERY ONE, AMERICAN, ENGLISH, OR TURK,
WHO WILL HELP TO HEAL
THIS OPEN SORE OF THE WORLD."

"OTHER SHEEP I HAVE, WHICH ARE NOT OF THIS FOLD: THEM ALSO I MUST BRING, AND THEY SHALL HEAR MY VOICE."

"TANTUS AMOR VERI, NIHIL EST QUOD NOSCERE MALIM, QUAM FLUVII CAUSAS PER SÆCULA TANTA LATENTES."

David Livingstone's Grave, Westminster Abbey. Waller went to see the newly installed gravestone early in January 1875 with Edmund Sturge, an Honorary Secretary of the Anti-Slavery Society. The words captured the Livingstone legend and carved it in stone.

LIVINGSTONE'S LEGACY

Horace Waller
and Victorian Mythmaking

DOROTHY O. HELLY

OHIO UNIVERSITY PRESS
ATHENS, OHIO   LONDON

Library of Congress Cataloging-in-Publication Data

Helly, Dorothy O.
    Livingstone's legacy.

    Bibliography: p.
    Includes index.
    1. Livingstone, David, 1813-1873. Last journals of
David Livingstone, in Central Africa, from 1865 to his
death.   2. Waller, Horace, 1833-1896.   3. Editors—Great
Britain—Biography.   I. Title.
DT731.L7353H45   1986   967'.023'0924 [B]   86-12624
ISBN 0-8214-0836-4

For
WALTER and RANDI,
With Love

CONTENTS

MAP AND ILLUSTRATIONS

ACKNOWLEDGMENTS

The Frontispiece is used by courtesy of the Dean and Chapter of Westminster; illustrations 1, 6, 10, 14, 15, 20, 22, 23, 24, 25, and 26 are used by generous permission of the Royal Geographical Society; illustrations 2, 3, 4, 5, 12, 19, 27, 28, 31, and 34 are used by the generous permission of the United Society for the Propagation of the Gospel; illustrations 8 and 16 are used by the generous permission of the Yale Divinity School Library; illustration 11 is used by the kind permission of John Murray; illustrations 7, 9, 13, 17, 18, 21, 29, 30, 32, and 33 are used by kind permission of the Bodleian Library, Oxford University. Illustrations 7, 9, 13, 17, 18, and 29 are from Rhodes House Library, MS Afr. s16/9, fol. 79r, 76, 70, 66–67, 72, and 31r; illustrations 21, 30, 32, and 33 are from MS Brit. Emp. s 99n. · The map was prepared by Maureen Verity.

ABBREVIATIONS

Abbreviations are also introduced at the first mention of the source.

BFASSP	British and Foreign Anti-Slavery Society Papers, RH
BL	British Library, London
JAI	*Journal of the Anthropological Institute*
JMPA	John Murray, Publisher, Archives, London
JSA	*Journal of the Society of Arts*
LJDL	*The Last Journals of David Livingstone.* 2 vols. Edited by Horace Waller. London, 1874.
MP, SOAS	Mackinnon Papers, School of Oriental and African Studies Library, University of London
NAZ	National Archives of Zimbabwe, Harare (formerly National Archives of Rhodesia, Salisbury)
NLS	National Library of Scotland, Edinburgh
NMLZ	National Museum, Livingstone, Zambia (formerly Northeastern Rhodesia)
PRCI	*Proceedings of the Royal Colonial Institute*
PRGS	*Proceedings of the Royal Geographical Society*
SGM	*Scottish Geographical Magazine*
RGSA	Royal Geographical Society Archives
RH	Rhodes House Library, Oxford
Uj, NLS	Unyanyembe journal of David Livingstone, 28 Jan. 1866 – 5 Mar. 1872, Scottish National Memorial to David Livingstone, Blantyre, Scotland, microfilm NLS, MS. 10734
UMCA	Universities' Mission to Central Africa Papers, USPGA
USPGA	United Society for the Propagation of the Gospel Archives, London; now at Rhodes House Library, Oxford
UWL	University of Witwatersrand Library, Johannesburg, South Africa
WPRH	Waller Papers, Rhodes House Library, Oxford
WPYDS	Horace Waller Papers, Library of the Yale Divinity School, New Haven
ZEDL	*The Zambesi Expedition of David Livingstone, 1858–1863.* 2 vols. Edited by John P. R. Wallis. Oppenheimer Series of the Central African Archives, no. 9. London, 1956.

PREFACE

Late nineteenth-century European imperialism began to fascinate me when I was an undergraduate at Smith College in the early 1950s, studying with Vera Brown Holmes. I pursued these studies as a graduate student under David Owen at Harvard University, focusing on Africa. As I read modern theories about the economic and political roots of imperialism, I found myself increasingly curious about the ideas and assumptions exhibited by those who championed proimperialist policies outside as well as inside government circles. My research led me to focus on the attitudes expressed by an interconnected circle of British humanitarians—antislavery advocates and missionaries—geographers and explorers, businessmen, men in government circles, and men who believed that the introduction of new technological advances in transportation and communications—roads, railroads, telegraphs, and steam ships—would solve every economic and social problem of the day. Very often these men spoke of the need to introduce "civilization" into Africa; it was their shorthand for a conviction that they possessed the know-how that Africans would—or should—be glad to receive. In fact, they knew very little about African realities.

An important theme running through their discussions was the barrier presented by the continued slave trade in East and Central Africa. British humanitarians saw it as a horrific blot on the high civilization of the nineteenth-century world and believed the solution lay in the introduction of Christianity—pointing out the link between Muslim merchants and the slave trade. British businessmen interested in East and Central Africa saw the slave trade as a block to the widespread introduction of legitimate commerce. Without any real knowledge of the interrelated nature of the slave trade and trade in "legitimate" commodities, many expressed confidence that Africans would soon enough learn which trade was more beneficial to them and cease to engage in any trade in slaves. Those who called for government intervention to end the slave trade—coastal patrols, consular agents in the interior, armed ships on inland waters—saw in its prior extinction alone the hope of "regenerating" the continent. In each instance, the prescription involved greater European intervention on the African continent. By the last decades of the nineteenth century, "regeneration," like "civilization," became the asserted prerogative of European agencies and agents.

This book developed its present scope out of an initial decision to examine the choice of Horace Waller as editor of David Livingstone's *Last Journals* and how he handled that assignment. That research soon made clear that I was dealing with the self-conscious creation of a Livingstone legend to serve a purpose Livingstone would have applauded. Livingstone's life must be seen to symbolize the British antislavery cause in Africa so that his death would create a national legacy to carry on in his footsteps. I also discovered there were two dimensions to Livingstone's legacy. If the first had to do with leaving to his country the conviction that England had a mission in Africa that must not be shirked— to end the slave trade of the Eastern interior—the second was a personal legacy for Horace Waller. Participation with Livingstone in antislavery efforts gave a point and purpose to Waller's life. He encouraged opening Malawi to renewed mission activity and became a propagandist for all the British interests that developed there. He encouraged other men to carry out Livingstone's legacy in Africa. In the first decade after Livingstone's death, he sought to place Livingstone's mantle on the shoulders of Colonel Charles Gordon; in the next decade he turned to Captain Frederick Lugard. Throughout, he remained a gadfly among British antislavery men. To examine what happened to Livingstone's legacy in the years of developing imperialism in East and Central Africa is to explore the activities of Horace Waller on behalf of British intervention in those regions. What began as the story of the editing of Livingstone's *Last Journals* became the history of Livingstone's legacy for the growth of empire in Africa.

I am indebted to many institutions, organizations, and individuals for making it possible for me to do the research, thinking, and writing of this book. I became aware of Horace Waller as an active member of various circles of Englishmen interested in tropical Africa while doing the research for my doctoral dissertation. My next, more careful look at African history came by way of a faculty seminar conducted at Columbia University in 1964, sponsored by the New York State Department of Education and funded by the Ford Foundation. To these same sources I owe the opportunity for a special "reading summer" under the direction of Prof. Graham Irwin of the African Studies Program at Columbia University.

My first research efforts exploring the life of Horace Waller were aided by a Faculty Summer Research Fellowship awarded to me by the

Research Foundation of the City University of New York in 1968. Thereafter I received grants from the Hunter College Schuster Fund for Faculty Research (1974) and from the Penrose Fund of the American Philosophical Society (1976), which enabled me to make further trips to archives and libraries in England and Scotland. An NEH Summer Seminar in Psychohistory and Quantohistory, conducted at the Graduate School of the City University of New York by Bruce Mazlish and Herbert Gutman, helped to sharpen my methodological tools, as have extensive reading and discussion over the last decade with the Methodology and Family History Research Groups of the Institute for Research in History. To my colleagues in those groups, with whom scholarly exchange has ever been lively, I extend special thanks; and I thank Marjorie Lightman for early involving me in the creation of an organization which has nurtured me intellectually ever since.

I am grateful to a number of librarians and archivists who made my research possible in person in Great Britain and, by mail, in Africa. In London, Isobel Pridmore and her successor, Brenda Hough, introduced me to the treasures of the UMCA papers stored in the archives of the United Society for the Propagation of the Gospel and unfailingly filled the many orders for xerox that trailed my visits. More recently, Miss Mary Harrison, in charge of the USPG photograph archives kindly assisted me. Mrs. Brown and Mr. Blumfield at the Library of the School of Oriental and African Studies of London University aided my early searches through the Mackinnon Papers. At the British Library, D. J. Edwards, Esq. of the Department of Printed Books and Edward Telesford of Photographic Services were helpful, as was Ms. C. H. Olorenshaw, the superintendent of the Manuscript Room, who enabled me to find pertinent Gordon and Gladstone letters there and to locate the Gordon Collection at the Royal Engineers Museum at Brompton Barracks, Chatham, Kent. At that museum, my searches were aided by Lt. Col. H. S. Francis, OBE.

I am particularly grateful to Mrs. Virginia Murray, archivist at the publishing house of John Murray, whose untiring attempts to find what I was looking for helped me unearth the story of the choosing of Waller as editor of Livingstone's *Last Journals*. I am also greatly indebted to Christine Kelly, archivist at the Royal Geographical Society, whose knowledge of that collection makes her an invaluable guide, and whose encouragement to this researcher made her a real friend. Also in London, for truly invaluable hints and serious discussions about Livingstone, I count Donald H. Simpson, Chief Librarian at the Royal Commonwealth Society, as a mentor as well as an unfailing resource. I am grateful to the head archivist of the Greater London Record Office for giving me access to the Search Room, where I was able to locate parish records for St. John the Baptist and All Saints, Hyde Park Crescent.

In Oxford, at Rhodes House, for over a decade and a half Librarians Lewis Frewer and, more recently, Alan Bell, have been generous and flexible in meeting my scholarly needs, while Mr. F. E. Leese and his successor Alan Lodge have shepherded my requests for materials, microfilming, and xeroxing with patience, good will, and a kindly attention to many details. At Cambridge, at the University Library, I am indebted to Mr. J. Claydon and the staff of the Anderson Room; while Prof. Owen Chadwick, on more than one occasion, has been generous with his time and help in my researches. In Edinburgh, Prof. George Shepperson has been equally generous over the years, supplying me with information and reading my work. Mr. Ian C. Cunningham of the Department of Manuscripts at the National Library of Scotland, has also aided me for over a decade and half, in locating materials and obtaining permission to copy them. He has responded to telephone calls, letters, and visits with unstinting assistance. I am indebted to Mr. William Cunningham, Warden, and the Trustees of the David Livingstone Trust at the Livingstone Memorial, Blantyre, Scotland, for permission to have microfilmed various Livingstone papers, including the field diaries and journals of Livingstone's last journey. I am also grateful to Mr. P. I. King and Mr. Clive Burch of the Northamptonshire Record Office and Mr. Felix King of the County Archives Office at Maidstone, Kent, for facilitating my research in these places. I am also deeply grateful for the courtesy extended to me by Mrs. Daphne Foskett, a granddaughter of Sir John Kirk, in allowing me to spend several days with Kirk's Papers, and to Mr. Valentine Baker, Esq., for allowing me to visit his home in Salisbury to read the Sir Samuel Baker Papers. I would like to thank Rozina Visram, who allowed me to read her copy of her University of Scotland Master's thesis on Livingstone and India and helped me understand how cross-cultural misunderstandings underlay some of Livingstone's difficulties with his Indian Marines. I must also acknowledge a spritely correspondence with Richard Hall during the time when he was preparing his book on H. M. Stanley.

I am indebted to many librarians and archivists in Africa who helped supply me with microfilm and xerox that I was unable to obtain in person. These include Mrs. J. West and the staff at the National Archives of Rhodesia, now Zimbabwe, R. Musiker and Mrs. Cunningham at the Witwatersrand University Library, and Canon C. T. Wood, Provincial Archivist of Cape Town, who directed me to Witwatersrand University in Johannesburg, South Africa. In the United States, Mrs. Mary Stevens of the Florida State Bank of Sandford and Mrs. Irene Brown, her administrative assistant, are to be thanked for their efforts at helping me obtain microfilm of materials from the General Sandford Library. At Hunter College of the City University of New York, librarians David Lane, Milton Mittleman, Joseph Weiss, and the late Magda Gottesman generously offered their time and expertise over many years.

It is my pleasure to acknowledge the help given me by a number of readers of this book in manuscript form, absolving them uniformly from any faults that remain in the final book, which are entirely mine. Gary Clendennen, the compiler of the *David Livingstone Catalogue*, was one of the first to respond to my work with heartening enthusiasm, and I am particularly grateful to him. Also in this country, Professors Norman R. Bennett (Boston University), James Casada (Winthrop College), Robert O. Collins (University of California, Santa Barbara), John S. Galbraith (University of California, San Diego), Barbara Harris (Pace University), Robert July (Hunter College), Suzanne Miers (Ohio University), and Robert I. Rotberg (M.I.T.) generously read and commented on the first draft of this manuscript, and offered many, detailed, and extremely helpful suggestions for which I am deeply grateful. In Great Britain, Greville Freeman-Grenville, George Shepperson (University of Edinburgh), and Donald Simpson read and commented on the first draft of the manuscript. Professor Dolores Greenberg (Hunter College) supplied invaluable suggestions about Livingstone's ideas on the economic development of Africa. Professors Darline Gay Levy (New York University), JoAnn McNamara (Hunter College), and Marcia Wright (Columbia University) offered important advice about the structure and content of the manuscript in its final stages. To Dr. Deborah Gardner for her generous encouragement at the first-draft stage I extend my particular thanks. To Barbara Wilcie Kern, who began as my student and became my friend, I owe an enormous debt for careful reading, copyediting suggestions, and turning my strictures to her about writing and meaning against me as a peer and a colleague whenever I needed it. I also wish to thank W. Scott Morton for allowing me to use over an extended time period his personal copies of David Livingstone's *Missionary Travels* and *The Zambesi and Its Tributaries*. To Margot Badran I owe the pleasure of a joint trip to East Africa in the summer of 1985, where her fluent Arabic and knowledge of the Middle East added a special flavor to visiting some of the places (Mombasa, Freretown, Malindi, Lamu, Zanzibar, and Dar es Salaam) hitherto familiar to me only in terms of their nineteenth-century past. Deborah Palmer, Jamie

Lehman, Ayna Soskin, and Judi Dovan have my gratitude for clerical support cheerfully undertaken. From my brother Daniel, who has also discovered the pleasures of history, I received the loving support of early mentoring. Finally, to my husband and my daughter, I am especially endebted for gifts of time and love.

Dorothy O. Helly
New York City
October 12, 1986

Introduction:
Slave Trade in East Africa,
the Humanitarian Impulse,
and Imperialism

In the last three decades of the nineteenth century, humanitarians in Great Britain who might otherwise have been inclined to look askance at imperialist ventures clamored for the advance of the British flag over African territory in order to stop the slave trade in East Africa.[1] Missionaries, concerned about the safety of new centers of proselytization in East and Central Africa, looked to the presence of a British consul near their mission stations for the exercise of supreme civil authority to assure them the peaceful conditions so necessary for their work. In the 1860s and 1870s, British humanitarians, concerned about missionary and antislavery efforts in East Africa, understood that any assertion of British power would be at the expense of African and Arab sovereignty. They also knew that political interference would involve them with the commercial and territorial claims of the Portuguese and the French. By the mid-1880s, Bismarck in Germany and Leopold II in Belgium had entered the scene as major competitors for spheres of influence in East and Central Africa. Impelled primarily by Eurocentric diplomatic strategy, European powers sought in Africa useful chess pawns in their games of nationalist competition. In the diplomatic moves that ensued, the clamors of humanitarian groups in Great Britain for the protection of the British flag for their East African missionary and commercial ventures, established in the name of antislavery, could be used by British statesmen to press claims to national—imperialist—control over such areas as Malawi (Nyasaland) and Uganda.

The history of the friendship between David Livingstone and Horace

1

Waller is the history of two members of the British humanitarian community who devoted their lives to the cause of antislavery in East Africa
and, thereby, helped lay the foundations for imperial expansion. By exploring the conjunction of these two lives—one the famed missionary
explorer who exposed the expanse and nature of the East African slave
trade and the other the editor of the posthumous publication of Livingstone's *Last Journals*—we gain some insight into the dynamics of the
antislavery cause in Great Britain and East Africa and its integral relationship to British imperialism. This study consists of the story of that
friendship, the choice of Horace Waller as the editor of the *Last Journals*,
Waller's decisions and omissions in shaping the Livingstone legacy for
posterity, and Waller's continued involvement in humanitarian and imperialist causes in the name of Livingstone and the expansion of British
influence in East and Central Africa.

From the late 1860s, the organized voice of antislavery in Great Britain was the British and Foreign Anti-Slavery Society, dominated by
Quakers advocating pacifist policies in the conduct of foreign policy.
Numbered among the members of the Committee of the society, from
1870 to his death in 1896, was the Reverend Horace Waller, an Anglican
who shared his colleagues' antislavery fervor but not their commitment
to pacifism. Waller confessed to having three heroes—Lord Palmerston,
Napoleon III, and Dr. Livingstone.[2] Each, for Waller, represented what
could be achieved by a man of action committed to a great ideal.

Palmerston's claim to greatness lay in his use of his position as prime
minister to shape a foreign policy that used national power as a force for
moral good. Palmerston's pursuit of a firm British antislavery policy in
African coastal waters won the admiration of Waller, who also admired
Palmerston's broad vision of a *Pax Britannica* that championed the rights
of British subjects anywhere in the world to claim the protection of their
flag. Waller's second hero, Napoleon III, while living in London as the
untitled Louis Napoleon in the late 1840s, had actually been befriended
by Waller's father, a City stockbroker. Once the French leader acquired
his title and his palace at the Tuilleries in the early 1850s, he invited the
senior Waller and two of his sons, Horace and Edmund, to visit.[3] The
emperor's antislavery actions, part of his policy as an enlightened mon-
arch, appealed to Horace's moral principles and political conservatism.

The magnetic appeal of Scotland's David Livingstone, Waller's third
hero, may have been the sheer possibility of imitating him. Livingstone
had captured the imagination of the British public in 1857 with the tale of
his missionary adventures, including the feat of crisscrossing the southern part of the continent accompanied by a band of loyal African followers. *Missionary Travels and Researches in South Africa* embodied

the personal bravery, evangelical dedication, humanitarian ideals, and geographical prowess that both defied and challenged emulation. Livingstone was a hero whose exploits Waller might not match, but he was one in whose path it might be possible for him to follow.

Waller's three heroes had in common their ability to impress their personalities on the world to make it a different place. A modern biographer of Palmerston, for example, sums him up as a politician who believed English institutions were the best in the world.

> That it was his country's high destiny, under Providence, to police the seas, to abolish the slave trade and so put an end to slavery, to assure that a subject of the Queen was safe however hostile or barbarous the region into which he ventured, [and] to take the leading part in bringing commerce, and with it, Western civilization, to Asia and then to Africa. . . .[4]

This combination of patriotism and proselytism stirred Waller's imagination and admiration. In 1859, when he experienced a personal religious conversion experience, the young City stockbroker formulated a new vision of himself in keeping with such ideals. He dreamed he might become an African missionary. David Livingstone's travels in South Africa clearly had set the shape of this goal. The missionary spread the word of personal salvation to those who would otherwise never have heard it; it was a suitable goal for someone himself so newly awakened to the power of that salvation message. By 1859, Livingstone had also publicized in his letters home from the Zambezi his formula for preventing the spread of the slave trade in the interior of Central Africa, legitimate commerce working hand in hand with Christianity. The activity among Church of England enthusiasts for a new kind of mission to Central Africa, a mission which would embody Livingstone's prescription for the regeneration of Africa through Christianity and legitimate trade, would become the vehicle, in 1861, by which Waller would actually meet his hero in Africa.[5] There he would become a friend as well as a fellow worker. By the time Waller left Africa in 1864, his personal experiences had confirmed him as an anti-slave trade crusader, and with that cause he identified himself the rest of his life.

What did British humanitarians like Livingstone and Waller know about the meaning of slavery and the function of the slave trade in the African context? The question is basic to understanding nineteenth-century cross-cultural interactions, yet historians have only recently begun to examine it as an interpretive issue for their own research.[6] One aspect of the question involves the social as well as the economic value of slaves in Africa and the Middle East. Slaves not only provided labor for these societies, but their ownership also gave status and offered a great variety of ways of serving social needs involving kinship and households. Slave women might become concubines and increase the number of the owners' children. Slaves might be employed as domestic labor in a way that emphasized the wealth and position of the house they served. As one European observer in Egypt in the 1870s explained, "The possession of one or more slaves is as essential to 'respectability' amongst one's neighbours as is that of a servant for menial work in a European family. . . ."[7]

The question of understanding what slavery and the slave trade involved in any one place and time in Africa in the nineteenth century includes but goes beyond the problem of cross-cultural meanings. It entails issues of methodological interpretation. For example, it has been suggested that, "The only real chattel slave . . . was probably the trade slave in the hands of the dealer . . . a saleable commodity like any other object of commerce." Once that slave was removed from the dealer and found a permanent master,

> his integration into society as a human being began. He might remain saleable but in fact have considerable freedom, power and responsibility or he might be poor and hardworked and forbidden to leave but be sold only as a last resort just as free man might be.[8]

One recent study of African slavery makes clear the extent to which ordinary patterns of kinship, adoption, and the acquisition of wives and children by African men all involved cultural exchanges that had "precise equivalencies in goods and money." Another historian, reviewing this and other works on the subject, comments that "no slave-owning class, no matter how powerful, has ever made slaves into chattels and nothing more."[9] The authors of the study under review, however, suggest the difficulties in using the Western concepts of property and salability to describe "slavery," as distinct from "kinship," by stating that in general in the traditional societies of Africa

> . . . rights in wives, children, and kin-group members are usually acquired through transactions involving material transfers and in which kin groups "own" and may dispose of their blood members in ways that Westerners consider appropriate to "property." These rights and transactions are an integral part of the traditional social organization of African societies.[10]

Part of the problem of understanding slavery in African societies in the nineteenth century stems from the fact that it was possible to acquire people in Africa in numerous ways. For example, children and even some adults might be bartered as the purchase price for grain in times of famine "to save the rest of the group"; children might be used to compensate for homicides or other crimes and become slaves; or children or young women might be kidnapped and end as slaves. People might become slaves as prisoners of war or as tribute demanded by rulers. Some societies might simply "buy" slaves from their neighbors. In all these instances, people were acquired as slaves because they were desirable: to expand their masters' kin groups, to till their fields, or to become their retainers, soldiers, canoe paddlers, servants at court, or victims for human sacrifice. The demand for slaves was the demand for human resources adaptable to the widest variety of uses, including social and political as well as purely economic ones. Perhaps one of the more striking breakthroughs of recent scholarship on this subject has been the recognition that "Not only were women more common in the African internal slave trade, but they were also in higher demand."[11]

Once acquired, slaves occupied a marginal status as strangers in the societies into which they were sold or given. They were also incorporated in ways that integrated them into their new society while maintaining their "outsider" status. Attached to a kin group or placed within a definite social framework, slaves "belonged" to those who now gave them protection. In this way, "slaves" could become wives, daughters, and sisters; or fathers, sons, and brothers to the "free" of the new society. The crucial difference underlying their status in contrast to nonslaves was that they retained no choice or options to change this new relationship. Yet slaves might act as important agents of their owners, both female and male, and acquire the wealth that allowed them to become the owners of slaves in their own right. This situation came as a surprise to Western observers who noticed it, because the stereotype of "slavery" in the Western sense meant only one thing: low social status, relative poverty, deprivations, and ill-treatment. Livingstone, for example, when staying with the Kololo in Central Africa in 1855, noted:

> The servitude rendered from time immemorial by the poorer to the richer classes cannot be called slavery, though akin to it. The poor man is called the child of the rich man, and their intercourse is on a sort of equality. . . . The poor man has his own garden, hut, &c, and eats his own produce, having the advantage [of] recourse to his master in case of need. The services rendered are assistance

in sewing & preparing skins, in erecting cattle pens, in service in case of going to visit other towns, or in war as squires. The wife assists the mistress in the same way. The arrangement is absolutely necessary for the poor who cannot conveniently be independant [sic]. It is like slavery only in no specified wages being paid, but the obligations are well understood.[12]

Slaves who were captured or bought for immediate resale occupied the most marginal status in African society, coming close to use only as commodities. In this circumstance, they might be used as human sacrifices or killed if the situation warranted that action. In the limbo before transition to a socially integrated status, escape was always possible. A concern of this kind led masters to prefer to acquire women and children from distant areas and to sell off adult men as quickly as possible for removal to distant regions, especially when they were captives of war or victims of kidnapping. In fact, children were often preferred as more readily subject to acculturation to their new homes and less resistant to acceptance of their servile status. The acquisition of people as social and political resources could coexist with the acquisition of slaves as commodities. Changes in the social situation of the owners could tip the balance in the use of those acquired, from one function to the other.[13]

Although this kind of analysis has been criticized as being ahistorical because it is functional, it is useful for raising many questions about the exact nature of the local changes that were occurring in East and Central Africa in the 1850s and 1860s. Livingstone became convinced he was witnessing a significant increase in slave trading in the Zambezi and Malawi regions, and his explanations for the phenomenon were crucial to the development of British humanitarian responses to the situation. The examination of the history of the region during these decades, however, though important to the understanding of contemporary European interpretations of African realities, lies beyond the scope of the present work. Here it is important only that Livingstone believed that the primary cause of the increasing slave trade in the interior was a deliberate effort by two main agencies, Portuguese agents in the Zambezi area and—farther north—Arab slavers, financed by British Indians at Zanzibar, to acquire more slaves for export.[14]

Whatever these institutions constituted in terms of the political, social, and economic changes occurring in contemporary Africa, therefore, for British humanitarians, "slavery" and the "slave trade" meant the use and sale of human beings as chattel property; and these concepts roused great moral passion. At the end of the eighteenth century, the first British abolitionists invested the physical enslavement and trade in human beings with an aura of horror. These evangelical Anglicans and noncon-formists, like the Quakers, viewed slavery as the most blatant denial of the possibility for personal salvation and thus the right to equality in the eyes of God. Abolitionism did not involve a belief in equal status in this world, but it did imply the equality of humanity. By the nineteenth cen-tury, such equality meant personal freedom of movement and individ-ual autonomy—the ability to act rather than simply to be acted upon. By extension, it also implied each person's responsibility for ensuring the enjoyment of these blessings by others. By the second quarter of the nineteenth century, reflecting a growth of secularization in society gen-erally, the notion was increasingly tinged with the belief that ending slavery everywhere could contribute to the sum total of human "pro-gress." The logo of the British and Foreign Anti-Slavery Society, estab-lished in 1839, was an engraving of a black man in chains, kneeling, with the motto: "Am I not a man and a brother?"[15]

Also intermingled with such concepts as freedom and autonomy in the third quarter of the nineteenth century was a keen awareness of how different the modern age was from its preindustrial past when translated into fundamental legal principles. In 1861, in his book *Ancient Law*, Henry Sumner Maine, professor of civil (Roman) law at Cambridge University, summed up this great change with an idea that immediately became popular in intellectual circles. The difference in legal principles that separated ancient and modern Western society was characterized by a shift "from status to contract." According to Maine, persons no longer took their status in law from their membership in kinship groups (that is, acted only through and as members of a corporate body), but were now legally treated as individual, autonomous units whose rela-tions with other individuals could be defined contractually under the law.[16]

Maine grasped what was already a fact in law and confirmed it in theory. This mid-nineteenth-century interpretation of individual action and responsibility had become so commonplace that most British ob-servers, whether explorers, missionaries, traders, or consuls, failed to recognize the implications of the corporate identity and responsibility that still characterized African societies. That this kind of structure had become, as it were, largely invisible to their eyes is all the more remark-able given the popularity of Maine's thesis and the prevailing contem-porary analogy—used at times by Livingstone—that the peoples of Africa were to be compared with the early inhabitants of Britain.

Furthermore, the idea of "progress" also came to be identified in spe-cifically material terms in an increasingly industrialized Great Britain. By 1851, half the population of the nation no longer lived in rural areas;

they inhabited increasingly larger-scale urban places organized around industrial and commercial occupations making new use of natural, human, and animal resources and based on the unique development of Western capitalism. From these legal and material perspectives, nineteenth-century British observers of African societies saw them as doubly backward. Not only did they lack the essential respect for individuals that would prevent the sale of persons as chattel property, but also they had failed to develop in modern Western material ways. Together, these British convictions concerning the failures of African development fed readily into the notion that it was the responsibility of those who possessed the more advanced material civilization to take the lead in "opening up" Africa to the factors identified as key to British progress: commerce in goods, not persons; the message of personal salvation expressed by Christianity; the benefits of the modern, mechanized world, especially the telegraph, steamships, and railways. These ideas held great attraction for the British and for other Europeans (and Americans) who used them, but the extent to which they answered the needs of contemporary Africans was another matter.

If we hope to understand British attitudes toward slavery and the slave trade in the second half of the nineteenth century, and in particular the attitudes of the Scotsman David Livingstone and the Englishman Horace Waller, we must keep in mind that their ideas and attitudes had a reality for them that only partially coincided with the African world they sought to change. The ensuing analysis of the events that led up to the publication of Livingstone's *Last Journals* together with the subsequent use of the legend created by Waller in those pages attempts to suggest the complexities of understanding the African scene through European eyes. As part of this process, it is important to understand the character of these men, since it is through them that we will appreciate their humanitarian concerns and through their eyes that we will see Africa.

Livingstone was born in 1813 and spent his first twenty years in Blantyre, a Scottish mill town eight miles from Glasgow. During his youth, Blantyre numbered some two thousand people, its population making it only twice the size of the large village of Chief Mataka, a major market place halfway between the East Coast and Lake Malawi which was visited by Livingstone in 1866. The scale of Livingstone's Scottish surroundings as a boy, therefore, was in some ways not enormously different from that of the African world in which he spent the larger part of his adult life. The character of his Scottish village, however, was that of early industrial enterprise set in a rural community. From the age of ten, to augment his father's meager income, David Livingstone worked first as a piecer in the cotton mill (piecing broken cotton threads together on the spinning frames) and then as a spinner. He shared a one-room apartment in a multistory building with his parents, his two brothers and two sisters. In early adolescence, he and his older brother John moved in with their nearby grandparents because of the crowded conditions at home. A rich religious heritage and a strong sense of his Scottish forebears balanced the harshness of his material environment. Despite his twelve hours of work daily at the mill, young David was determined to take advantage of the two hours of class offered after work, from 8:00 to 10:00 P.M., to learn Latin and lay claim to a share in the intellectual patrimony of the educated classes.

The pattern of Livingstone's family life was not an unfamiliar one in the nineteenth century. His father played a dominant psychological role at home, and his intellectual pretensions in particular were important for all his sons. David's mother is recorded as remaining relatively unobtrusive; but with an unsuccessful provider for a husband, she had to spend her days making ends meet. She was a tailor's daughter, and one distinctive expression of her personality was her determination to dress her children on Sundays in a style that seemed, to the mill master, to be above their station. From these lowly beginnings, all three male siblings escaped to make their way in the world with some success (both of David's brothers emigrated to North America). The daughters, however, remained single, devoting their lives to the care of their elderly parents—especially their mother—and, in time, to David's children when his wife, Mary Moffat, died.

David's father, Neil Livingstone, was a traveling tea merchant whose lack of business success did not prevent him from playing a vigorous role in the religious life of his small community. During a period of religious revivalism in the early 1830s, he became a member of the new "Free Kirk" that broke away from the established Presbyterian Church of Scotland. His sons accompanied him in becoming members of the new congregation in nearby Hamilton, and there they met settled men of substance who would be of use to ambitious young men.

The shape of David Livingstone's particular ambition soon crystalized; he wished to become a medical missionary. His interest in science had developed from an early fascination with nature and with travel books, but medicine and missionary labor became the fixed focus of his life only after a personal conversion experience. As he explained at the beginning of his first book, *Missionary Travels*, his parents taught him the religious theory that free salvation was guaranteed to all by "the atonement of our Saviour," but, he continued:

it was only about this time that I really began to feel the necessity and value of a personal application of the provisions of that atonement to my own case. The result was like what may be supposed

would take place were it possible to cure a case of 'colour blindness.' . . . In the glow of love which Christianity inspires, I soon
resolved to devote my life to the alleviation of human misery.[17]

David's father, suspicious of science as a rival to religious belief, would
have opposed his son's medical education had it not been argued as an
important skill for missionary labor.

Once the hurdle of parental consent was passed, there followed years
of struggle to earn the money to take the necessary science courses at
Anderson's College in Glasgow. Two years of medical school in Scotland
and a further year of preparation in London earned Livingstone his Scottish medical degree in 1840. More difficult for him were the courses in
theology, Greek, and preaching to which he was sent by the London
Missionary Society. A poor memory for a set text and a rather thick,
somewhat indistinct speaking voice were sore impediments to an aspir-
ing missionary, but in the end his medical training made him too valuable to keep away from the field.[18] By the time Livingstone had left for
South Africa, he had learned that dogged determination in pursuit of his
goals secured success. Yet his trials were great. He could believe that his
success was linked in no small part to the divine inspiration of his goals.

Once in Africa, Livingstone followed the expected pattern of missionary life for a decade, although with increasing unease that what he
was doing was not enough, would not effect significant change in African societies to allow the message of the Christian gospel to be heard and
grasped by Africans as their own. In the progress of his discontent,
he moved ever forward, beyond the path of other men's work. Heading north, he became involved in the discovery of lakes and rivers and
peoples unknown to him and to those at home. By the early 1850s, he had
determined upon a new course. He sent home his family, his wife and
four children, to live on the dour generosity of his own family in
Scotland. He had met the Kalolo people in the heart of Central Africa
and was determined to help them find a way to communicate readily
with the outside world. He was already formulating what would become his singular contribution to thinking about Africa, a challenge to
Europeans to intervene on behalf of African regeneration by means of
"civilization, Christianity, and commerce." As we shall later see, these
ideas did not originate with Livingstone, but they acquired their later
attractiveness to an imperial age by virtue of his characteristic presentation of them to the British public.

Livingstone saw the need to find a "highway" that would lead Europeans into the interior and allow Africans to trade beyond their contin-
ental borders. He came to believe, with all the passion of an early-

nineteenth-century convert to science and industry, that the material problems of Africans must be solved—by opening the region to world (and free) trade—in order to free them to open their hearts and minds to Christianity. As a missionary and an explorer, he would offer an economic solution to the conundrum of material and spiritual change in African societies. Part of that solution would also be a vision of sturdy, Christian Scots, "honest," respectable poor from Great Britain, as settlers and civilizers in the African interior, where he saw highlands as the locations for European health and the management of large-scale agricultural production and food processing by African labor. It was a capitalist's dream: to open new markets and create new demands for British manufactured goods while obtaining in exchange the raw materials on which the new industrial system was being built. The means would entail the use of such new technology as sugar mills and steamships, an aspect of his own European world that excited Livingstone's imagination and convinced him of the inevitable progress of the world once the right lines were followed. Livingstone saw himself in the great reform tradition of his age, and he spent the rest of his life producing the propaganda necessary to move his countrymen to follow his lead. The man who would edit his *Last Journals*, Horace Waller, would meet him in Africa, be captured by his great vision, and spend the rest of his life ensuring that Livingstone's legacy was sustained as an active challenge to Great Britain to link its fate with Africa.

Waller was born in 1833, when David Livingstone was twenty years old and about to embark on his medical education. In contrast to the Scottish mill-town world of Livingstone's early years, Waller's childhood was spent in London in newly built, fashionable Tavistock Square. The young Horace was the firstborn son in a multiservanted household supported by an affluent stockbroker already in his late thirties. When his oldest son was seven, John Waller sent him to board at Eagle House in Hammersmith, an excellent preparatory school run by the scholar William Wickham. The school had a high reputation among men of learning; while Horace was there, one of his schoolfellows was Wickham's own son Edward, later the headmaster of Wellington College and Dean of Lincoln. Other schoolmates as well would become illustrious men of their generation: Dr. Edmund Warre, provost of Eton; Professor Montagu Butler, master of Trinity College, Cambridge; and Canon George Edward Jelf, master of Charterhouse.[19]

John Waller then removed his growing family into the fashionable nearby countryside in Leyton, Essex, still a rural area in the early 1840s and much occupied by gentlemen who held directorships in the East India Company. There, as a young man, Horace developed his love of nature and of all the sports connected with the life of nineteenth-century gentlemen—hunting, fishing, shooting, riding with the hounds, and attending steeplechases. His father apprenticed him as a clerk in the City to begin to learn the stockbroking business. Waller's diaries for these early years show him occupying his leisure time with betting on horse races, attending hunt balls and champagne breakfasts, dining out with friends, and keeping up with the world of painting, music, and the theatre.

What seemed a set pattern of life, that of an upper-middle-class gentleman with a profession in the City and pastimes in the country, was interrupted by events in May 1859, when Waller was twenty-six. On Whit Sunday that year, and presumably during the religious celebrations of Whit week, Horace Waller—like Livingstone some decades before— underwent an important religious conversion experience.[20] The Waller family (somewhat reduced in size by the departure of three of the older siblings) was now living in Cambridge Square, London where Horace and his father had become active members of the Church of St. John the Baptist and All Saints. There Waller found spiritual guidance and religious influence exercised by its incumbent clergyman, the Reverend Mr. Boone, and his curate, Alex Joseph. Waller's relationship with Joseph would be long-lasting, for eight years later he would become Joseph's curate at Chatham in Kent.

In the six months that followed Whit Sunday 1859, Waller's life was shaken out of its well-worn paths and literally turned upside down. In his desire to express his sense of a new spiritual commitment, he was caught up in the excitement being generated in the Church of England in response to Livingstone's call, in December 1857, to the young University men of England to follow in his footsteps. Under Archdeacon Charles F. Mackenzie, recently returned to England from Natal in South Africa, an Oxford, Cambridge, Dublin, and Durham Mission to Central Africa was being formed. A "Great Zambezi Meeting" was held in Cambridge November 1, 1859, to commemorate Livingstone's call two years before and to announce plans for a mission to Central Africa. Scarcely more than a week after Mackenzie was named to head the mission, he received a letter from Horace Waller, applying for a position as a lay missionary. Learning of the relatively recent nature of Waller's spiritual commitment, Mackenzie advised him to wait and see whether his newfound religious earnestness would last.

Ten months later, when he offered his services again, Waller gained permission to join the first party going out to Central Africa. His knowledge of country life as well as his City background proved a good recommendation for his post as lay missionary, for he was charged with implementing the secular, industrial goals of the mission. He was to oversee the work of cultivation, particularly of cotton, which Livingstone had reported as flourishing in the region above the Zambezi River that he recommend as a mission site. As a Livingstone-inspired mission, the group went in the faith that legitimate commerce would prove a powerful attraction to the people whose spiritual salvation was their goal. In late October 1860, Horace Waller, missionary, set out with his colleagues to take up Livingstone's invitation to found an Anglican mission in the highlands near Lake Malawi.[21]

David Livingstone and Horace Waller, men of strikingly different social origins and early life experiences, met early in February 1861 on the East Coast of Africa at the mouth of the Zambezi River. From that time forward, their lives became closely entwined. During the next three and a half years in Africa, a warm, kindly, teasing friendship developed between them that was uncharacteristic of Livingstone's more taciturn relationships with other European companions in Africa, especially those who accompanied him on his official Zambezi Expedition. The nature of the contrast is so striking that it is worth remembering that Livingstone always remained one of Waller's heroes. It may have been Waller's capacity to see men in heroic terms that proved to be the key to the relationship. It is a relationship that the rest of this book will explore.

Among the bonds that united Livingstone and Waller was a strong commitment to bringing to Africa the Christian gospel message of "freedom" and personal salvation. Both held a firm belief in the power of British commerce to create beneficent social change in Africa, a notion that sprang from a shared interpretation of slavery and the slave trade as the consequences of material backwardness. Only introduce a world-scale external market for the products of the African soil and African skills, Livingstone would argue—and Waller would agree—and producing goods for exchange would make obsolete the willingness of Africans to sell people away. Neither would comprehend the function of slavery or the slave trade in the East African economy they sought to affect. Just as their analysis of the ills of African society was based solely on their understanding of the material progress of their contemporary Western world, so Livingstone and Waller shared a commitment to ending slavery and the slave trade—the "great evil" shadowing Africa, which stemmed from their shared religious and cultural commitment to alleviating "human misery." As an idiom or a metaphor, their equation of the slave trade with "evil" resonated with their personal religious convictions as well as with an awareness of the significant material changes that marked nineteenth-century Britain.

Each man had made a break with his early life in order to construct a new social reality for himself in Africa. Each had experienced a conversion which suddenly gave the world new and bright colors, to paraphrase Livingstone, and daily gave deeper meaning to his personal life. The conversion experience led each to seek a new place in the world in order to establish a new identity. In the words of a perceptive analyst of this phenomenon, "To have a conversion experience is nothing much. The real thing is to be able to keep on taking it seriously, to retain a sense of its plausibility. This is where the religious community comes in. It provides the indispensable structure for the new reality."[22] In seeking in Africa a new definition and identity for their lives, Livingstone and Waller were not different from many others in the nineteenth century—explorers, soldiers of fortune, traders, and consuls—who sought in remote regions of the African continent the unknown frontier they needed for testing their personal endurance, shaping a new identity, and achieving fame.[23]

To what extent were such men as Livingstone and Waller motivated by hatred of an abstract concept of slavery and the slave trade and to what extent did their need to find solutions to personal problems explain their behavior? Motives are rarely unmixed, perhaps especially those we call altruistic; yet one scholar who has studied the British reaction to Central African society between 1840 and 1890 has called the antislavery impulse a British "obsession":

> Many of the British, in fact, possessed little short of an obsessional hostility to the slave trade and slavery. The conviction that the slave trade was an anachronism in a world undergoing constant improvement automatically placed the British, as judges and deliverers, in the vanguard of the moral progress of the world.[24]

If obsession it was, the British who ventured into Africa in the name of antislavery did so because, at some level of consciousness, they identified themselves and their fate with the power of their country to effect radical social change there. The role of the British nation in the suppression of the Atlantic slave trade since the early nineteenth century—so often identified in rhetoric as retribution for the national guilt of earlier complicity—became for many both a cause for pride and a spur to further action. For Livingstone and Waller and other champions of antislavery, the reasoning was clear: if it could be shown that the slave trade on the East Coast of Africa was but the smallest part of a traffic in human flesh that flourished on a grand scale in the heart of the continent, the British nation might be rallied to rededicate itself to the completion of its humanitarian task. Such a sentiment, reflecting the philanthropic politics of the day, led Waller to turn Livingstone's *Last Journals* in 1874 into a testament for an antislavery crusade in East Africa.

The conviction which lay at the heart of both men in planning for a broader involvement of Great Britain in Africa was an assumption about the nation's antislavery commitment, based on its past performance. For Livingstone and Waller it was axiomatic that the British flag carried with it an intolerance for the slave trade. This symbolism formed part of the assurance with which most Englishmen called for the presence of their flag wherever possible in Africa. The British flag promised a source of superior authority to which they could confidently turn, a disinterested arbiter, a rational judge to mete out justice as British subjects understood it. British missionaries who sought Africa as a field of labor felt the need for civil order. If the societies among whom they worked failed to provide it, they must seek it from the only other alternative power acceptable to them, the British flag. British traders who brought "legitimate commerce" to Africa, in theory to drive out the slave trade by encouraging the use of human resources at home, also wanted peaceful kingdoms. They faced a similar dilemma. Both, therefore, sought ways of bringing pressure to bear on the British government to provide them with the protection they—like Palmerston—believed was appropriate for British subjects anywhere in the world. Whether this was to be done by establishing a roving consul of Her Majesty's government to the interior chiefs or by asserting an imperial claim over the area, the important end to be gained was that the British nation should take a clear moral position in the face of a grave, continuing evil.

When international competition for territorial claims in Africa took a new turn in the 1880s, the presence of those British missionaries and men of commerce at crucial centers of African life could be part of a strategy of imperial expansion, if Her Majesty's government so desired. Whether it did so or not depended on new political circumstances and the men who made such diplomatic decisions. When the aims of diplomacy and humanitarianism coincided, the extension of the British flag into the interior of Africa to proclaim protection over British humanitarian enterprises became the language of empire. Thus, empire became the means to civil order, though the very presence of Europeans had often been the reason for its disruption. When competition became predominant, those who competed justified their new attitudes by asserting that African societies could no longer be left alone because they had proven themselves incapable of sustaining civil order or taking any other steps now deemed necessary to making "progress" on their own. European intervention, therefore, in the name of antislavery and developing African resources for commercial use, was justified as carrying out Livingstone's legacy to Africa. Horace Waller's contribution to this process was not only to shape the Livingstone legend but also to use it in an active role that furthered intervention in Africa on behalf of the British Empire.

Within this framework, the present study looks in detail at the relationship of David Livingstone and Horace Waller to understand not only why but how Waller shaped Livingstone's *Last Journals* into an instrument for advancing their shared humanitarian aims for Africa and how Waller carried forward that shared vision in his own philanthropic pursuits through the era of high imperialism on the African continent. Chapter 1 examines the formation and development of their friendship and the crisis posed by the entrance into their lives of Henry M. Stanley. Chapter 2 reveals the process by which Waller was chosen to be the editor of Livingstone's *Last Journals*, and suggests the complicated nature of the relationships that existed among Livingstone's children. Chapter 3 explores Waller's overall editorial plan for completing a two-volume work in five months' time. Waller's object from the beginning was to shape an antislavery legacy depicting Livingstone as a great missionary, geographer, explorer, natural scientist, ethnographer, and antislavery crusader.

Chapters 4 and 5 examine in detail the major editorial decisions which enabled Waller to carry out his overall conception of the work. Waller's choices of what to include and what to omit reveal the political nature of his decision to create a memorial powerful enough to carry the weight of the antislavery cause. It is possible here to argue that Waller's vision, in substance if not in style, was not far from that which Livingstone himself would have brought to the editing of his own work. A careful analysis of Livingstone's large Unyanyembe journal, which took his narrative from January 1866 to March 1872 (when he sent it home with Stanley), with the field diaries from which he wrote it up—diaries in large part not available to Waller at the time of editing—also suggests important ways in which Livingstone acted as his own first editor and censor.

Chapter 6 looks at a number of contemporary book reviews and compares two major ones to discover the first public reaction to the Livingstone legend as presented in Waller's edited volumes. Chapter 7 traces the evolution of Livingstone's views about the need for British involvement in Africa, not as the originator but as the propagandist of contemporary scientific and ideological currents of thought. His emphasis on the necessary links between the slave trade and legitimate commerce, slave labor and free labor, forms of transportation in Africa and bringing African resources into the paths of world trade became the formulaic incantation of European intervention, the "opening up" of Africa to Christianity, commerce, and civilization. Chapters 8 and 9 trace one thread of this history, analyzing the role Waller played in carrying forward Livingstone's legacy by means of his close ties to the missionary, antislavery, and commercial ventures created after Livingstone's death and heralded as monuments to his memory. Thus the book ends as it began, with the problems historians face in assessing the part played by the antislavery cause in empowering British humanitarians to take hold of Livingstone's legacy, embodied in the Livingstone legend, in the cause of British imperialist expansion in the late Victorian period.

NOTES

1. Howard Temperley, *British Antislavery 1833–1870* (London, 1972), 264.

2. Speaking of his admiration for Livingstone to James Stewart, whose own hopes for a Scottish mission to Central Africa in 1862 were dashed by his visit to the Zambezi, Waller wrote, "His heart is in the right place and he's the bravest man I ever saw or ever expect to see which for one who has longed to have a tithe of his pluck is a go-and-do-likewise object to gaze on. . . . " Waller to Stewart, October 5, 1864, Stewart Papers, St 1/1/1, fol. 182–85, National Archives of Zimbabwe, Harare (formerly National Archives of Rhodesia, Salisbury; hereafter, NAZ).

3. R. M. Heanley, "In Memoriam. Horace Waller, Fell Asleep February 22, 1896, Aged 63," *Central Africa: A Monthly Record of the Work of the Universities' Mission to Central Africa* 14 (April 1896): 54.

4. Donald Southgate, "*The Most English Minister . . .*": The Policies and Politics of Palmerston (London, 1966), xxviii.

5. Owen Chadwick, *Mackenzie's Grave* (London, 1959), 17. See also William Monk, ed., *Dr. Livingstone's Cambridge Lectures*, 2d ed. (Cambridge, 1860).

6. An important book to begin the exploration of this subject is Suzanne Miers and Igor Kopytoff, eds., *Slavery in Africa. Historical and Anthropological Perspectives* (Madison, 1977). Two critical review essays on the subject which appeared after the publication of this book are: Martin A. Klein, "The Study of Slavery in Africa," *Journal of African History* 19, no. 4 (1978): 599–609; and Frederick Cooper, "The Problem of Slavery in African Studies," *Journal of African History* 20, no. 1

(1979): 103–25. See also Paul E. Lovejoy, ed., *The Ideology of Slavery in Africa* (Beverly Hills and London, 1981).

7. Quoted in Suzanne Miers, *Britain and the Ending of the Slave Trade* (London, 1975), 59. For the multiple uses of slaves in Egypt, see Gabriel Baer, "Slavery in Nineteenth Century Egypt," *Journal of African History* 8, no. 3 (1967): 417–41.

8. Miers, *Britain and the Ending of the Slave Trade*, 144.

9. Igor Kopytoff and Suzanne Miers, "African 'Slavery' as an Institution of Marginality," in Miers and Kopytoff, *Slavery in Africa*, 11; Cooper, "Problem of Slavery in African Studies," 125.

10. Kopytoff and Miers, "African 'Slavery'," 12.

11. Claire C. Robertson and Martin A. Klein, "Introduction," in Claire C. Robertson and Martin A. Klein, eds., *Women and Slavery in Africa* (Madison and London, 1983), 5. Of particular interest in this collection is an essay which considers the methodological problems involved in turning a gender analysis on slavery in Africa: Marcia Wright, "Bwanikwa: Consciousness and Protest among Slave Women in Central Africa, 1886–1911," in *Women and Slavery in Africa*, 246–67.

12. Passage entitled "Moral Status," under date October 23, 1855, in *Livingstone's African Journal, 1853–1856*, 2 vols., edited by Isaac Shapera (London, 1963), 2: 320–21.

13. The preceding discussion is based on the introductory chapter in Miers and Kopytoff, *Slavery in Africa*.

14. Books that begin to deal with this issue include the following: Edward A. Alpers, *Ivory and Slaves. Changing Patterns of International Trade in East Central Africa to the Later Nineteenth Century* (Berkeley and London, 1975); R. W. Beachey, *The Slave Trade in Eastern Africa* (London, 1976); Frederick Cooper, *Plantation Slavery on the East Coast of Africa* (New Haven and London, 1977); Richard Gray and David Birmingham, eds., *Pre-Colonial African Trade. Essays on Trade in Central and Eastern Africa before 1900* (London, New York, and Nairobi, 1970); Bridglal Pachai, ed., *The Early History of Malawi* (London, 1972); and Bridglal Pachai, ed., *Livingstone: Man of Africa. Memorial Essays 1873–1973* (London, 1973). For an outline of the Swahili commercial system of "licit and illicit" trade after the slave trade treaties with Zanzibar in the 1870s, see Marcia Wright, "East Africa, 1870–1905," *The Cambridge History of Africa*, Vol. 6, Roland Oliver and G. N. Sanderson, eds. (Cambridge, 1985), 550–60.

15. For a discussion of the antislavery temperament in connection with men who founded the British and Foreign Anti-Slavery Society, see Temperley, *British Antislavery*, 66–67.

16. Theodore W. Dwight, professor of Municipal Law at Columbia University, in his introduction to the first American edition of the book, noted Maine's historical insight: "The unit of an ancient society was the family; of a modern society, the individual." Henry Sumner Maine, *Ancient Law* (New York, 1864), *xxxii*.

17. David Livingstone, *Missionary Travels and Researches in South Africa: Including a Sketch of Sixteen Years' Residence in the Interior of Africa, and a Journey from the Cape of Good Hope to Loanda on the West Coast, Thence Across the Continent, Down the River Zambesi, to the Eastern Ocean* (London, 1857), 4–5. The account of Livingstone's early life is taken from the introductory chapter of *Missionary Travels* and from Tim Jeal, *Livingstone* (New York, 1973), chap. 1. For similarities as well as differences in the patterns of nineteenth-century family life in England, see David Roberts, "The Paterfamilias of the Victorian Governing Classes"; Deborah Gorham, "Victorian Reform as a Family Business: the Hill Family"; and R. Burr-Litchfield, "The Family and the Mill: Cotton Mill Work, Family Work Patterns and Fertility in Mid-Victorian Stockport," in Anthony S. Wohl, ed., *The Victorian Family: Structure and Stresses* (London, 1978).

18. Jeal, *Livingstone*, 19–20. He had "a long uvula which caused a thick and indistinct speech." Michael Gelfand, *Livingstone the Doctor: His Life and Travels*, 2d ed. (Oxford, 1957), 20. Compare Livingstone in 1852 on "being incapacitated by a disease in the throat for public speaking." *Livingstone's "Private Journals," 1851–1853*, edited by Isaac Shapera (London, 1960), 80 n. 4.

19. Heanley, "In Memoriam. Horace Waller," *Central Africa*, 54. For recollections of Eagle House during these years, see Lonsdale Ragg, *A Memoir of Charles Edward Wickham*, London, 1911. Horace Waller graduated from Eagle House in May 1846. A. G. Malan, ed., *Eagle House, 1820–1908: A Register of the School* (London, 1909).

20. Heanley, "In Memoriam. Horace Waller," *Central Africa*, 54. Waller recorded in his diary for May 19, 1861, "Whit Sunday, what a day ever for me to remember." Waller Papers, vol. 4 (MS. Afr. s16/4), Rhodes House Library, Oxford (hereafter, WPRH).

21. Philip Elston, "Livingstone and the Anglican Church," in Pachai, *Livingstone*, 61–85. Evidence of Waller's application to Archdeacon C. F. Mackenzie is found in Mackenzie to Waller, November 11 and 13, 1859, WPRH, 3. The account of Waller's early life is a composite of information found in his early diaries, especially for the years 1849, 1851, 1856–1857, WPRH, 4.

22. Peter L. Berger and Thomas Luckmann, *The Social Construction*

of Reality: A Treatise on the Sociology of Knowledge (New York, 1967), 158.

23. Compare the discussion of this question in Robert I. Rotberg, "Introduction," in Robert I. Rotberg, ed., *Africa and Its Explorers: Motives, Methods, and Impact* (Cambridge, 1970), 5. See also James A. Casada, "British Exploration in East Africa: A Bibliography with Commentary," *Africana Journal* 5, no. 3 (1974): 195–239.

24. H. Alan C. Cairns, *Prelude to Imperialism: British Reactions to Central African Society, 1840–1890* (London, 1965), 140.

§ 1 ℬ

The Friendship

On his fifty-third birthday, March 19, 1866, Dr. David Livingstone, missionary explorer, sailed south from Zanzibar on his way to the mouth of the Rovuma River on the East Coast of Africa. With grants of £500 each from the Foreign Office and the Royal Geographical Society toward the cost of his expedition, Livingstone had undertaken the task of seeking definitive information on the sources of the Nile River and its watershed in the lakes region of East Central Africa. For almost a decade, the geographical puzzle posed by this question had been the subject of scientific controversy in Great Britain.

John Hanning Speke, exploring the lake regions of East Africa with Richard Burton eight years before, had spied from its southern edge a great lake he called "Victoria Nyanza." He decided that he had found the true source of the Nile. His senior partner on this expedition, Burton, had been ill and had not accompanied him on this excursion from their base camp. Though he did not see the lake himself, Burton decided that Speke was overhasty in making his claim, disputing the idea in his separately published account of their travels, *The Lake Regions of Central Africa.*

In the meantime, an enthusiastic Council at the Royal Geographical Society decided to send Speke back with a new companion, James Grant, to prove his hypothesis about Lake Victoria. Speke reached the northern end of the lake and located its outlet northwards, calling it "Ripon Falls" after the RGS president who had encouraged him. He then encountered difficulties of travel that made it impossible to trace the actual connection between the lake and the Upper Nile. Instead, Speke and Grant proceeded northward overland to Gondokoro in the Sudan, where, in February 1863, they met Samuel Baker, a wealthy sportsman travelling with a young Hungarian woman he had rescued from a Turkish slave market and whom he later married. The Bakers were heading

David Livingstone and Sir Roderick Murchison, attending the meeting of the Geographical Section of the British Association for the Advancement of Science at Bath, September 1864. On the mound, Dr. Livingstone stands left of center with his distinctive peaked cap and an umbrella. Murchison stands right of center, dressed in white, equally prepared for inclement weather.

south along the Nile in hopes of contributing to the unraveling of the mysteries surrounding its source.

Speke and Grant suggested that Baker head south and west, where they had heard tales of another large lake. A year later, the Bakers found this body of water and the waterfall on its east side that formed its outlet. Naming the lake "Albert" and the falls "Murchison" (after the late prince consort and the current RGS president) and claiming he had found the source of the Nile, Baker received a knighthood at the hands of a gratified Queen Victoria. It was to take over a decade more of exploration to confirm conclusively that the Nile originated in Speke's lake and that Baker's lake was a major but secondary source. Meanwhile, the geographical question remained open, and David Livingstone became a major figure in the search for a definite answer.

Speke and Burton agreed to meet in Bath in September 1864, where the annual meeting of the Geographical Section of the British Association for the Advancement of Science would be held that year. Because of the bitterness of the quarrel that had developed between them, there was every expectation that the meeting would be a dramatic confrontation. In the afternoon of the day before their scheduled meeting, Speke—who was staying on an estate of some cousins in the area—went out shooting and accidentally shot himself while climbing over a stone fence. David Livingstone had been asked to chair the Burton-Speke debate before presenting a report of his own on his recent Zambezi Expedition. He was asked to attend Speke's private funeral. In the next few months, he turned his attention to the Nile question and discussed it with the RGS president Sir Roderick Murchison. At a Royal Geographical Society meeting in November, Burton suggested that the real source of the Nile lay south of Lake Victoria in Lake Tanganyika, the location of which he had established on his expedition with Speke. When Murchison wrote Livingstone in January 1865, definitely proposing that he set out to establish whether the ultimate source of the Nile lay south of Lakes Victoria and Albert, Livingstone agreed.[1]

Once Livingstone made the decision to take up the geographical question of the Nile sources, he fitted it into the plans he had in mind for another journey to Africa. Livingstone's commitment to the Nile quest enabled Murchison to help him secure the contributions of the Royal Geographical Society and the Foreign Office; but it still required the private contribution of £1000 from Livingstone's friend James Young of Kelly (Scotland) to make the expedition possible. Had he wished to do so, Livingstone might have planned to go directly to the northern end of Lake Tanganyika to establish whether any water connection existed between it and Lake Victoria. From the beginning, however, Livingstone envisioned approaching Tanganyika from the south. He wrote of entering Africa again by way of the Rovuma River and pushing on to learn whether any rivers flowed northward linking Lakes Malawi and Tanganyika. Once he had established that, he could seek what water connection might exist between Lakes Tanganyika and Victoria.

By 1871–1872, Livingstone had found no rivers connecting the southern lakes of East Africa and, in the company of Henry M. Stanley, he found no river flowing northward out of Lake Tanganyika. By December 1872, he also discovered that Lakes Tanganyika and Albert were not linked. None of this evidence, however, convinced Livingstone that the watershed of the Nile did not arise from the region south of Lake Tanganyika and west of Lake Malawi. The more his travels were delayed, the more intently he brooded upon his own solution to the problem of the Nile watershed. Reading Herodotus and the Old Testament, attacked by fever and foot sores, Livingstone steadily convinced himself that he was about to find the place where four fountainheads arose, the watershed for all the great river systems of Central Africa.[2]

When Livingstone set foot again in East Africa in 1866, he was rather older than most travellers who embarked on these expeditions, but he was also extremely experienced in pitting his survival skills against the uncharted terrain. Since 1841, for a quarter of a century, he had been walking through the interior of Africa. He had crossed and recrossed the entire continent at its southern end, had navigated its rivers, and had the advantage of having lived among Africans during most of that time. No one, including Livingstone, had any doubts that he was a man who could complete the task he had set himself. His choice of routes, to enter from the East Coast and work his way northward from Lake Malawi, was determined in part by his past work. He clung to the hope that the Rovuma River would prove to be a useful water route into the interior, especially since it lay north of the Portuguese territorial claims. The Zambezi Expedition (1858–1863) had convinced him that to achieve the unrestricted entrance of British trade and missionaries into East and Central Africa, it was necessary to avoid the Portuguese. His distrust of the Portuguese developed when officials in Mozambique decided to impose tariffs on foreign shipping on the lower Zambezi River soon after he had successfully navigated it. His feelings turned to contempt when he found evidence that many local Portuguese officials and settlers were involved in an ongoing slave trade with the interior.[3]

In making his choice of route along the Rovuma River in 1866, Livingstone found himself in the middle of an even larger-scale longer-distance slave trade between the East Coast and the Malawi region in the interior. This slave trade was organized by Arabs from the East Coast and Zanzibar and financed by British Indian subjects in Zanzibar. Livingstone's exposure of the volume and cruelty of this Central African slave trade during his last journey gained wide public attention early in the 1870s, at a time of critical importance for British antislavery circles. Livingstone's dramatic portrayal of the facts of the Arab slave trade fueled the efforts of the British and Foreign Anti-Slavery Society to pressure the Foreign Office into more direct action against the sultan of Zanzibar, through whose domain the slaves were channelled for export as well as domestic use on clove plantations.

Historians have generally agreed that the publicity accompanying the final years of Livingstone's last African journey helped to increase vocal British enthusiasm for national intervention in East and Central Africa. In his biography of Livingstone, Tim Jeal emphasizes that Livingstone's primary goal on his last journey was to find the Nile sources, but he also admits that "in time it would be hard to judge whether the search for the Nile's source or his desire to expose the slave-trade was his dominant motive." Jeal argues convincingly that Livingstone was motivated by a desire to show up Burton, Speke, and Baker. That desire was stoked, however, by Livingstone's scorn for the much publicized views of Burton—and later of Baker—denigrating the possibility of African conversion to Christianity. Livingstone understood that public acclaim for his geographical achievements would give his views about Africa important leverage against the more negative ones of these British explorers. To accept Jeal's proposition that for Livingstone "the Arab slave-trade was a convenient excuse" for his plans for exploration is to fail to grasp how central was the choice of Livingstone's Rovuma route in 1866 in his long-held conviction that Africa's future lay in its development as a producer of raw materials for British commerce and industry.[4]

Livingstone in Africa and his supporters in Britain understood his need for recapturing a positive image in the public's eyes. His original fame of the late 1850s lost its luster in the wake of the public criticism that accompanied the Government's recall of his Zambezi Expedition in 1863. The famine, local wars, slave raiding, and depopulation of the Shire Highlands and Zambezi River of the early 1860s, reported by Livingstone and the Oxford, Cambridge, Dublin, and Durham Universities' Mission he had directed to that region, led to highly critical commentary in the press concerning Livingstone's judgment and the use of government funds to open so unpromising an area to British trade. Only a false report of his death early in his last journey began to revive public enthusiasm for the hero of 1857.[5]

The concern for a lost hero roused by the false story of his death in 1867 was revived early in 1872 by the determination of the Royal Geographical Society to send him a relief expedition. By summer, with the tale of Henry M. Stanley's meeting with Dr. Livingstone in the heart of Africa, the excitement reached fever pitch. Eager public curiosity was fed by the publication of the sensational newspaper stories Stanley wrote for the *New York Herald* of his search and finding of the "lost" missionary hero. Stanley's dramatic prose describing the man and his adventures led to a resurgence of Livingstone's original popularity, while the newspaper stories from inner Africa riveted public attention once more on the great Nile question and assured intense public notice for both his travels and the East African slave trade. Livingstone's death in 1873, which became known early in 1874, was equally sensational, involving as it did the carrying of his body down to the East Coast by his African "faithful followers." The outpouring of public acclaim culminated in the organization by the Royal Geographical Society of a full-scale burial for Livingstone in Westminster Abbey in April 1874.

By the time of his state funeral, Livingstone's name had come to stand for the exposure of the slave trade in East and Central Africa. When Stanley arrived in England at the beginning of August 1872, he carried with him a letter from Livingstone describing the massacre of hundreds of market women by Arab ivory and slave traders in Manyema, an area west of the northern half of Lake Tanganyika. Widespread publication of this letter on both sides of the Atlantic effectively dramatized Livingstone's message concerning the brutality and horrors of the interior African slave trade. Livingstone's vivid characterization of the wholesale bloodshed that could disrupt daily life in Africa as a consequence of the slave trade came at a critical moment. His words fed into a well-planned campaign recently launched within antislavery circles to stir up public clamor for ending the seaborne slave trade that supplied the Middle East from the island of Zanzibar and its sources on the adjacent East Coast of Africa. The British antislavery assumption, which proved to be incorrect, was that this overseas demand, more than the use of slaves on coastal and island plantations or for caravan porterage, created the increased slave-trade demand in the interior.

Livingstone's descriptions of the extreme brutalities of the slave trade, drawn from his previous publications, his private letters, and his description of the Manyema massacre, became basic texts for the antislavery meetings held in the course of the next year to sustain public pressure for a new antislave trade treaty with the sultan of Zanzibar. The man most instrumental in mounting this campaign, Livingstone's friend Sir Bartle Frere, former governor of Bombay, was sent by the Foreign Office in late 1872 to negotiate such a treaty. By June 1873, antislavery pressure in Great Britain was rewarded by the signing of the treaty, but success with the sultan of Zanzibar was actually achieved by the direct diplomatic threats manipulated by Dr. John Kirk, formerly of Livingstone's Zambezi Expedition, who had become H. M. vice consul and acting political agent at Zanzibar. Nonetheless, the repeated use of Livingstone's graphic eyewitness accounts of Arab slaving coupled his name in British minds with the antislave trade crusade in East Africa in a more enduring way than ever before. Dr. Livingstone and the cause with which he became identified would thereafter remain synonymous, just as Wilberforce's name had come to symbolize the antislavery cause on the Atlantic coast of Africa earlier in the century.[6]

Within a decade of Livingstone's death and the publication of his *Last Journals* late in 1874, British missionaries, explorers, consuls, and businessmen initiated important new advances into East and Central Africa. Within two decades these activities became part of the European scramble to carve out spheres of interest and eventually colonial empires in tropical Africa. These initiatives, made as living memorials to Livingstone's aims for Africa, established British influence in areas over which diplomats then bargained at European conference tables, bringing under the British imperial flag Zambia (Northern Rhodesia), Zimbabwe (Southern Rhodesia), Malawi (Nyasaland), Kenya, Zanzibar, and Uganda.

Livingstone's legacy—his commitment to ending the slave trade in Central Africa and introducing the message of material and spiritual advancement—inspired his countrymen to follow in his footsteps. It provided a direct link between British humanitarians, advancing in the name of missionary and antislavery causes, and British imperialists, advancing in the name of international competition. The image of Livingstone the great missionary explorer that remained fixed upon public memory was of a gentle, saintly man who, in his relationships with Africans, embodied the highest ideals of human behavior. It was an image first made popular by the journalism of H. M. Stanley in 1872, but its final shape and the legacy for which it became the symbol were given permanent form in the pages of Livingstone's *Last Journals.* Livingstone's death in Africa left to the person who would edit those last journals in 1874 the task of handing on the legacy by locking the image of Livingstone the heroic missionary into the national consciousness. The gaps that were evident between the image and reality, between the saintly missionary explorer and the flesh and blood and all too human Livingstone, made it necessary to give explicit editorial shape to that legend.

✿   ✿   ✿

A missionary by vocation and an African traveller by inclination, David Livingstone had earned his first national acclaim in the late 1850s with a long journey crisscrossing South Central Africa. His book *Missionary Travels and Researches in Southern Africa*, published in November 1857, soon went into a second and a third printing of the expensive guinea edition, selling twenty-eight thousand copies by the following June.[7] It established Livingstone—who appeared in public as a rather laconic Scot who did not hide his relatively humble origins—as a heroic figure in the worlds of geographical and missionary labor. Livingstone's fame derived from a public appreciation of his peculiar brand of piety, perseverance, and physical daring. His origins as a Scottish mill worker, his simple mode of dress, the distinctive blue peaked, rather military-looking cap he always wore, and his direct, plain speech captivated his audiences. His unassuming figure, belying his fame as both a renowned explorer and a missionary hero, seemed to add to his public's delight; here was an ordinary man who had reduced the terrors of unexplored Africa by sheer grit and had preached the gospel in a frank and friendly way to the peoples among whom he passed.

Livingstone understood the value of his reputation. Though he protested that he had not sought it, he accepted it as a mark of divine favor. Accordingly, he set out to use it for the goal to which he now dedicated himself: to end what he saw as an unChristian reluctance on the part of the British nation to intervene in Central Africa. The human misery he encountered in his travels Livingstone identified with the steadily increasing activity of alien Portuguese and Arab slave dealers and their African agents. The solution seemed clear to him: the British government must intervene, and British power must end the slave trade here as it had done on the West Coast. Ending this "open sore" in the heart of Africa, a metaphor used by Livingstone which captured the dual perspective he brought to Africa as a doctor and a missionary, would make it possible for Africans to live what he as a European envisioned as productive, industrious, and ultimately Christian lives.

Livingstone's ideal solution was the presence of individual British colonists, missionaries, and merchants—and friendly government consuls—who were free to act in the "English name" and by their example help release Africans from both material and spiritual bondage. At various times, he prescribed colonies of sturdy Scots or Christianized West Africans to act as catalysts to set in motion the regeneration of an African Christian society. He saw no contradiction between introducing a British presence and at the same time encouraging Christianized Africans who would follow the British model of "work" and "progress," but act on their own behalf.

Livingstone's vision of African regeneration provided an important link between the ideas propounded by abolitionist Thomas Fowell Buxton in the late 1830s and early 1840s and the ideas of British expansionists of the 1870s and 1880s. Buxton called for British intervention in Africa to introduce free trade and legitimate commerce, working as equal partners with Christianity for the salvation of its inhabitants. He envisioned Africans as producers of the raw materials that the industrializing world would need.[8] Later imperialists, such as Sir William Mackinnon or Buxton's grandson and namesake, Sir Thomas Fowell Buxton, would also view commerce as a civilizing force needed to create a Christian society in Africa. They too saw Africans as suppliers of the products of the soil, but they also saw a need to create a protected field of enterprise to make this economic system work. Both generations of interventionists, Eurocentric in their assumptions, viewed such an economic relationship between Africa and the European world as a fair exchange. If anything, they were convinced that the greater value—in terms of the changes that they would experience—would accrue to the Africans who took part in the exchange.

Once Livingstone the man was gone, Livingstone the Victorian hero provided the ideological bridge which interpreted British intervention in Africa, whether by missionary, consul, or merchant, as a national duty, the just use of great national power for humanitarian ends. That powerful myth was embodied in the *Last Journals of David Livingstone*. The theme that emerged from these journals was that of a great missionary traveller whose geographical and scientific exploits, though remarkable, paled in importance compared to the selfless dedication to the moral and material regeneration of the people of Africa. This theme was Livingstone's legacy to the cause of Britain in Africa. To honor Livingstone was to rededicate the nation to a great moral mission, a true battle against the forces of evil in the world, the destruction of the hydra-headed slave trade. To honor the memory of that great hero was to intervene in Africa in the name of British humanitarian goals.

By the time Livingstone's body was laid to rest in Westminster Abbey on April 18, 1874, the events of his last journey had become matters of lively interest to a large cross section of the literate British public. The mythic qualities of Livingstone, the Victorian missionary hero, first shaped by the prose of H. M. Stanley in the pages of the *New York Herald* in July and August 1872, took final form from his pen in the book *How I Found Livingstone*, published in November 1872. Stanley's journalistic triumph was to build upon the renewed public enthusiasm for Livingstone so completely that his image of the heroic missionary explorer effaced from public memory the more critical public assessment

Horace Waller, c. 1860. Just before leaving for Central Africa as a lay missionary in October 1860, Waller already had the beard that would remain a characteristic feature the rest of his life. Six-feet tall, lanky, and determined to set a new life course for himself, he joined the first UMCA party for a farewell service at Canterbury Cathedral and sailed for Cape Town. He knew he would meet his hero, David Livingstone, on the Zambezi.

of Livingstone of the mid-1860s. The popular image Stanley conjured up was of a white-haired, humble but determined Christian missionary, travelling alone in the dangerous interior of a "dark" and often treacherous continent, single-handedly waging a campaign against evil that was embodied in barbarism and slavery, while brilliantly solving Africa's geographical riddles. By his saintliness, the missionary hero contributed to the first ties of friendly contact wherever he went, while his complete dedication to his mission excluded all personal considerations of safety, health, comfort, and kin. He was scarcely a flesh and blood man any longer; he was a truly powerful legend.[9]

❁   ❁   ❁

The Reverend Horace Waller was the man whose task it became to engrave that heroic myth for posterity in the volumes of the *Last Journals*. The task could not have fallen to more willing hands. A self-confessed enthusiast, Waller called himself "a philanthropist at heart of the most florid order."[10] Livingstone had become a compelling hero to Waller fourteen years before Waller was chosen to be the editor of Livingstone's last journals.

By coincidence, both Livingstone and Waller entered Africa for the first time at the age of twenty-seven. Although their experiences were separated by two decades, the initial impact of that land and its people changed both their lives. It was the capstone of Waller's conversion from businessman to missionary to meet his hero on the shores of Africa in February 1861, and their friendship—like Africa itself—ultimately determined the shape of the rest of his life.[11]

Although Waller never returned to Africa after his three and a half years there as a lay missionary, his relationship with David Livingstone continued and deepened, as did his commitment to what became their shared goals for African development. Against a background of African scenes that remained vivid in Waller's memory for the rest of his life—on the Zambezi and Shire rivers and in the highlands beyond them—Waller and Livingstone talked for hours on end about the strategies Englishmen might use to bring about the regeneration of Africa. To the editing of Livingstone's *Last Journals*, Waller brought the wealth of these experiences in Africa and his dedication to the eradication of what he, like Livingstone, believed to be the root of all evil there: the continuing trade in slaves between the interior and the East Coast. When the possibility of becoming the editor of these journals arose, with a publication deadline a few months away, Waller was well prepared, not only to undertake the task but also to impress upon the finished work his personal appreciation of Livingstone the missionary hero. The choices Waller made as editor reflected his understanding of the politics of the philanthropic world of his day and his mature opinions about Livingstone and Livingstone's Africa.

Waller also brought to the editing of Livingstone's *Last Journals* the special friendship which had developed between the missionary hero and the ardent hero-worshipper. Their friendship was important to Waller's choice of a career after returning from Africa, and it shaped the place Waller made for himself in British antislavery and missionary circles. The friendship had matured and shifted over time from that of master and disciple to that of partners in the common cause that obsessed them. The quality of Livingstone's regard for the younger man whose background was so different from his own was marked by playful humor, a trace of kindly condescension, and sincere regard. The extraordinary nature of their relationship can be measured only against the awkward, uncommunicative quality of Livingstone's ties with the other Europeans with whom he worked in Africa.

Especially on the Zambezi Expedition, during which Livingstone was at times surrounded by European colleagues, including his younger brother Charles, his interactions with those who reported to him were at best strained and more often disastrous. He exchanged bitter words with his brother, dismissed three members of the expedition—for failing to take orders, for cheating him of supplies, and for laziness—and treated with small consideration even his closest associate, Dr. John Kirk. The Anglican missionaries he had encouraged to come to Africa were not spared his biting criticisms. His fellow Scotsman James Stewart, who sought out Livingstone on the Zambezi for advice about establishing a Scottish mission there, became so disappointed and discouraged and so disgruntled with the great missionary hero that he threw his copy of *Missionary Travels* into the river in disgust. Most historians and biographers, with the exception of Tim Jeal, have tended to gloss over Livingstone's inability to get along with other Europeans on the grounds that his strength lay in his facility for creating trust and establishing leadership with Africans.[12] The character of Livingstone's various relationships with both Europeans and Africans will be the subject of following chapters. Here what is significant is simply the contrast between Livingstone's general attitude toward his European colleagues in Africa and his specific enjoyment of his developing friendship with Horace Waller.

The course of their friendship is revealed by a decade-long correspondence (1862–1872), letters in which Livingstone was at his most informal—teasing, lively, and amiable—but letters which also show him as serious and concerned about the views of the younger man. One fairly long sample of this correspondence provides an idea of the texture of the relationship they had established. I will explore it in some detail for what it reveals about both men. It is a letter Livingstone wrote to Waller, begun shortly after the Welsh-born "American" journalist Stanley had discovered him at Ujiji, an Arab trading center on Lake Tanganyika, in November 1871. Stanley had, quite literally, relieved him, supplying him with all kinds of goods and with news of the outside world as well, bringing him a batch of magazines and letters that had been long delayed in reaching him. Livingstone wrote:

My dear Waller

I recieved [sic] two letters from you in February last [and] answered them, but in September I found them in the spot they were left. The Post Office authorities in Manyuema had neglected to furnish the postman with velocipedes, and as I never saw these machines I could not urge their adoption and brought the answers to Ujiji myself.[13] . . . you mention your exertions for a missionary bishop for Madagascar. . . . It is a pity that you do not see that sending a bishop into a part where missionaries have laboured with great success . . . to steal the flocks . . . would be a piece of monstrous dishonesty. . . . What an out-rage to intrude into this field in Madagascar and so many millions of Heathen untaught elsewhere. I am ashamed of you but you are only a poor Tozerite. I thank you heartily for offering to help me at "proof" &c but I fear that you have not yet won your spurs as corrector of the press. What a hash "Rev Horace Waller" made of Young's book. You saw the review of course. Could you not manage a few pages for him without "Buffon's dogs & tails curled over the left side" "flutter of the Union Jack annually decimates"–what on earth do you mean? . . . But I thank you for your offer very sincerely. I cannot for a moment doubt your willingness to aid me in every way you can. . . . Give my kind love to your wife—she must be a brave woman to take charge of one like you. . . .

19th February 1872, Unyanyembe, P.S. All your past misdemeanours faults failings and nonsense of every degree are hereby pardoned and obliterated. I could trust you even in sight of a dead bear. . . . I got the boots you most kindly sent. . . . We came here yesterday and I who had sore feet blessed you when I found your most considerate and welcome present. I voted you to be a gentleman and if you have really become a parson I shall vote you to be a bishop . . . whenever my vote is asked. . . . I have just seen Young's book. He did his work right nobly & well and feel grateful to him. . . . He writes like a gentleman. . . .[14]

Rev. Henry Rowley, c. 1860. After earlier being a Baptist and a Quaker, Rowley joined the first UMCA party as an Anglican deacon with High Church views in 1860. He was soon writing friends that Livingstone's enthusiastic claims for the Zambezi as a water route into the interior and for the cotton of the Shire Highlands were not well founded. Rowley published a book about his Central African missionary experiences in 1867 and worked for the Society for the Propagation of the Gospel for thirty-six years.

The book in question was *The Search after Livingstone*, by Edward D. Young, published in 1868. It was the journal of a coastguardsman who asked for leave from his service aboard the Prince of Wales' yacht in 1867 to volunteer to lead an expedition to Africa to check out a report of Livingstone's murder near Lake Malawi the year before. Young had joined Livingstone's Zambezi Expedition in 1862, had met Waller at that time, and came forward in 1867 at Waller's suggestion.[15] Young's journey traced Livingstone's steps around the southern end of Lake Malawi in order to prove false the story of his death; and Waller undertook to revise Young's expedition journals for publication. Livingstone's first censure of Waller for the book's style, writing from Ujiji, occurred when his acquaintance with the work came from some reviewer's criticisms. Many months later, when Livingstone and Stanley arrived at Unyanyembe, east of Lake Tanganyika, Livingstone found more mail and packages awaiting him. For the first time, he saw Young's book and, whatever he may have thought of its style, he expressed his appreciation for the effort that had gone into the search expedition.

Livingstone's acerbic comments about the possible Anglican bishopric for Madagascar were particularly pointed because he not only deeply disapproved of one missionary society's "poaching" on the province of another, but he also particularly disliked the candidate in question, the Reverend Henry Rowley. Another member of the (Oxford, Cambridge, Dublin, and Durham) Universities' Mission to Central Africa in the early 1860s, Rowley wrote, and allowed to be published, his strongly held view that Livingstone had misled both the missionaries and the nation about the navigability of the Zambezi River. To the extent that Livingstone's enthusiasm and concern for making the Zambezi a highway into the interior had led him into sweeping pronouncements on the subject, Rowley felt justified in making these accusations; for the same reasons, in defending himself against these attacks, Livingstone was furious at Rowley's audacity. But Rowley was undaunted at taking on a national hero. In the early 1860s, he wrote a friend at the Cape, defending warlike acts of his missionary colleagues—who had taken sides against the slave-trading Yao—on the grounds that they were merely following the precedent set by Livingstone when he was with them in the Shire Highlands. Rowley was unrepentant when the letter— which caused a furor—was published in a Cape newspaper. Early in 1865, Livingstone's deep distaste for this former dissenter turned High Church Anglican was compounded when an official Portuguese newspaper in Lisbon reprinted Rowley's letter implicating Livingstone in missionary aggression. The aim of the Portuguese was to discredit Livingstone's public indictment of their African slaving activities, which had formed a prominent part of his British Association speech at Bath the previous year.[16]

Bishop William G. Tozer, referred to in Livingstone's letter, had also publicly criticized Livingstone in the mid-1860s for misleading missionary circles in Britain about the geography, terrain, and healthfulness of the area to which he directed the first UMCA missionaries. Like Rowley, Tozer maintained that Livingstone had taken the lead in the first missionary fighting which occurred in the Shire Highlands under his predecessor, Bishop Mackenzie. Livingstone's dislike of Tozer was so great that, in his book *The Zambesi and Its Tributaries*, he compared the bishop's decision to transfer the Universities' Mission from Central Africa to Zanzibar in 1864 to what it would have been like if St. Augustine had decided to locate himself "on one of the Channel islands when sent to christianize the natives of Central England."[17] To call Waller a Tozerite was outrageous and a prime example of Livingstone's extremely wry humor. He was well aware that Waller disliked Tozer as much as he did, and that Waller had not forgiven the bishop for removing the mission from its original location in the Shire region and for refusing to accept the care of a few women and children dependent upon the original mission.[18]

The use of quotation marks encircling the phrase "the Rev Horace Waller" was Livingstone's way of responding to the news that Waller had taken Anglican orders in December 1867, another piece of information brought him in the delayed letters delivered by Stanley. The mention of Buffon's dogs referred to a long-standing private joke between the two, sustained since their Zambezi days, on the question of whether all dogs' tails curled to the left, as the eighteenth-century French naturalist Buffon had maintained.[19]

Waller's missionary experience was marked by many anxieties and sorrows as well as close friendships and good fellowship. Bishop Mackenzie, with whom he had entered Central Africa, and four of his missionary colleagues died after sickness and fever. Waller felt impelled to resign from the mission when its new head arrived from England, because he so strongly disagreed with the policies of the Bishop Tozer. Vitally important to Waller's future role as Victorian Africanist in humanitarian circles was the fact that he had witnessed at firsthand the brutality of the Portuguese slave trade, and—good Palmerstonian that he was—left Central Africa convinced that British intervention was the answer to African salvation. Full of hardships and tragedy though they were, Waller enjoyed his African years. As a lay missionary, he was able to act out his dreams of sharing the gospel message of salvation with those who had not heard it. In a new location, among strangers, he was able to continue the process by which he freed himself from his past as a stockbroker. Accepted on these new terms, he had the opportunity to begin thinking about a career more in keeping with his changed aspirations. Back in England in 1864, Waller was unable to make plans for his future until he found the means—as we shall see—of permanently linking his life to the cause of British antislavery in East Africa.

While Livingstone was in England in 1864–1865, writing his book on the Zambezi Expedition and arranging for his return to East Africa, he kept up his friendship with Waller. It was a natural continuation of the friendship they had been able to establish during the time spent together, characterized by story telling, teasing, and philosophizing about the problems of evangelizing the peoples of Africa. In Waller, Livingstone found a ready audience for the wealth of stories he liked to tell about his previous adventures in Southern Africa. Each man enjoyed the other's sense of humor and delighted in light, mutual banter. Waller teased Livingstone about a predilection for poaching, in response to stories about Livingstone's boyhood in Scotland. Livingstone teased Waller about his enthusiasm for hunting and shooting (as when he referred to trusting Waller with a "dead bear") and for his "young-man-about-town" manner (when both were back in England). Livingstone also chided his friend that any man in his early thirties who had no wife or settled career was not yet a responsible person. Since Waller married in 1869, Livingstone would have learned about his wife's existence only from the mail delivered by Stanley. This news precipitated the comment about how "brave" she must be "to take on one like you."[20]

While in Africa together, the two men had shared important experiences, including the unexpected death of Livingstone's wife Mary, shortly after she rejoined him in 1862. There occurred a major dispute between them, a year later, over the activities of a small number of Livingstone's Kololo followers. These were a few of the Africans who had decided not to return to their Central African home, but to stay behind and settle on the Shire River, near the UMCA mission station. The missionaries viewed them as very troublesome because of their effective aggrandizing activities, undertaken in the eyes of the local people as "Black Englishmen." They rescued slaves, just as the English had, by means of guns given them by Livingstone, only to set themselves up as local chiefs on the basis of these ready-made followers. When Waller undertook to complain to Livingstone that it was his responsibility to discipline the Kololo, Livingstone replied that he saw no proof that they had committed the crimes specifically complained about by the missionaries. The measure of the regard Livingstone had come to have for Waller by April 1863, when this matter reached the proportions of an open dispute, is clear from the tone of his written apology:

> My dear Waller,
>
> My conscience reproved me for saying some things to you which I ought not to have said but I was too much of an ass to confess it.[21]

What is striking about this contrite note is that Livingstone was apparently never able to speak as directly and simply to the Europeans of his own party, whose peace had been marred by many unpleasant quarrels. Livingstone's intimacy with Waller may have deepened because of his appreciation of the younger man's ardent admiration and real affection for him. Waller must have seemed to Livingstone an open, warm-hearted, truly dedicated younger man whose level of cultivation and status as a gentleman gave a pleasurable tinge to his obvious desire "to sit at his hero's feet." Waller's loyalty and sympathy were so forthright and generally so uncritical that Livingstone, otherwise rather laconic and prickly with his European companions in Africa, was put at his complete ease. Among the more complicated and tense relationships of the missionaries and the members of Livingstone's own expedition on the Zambezi, Waller's gift for friendship and loyalty marked him as unique.

One exception to Waller's amiable capacity to get along with people who bitterly criticized each other—like the missionary Rowley and Livingstone—was his unhappy relationship with Bishop Tozer. When Tozer arrived in Central Africa, he found a beleaguered mission party trying desperately to sustain themselves in the year and a half since the death of their episcopal leader. Tozer's response was a rather dry account taking and the decision to move on, repudiating any official responsibility for the small number of dependent women and children who had been attached to the mission when they were rescued from slavers in the Shire Highlands by his predecessor, Bishop Mackenzie. In contrast to Tozer's cool appraisal of the situation, Waller saw the sending of these dependents back to what he was sure would be immediate reenslavement as symbolic of a pronouncement on his own reach for freedom from the bonds of the past. The depth of his feeling was marked by his willingness to resign over this issue from the very position as lay missionary which had emblemized his own changed status. He turned to Livingstone for assistance in relocating them to safety. Livingstone eventually agreed, adding to Waller's small group a larger number of young men, Africans whom Tozer had at first consented to take along but then found it expedient to leave behind when he departed for Zanzibar. Before returning home from South Africa in June 1864, Waller placed one young girl in an orphanage and the rest of his charges as servants with families in Cape Town.[22]

✿   ✿   ✿

In England, Waller and Dr. John Kirk—the medical botanist of Livingstone's recent expedition and a man Waller's age—were the only "Zambezi" men Livingstone saw with any frequency in 1864–1865. While a tone of mutual bantering continued to characterize their relationship, Livingstone put Waller to work for him in a number of ways. He asked him to make drawings for the engraver at work on his book on the *Zambesi and Its Tributaries*, consulted with him on the spelling and meaning of Yao and Mang'anja words, solicited his help in reading proof and making suggestions about passages that concerned the Universities' Mission, and sent him on various errands in London. One of the first commissions Waller undertook was to sketch a head of an African woman with a lip ring, huge enough to be visible to the larger part of Livingstone's audience during his talk at Bath September 19, 1864. For the *Zambesi and Its Tributaries*, Waller made drawings of an African cotton loom, a smelting furnace, and a pair of bellows.[23]

Because of Livingstone's strained relations with Bishop Tozer and the controversy triggered by Rowley over his responsibility for the fighting engaged in by the first UMCA party under Bishop Mackenzie, Livingstone looked to Waller for help writing passages which would deal with the missionaries. He was especially concerned about the period during which he had led them to find a site for a station in the Shire Highlands, when together they released slaves from their captors and engaged in an exchange of gunfire with marauding groups. Livingstone sent Waller proof "which you may amend if you can & make faces at if you dare— but any fault or improvement if pointed out will much oblige. . . ."[24] Two weeks after this note, Livingstone acknowledged, "I have put in the lines you gave. . . . If you think anything wrong I don't [sic] want that, but I think I need not submit to the assertions of old Tozer & say nothing."[25]

In turn, Waller sought Livingstone's aid in thinking about establishing a new career. Livingstone was direct and sympathetic. He wrote him, "Had you been of my party I should have tried to get a consulate for you."[26] By his own admission Livingstone was able—at least indirectly— to help his brother Charles get an appointment as British consul at Fernando Po in West Africa, and he vigorously pressed the case for Kirk's

Rev. Charles Frederick Mackenzie, c. 1860. Only eight years older than Waller, Mackenzie joined Bishop Colenso of Natal in 1855 after earning high honors at Cambridge University. Consecrated the first missionary bishop to Central Africa in January 1861, he was dead a year later. To Livingstone and Waller he symbolized the continued hope that, through European agency, Christianity and commerce would be introduced into the Malawi region.

Bishop William G. Tozer. Disapproved of by Livingstone for having relocated the UMCA mission in Zanzibar in 1864 and disliked by Waller for having "repudiated" the women and children brought under the mission's protection by Bishop Mackenzie, Tozer nonetheless managed to establish a solid base for this relatively new missionary venture before forced to retire from the field in April 1873 because of ill health.

acquiring a consular post. He did try to aid Waller. He presumed upon his acquaintance with Baroness Angela Burdett-Coutts and personally, though unsuccessfully, wrote her friend Rajah Brooke of Sarawak on Waller's behalf.[27] Even as he was about to embark from India to East Africa, early in January 1866, Livingstone sent Kirk a few sentences of recommendation on behalf of Waller to share with William H. Wylde, the officer in charge of antislave trade affairs at the Foreign Office. Livingstone's opinion of Waller was clear: "If Waller should get the appointment on the west coast I think he would always act consistently against slavery & the slave trade. . . . I don't know anyone on whose principles I could rely more confidently. . . ."[28]

While Waller searched for a new direction for a career at home, his friendship and correspondence with John Kirk, who became vice consul and agency surgeon at Zanzibar in 1866, brought him a steady flow of information about the East African slave trade. His access to this intelligence soon made Waller a valuable addition to antislavery circles in England. The next step in expanding his new role as Africanist occurred early in 1867, when a report arrived from Zanzibar that Livingstone had been killed in the interior. Concern for his hero's fate brought Waller with frequency to meetings at the Royal Geographical Society—where his membership had been sponsored by Livingstone in 1864. He was a consultant who knew firsthand both the area where the murder was said to have occurred and the Comoran porter on whose report the story rested.[29]

After E. D. Young's Livingstone Search Expedition confirmed that the tale of his demise was false and, by 1869, letters from Livingstone once again appeared in England, Waller wrote to him with enthusiasm: "[T]he interest in this country about you is as intense as ever I could wish it to be and no one has a better chance of gauging it than myself. The Geographical Society might in short be called the Livingstone Society for the last two years."[30] Waller clearly perceived the link between this heightened public interest in Livingstone and British antislavery efforts directed toward East Africa. He ventured to predict that, "Slowly but surely, and mind you mainly owing to Kirk and others whom you first aroused to think and work, this horrid slave trade may be put 'down.' " He included himself in those "others." Although a Conservative in politics, Waller believed that the Liberal party which took office in 1868 included "just the right men" to take up the question. The publicity which accompanied the general interest in Livingstone's fate provided useful leverage to hold public attention for the antislavery cause. Writing Livingstone in late October 1869, Waller confessed, "I have not missed many opportunities of keeping the matter open & your name before the Public. . . ."[31]

Waller returned to this theme in another letter to Livingstone a month later, reporting the "tremendous" reception at the Royal Geographical Society upon receipt of Livingstone's letter announcing his discovery of the existence of Lake Bangweulu. With a use of hyperbole very much in the spirit of their early exchanges, he warned Livingstone—whom he knew to be reticent about appearances before large audiences—that when he came home he should expect to address the multitudes: "I think a balloon with about 20 fathoms of cable will be the only thing . . . say on Salisbury plain. . . ." Waller continued on a more sober note, "People are alive to the East Coast slave trade. . . . Whatsoever you say on your return will not easily be forgotten . . . you will be able to do a work in this way which will stand when all Lakes have become old."[32]

For Waller, Livingstone's geographical feats were important, but primarily because they provided the means of commanding the attention of the people of England. Once captured, the public attention might be turned to an appeal to the public conscience to help bring an end to the slave trade in East and Central Africa. It is a focus that Waller, once chosen as editor of Livingstone's *Last Journals* in 1874, would bring to his work of shaping those volumes as an antislavery document. Waller's assessment of this process of capturing the public imagination—and his graphic account of the way he saw it function in the late 1860s—may have helped Livingstone see the powerful publicity value of his geographical work in Africa. At least, it was after he would have read this letter from Waller that Livingstone wrote his brother John in Canada in December 1872, "The Nile sources are valuable to me only as a means of enabling me to open my mouth with power among men. It is this power I hope to apply to remedy an enormous evil. . . ."[33]

Writing to Livingstone in November 1869, Waller confessed, "I am jealous of your fame and . . . I know the feeling here in England about you so well and watch it for you if by chance I can turn it to use for you." Revealing how personally involved he felt, he added, "It is the only recompense I can make to you because every one seems kind to me and glad to see me because I have in some little way had my name associated with your doings at times."[34] Waller understood that his relationship with Livingstone and Kirk had opened the doors to a resolution to his search for a new way of life at home. By being ordained an Anglican clergyman late in 1867, Waller could follow a profession that assured him the three things he needed in a new career. It confirmed his new religious identity; it promised him enough money to marry and raise a family if he could secure a good church preferment or "living"; and it provided him with the status and leisure necessary to allow him to connect his life in useful ways to the scenes and events of his African days. The clerical profession also permitted Waller to continue to fulfill his family obligations to his widowed mother and a younger sister and brother, the initial considerations which had tied him to England after his return from Central Africa. His choice freed him, at last, to establish what would be a long career as a leading Africanist in the antislavery and missionary causes of Victorian humanitarian circles.

*   *   *

The first major public platform on which Waller appeared as he evolved his new plan of action was the Paris Anti-Slavery Convention in August 1867. The agenda ranged widely, involving information about Jamaica, Egypt, Turkey, Cuba, Brazil, and the Far East. "But," as Temperley describes it, "what really fascinated the delegates was Africa, in particular the recent revelations of Dr. Livingstone respecting the East Coast slave trade and the way in which slave-traders operated in the interior." Waller provided part of that excitement. He spoke at length to a large audience about his personal experiences with African slave traders and the adventures he shared with the great missionary hero, David Livingstone.[35] Waller was already in touch, on a steady basis, with Sir Thomas Fowell Buxton, grandson of the man whose views had made such an impression on Livingstone in 1840. Buxton was a member of Parliament at this time and deeply involved in the councils of the British and Foreign Anti-Slavery Society, an important link between the men in antislavery and government circles who took an interest in East Africa. As John Kirk—from early in 1866—began to supply Waller regularly with news of the slave trade at Zanzibar and the politics in which it was embedded, Waller shared his reports with Buxton.[36] Kirk knew what use Waller made of this slavery intelligence and advised Waller only to make sure that the source of the information be kept "confidential" because of the official nature of his position at the British Consulate. To maintain concern about the East African slave trade in the minds of prominent men in England, as well as an awareness of his own role at Zanzibar, served Kirk's ambitions.[37] Each in his own way, therefore—Livingstone, Waller, and Kirk—identified his career with the antislavery cause in East Africa.

By 1870, Waller was invited to sit on the Committee of the British and Foreign Anti-Slavery Society. Because he was an Anglican clergyman, his presence was noteworthy. Since its founding in 1839, the society was the organ of nonconformists, and just under half of its sixty-seven Committee members, down to 1870, were members of the Society of Friends, Quakers. Aside from the Buxtons, who were Anglicans inter-married with Quakers, the members of the Society of Friends ran the organization.[38] Waller's election to the Anti-Slavery Committee repre-sented a deliberate effort to broaden their representation and to bring in a new figure of public importance to the regular work of the antislavery cause. Waller was the first Anglican clergyman to sit on the Committee, and he retained his seat until his death twenty-six years later.

Within the expanding circle of acquaintances that became part of Waller's new life in England was Sir Bartle Frere, who had returned from India in 1869. Frere had spent several years as the British governor in Bombay and while there, in 1864–1865, he had offered hospitality to Livingstone, who was making preparations for his last journey into East Africa. Livingstone first met Frere in 1864 when he sailed to Bombay on the *Lady Nyassa*, having failed to install the steamship on Lake Malawi before his recall from the Zambezi. Having paid for its construction out of his profits from the publication of *Missionary Travels*, Livingstone hoped to sell the ship in India and recoup some of its cost to help defray the expenses of his new expedition. In 1864, Livingstone left in India the Africans who had helped him sail there, Chiko, Amoda, and Susi, river men from Shupanga (a village on the Zambezi) and Wikatani and Chuma, boys rescued from a Yao slave gang. Livingstone returned in 1865, therefore, not only to sell his ship but also to pick up these Africans and take them back with him.[39] While in Bombay in 1865, at Frere's suggestion, Livingstone visited the Church Missionary Society's orphan-age for freed slaves at Nasik. There he recruited nine more young men for his expedition. Again at Frere's urging, Livingstone asked a small group of Indian marines from the Marine Battalion at Bombay to ac-company him to Africa. Before he left Bombay early in 1866, Frere an-nounced that Kirk, recommended to him by Livingstone, had been ap-pointed vice consul at Zanzibar, a position in the control of the British Indian government at that time.

Once Sir Bartle Frere returned to England in 1869 and, as a knowl-edgeable Anglo-Indian official, took up a active role at the Royal Geo-graphical Society and in British antislavery circles, it was inevitable that Waller should make his acquaintance. In 1871, both men were among the expert witnesses called before a Select Committee of the House of Commons to give evidence about the East African slave trade. The Committee had been established in response to pressures brought by men who served as links between government and antislavery circles in England. Waller was well aware of the political tensions that existed between the India Office and the Foreign Office over the issue of a

Sir Henry Bartle Edward Frere. While Governor of Bombay in 1865, he suggested to Livingstone that he take young Nasik-trained Africans and Indian Marines on his last journey. He spearheaded the 1872 Anti-Slavery Society campaign to pressure the Foreign Office into making a new antislave trade treaty with the sultan of Zanzibar and while there officially investigated and exonerated Kirk from Livingstone's charges against him, recommending Kirk's promotion as H.M. Consul. Frere encouraged the Church Missionary Society to set up a freed slave settlement on the East Coast of Africa and urged the Free Church of Scotland to consider missionary work there.

British antislavery policy in Zanzibar. He had gained insight into this issue from Kirk's Zanzibar correspondence and from his new antislavery allies in England. The Anglo-Indian establishment wished to safeguard British influence in the Middle East and Indian Ocean at a time of Muslim unrest in the area; its concern was to keep Turkish influence, already present in Yemen, from spreading. The slave trade was not a major issue in these considerations. The Foreign Office and a few old India hands like Frere, however, believed that intervention against the slave trade on the East Coast of Africa, including the coasts of the Arabian peninsula, provided a sound basis for strengthening British power in the entire region.[40]

When Frere pushed his policy views by enlisting the aid of the British and Foreign Anti-Slavery Society in 1872, to plead for renewed British intervention in Zanzibar, he called upon Waller to aid him on the public platform. Waller was not only an eye witness to the slave trade organized in the East African interior to supply coastal markets, but also a platform speaker who could provide a personal account of Livingstone's antislavery efforts. Waller's remarks were featured at a great meeting sponsored by the Anti-Slavery Society on July 25, 1872. The next day, he accompanied an antislavery deputation which waited upon the Liberal Foreign Secretary, Lord Granville, to deliver the resolutions passed at the meeting. During the fall and early winter months of 1872–1873, Waller—who asked to be described as "vicar of Leytonstone, formerly with Dr. Livingstone on the slave hunting grounds of East Africa"—continued to lecture at antislavery meetings held throughout the country to keep public interest aroused to maintain pressure on the government to stem the East African slave trade. In November, he travelled to the north of England (Manchester, York, and Newcastle); in January, he spoke in the industrial midlands (Birmingham and Bradford); while in February, he visited several southern cities.[41]

By early November 1872 the Foreign Office authorized Sir Bartle Frere to lead a mission to the sultans of Muscat (on the Arabian coast) and Zanzibar to negotiate treaties ending the seaborne slave traffic which operated along the East Coast of Africa, in the Red and Arabian seas, and in the Persian Gulf. By implication, these treaties would also confirm British influence over the area. Success eluded the mission at Zanzibar because its sultan believed he could rely on the power of the French representative there to protect him from the British. After Frere left Zanzibar, he sent Kirk orders to enforce a British naval embargo on the coast south of Zanzibar to prevent the export of slaves to the island during the month of May. On June 2, Kirk received authorization from Lord Granville to order a naval blockade of the entire island should the sultan continue to refuse to sign the new treaty. Kirk managed to convince the sultan and his advisors that the French could not save them from this threat, and by June 5, 1873, the treaty was signed.[42]

Coinciding with the Anti-Slavery Society meeting late in July 1872, came the publication of the news that Henry M. Stanley had met and brought succor to Dr. Livingstone in the heart of Africa. The newspapers were flooded with stories about Stanley, Stanley's account of his meeting with Livingstone, Stanley's narrative of Livingstone's travels since 1866, and Livingstone's two widely-published letters to James Gordon Bennett, Jr., the manager of the New York Herald, who had sent Stanley to find him. The first, written in November 1871, thanked his American benefactor for his kind interest in the traveller's fate. The second letter was written in February 1872 and was twenty-two pages long. It described in graphic detail the massacre of hundreds of Manyema market women by Arab slavers, witnessed by Livingstone in July 1871. The public interest and excitement caused by this revelation of bloodshed and cruelty could not have come at a more opportune moment for the British antislavery forces.[43]

This well-timed exposure of the human misery that could be laid at the feet of slavers in the heart of Africa was a stroke of good fortune that was not without unpleasant aspects for Waller. At Zanzibar, Stanley found Kirk, acting consul in 1871–1872, to be a brusque and opinionated Scotsman. Stanley believed Kirk might have been more energetic than he seemed about ensuring that supplies sent to Dr. Livingstone would arrive safely and expeditiously in the interior. Once Stanley found Livingstone at Ujiji, on the eastern shore of Lake Tanganyika, he conveyed his dismay that Kirk had not supplied the Doctor a fraction as well as the American consul at Zanzibar had managed on behalf of his "countryman," Stanley. The latter interpreted Kirk's attitude as lukewarm toward Livingstone and his behavior, at best, as negligent. In his case against Kirk, Stanley expressed all the resentment he had stored up against seemingly supercilious Englishmen of the kind he had encountered in the Abyssinian campaign a few years before.[44]

Perhaps to Stanley's surprise, it was not difficult to convince Livingstone of Kirk's incompetent management. Livingstone had already convinced himself that his failure to accomplish the geographical task he had set for himself was in large part due to this lack of provisioning. In fact, the blame and the brooding which Stanley's accusations triggered were not uncharacteristic of Livingstone, but on this occasion they were undoubtedly aggravated by the severe toll on his general health made by his last years of exploring without adequate provisions or medicines. Complaints that Livingstone would not ordinarily have considered appropriate to air to the general public, therefore, were being read by thousands and thousands of strangers in newspapers on both sides of the Atlantic as a result of Stanley's meeting with him in Africa and Stanley's desire for good newspaper copy.

Thus, in the midst of events that promised to have a positive effect on British policy regarding the East African slave trade, Waller received two unpleasant blows. The first affected his self-esteem; the second, his sense of himself as bound in an enduring relationship with Kirk and Livingstone to end the slave trade in East Africa. First, he learned of a derogatory reference to himself made by Stanley in his tale of Livingstone's travels. The remark came in connection with the African Wikatani, who chose to leave Livingstone in Africa to remain with the relatives he had discovered at the southern end of Lake Malawi early in the course of the expedition. Stanley's identification of Wikatani as both "one of the 'nice honourable fellows' of Mr. Horace Waller" and as a lad who had "deserted" Livingstone caused Waller a deep sense of chagrin.[45] In part, the reason lay in Waller's own mixed feelings about Wikatani's choice. Livingstone had rescued him from slavery in 1861, when he was perhaps ten years old; Waller himself had cut the chains that bound him. Wikatani then lived with the missionaries until 1864, when he accompanied Livingstone to India. Once in Bombay, Livingstone placed Wikatani and Chuma, rescued at the same time, with a Scottish missionary, the Reverend John Wilson of the Free Church of Scotland, for further Christian education. When Livingstone returned to India the next year, he reported to Waller on their progress. As a result, Waller sent encouraging letters and some pocket money to them, and in turn received grateful letters.[46]

In 1867, Waller expressed doubts about the story of Livingstone's murder because it also involved Wikatani's apparent desertion of the man who had rescued him from slavery only five years before. Waller had looked upon Wikatani as a favorite among the African dependents sheltered by the UMCA mission. Aware that Wikatani had also received a Christian education in Bombay, Waller found it difficult to imagine that as a grown youth he might wish to sever his ties with his European savior, especially to remain among the kin who had probably sold him into slavery in the first place. Only after Waller received confirmation from Livingstone had he been convinced that Wikatani had freely chosen to leave him. Because they were disappointed, neither Livingstone nor Waller could understand Wikatani's desire to remain with his kin on his home ground. To their European eyes, the decision was an act of disloyalty, plain ingratitude; they simply could not understand Wikatani's need to stay where he was a full part of the culture. This failure of empathy was an ethnocentric blind spot, and it left Waller sensitive to Stanley's rough-edged sarcasm.[47]

If Stanley's first published descriptions of Livingstone's trials in Central Africa stung Waller on his own account, graver still was Stanley's claim, publicly made and reported from France before his arrival in England, that he returned from Livingstone with a mission to expose Kirk as a traitor to his old chief. To gauge the effect such a declaration made on Waller, it is necessary to listen to Waller's own words from a public platform, uttered just three months earlier, when he laid claim to a bond that linked him, inextricably, with David Livingstone and John Kirk in the name of antislavery. Speaking first of Livingstone, Waller had declared:

> I feel as though his gaze was upon me now, because it was a compact which we entered into in Africa, which we again signed and sealed in this country, that . . . whether it be Livingstone in Africa, or Dr. Kirk reporting from the coast of Africa, or he who stands before you, it is a common duty that we are engaged in. I am bound with these men in a common cause.[48]

In Waller's view, the stranger Stanley had appeared out of nowhere to endanger that solemn compact. He had turned one man against the other. He had filled a weakened Livingstone with stories of Kirk's half-hearted concern for his welfare. He had insinuated himself so well into Livingstone's good graces that the Doctor enjoined Waller, in a letter entrusted to Stanley, to do his utmost to make Stanley welcome in London. Highly distressed by this turn of events, in which both he and Kirk were attacked by an outsider on faulty premises, Waller could come to only one conclusion: Stanley was an untrustworthy schemer and very dangerous.

In his letter from Livingstone, Waller was instructed, with regard to Stanley, to "bestir yourself and . . . show him all the attentions you can," while Kirk's handling of the money entrusted to him to keep Livingstone supplied in the interior was disparaged as, at best, carelessness and, at worst, deliberate sabotage.[49] Livingstone's broodings in Africa had somehow convinced him that Kirk, an ambitious and vigorous man twenty years his junior, meant to force him to leave so that he, Kirk, might finish up the geographical work and claim the great reputation that must result.[50] For Livingstone to conjure up the notion that Kirk might harbor these particular designs, however, reflected more the intensity of his own ambitions than any realistic assessment of Kirk's. That Livingstone's painful doubts about his failures and his suspicions of Kirk should become common newspaper fare and general gossip in England and America left Waller genuinely disturbed and quite fearful lest Kirk's career be jeopardized.

Waller's fierce loyalty to Kirk was fueled less by the marriage tie created five years earlier, when Waller's younger sister Ada married Kirk's older brother Alexander, than by the whole shape of Waller's life since his Zambezi days.[51] Imbued with the vision he had of himself, as "bound together with these men in a common cause," Waller became convinced that Livingstone's words could destroy hard-won antislavery efforts just as they were on the brink of success. He was aware that what Livingstone said now carried a "terrible weight," and that he himself had helped to give him that power. This knowledge led Waller to defend as vigorously as he could the reputation of a man believed to be falsely accused.

He laid his case before Livingstone, the judge who had dealt with him so fairly in their fierce disagreement over the Kololo on the Zambezi, the hero whose name symbolized to the world both generosity and mercy. In a letter to Livingstone that must have been painful to write, Waller called upon the man who had been for so long his hero and admired friend to reject Stanley's false allegations and to make public amends for the harm already done.

> If he has in any way aided to unsettle your mind respecting one of the best friends you ever had, it is hard, very hard to forgive him . . . Kirk . . . did all he could to relieve you; he failed, and in all probability his career is blighted by what you have said. . . . With our friendship such a sacred thing to me . . . I dare not speak this if I were not well assured of Kirk's singleness of purpose. . . . I feel for you and the misery you have been in as few can, but I also feel this, that the powers of darkness are lashed into fury at such lives as yours and such exertions as yours and Kirk's and our own here against the slave trade and that if they can break us up and set us one against the other . . . the screams of the women and children in the forests you have trodden will be more sweet to their ears than ever. . . . You must believe me when I say it must be utterly intolerable to any gentleman to be dealt with as he has been by Stanley in your name – it has really been outrageous. . . . Forgive all I have said but the highest service is to stand by the weaker side. . . .[52]

Ultimately, of course, Waller's reactions tell us more about his personality than about the two men with whom he identified. Both had made strong and bristling comments about each other in the past, albeit in private. Both were strong-minded Scotsmen, well able to take care of themselves in such a fray. Waller's gift was a capacity for empathy which enabled him to sustain close friendships. This capacity for identification may have been, at least in part, the wellspring of his commitment to end the enslavement of Africans in their homeland and their sale to distant shores. He mourned the misunderstanding between Livingstone and Kirk and called upon the party he deemed to hold the superior position to be generous. He based his judgment, however, not on what may or may not have happened, but upon his personal friendship for Kirk and what he knew of Livingstone's previous difficulties with his European companions. As Waller confessed in 1864, in response to a disgruntled friend who accused Livingstone of acting "cool" toward him, "he's the bravest man I ever saw or ever expect to see. . . . So I always stick up for him tho' I confess with more tact in dealing with his companions he might make a much greater and more lasting mark."[53]

By November 25, 1872, Waller could write Livingstone, with somewhat greater equanimity. Livingstone had written Lord Granville at the Foreign Office, in a letter dated July 1, 1872, that he regretted that Kirk viewed his formal complaint against the British Indian money lenders at Zanzibar as "a covert attack upon himself . . . I had no intention to give offence. . . ." Waller was delighted: "Your last letters written at Unyanyembe . . . respecting Kirk have caused the greatest delight and satisfaction . . . I never can acquit Stanley . . . and I accuse him of trying at all times and in all ways to ruin Kirk." As for the antislavery cause, Waller continued,

> if it please God that you return to us and are able to repeat in person your own experiences there is not a man in the civilized world but will not try to take up your words and act them out. It is not everyone to whom it is allowed to be the regenerator of a Continent, yet to you it is allowed, for, once stop the slave trade, and what may not Africa be?[54]

Of the Frere mission to negotiate a new slave trade treaty with Zanzibar and his own part in forwarding it, Waller remarked, "I have been (at Sir Bartle's instigation) stumping the country of late and speaking on the slave trade . . . to stir up a feeling . . . by all means. . . . the most hearty sympathy prevails everywhere and mention of your name always makes the rafters shake!"[55] Livingstone never read this letter, nor the previous one written in July on behalf of Kirk, for he died in Africa at Ilala, May 1, 1873, before either could reach him.

When he became the editor of Livingstone's last journals, Waller's convictions about the power of Livingstone's words would impel him to make that record a permanent testament to a missionary hero whose remarkable geographical exploits were of lesser importance than the man's selfless dedication to the moral and material regeneration of a continent. To honor the memory of such a hero, the British would have to rededicate themselves to the unfinished task of destroying the interior slave trade of Africa. The public which avidly read Stanley in 1872 would be eager, after the nation's tribute to Livingstone at Westminster Abbey in 1874, to read in his own words the story of his last journey. The editor of those words, therefore, had a duty to take advantage of the country's interest in Livingstone the man, to transform it into a national inspiration. The means by which that might be done was to emphasize Livingstone the missionary hero, Livingstone the antislave trade crusader, and Livingstone the larger-than-life legend—without human failings. To shape that legend, Livingstone's journals should convey the higher meaning of Livingstone's life and the legacy of his vision for England and Africa.

NOTES

1. Alexander Maitland, *Speke* (London, 1971), chaps. 8–10; Richard Hall, *Lovers on the Nile: The Incredible African Journeys of Sam and Florence Baker* (New York, 1980); Roy C. Bridges, "The Sponsorship and Financing of Livingstone's Last Journey," *African Historical Studies* 1, no. 1 (1968): 84–85 (hereafter, Bridges, "Sponsorship"). Livingstone to Murchison, November 28, 1864; January 6 and January 16, 1865, Livingstone Papers, LI 1/1/1, fol. 1957–60, 2010–21, 2026–29, NAZ. For a synopsis of these letters, see *David Livingstone: A Catalogue of Documents*, comp. G. W. Clendennen, assisted by I. C. Cunningham, National Library of Scotland, Edinburgh (hereafter, NLS) for the David Livingstone Documentation Project, 1979, 180 (hereafter, *Livingstone Catalogue*). The compilers located Livingstone documents around the world. An addendum has recently been issued: *David Livingstone: A Catalogue of Documents. A Supplement*, comp. I. C. Cunningham, Edinburgh, NLS, 1985 (hereafter, *Livingstone Catalogue Supplement*).
2. See "Central African Watershed As It is" and "Watershed As Livingstone Believed It To Be," Jeal, *Livingstone*, 324, 325n.
3. Bridges, "Sponsorship," 83–84; Jeal, *Livingstone*, chap. 19. Livingstone wrote Charles Alington, an Anglican missionary he had met on

the Zambezi, "I am going out again to try and get an opening in by way of Rovuma or elsewhere north of the Portuguese. . . ." Livingstone to Alington, Newstead Abbey, February 3, 1865, copy, Livingstone Papers, A347, University of Witwatersrand Library, Johannesburg, South Africa (hereafter, UWL). Original, MS. 3651, fol. 81–82, NLS.

4. Jeal, *Livingstone*, 287. For the historical assessment of the significance of Livingstone's activities on later imperialist expansion, see Jeal, chap. 24; Pachai, *Livingstone*, chaps. 9–10; Andrew Roberts, *A History of the Zambia* (London, 1976), 151–55; Beachey, *Slave Trade of Eastern Africa, passim*; John McCracken, *Politics and Christianity in Malawi, 1875–1940* (Cambridge, 1977), esp. chap. 2. Roland Oliver pioneered this interpretation of events in relation to missionary expansion in *The Missionary Factor in East Africa* (London, 1952), 9–15. Margery Perham developed it in setting the stage for the first volume of her biography of Frederick Lugard, *Lugard: The Years of Adventure, 1858–1859* (London, 1956), 78ff. More recent scholarship explores the implications of missionary and antislavery activities for the national and international politics that accompanied the acquisition of empire.

5. Within four months of his arrival on the Zambezi in 1863, Bishop Tozer wrote T. Parry Woodcock, UMCA honorary secretary, "I much fear that the 'Examiner' was not very far wrong when it called the Zambesi 'a giant humbug'. It has fulfilled no prediction or hopes once entertained with respect to it and does its chief Sponsor no credit whatsoever." Tozer to Woodcock, September 30, 1863. UMCA Papers, United Society for the Propagation of the Gospel Archives (hereafter, UMCA, USPGA). Jeal suggests that Lord John Russell ordered Livingstone's recall in February 1863 because "The deaths and dismissals had already persuaded him that nothing more would be achieved. . . ." Jeal, *Livingstone*, 266. But Roy Bridges discovered a study made within the Foreign Office in 1870 which ". . . suggested that Livingstone had been recalled . . . in 1863 through difficulties his activities caused in [Anglo-] Portuguese relations but that Russell and Palmerston had been pleased with his work." Bridges, "Sponsorship," 95.

6. Before Stanley left, Livingstone wrote two letters to James Gordon Bennett, son of the founder of the *New York Herald* and the initiator of Stanley's trip, one in November 1871 and one in February 1872. The latter described the slave trade and the Nyangwe massacre of Manyema market women. The letters appeared in the *New York Herald*, July 26 and 27, 1872; they were published in *The Times*, July 27, 1872. The *Daily Telegraph* carried the Manyema massacre letter July 29, 1872. Livingstone wrote a third letter to Bennett April 9, 1872—sending it to catch up with the departing Stanley. It was published in *The Times*, April 10, 1874,

eight days before the Westminster Abbey burial. *Stanley's Despatches to the "New York Herald," 1871-1872, 1874-1877*, edited by Norman R. Bennett (Boston, 1970), *xxiv*, n. 48; Reginald Coupland, *Livingstone's Last Journey* (London, 1945), 170-71, 263 n. 170 (1); *Livingstone Catalogue*, 84-85, 96, 318, 332-33; *Livingstone Catalogue Supplement*, 1, 14-15, 16. Contemporaries and historians have commented on the influence of Livingstone's timely letters describing the slave trade. Good examples are: *Anti-Slavery Reporter*, October 1, 1872, 68; R. J. Gavin, "The Bartle Frere Mission to Zanzibar, 1873," *Historical Journal* 5, no. 2 (1962): 140-41, 147; Jeal, *Livingstone*, 345, 353; and Miers, *Britain and the Ending of the Slave Trade*, 89. In a letter published in the *New York Herald* December 26, 1874, Stanley quoted the sultan of Zanzibar as blaming the publication of these Livingstone letters for precipitating the British demand for a treaty ending the seaborne slave trade. *Stanley's Despatches*, 168 n. 1; 178. By ascribing the treaty directly to Livingstone's letters, Stanley gave the impression that by his agency in getting them published he played a significant role in the signing of this treaty; the efforts of Frere and Waller and the consular pressure brought by Kirk were thereby ignored.

7. Ledger Journal, John Murray, Publisher, Archives (hereafter, JMPA). In all, 30,000 copies of the guinea (21-shilling) edition were sold; by 1861, there was an additional sale of 10,000 of a cheap, abridged 6-shilling edition. Richard D. Altick, *The English Common Reader* (Chicago, 1957), 388. George Shepperson has remarked that the publication of nine editions in quick succession indicated the kind of infectious excitement generated by Livingstone's exploits. "Livingstone and the Years of Preparation, 1813-1857," in Pachai, *Livingstone*, 11. According to Altick, the only other travel books to sell 10,000 copies or more in Britain in the nineteenth century were Sir Francis McClintock's *Voyage of the "Fox" in the Arctic Seas*, 1859 (12,000 to 1863) and Paul B. Du Chaillu's *Explorations in Equatorial Africa*, 1861 (10,000 in two years). The popularity of these travel books, published so soon after *Missionary Travels*, may have resulted in part from an appetite for travel literature stimulated by Livingstone's book. For the publication record of Livingstone's *Last Journals* and further cheap editions of Livingstone's first two books, see below, chap. 6.

8. Jeal, *Livingstone*, 22-23; John Gallagher, "Fowell Buxton and the New African Policy, 1838-1842," *Cambridge Historical Journal* 10, no. 1 (1950): 36-58.

9. Jeal, *Livingstone*, 163-65, 293, 333, and chap. 22, esp. 346-47, 351-52; Henry M. Stanley, *How I Found Livingstone. Travels, Adventures, and Discoveries in Central Africa; Including Four Months' Residence*

with Dr. Livingstone (London, 1872, 1874, 1890). The 1890 edition is most often cited, but the major revision occurred in 1874. Richard Hall, *Stanley: An Adventurer Explored* (Boston, 1975), 193–207.

10. Waller to Stewart, October 18, 1864, Stewart Papers, ST 1/1/1, fol. 195–202, NAZ.

11. Waller's African experiences were critical to his later views. Space does not allow me to develop the events this period, but I plan to make a reassessment of the UMCA missionary experience on the Zambezi in the early 1860s the subject of another book.

12. A major theme of Jeal's biography is Livingstone's difficulties with Europeans. Trying to sum up this important characteristic in Livingstone's life, he writes, "As a man, Livingstone had been marked for life by the harshness of his childhood. . . . His loyalty to Africans and his faith in their capacities were limitless, but he was easily swayed, on the scantiest of evidence, into believing the worst of his fellow–countrymen who had previously served him well." Jeal, *Livingstone*, 372–73. In contrast, Jeal accepts with little analysis the relationship between Livingstone and his African followers, especially on his last journey, as depicted in the *Last Journals*. Jeal, *Livingstone*, chap. 20. The historian Roy Bridges, however, wrote in 1968, "In fact Livingstone was a very poor leader of men—and not just of other Europeans as is conventionally asserted; only a few individuals like Kirk or Susi or Chuma found it temperamentally possible to remain unswervingly loyal to such a withdrawn, self–sufficient character as he had become." Bridges, "Sponsorship," 92. Before Jeal's focus on Livingstone's relationships with all the Europeans he met in Africa, John P. R. Wallis examined these clashes on the Zambezi Expedition in: *Thomas Baines of King's Lynn: Explorer and Artist, 1820–1875* (London, 1941); *The Zambesi Journal of James Stewart, 1862–1863*, edited by J. P. R. Wallis, Oppenheimer Series of the Central African Archives, no. 6 (London, 1952); and *The Zambesi Expedition of David Livingstone, 1858–1863*, 2 vols., edited by J. P. R. Wallis, Oppenheimer Series of the Central African Archives, no. 9 (London, 1956) (hereafter, *ZEDL*). Examination of the Stewart Papers reveals that Wallis edited out some of Stewart's comments. Since Jeal wrote in 1973, some of Livingstone's difficulties with his African followers during his last journey have been described by Donald H. Simpson, *Dark Companions: The African contribution to the European exploration of East Africa* (London, 1975), chaps. 6 and 8. Simpson draws upon Livingstone's unpublished diaries for this story, as do chaps. 4–5 below.

13. Among the batches of delayed mail Stanley delivered to Livingstone may have been *The Times* of February 19, 1869, in which there was an account of a trip from London to Brighton made on an experi-

mental bicycle called a velocipede. Frederick Alderson, *Bicycling: A History* (Newton Abbot, England, 1972), 26.

14. Livingstone to Waller, November, 1871, with two postscripts dated February 19 and March 8, 1872, WPRH, 1. The letter appeared in *The Times*, August 2, 1872; see *Livingstone Catalogue*, 84–85. The only change made here and elsewhere in Livingstone's letters is to introduce whole stops (periods) where they are appropriate but where Livingstone uses dashes.

15. Committee Minute Book, Livingstone Search Committee, April 15, 1867, Royal Geographical Society Archives (hereafter, RGSA). When Young led the Scottish Memorial Missions to the Shire Highlands and Lake Malawi in 1875, Waller again aided him in producing a book, *Nyassa: A Journal of Adventures* (London, 1877). Young was awarded the rank of honorary lieutenant when he retired from the coastguard in 1891. *Livingstone Catalogue*, 254.

16. David and Charles Livingstone, *Narrative of an Expedition to the Zambesi and Its Tributaries; and of the Discovery of the Lakes Shirwa and Nyassa, 1858–1864* (New York, 1866), 499–500 and note (hereafter, *Zambesi and Its Tributaries*). Livingstone to Waller, February 3, 7, and 9, 1865, WPRH, 1; Livingstone to W. C. Oswell, February 8, 1865, Livingstone Papers, National Museum, Livingstone, Zambia (formerly Northeastern Rhodesia), photocopies in Rhodes House Library (hereafter, NMLZ, RH). Chadwick, *Mackenzie's Grave*, 172–73.

17. *Zambesi and Its Tributaries*, 601. A letter from Livingstone to W. Cotton Oswell, February 15, 1865, suggests why he felt free to criticize Bishop Tozer so openly in his book: "I found Tozer not in high repute in high quarters. It is known how he would have left some 30 or 40 boys and 5 widows whom I brought away." E. Edward Oswell, ed., *William Cotton Oswell: Hunter and Explorer*, 2 vols. (New York, 1900), 2:82. The internal date of the letter in which this remark was made was "18th." Livingstone to W. C. Oswell, February 15, 18, 1865, Livingstone Papers, NMLZ, RH. See Livingstone to Waller, February 3, 1865, WPRH, 1.

18. Chadwick, *Mackenzie's Grave*, 169–76, and chap. 6; Philip Elston, "A Note on the Universities' Mission to Central Africa: 1859–1914," in Pachai, *History of Malawi*, 345–48; Elston, "Livingstone and the Anglican Church," in Pachai, *Livingstone*, 76–79.

19. Comte de Georges Louis Leclerc Buffon (1707–1788), *Histoire naturelle generale et particuliere, avec la description du Cabinet du roy. . . .* (Paris, 1747–1789). When Young's report on his Livingstone Search Expedition was read at the Royal Geographical Society January 27, 1868, Waller referred to Livingstone's enjoyment in carrying out this

dispute, and said that the Doctor was ever on the lookout for dogs whose tails curled to the right. *Proceedings of the Royal Geographical Society* 12 (1867–1868): 90 (hereafter, *PRGS*). Compare Edward D. Young, *The Search after Livingstone*, revised by the Reverend H. Waller (London, 1868), 204–5.

20. David's sister Janet recollected an occasion "when he and his brother Charles had poached a salmon; [and] to disguise it, David stuck it down Charles's trouser leg and got the boy to limp painfully to persuade anybody they might meet that the concealed fish was a monstrous swelling." Jeal, *Livingstone*, 10. Janet Livingstone wrote this memoir of her brother's early life for use by William Garden Blaikie. See *The Personal Life of David Livingstone, LL.D., D.C.L., Chiefly from His Unpublished Journals and Correspondence in the Possession of His Family* (New York, 1881), 12–13 (hereafter, Blaikie, *Personal Life*). Another biographer has suggested that Livingstone regretted that Waller did not marry his daughter Agnes. Oliver Ransford, *David Livingstone: The Dark Interior* (London, 1978), 181. James Casada suggests that Livingstone may have seen in Waller some of the characteristics he wished for, but did not find, in his own sons. Personal communication.

21. Livingstone to Waller, April 28, 1863, WPRH, 1. Chadwick thinks the date wrong and that this letter from Livingstone reached Waller a week earlier, *Mackenzie's Grave*, 185 n. 1. Compare Kirk's reference to the letter in an entry which precedes that of April 27, 1863: "Dr. L. has made an abject apology to Mr Waller for the expressions used in re Makololo." *The Zambesi Journal and Letters of Dr John Kirk, 1858–1863*, 2 vols., edited by Reginald Foskett (Edinburgh and London, 1965), 2:514. Livingstone wrote in his Zambezi Journal for April 6, 1863, "Mr Waller asserted that his common sense assured him that the Makololo [sic] plundered the Manganja [sic] . . . and had killed a chief up near the [Murchison] falls, though he confessed that he could not swear to any one deed of plunder by any one." In a separate, undated note, Livingstone put the allegations down to "certain reports given by a few disreputable Cape blacks between whom and the Makololo there seems to have been a feud about women." *ZEDL*, 2:230, 242. How much Livingstone regretted the bitter quarrel can be gauged by the several ways in which he sought to express his feelings in his letter of apology: "It is possible you may have taken up reports with too much facility but I ought not to have said that you did or anything else that might give you pain. I am heartily sorry for it and have grieved over it again & again. I hoped to tell you so when we met but might then lack an opportunity."

22. Chadwick, *Mackenzie's Grave*, 208–16, 236–37. Waller arrived in Cape Town April 15, 1864; he spent the next month placing the Africans

with him as apprentices (servants) in local households. Reflecting on this activity at sea on his way home to England, he wrote in his diary for May 26, 1864, "there they are in health and strength safe on English soil in English homes. . . . say what one like it is a noble splendid deed of benefaction done by God's grace." WPRH, 5.

23. Livingstone asked Waller to sketch for his Bath speech, "a gigantic human head—not an ugly one—with a lip ring in it to show the Theatre tonight." Livingstone to Waller, Monday morning, n.d. (by inference, September 19, 1864), WPRH, 1. Waller later lamented that "the girl's head at Bath was walked off with. . . ." Waller to Stewart, October 18, 1864, Stewart Papers, ST 1/1/1, fol. 195–218, NAZ. Some Waller-Stewart correspondence was published (with portions edited out) in *Zambesi Journal of James Stewart*; this letter appears on pp. 233–34. Livingstone supplied Waller with a description of Speke's private funeral: "There were no sobs so loud as the poetical reporter or penny a liner reported – nor did Grant who is a fine fellow & a Scotchman the equivalent of all thats good &c &c go down into the vault. He put a small 'immortelle' of violets & migonette on the coffin as it was borne past us in the church. So much for contemporary history." Livingstone to Waller, September 24, 1864, WPRH, 1.

For the occasions on which Livingstone requested Waller to make a sketch for the engraver for his book, see Livingstone's letters, WPRH, 1, as follows (compare *Zambesi and Its Tributaries*, 124, 125, 127, 333):

Nov. 8, 1864: "can you give me a sketch of the little loom for weav[ing] cotton which you sent home . . . also if you can a furnace for smelting iron or anything else you like. . . ."

Nov. 18, 1864: "draw a pair of native bellows – looms – spinning apparatus. Foundery [sic] for smelting iron – &c.

Dec. 8, 1864: "Many thanks for the drawings they are in the artists hands – and also for the loom you are going to do for me. If it is done by Christmas I mean the Head – That will do."

Dec. 14, 1864: "Can you send an original lip ring with the 'Manganja head' . . . Thanks for your kindly intentions about the Loom . . . Can you make a man spinning of course you can & will you"

Feb. 24, 1865: "Thanks for going to the artist – Did you enlighten him on fish baskets"

Mar. 8, 1865: "Tell [the artist] I shall be much obliged if he make the faces marked . . . less prognathous otherwise I shall put it in the Int[roduction that] in spite beseeching [by] Mr W. with tears in his eyes he would make them like baboons. Also the fish basket put to rights please."

Apr. 6, 1865:   "Will you call at Mr Cooke's in Mr Murrays for your
                drawings in a few days – I will write to have them . . .
                ready & many thanks for them."
May 11, 1865:   "Will you at your earliest convenience make a small
                drawing for the outside of the book. I think a man in a
                slave stick with hands tied behind and the slaver with a
                hold of the other end of the goree [slave stick] & a
                musket in his right hand will be best. . . . There my fine
                fellow dont oppress me so with thanks for offering to set
                your work in gold – and send it down to posterity (or the
                butterman's shop) – Quick now." WPRH, 1.

24. Livingstone to Waller, October 31, 1864, and January 25, 1865,
WPRH, 1. Livingstone consulted Waller on the exact meaning of some
words in the Yao and Mang'anja languages they encountered. "You will
know the exact meaning of the words – Ambuiatu – our Father or master?
(moio life? or amae mother) said by Manganja chiefs on recieving [sic]
one better than I do. Am I right in the meaning here given. What was the
name of the old man at Mankokwe's whose wife was given to [the spirit]
Bona & what was Bona's legend – if any." Livingstone to Waller, November 23, 1864, WPRH, 1 (compare *Zambesi and Its Tributaries*, 121–
22). "Can you translate vacheryera na chanjera kale – Ninga & Nyama
Sambe – Thou are slippery [sic] always – or thou art roguish (too clever
by half) (or Tozery) of old like meat sumbe. What is sumbe? Does this
boat song mean that the Busunga were always a slippery lot?" Livingstone to Waller, January 24, 1865, WPRH, 1. Waller consulted John Blair,
an English artisan who had accompanied the Universities' Mission and
was back in England at St. Augustine's Anglican Divinity School in Canterbury. There he exercised supervision over some black men from the
Zambezi brought back by a few of the missionaries and left there with
him. For Blair's response, see Livingston Papers, LI 1/1/1, fol. 2034–37,
NAZ. Also among these papers are two of Waller's letters to Livingstone
from this period, not dated but probably written in February, 1865,
supplying comment on Livingstone's narrative as it concerned the fighting by the UMCA missionaries. In addition, Waller wrote, "The name of
the Potamus hunters is Akombwe or Ma Podzo," and "Don't know what
MTungu means . . . Olendo is a traveller: Ku chesa to visit – I think its
Magomero . . . the beginnings or outside boundaries I believe: it ends
with an o." Livingstone Papers, LI 1/1/1, fol. 2160–63, 2168–71, NAZ.

25. Livingstone to Waller, February 3, 1865, WPRH, 1. Livingstone
first wrote *surrender* and then crossed out and substituted *submit to*. He
sent Waller more proof on February 6 and wrote him the next day,
promising to send the "matter in proof about the Manganja which per-

haps you have a suggestion for." Livingstone to Waller, February 7, 1865, WPRH, 1. The issue involved the first encounter Livingstone and the missionaries had with warring Yao and Mang'anja in the Shire Highlands. See *Zambesi and Its Tributaries*, chap. 18, esp. 382.

26. Livingstone to Waller, October 13, 1864 (along the margin), WPRH, 1.

27. For Livingstone's efforts on behalf of his brother and John Kirk, see Livingstone to Kirk, March 24, April 5, April 14, September 20, and November 15, 1865, in *The Zambesi Doctors. David Livingstone's Letters to John Kirk, 1858–1872*, edited by Reginald Foskett (Edinburgh, 1964). Livingstone was an enthusiastic admirer of Sir James Brooke (Rajah Brooke of Sarawak) and may have met him through Baroness Burdett-Coutts in late 1857 or early 1858 when they both were in England. Steven Runciman, *The White Rajahs* (Cambridge, 1960), 136. Sir James wrote to Livingstone from Baroness Burdett-Coutts's residence, Holly Lodge, July 18, 1865, saying that he had no appointment to offer Horace Waller. The note is found with Livingstone to Waller, July 21, 1865, WPRH, 1. See Edna Healey, *Lady Unknown: The Life of Angela Burdett-Coutts* (London, 1978), 157–60. A letter from Livingstone to Baroness Burdett-Coutts, recommending Waller "as the man to carry out her plans for sending a mission to Borneo," is listed as no. 1719 in the *Livingstone Catalogue*, 104.

28. Livingstone wrote Waller that he had written Kirk on his behalf; a letter fragment of this sort is found with Livingstone to Waller, January 1, 1866, WPRH, 1.

29. Waller was elected a fellow of the Royal Geographical Society November 28, 1864. RGS Council Minute Book, 1859–1867, RGSA. In his diary for March 8, 1867, Waller recorded, "This morning at breakfast I read Kirk's letter saying the Dr has most likely been killed at Lake Nyassa [Malawi]. . . ." WPRH, 4. To James Stewart, two months later, Waller confessed, ". . . Chibisas, with the little crosses and the graves! What an unworthy wretch I feel as I write these words, how can I decide what I ought to do to follow such men who have gone before me. . . ." Waller to Stewart, May 8, 1867, Stewart Papers, ST 1/1/1, fol. 378–91, NAZ (extract in *Zambesi Journal of James Stewart*, 244.) For Waller's role in helping E. D. Young to plan his search expeditions, see P. A. Cole-King, "Searching for Livingstone: E. D. Young and Others," in Pachai, *Livingstone*, 159. Livingstone had obtained porters from the island of Johanna (now Anjouan) in the Comoros Islands.

30. Waller to Livingstone, October 25, 1869, WPRH, 1.

31. *Ibid.*

32. Waller to Livingstone, November 24, 1869, WPRH, 1.

62LIVINGSTONE'S LEGACY

33. Blaikie, *Personal Life*, 444.

34. Waller to Livingstone, November 24, 1869, WPRH, 1.

35. Temperley, *British Antislavery*, 261; British and Foreign Anti-Slavery Society, *Special Report of the Anti-Slavery Convention held in Paris . . . 26–27 August 1867* (London, 1869), 15–16.

36. "Sir F Buxton M.P. and one or two other influential people will not let the knowledge they at last have of E African evils die out without a struggle to produce an effect. I have been a good deal with Sir Fowell and he is very enthusiastic about it." Waller to Stewart, May 8, 1867, Stewart Papers, NAZ.

37. Kirk to Waller, Zanzibar, August 29, 1868; Waller to Buxton, January 28; June 19, 1868. British and Foreign Anti-Slavery Papers, MS. Brit. Emp. s22/G7, Rhodes House (hereafter, BFASSP, RH).

38. Temperley, *British Antislavery*, 68.

39. Simpson, *Dark Companions*, 54–56.

40. Gavin, "Bartle Frere Mission"; *Anti-Slavery Reporter*, October 1, 1872, 61–66.

41. For Waller's request regarding how he was to be described, Waller to Benjamin Millard, November 8, 1872, MS. Brit. Emp. s18 C46/97, BFASSP, RH. On November 15, 1872, Waller wrote Bates, RGS secretary, of the "most enthusiastic meetings at Manchester, York, and Newcastle about the slave trade." Letter Books, 1865–1878, RGSA. For the antislavery meetings of late 1872 and early 1873, see *Anti-Slavery Reporter*, January 1 and April 1, 1873. The opening page of the April 1 edition featured a drawing of a slave gang and an extract from a speech by Waller, recounting the tale of the first liberation of slaves by Livingstone and the UMCA missionaries in the Shire Highlands in July 1861.

42. Reginald Coupland, *The Exploitation of East Africa, 1856–1890: The Slave Trade and the Scramble* (London, 1939), chap. 10. See also, "Correspondence respecting Sir Bartle Frere's Mission to the East Coast of Africa, 1872–1873." Parliamentary Papers, Slave Trade 91: *Reports, Correspondence, and Papers relating to Slavery and the Abolition of the Slave Trade, 1861–74* (Shannon, Ireland, 1971), 293–449.

43. See n. 6 above.

44. Hall, *Stanley*, 201–2.

45. Waller to Livingstone, August 12 and 28, 1872, WPRH, 1. Someone in New York, possibly his brother Ernest, sent Waller the *New York Herald* for July 15, where these remarks first appeared. For the complete letter, see Bennett, *Stanley's Despatches*, 50–60; for the specific remarks, 53.

46. *PRGS* 12 (1867–1868): 24. Compare Young, *Search after Livingstone*, 163–64, 198–99, 204–5. In a postscript to Young's book, Waller an-

nounced cryptically that Wikatani had decided not to live among "those who remind the black man how black he is." Young, *Search after Livingstone*, 261.

47. Livingstone wrote Waller of Wikatani's decision: "[H]e met a brother & found that he had two brothers and one or two sisters living down at the Western shore [of Lake Malombe] . . . under Kabinga. He thought that his relatives would not again sell him. I had asked if he wished to remain & he at once said yes, so I did not attempt to dissuade him. . . . In the event of any mission coming into the country of Mataka he will go there. . . . I was sorry to part with him but the Arabs tell the Waiyao [Yao] chiefs that our object in liberating slaves is to make them our own and turn them to our religion. I had declared to them through Wikatani as interpreter that they never became our slaves & were at liberty to go back to their relatives if they liked, and now could not object to Wikatani going without stultifying my own statements." Livingstone to Waller, November 3, 1866, WPRH, 1.

48. *Anti-Slavery Reporter*, July 1, 1872, 51.

49. Livingstone to Waller, November, 1871, P.S. March 8, 1872, WPRH, 1.

50. An earlier hint of some brief moment of rivalry was in Waller's mind when he wrote James Stewart November 13, 1864, "[T]here's to be a grand meeting of the Royal Geo: tomorrow night at which a new Nile Expedition is to be proposed via Zambesi Shire Nyassa &c with Kirk at its head. . . . Livingstone [will be there] and to propose Kirk to head another expedition before his chefs [sic] face—rayther [sic] awkward thing I think?" Stewart Papers, ST 1/1/1, fol. 219–26, NAZ.

51. Waller to Livingstone, August 12 and 28, 1872, WPRH, 1. For the fullest version of the controversy, see Coupland, *Livingstone's Last Journey*, esp. 197–216. Coupland defends Kirk, while Richard Hall offers a more sympathetic treatment of Stanley—but not Waller. Hall, *Stanley*, chap. 15.

52. Waller to Livingstone, August 12 and 28, 1872, WPRH, 1.

53. Waller to Stewart, October 5, 1864, Stewart Papers, ST 1/1/1, fol. 182–5, NAZ.

54. Waller to Livingstone, November 25, 1872, WPRH, 1; Coupland, *Livingstone's Last Journey*, 202.

55. In his last letter to Livingstone, written—though he did not know it—after Livingstone had died in Africa, Waller spoke his heart, "So much hangs on your presence here. Your word about the slave trade will lead the English people as one man I am convinced . . . meanwhile we have been pegging away in season and out of season about it and mean to do so still." Waller to Livingstone, October 23, 1873, WPRH, 1.

§ 2 §

Choosing An Editor

In August 1872, Henry M. Stanley brought to England a large journal entrusted to him by Livingstone. It contained Livingstone's official account of his travels from March 1866 to March 1872. A substantial portion of this journal had been written up by Livingstone from his field diaries after Stanley had put new supplies at his disposal at Ujiji in the autumn of 1871. The journal was completed only on the eve of Stanley's departure from Unyanyembe in March 1872. In the meantime the two men had travelled around the northern end of Lake Tanganyika and, without retracing their steps to Ujiji, had settled east of the lake at Unyanyembe, the capital of a Nyamwezi state where some trading Arabs were headquartered. Livingstone had asked Stanley to deliver the Unyanyembe journal (as it will be called henceforth) to his daughter Agnes. As she was in Scotland with James Young and his family when Stanley arrived in London, she sent her brother Tom to get it, as well as to meet their brother Oswell on his return from Africa. Agnes received the journal August 7 and, still sealed, it was then stored in a Glasgow bank vault to await Livingstone's return.[1]

When Livingstone died at the beginning of May 1873,[2] his servants carefully preserved his personal possessions and the astronomical instruments and field diaries he had been carrying with him. On their way back to the coast and Zanzibar in October, they met at Unyanyembe Lt. Verney Lovett Cameron, leader of the Royal Geographical Society's second Livingstone East Coast Expedition—the first Livingstone Search and Relief Expedition having dispersed upon meeting Stanley on his return to the coast in 1872. Susi and Chuma, who shared the organization and leadership of the caravan carrying Livingstone's body to the coast, told Waller that they had had to resist Cameron's advice to bury Livingstone's remains at Unyanyembe.[3]

The three Englishmen at the head of the RGS Expedition had experienced several violent attacks of fever, diarrhea, and in two cases, partial blindness. While his two companions, Dillon and Murphy, now decided to accompany the caravan carrying Livingstone's body to the coast, Cameron remained determined to push forward to Ujiji to rescue the boxes Livingstone had left there.[4] Therefore, much to the subsequent regret of Livingstone's family, he laid claim to most of the instruments by which Livingstone had made his scientific observations over the previous seven years—"aneroid barometers, compasses, thermometers, [and] the sextant. . . ."[5]

In addition, at Zanzibar, a number of other items brought down by Livingstone's porters were retained at the English consulate and, it seems, auctioned off before they could be claimed by Livingstone's family.[6] When the body arrived in England in April 1874, it was accompanied by some clothing, one thermometer, the field diaries dating from Stanley's departure in March 1872 to Livingstone's last entry in April 1873, a brief account of the lake trip with Stanley, some maps, and some makeshift papers relating to the period in 1871 before Stanley arrived.

The field diaries for 1866 to 1871, from which Livingstone had written up his large journal from time to time, were stored in a box at Ujiji before he set forth on his lake trip with Stanley. Later in 1872, when he set off southward once more, Livingstone decided to leave them in Ujiji; thus he did not have them with him when he died. Having learned of the box at Ujiji from the men carrying Livingstone's body to the coast, Cameron set out in November 1873 to salvage it. He reached Ujiji in late February 1874. Here he decided to continue exploring Lake Tanganyika and the interior. He did not feel secure enough to entrust the box to anyone to take back for him until May, when his personal servant Mohammed Malim left him to return to the East Coast.[7]

The contents of Livingstone's Ujiji box reached England in late January 1875, after the initial publication of the *Last Journals of David Livingstone*. Waller received the box at the Foreign Office January 28 on behalf of the Livingstone family. It contained ". . . 14 memorandum books, 1 on the Zambesi & the rest from leaving London to far on in his last travels. Then a map—the map beautifully laid down from the coast to . . . Lake Nyassa which we wanted."[8] Waller recorded in his diary, "Read through a good deal of Livingstone's sojourn at Chitimba's [sic] from his pocket books. A great pity I had not got them before." He did not express this view in public, however. When he reported on the contents of the box at a meeting of the Royal Geographical Society, he said it contained "a missing [map] section . . . of much importance," but that the notes were "in great measure duplicates of the Journal which had been published."[9] The *Last Journals* had been set in type; its editorial shape served a humanitarian purpose. Waller must also have realized that to say otherwise would only jeopardize the sales of the book as it stood. As the following chapters will demonstrate, such a pronouncement obscured the way in which editorial changes, beginning with those made by Livingstone himself, made inaccessible much of interest and value that the traveller recorded during his last journey.

*　　　　　*　　　　　*

The official telegram from Zanzibar confirming the death of David Livingstone arrived in England in late January 1874. In February the Foreign Office wired its consulate at Zanzibar to send home Livingstone's body at Government expense. Dr. John Kirk had arrived in England on leave in early January. The charges raised by Livingstone regarding Kirk's behavior in supplying him from the coast—that he had hired slaves to lead the caravan and had been dilatory in making sure that it set off inland—had been officially investigated by Sir Bartle Frere as part of his Foreign Office mission to Zanzibar the previous year. On Frere's strong recommendation, Kirk was completely exonerated and his permanent appointment as consul-general and political agent at Zanzibar confirmed. The Government was then gratified by Kirk's able diplomacy in convincing the sultan that he must sign the new slave trade treaty prohibiting seaborne slave traffic in his dominions. Now secure in his career, Kirk had returned home for the first time since 1866 bringing his family. When he learned at the Foreign Office that Livingstone's papers would be accompanying his body home, he wrote to John Murray, Livingstone's publisher and family friend, "[I]t is little matter with men of his stamp where his body is left . . . his real monuments" were his journals.[10]

Kirk added that he anticipated a visit from Agnes Livingstone and promised to speak to her about placing all her father's papers in Murray's hands, "for there has been no one more intimate with her father than I." Whatever Kirk may have had in mind regarding Livingstone's journals and any role he might play in their publication, he underestimated the harm which Stanley's charges had done to his relationship with Agnes. Official exoneration had not erased from her memory the bitter accusations Livingstone had levied against him in letters written in 1871 and 1872. One sign of the continuing strain caused by this affair was that Agnes did not visit Kirk in February 1874. In fact, she had written Murray the year before that she was still convinced that Kirk had not "exerted himself as he should have done. Mr. Stanley told me one or two things privately which pained me much but it may rest till Papa returns."[11]

While staying at Waller's vicarage in Leytonstone, Essex, early in April 1874, Agnes did write to John Murray about the publication of her father's last journals. She informed him that just that day James Young, her father's old friend and one of her guardians, had delivered the sealed Unyanyembe journal to her, but that she had decided to await the arrival of her brother Tom before opening it.[12] With the death of his brother Robert in 1864, Tom had become David Livingstone's oldest surviving son. Upon learning of the death of his father, Tom had joined the P. & O. steamer *Malwa* at Alexandria in Egypt, where he worked for a mercantile firm, to accompany the body home. Although Agnes was two years Tom's senior—in 1874 she was 27 and he 25—and despite the fact that she was closer to her father than any of his children, she was clearly prepared to defer to Tom as the male head of the family.

By the time Agnes wrote this letter to the publisher, she had received more advice on the subject in a letter of condolence from H. M. Stanley. He confessed, "I loved him as a son . . . and while I think of him I shall think of his children, more especially his favorite daughter, and friend, and of the deep, deep love he bore for her." He then cautioned her to "be careful to whom you show the Journal, for it is now of pecuniary value to you. . . . If Murphy brings all of your father's notebooks, one of your brothers should be deputed to receive them, and guard them in like manner." He wrote the day after returning to England from West Africa in mid-March, unaware that Murphy was not accompanying the body to England and that Tom Livingstone was arranging to meet it in Egypt. He was certain, however, that "the book is worth £10,000 at the least for you."[13]

A week after Agnes wrote John Murray, early Wednesday morning, April 15, the *Malwa* docked at Southampton. Agnes did not accompany her brother Oswell and Horace Waller to join the small party of men who boarded the *Malwa*. W. F. Webb of Newstead Abbey and Livingstone's father-in-law Robert Moffat also represented the family, while General C. P. Rigby, British consul at Zanzibar in the 1860s, and explorer Colonel James A. Grant represented the Royal Geographical Society. The Reverend Mr. W. Salter Price of Nasik Asylum represented the Church Missionary Society, which had paid the passage from Zanzibar for Jacob Wainwright to accompany Livingstone's remains. A naval official and some newspaper reporters, including H. M. Stanley, made up the group waiting to receive the body. This solemn entourage accompanied the coffin to the Royal Pier, where it was ceremoniously received by the mayor of Southampton and his corporation officials in robes and regalia. This procession, augmented by other local dignitaries, marched

"Arrival of Dr. Livingstone's Remains at Southampton," front page, *London Illustrated News,* Saturday, April 25, 1874. From the text, Waller is identified as the tall bearded figure in the center of the second row behind the carriage carrying the coffin. The man in the white beard directly in front of him was probably Dr. Robert Moffat, Tom Livingstone's grandfather.

through the streets to place the coffin on a special train for London. There a hearse and mourning coaches delivered the party to the Royal Geographical Society on Saville Row.

Later that afternoon, Waller joined the medical men, including Dr. Kirk, at the official physical examination to ascertain the identity of the body before it was placed in its final solid coffin. Waller, Rigby, Grant, and Webb had been asked by the RGS to manage the state funeral arrangements. The following Saturday, Waller rode in the third of the twelve official mourning coaches that accompanied the hearse to Westminster Abbey, along with three other men who had known Livingstone in Africa—W. Cotton Oswell, Edward D. Young, and Henry M. Stanley. At the Abbey, they joined four other men who had known Livingstone in Africa to act as the pall bearers—John Kirk, W. F. Webb, Major-General Sir Thomas Steele (who had accompanied W. Cotton Oswell to Africa), and Jacob Wainwright. The pall bearers made a memorable sight, four of them—Webb, Oswell, Waller, and Kirk—being over six feet tall.[14]

Two days before the *Malwa* docked, Sir Bartle Frere, addressing a meeting of the Royal Geographical Society as its president, announced that everyone interested in Dr. Livingstone's last days and travels would be glad to know that "an immense mass of information had been safely brought to England." He predicted:

> When his literary remains were collected and examined by competent geographical authorities in this country, they would form a monument to his memory such as no other traveller in our day, or even for ages past, had left behind him.[15]

Soon after Tom arrived in England, he agreed to undertake the task of editing his father's papers for publication. Frere announced his decision at the Royal Geographical Society on April 27, with praise for the "most worthy son . . . who had given up for a time a very promising career in Egypt to perform this pious duty to his parent, to his country, and to all mankind." Frere also referred to the "very valuable materials" Jacob Wainwright would contribute to the narrative in the shape of his own journal and "his oral communications."[16]

Within three weeks of the funeral, therefore, Tom was housed at Newstead Abbey, where his father had enjoyed the hospitality of the Webb family while writing *The Zambesi and Its Tributaries* in 1864 and 1865. From there, in a letter written May 7, Tom announced to John Murray, that he had "all the papers arranged" and would "begin the steady work at once."[17] Conscious that a significant part of the task was

Jacob Wainwright posed beside Livingstone's coffin, 1874. The coffin in the photographic studio, set in front of painted scenery and flanked by potted palms, is probably empty. The Church Missionary Society paid for Wainwright's passage to England to use him to help raise funds for establishing a freed slave settlement on the East Coast. Like Susi and Chuma, he looks a trifle uncomfortable in his stiff English clothing.

to supply a narrative of his father's last days and the journey undertaken by Livingstone's men in carrying his body to the coast, Tom urged Murray to secure Jacob Wainwright's diary on his behalf.[18]

An East African slave liberated by the British coastal squadron, Wainwright had been taught English and Christianity at the CMSNasik Asylum in India and had responded to a call for volunteers to join Livingstone early in 1872. He was described by the Nasik superintendent, Price, as "a well-educated, thoroughly reliable, earnest, good young man." He arrived in Zanzibar with five other Nasik youths to join the first Livingstone Relief Expedition under Lt. Llewellyn S. Dawson. Upon the breakup of that expedition, he and his Nasik colleagues were hired by Stanley to accompany the other men and goods he was dispatching to Livingstone before leaving Zanzibar.[19]

On the day Tom wrote Murray urging him to acquire Wainwright's diary, however, the publisher was already writing him from London advising against purchasing it. Early that day, Edward Hutchinson, lay secretary of the Church Missionary Society, had sent Murray the diary and some additional information he had obtained by cross-examining Wainwright. Two weeks earlier, Murray had suggested to Hutchinson that so long as the diary was not published before Livingstone's journals "the Livingstone family . . . are disposed to do justice to all parties concerned." He asked only to be allowed to read the diary before settling the matter.[20]

When Murray received the diary from Hutchinson on May 7, he read it swiftly and concluded that it "contains very little of your Father's last moments, sayings or doings." He decided that he could not in conscience advise buying the journal for the asking price of £200 "unless expressly authorized by you to do so." The contents of the diary outlined the process of preparing the body and the subsequent march, "but the whole together if printed would not make more than a sheet of the Zambesi volume." He further noted that he also had reason to expect that Wainwright's diary would actually be published in Germany in a few weeks.[21]

Murray did not mention to Tom how he had become aware of the possibility of a German publication. Edward Hutchinson himself had sent Murray a letter that had been written by Dr. August Petermann to Sampson, Low, Marston & Co. in London, dated April 28. Petermann offered to sell the English copy of Wainwright's diary to Sampson, Low for exclusive use or for an arrangement that would allow him to publish a German translation of it in his geographical journal, *Geographische Mittheilungen*.[22]

Murray consoled Tom with the thought that the *New York Herald* interview with Wainwright at Suez, where he boarded the *Malwa*, contained "very nearly the substance of all J. W. has to say." That dispatch had appeared in *The Times* March 30, 1874. Murray ended by commenting that Tom would have "to gather information elsewhere in order to complete your narrative."[23] If he anticipated that Susi and Chuma, on their way to England, might serve Tom as sources of information, he did not raise the possibility.

Tom Livingstone was not so easily deterred, especially when urged on by H. M. Stanley, who joined him at Newstead Abbey. He wrote Murray May 9, laying claim to Wainwright's diary on the grounds that its author was in Dr. Livingstone's employ when it was written. In a letter which arrived the day he had written Tom recommending against purchasing the diary, Murray had learned Stanley's views on this subject. Stanley said he wrote at Tom's request and spelled out his reasoning: Wainwright had been discharged by Oswell Livingstone at the breakup of the RGS expedition in 1872; he was then hired by Stanley to serve Dr. Livingstone. These events left Wainwright, though originally sent from the Nasik Asylum, a free agent—that is, not under the wing of the Church Missionary Society. After Livingstone's death, his servant was not automatically "discharged." Hence "whatever Jacob . . . wrote belongs to the Doctor's family - and the Church Mission has nothing whatever to do with him."[24]

When, in late May, a meeting on the diary was held with Edward Hutchinson, attended by Tom, John Murray, W. F. Webb, and Sir Bartle Frere, the question of "ownership" was not raised. Hutchinson felt it necessary to point this out when he replied to Tom's letter of May 31, which did raise the issue. As the representative of the Church Missionary Society, Hutchinson made his position clear. He could not see that Tom "was entitled to the benefit of the cow driver's diary after his master was dead." He then added, "[I]f you intend to do nothing for the boy in fairness let me know in time to bring out the Diary for his benefit. . . . No allusion shall be made to the march from Unyanyembe to Bemba and I will send the Proofs to you. . . ."[25]

Protracted negotiation had settled nothing. In the meantime, however, the situation changed dramatically. By the time Tom received Hutchinson's letter, which was written June 9, Tom had decided not to press the matter, but to turn it over entirely to John Murray. Tom was now convinced that Wainwright's diary was not essential to him. He had found a better solution to the problem of writing about Livingstone's final days and the journey his men made carrying his body to the coast. Two of his father's "faithful followers," men who had accompanied Livingstone since the beginning of his last journey in 1866, had arrived in

England, brought there through the good graces of James Young of Kelly. Just as Young's contribution of £1000 had been crucial in launching Livingstone on his last journey into Africa, so his willingness to pay the passages of the men Waller claimed were the leaders of the caravan that brought Livingstone's remains home would prove crucial to the shaping of Livingstone's last testament.

Waller had been indignant when he first learned from *The Times* of March 30 that the *Malwa* would be bringing home Livingstone's body accompanied by Jacob Wainwright. He hastened to send the editor of *The Times* a letter that was published the next day, expressing concern that the real leaders of the caravan that carried Livingstone's remains to the coast, Susi and Chuma, had been overlooked. "Why are the officers passed over," he had asked, "while a private is preferred before them?"[26] On the face of it, it must have been Waller's views that convinced Young that the wrong person was on his way to England if they were to learn all the details of what had happened. Young had responded to Waller's conviction in 1867 that the tale of Livingstone's death had a false ring to it and had financed E. D. Young to check out the story. Now the arrival of Susi and Chuma gave Tom an opportunity to listen to them talk about their last days with his father and convinced him that he no longer need worry about obtaining Wainwright's diary.

Tom wrote the publisher from Newstead Abbey, June 10, while Susi and Chuma were staying there. He had concluded that these men would be "of immense service to us," for ". . . they are particularly intelligent, speaking English well. Susi's Geographical knowledge is something wonderful and will be of great use in discussing the Tanganyika question." Tom assured Murray, "I can get four times as much from Susi and Chuma as they can from Jacob."[27] Thereafter, nothing more is heard of Wainwright's diary in the editing of Livingstone's *Last Journals*.

Shortly before Tom made this decision, Waller gave a lecture on David Livingstone in London, on the evening of May 29 at the National Temperance League. Both Tom and Stanley showed up to listen. According to a newspaper report the next day, Stanley made his appearance with his African servant Kalulu after Waller had begun speaking. After the talk, Tom proposed a vote of thanks to Waller and Stanley seconded it. Tom referred to Waller, the newspaper continued, as "one of the best friends of his family and one of the most intimate friends of his father."[28] Tom's expression of good will toward Waller at this time might be noted. It suggests that Tom anticipated no problems in planning a close collaboration with Waller, with whom Susi and Chuma would be staying.

Coverage of the same lecture in *The Times* emphasized different as-

Chuma (left) and Susi at Newstead Abbey, 1874, with Livingstone's Unyanyembe Journal and field diaries. The relics included Livingstone's famous peaked cap, his consular sword, his rifle, instruments for recording his route, maps, and some surgical tools. The lion skin was probably a trophy of William F. Webb, the Abbey's owner, who had been a big-game hunter in Africa.

pects of the occasion. For example, *The Times* noted that Waller told his audience that Susi and Chuma had just arrived at the Victoria Docks that very afternoon, and that he had seen them. He excused himself for not bringing them along that evening, saying they were "not presentable for want of clothes, and there had not been time to procure them any." *The Times* did not report the votes of thanks given to the lecturer. Instead, the reader learned that Stanley rose to make a point of differing from the speaker's views. First, Stanley disagreed that the missionary "ought to go to Africa before the Manchester man." In Stanley's opinion, the merchant's encouragement of "industry, thrift, and comfort among the African population" would prepare the way for the missionary's labors. Then, he said, he must differ with Waller, who had "eulogized Chuma." Stanley would give "the preference to Suzi [sic], who he also knew was Livingstone's favourite servant, and the spirit that gave the impetus in that trying journey of 1,500 miles."[29] The adversarial nature of the exchange is not lost on the reader.

When Tom wrote John Murray June 10 about his hopes of obtaining what he needed from Susi and Chuma, he also stated that he had made an important decision regarding his father's journals. After working on them for a month, he had given up his first inclination "to render the book as popular as possible." Instead, "on the advice of friends," he agreed that to do justice to the geographical and other aspects of the journals he would have to make the book "an Historical work." He wrote Murray that he would turn over the task of "merely copying" the journal to "an amanuensis," while he devoted his time to arranging the papers "in their relative places."[30]

These remarks may mean that Tom first envisioned reading the Unyanyembe journal and field notebooks available to him and writing the story presented by them. Urged to produce an accurate account—in Tom's words, a "Historical" one—he decided not to depart from his father's own words. At this stage, John Murray must also have suggested that it would be easier to work from printed copy. There was no need to waste time copying the Unyanyembe journal; it could be set directly into type. By mid June, Tom had agreed to this procedure and announced that he was moving into lodgings in Leytonstone, taken for him by Mr. Waller, at whose vicarage Susi and Chuma were now staying.[31]

It is possible that as July approached John Murray may have begun to feel some concern about Tom's ability to organize and carry out his editorial tasks in time for publication in November, the beginning of the next "publishing season." Murray and all those concerned about the welfare of Livingstone's children believed it was necessary for the *Last*

Agnes and Tom Livingstone, Susi (left) and Chuma, and the Rev. Horace Waller (sitting on the ground) at Newstead Abbey, Nottinghamshire, 1874. At this time Susi may have been in his early forties, while Chuma was in his early twenties.

Journals to appear at that time in order to take advantage of the enthusiasm of readers who had already that year followed so avidly the events connected with Livingstone's life and death. Both as Livingstone's publisher and as one of his children's friends, John Murray knew that substantial earnings from the book would be a welcome legacy from their father.[32]

The decision to make Tom the editor of his father's last journals presumably involved family discussions about his availability, his willingness, and the advisability of having the task done by a family member. Yet of the two surviving sons—and no one, including Agnes herself, seems to have suggested that she undertake the literary work—Oswell had carried off the school prizes, while Tom's history of poor health had prevented him from completing his formal education. Oswell, however, had returned from East Africa in 1872 in an "unsettled" state of mind, and that fall, a time when Tom was gravely ill, there was some anxiety about Oswell's returning to his medical studies. Tom's employment by a mercantile firm in Egypt was viewed as an important opportunity to pursue a career in a warm climate. It is likely that the family did not wish Oswell to take any further break in his medical training, which he had resumed. Tom's quick agreement to becoming his father's editor, therefore, may have pleased everyone. Yet his health did not hold up, even in Egypt, where he died in March 1876. Oswell survived him by only fourteen years.[33]

Even with the best of health and a more extensive formal education, Tom might have found the task he had undertaken a tedious one. Despite the long letters his father had written him, Tom's imagination was not stirred by the scenes or the problems that constituted his father's African career. At one point, once the editing of the Unyanyembe journal was underway, Agnes complained to John Murray that Tom ". . . was inclined to leave out too much, such as descriptions of scenery."[34]

Other family tensions underlay the choice of the editor of Livingstone's *Last Journals*. Tom and Oswell had openly clashed in 1872 over the Kirk controversy. Robert Cooke, a cousin of John Murray and his publishing partner, had written Murray at the time of Stanley's arrival in England in early August 1872 that "Tom & Oswell Livingstone have had a bit of a row. The former, who is more like his Pa, [sic] than the latter thought O had come forward too soon in defense of Kirk."[35]

Oswell Livingstone had been in East Africa with the RGS Livingstone Search and Relief Expedition under Lt. L. S. Dawson. When his superiors all resigned their commands upon learning that Stanley had anticipated them, Oswell briefly contemplated taking up the supplies to his father himself. After discussion with John Kirk at the British consulate in Zanzibar, however, Oswell decided it was useless to risk his own life by venturing inland in the rainy season. Kirk allowed Oswell to read his official correspondence from Livingstone, accusing him of sending only slaves as porters, men who freely made off with his property and seemed by their behavior to be following orders from the consul to force him back to the coast before his work was done. Such documents may have convinced Oswell, then only twenty-one, that even a personally delivered plea to his father to return home—for such was his intent—would fail.

Because of David Livingstone's dedication to his African work, his son Oswell had first consciously made his acquaintance at the age of six in 1857 and 1858; at the age of thirteen the boy saw him again in 1864 and 1865. Harboring what must have been a complicated set of disappointments in 1872, Oswell returned home without seeing his father, convinced that Livingstone had been quite unfair to Kirk. When Stanley made his public accusations against Kirk in France, a few days before he appeared in London, Oswell sent a defense of Kirk to the *Daily Telegraph*.[36] On the other hand, Agnes, who had been seventeen when she lived with her father during his 1864 to 1865 stay in England and had maintained close ties with him in their correspondence, tended to believe her father about Kirk and to accept Stanley's accusations. On this point she and Tom, two of the principal participants in the events which led to the choice of Waller to edit Livingstone's *Last Journals*, were agreed. Of the two, as we shall see, Tom was less happy with that choice.

While Tom was settling in next door to Waller's vicarage in Leytonstone, John Murray's anxieties about Tom's editorial skills had mounted high enough to cause him to write W. F. Webb on the matter. At this time, Agnes was staying with Webb at his summer home in Scotland. Webb confessed to Murray that he too had "many anxious thoughts" about the editorial work in progress. In reply to what must have been a suggestion that the family consider placing the editorial task in other hands, and to a question about his views on Stanley as a possible editor, Webb declared Stanley

> . . . a most zealous and true friend of the Dr and staunch and loyal to the backbone in all that concerns his memory; & I have little doubt but that his name being associated with the book would be popular with the public. We must not however be unmindful of the fact, that there are a party who still detest the name of Stanley, and who look upon all he had done, & ever will do, with suspicion. . . . the question seems to be[:] displease the Geographers, or

the British public. Chuma and Susi are under Waller's care, and most unfortunately he hates Stanley in a manner that I cannot understand. Chuma and Susi will be invaluable for the book. . . . The only question with regard to Stanley as Editor is will he forgoe Americanisms and personalities? I have no doubt if he undertakes the task every effort will be made to provoke him. What does Tom Livingstone intend doing in this matter. . . [?][37]

With this reply, Webb enclosed a letter to Murray from Agnes. She wrote, "I fully endorse all he [Webb] says to you, & I think Mr Stanley will do anything for our benefit for our father's sake, & would not do us any harm." Agnes, too, was uneasy about the book's progress: "I have been feeling very anxious about the book, because for one thing my brother is physically unfit to write it himself. Mr. Stanley would be sure to get it finished in time & could get much information from Susi and Chuma. . . ."[38] Is is possible to conclude from Agnes's remarks that Tom's designation as editor had been more his own idea than a family choice, and that the family had not wished to challenge his decision as eldest son?

There are no letters in the publisher's archives to suggest that Stanley was approached. Webb and Agnes wrote their letters June 25, 1874. At that time Stanley was deeply involved in planning an African expedition under the joint sponsorship of the *New York Herald Tribune* and the London *Daily Telegraph* to settle the outstanding questions about the Nile sources, a geographical issue still unresolved at Livingstone's death. In late June Stanley was planning a quick visit to the United States and intended to leave for Africa within two months. A few discreet inquiries by Murray would have revealed this situation.[39] In any case, Webb's cautions about Stanley's standing with the British geographical community—within which John Murray moved—and his reminder that Susi and Chuma were staying with Waller may simply have convinced the publisher that it would be wise to look elsewhere for an editor.

What Murray had observed of Tom's progress, and what Agnes hinted, expressed in terms of her fear about his "physical fitness," now led him to move with alacrity. When Murray wrote Agnes again on July 3, 1874, he proposed that Horace Waller become the editor of her father's last journals. By that time he must have spoken to Tom, for when Agnes wrote her reply on July 6, she had already heard from her brother on the subject.

I have this morning received a letter from my brother on the same subject. . . . Tom objects to Mr Waller being chosen as editor.

... For my part, as Mr Stanley is now out of the question, I think that under certain conditions, Mr Waller would be eligible. .... I should stipulate ... before he undertakes it that he should strictly adhere to the original as far as possible, & then send the proof sheets along with the originals to my brother & myself, so that we may ... judge what should be left out or retained. ... Mr Waller I know would do justice to the papers, but I know also that he would in his anxiety to spare the feelings of many parties mentioned, erase facts which ought to be made public. I wish my father's own words to be used as much as possible. . . .[40]

Clearly Agnes viewed Waller's championship of Kirk as a potential problem in the editing of her father's last journals, fearing he would take advantage of his position as editor to tone down or even censor any condemnations of Kirk in Livingstone's journal or diaries. Agnes also believed that the existence, in some instances, of what she called the "duplicate notes"—probably a reference to the loose papers and newspaper-turned-diary that Livingstone had constructed for himself early in 1871 when he ran out of proper paper—indicated that her father had prepared his last journals with care, just as he wished them to be read by the public. This was a wish she shared, believing that the only course necessary was to ensure the publication of a full account of events as her father recorded them.

Agnes made one further suggestion in light of her own and Tom's hesitation to turn over the editing task to Waller. She wanted time to inquire whether her father's old friend William Cotton Oswell, someone she knew well, would undertake it. She asked Murray to delay any action regarding Waller until she had an opportunity to sound out Oswell.[41] Her hesitation, despite all the arguments in favor of Waller as an appropriate choice, makes clear how the controversies involving Kirk, Stanley, and Waller in 1872 affected choosing an editor for Livingstone's *Last Journals*, just as they affected the editorial process itself.

John Murray, extremely anxious that he make a November publication date, had already asked Waller to look over the papers brought home with Livingstone's body and to comment on the publication problems they presented. In his response of July 10, Waller noted particularly that there was some difficulty about the legibility of the field diaries that Livingstone had put together early in 1871 without proper paper or ink. "Of course I am speaking with reference to the amount of time we have at our disposal," he continued, making clear how involved he felt. He then positioned himself carefully: "The valuable matter is contained in these obscure writings. I suspect the 'journal' will prove a lode of very poor stuff whilst we must rely upon small pockets and nuggets (—to be looked for in notes, on scraps of newspapers and in the brains of Susi & Chuma) for the real payable gold." He capped his analysis with an urgent warning, "A book can be made and a good one, but I am sure one ought not to lose an hour in arranging some definite work plan for the Editor whoever he is to be."[42]

To an anxious publisher, Waller must have sounded like a man both competent and available. From Waller's carefully worded remarks—emphasizing the difficulties of deciphering the most valuable material, stressing the importance of what Susi and Chuma, staying with him, would be able to contribute, and remarking on the need for an immediate plan of action by an editor—we can conclude that he meant to sound that way.

By July 16, Agnes had to acknowledge her failure to secure W. C. Oswell.[43] In response to her request, he had declared that much as he was touched by this expression of confidence, careful consideration led him to decline. His reasons, according to his son and editor, were based ". . . on the grounds of his inability to do justice to it, of the health of his wife, which rendered a winter abroad a probability, and of the expressed view of the publishers that Mr. Waller was the most competent and suitable person for the task."[44] Later, when Oswell received the completed volumes, he wrote to Agnes, referring to his decision not to accept the editorship. "I was not fit for it, and," he remarked pointedly, "in the face of what Mr. Murray said it would have been an impertinence to put myself forward." He then added generously, "Now . . . all has been done so much better than I could have done it. . . ."[45] Oswell's statements make it evident that the publisher had already made up his mind who should edit Livingstone's *Last Journals.*

Despite the fact that Agnes, in Scotland, continued to press Murray to wait upon her brother Tom's views, John Murray decided that there was no more time left. Tom had been using his energies for what at this phase could only be called tangential questions. He had requested the Council of the Royal Geographical Society to ask General Christopher P. Rigby, former Zanzibar consul, and John Kirk, still in England on leave, to examine Susi and Chuma in their own language regarding the articles Cameron had removed from Livingstone's boxes at Unyanyembe. At their meeting on July 13, 1874, the members of the Council formally declined the request.[46]

Cameron's expedition had become an explosive issue in its own right. His bills were mounting to a level of indebtedness that caused shock and dismay at the society. However, Cameron was the only African explorer the RGS now had in the field, and they needed to gather still more public

John Murray III by Sir George Reid RA. Murray played a pivotal role in choosing an editor for the *Last Journals* and in the decisions concerning its publication. His activities within the British geographical and religious communities and his choice to be painted at work at his desk, surrounded by manuscripts, suggests a Victorian dedication to industry and good works.

support for his expenses. They were not about to precipitate any public recriminations involving Livingstone's family. In addition, since Susi and Chuma were staying with Waller, who knew enough of their language to converse with them,[47] it must have been painfully clear to the Council that encouraging Tom was unwise; he obviously had several axes to grind. The Council had enough problems of their own with Cameron; they were determined to take no part in these quarrels.

Tom Livingstone's employment of his time in this direction may have settled the issue in Murray's mind. He discussed the matter further with Waller and on July 17, 1874, he sent him a formal offer:

> With the knowledge and consent of Dr. Livingstone's children, I have the pleasure of proposing to you to become the Editor of their Father's posthumous journals or Travels for which your knowledge of him and of the people and country seems peculiarly to fit you. The transcribed journal will, I think I may state, require very little editing, though you will necessarily be called upon to see it through the press and there are some questions of omission and insertion. This part is already in the printer's hands. The later narrative will, as you are already aware, require greater care and labour on the Editor's part, owing to the disjointed condition of the M.S.S. and the difficulty of deciphering parts of it. Besides this to the Editor will devolve the duty of writing the account of the last days of the lamented traveller down to his death as far as it can be derived from his faithful Black attendants. This ought obviously to be narrated in as simple a style as possible—as becomes the character of the hero of the work, equally obvious is it that as few changes as possible should be made in what he has written.
>
> It is of the greatest consequence to the success of the work, in which the interests of the children of Dr L. are so largely involved that it should be ready for publication by November next.
>
> If you can kindly undertake this task I shall with pleasure offer you the sum of £250—for your time, labour, for the compensation which you must of necessity make to a curate in relieving you of part of your other duties. It is scarce necessary to add that I will afford every assistance in my power to aid you in your work.

At the bottom left-hand corner of the publisher's copy of this letter, initialled J. M., is the note: "Chuma & Susi are to be paid at the rate of £5 per month in lieu of wages during their stay in England." At the bottom right-hand corner, also initialled J. M., is another note: "read over to Th S Livingstone by me July 24."[48]

John Murray had acted with less of the knowledge and consent of Livingstone's children than his formal letter to Waller indicates. He had the force of logic on his side, however, and Agnes was the first to concede it. She wrote Murray that she had learned of what had been done from a letter written by Waller to Webb, dated July 21. She assumed, however, that Tom had been consulted in person and had given his consent. She again expressed her concern that Waller not leave out anything in the last notebooks, and that he should ". . . in justice to Mr Stanley, write down all that my father says about him."[49]

Tom Livingstone wrote an angry letter to Murray on July 23, expressing dismay at the way the publisher had finally taken matters into his own hands. The primary sentiments expressed, however, involved Tom's dislike of being ordered about by Waller and his concern—shared by Agnes—that Waller not use his editorial role to change Livingstone's presentation of his relations with Stanley. More strikingly, Tom did not protest the essential decision to make someone else the editor of his father's last journals. His silence on this point suggests his tacit acknowledgment that if the publishing deadline were to be met, the editorial tasks had to be placed in other hands:

I have your letter of yesterday's date in reference to the Editing of my Father's papers. I have not called on you simply because, as far as I can judge, you had already made the requisite arrangements with Mr. Waller without its seeming necessary to ask my opinion or my consent. I am quite aware of the difficulties of getting my Father's papers properly put together (its [sic] long since I pointed that out to you) and as I think you know am quite as anxious that it should be properly done, but I scarcely like the way you honour me in consultation; the first intimation I got is a sort of "stand & deliver" request from Mr. Waller as regards all journals, maps, papers &c I have in my possession; however this is a matter of secondary moment. I am quite disposed to advise my Sister & Brother to acquiesce in the arrangement you propose, but there is one point on which I should like to be precise & on which I am sure I speak with the authorization of the whole family & friends & that is that we (the family), [sic] *must* have the right & power to cut out of the journal any parts we think fit & that without any question. We have quite as many objections to Mr Waller as the Rev. Gentleman has to Mr Stanley & we ask no more than he would have wished had it been in Mr Stanley's hands.[50]

Three days before Tom wrote this letter Waller had conferred in person with Murray and had written him a formal letter of acceptance: "I will merely add that as a result of my interview with you this morning it is further understood between us that all Dr. Livingstone's M.S.S. will be placed at my disposal to use in the undertaking and that no interference will take place on the part of any one whatever. . . . You were also kind enough to say that you would allow my name to appear as Editor of the Doctor's journal when published."[51]

The next day Murray wrote to Tom and to James Young. Young had been a natural choice for Livingstone to make in naming trustees to take charge of his children's finances in the late 1850s when his first book, *Missionary Travels*, a Victorian bestseller, produced a large capital sum to be invested. With the characteristic humor he employed toward those with whom he felt at ease, Livingstone had dubbed his old friend "Sir Paraffin" for having made his wealth from the discovery of a method by which to make paraffin from coal shale. Young had been generous to his friend over the years. Not only had he contributed the initial £1000 to send Livingstone back to Africa in 1865, but he had also financed the E. D. Young search expedition in 1867 and had borne the cost of a West Coast Rescue and Relief Expedition under Lt. W. J. Grandy in 1873–1874 to complement Cameron's efforts from the east. Finally, it was Young who agreed to bring Susi and Chuma to England in the spring of 1874.[52]

James Young had met Waller through Livingstone in the mid-1860s. Because he knew Waller and Livingstone had been in Africa together, he took Waller's advice in connection with E. D. Young's 1867 expedition and used Waller as his intermediary with the Royal Geographical Society in setting up the Grandy expedition in 1873. Young's reply to John Murray concerning the choice of Waller to edit Livingstone's *Last Journals* was therefore important, but not surprising: "I quite approve of the course you have taken with regard to Dr. Livingstone's book & I expect the other trustees here will do the same when they understand about Tom's attempt breaking down & the other circumstances connected with the matter. I know of no one so well fitted for the task as Mr. Waller. He will have a hard task to get through the work so as to be ready for publishing in November."[53]

Agnes Livingstone's final capitulation to Murray's decision came with more grace than her brother had managed. "I am truly thankful," she wrote Murray on July 28, "to hear that all is settled with Mr Horace Waller. I wrote to him offering to aid him in any way, & hope he & Tom will pull together." Unlike Tom, Agnes did not mention her brother Oswell as someone involved in receiving Tom's advice on the subject. Agnes wrote the publisher again two day later to say, "I received a letter from Mr Waller. . . . I do not presume to alter anything, unless I think it ought to be omitted. Mr Waller enters into my feelings completely, so I feel more at ease than I did." The next day, when she had begun to read early proof, she commented, "So far there has been nothing to omit, & I do hope my brother will judge rightly, because he is so apt to erase what does not interest him without thinking it will probably interest the majority of people."[54]

Tom was not so easily mollified. In fact, at the end of July he wrote Murray to suggest that he see all the proof first, expunge as he saw fit, and then have the corrected proof sent to Waller to "save him a considerable amount of unnecessary trouble." He expanded on this theme: "I would also correct the *lapsus pennae* which occur & in hazy sentences I could easily supply what is necessary & I venture to assert without fear of seeming to "brag" that I shall do so better than Mr. Waller or rather I should say more in my Father's own words. . . . it seems to me that there is no necessity for his seeing what we purpose to exclude & I think will be less likely to hurt what I know are the very tender 'feelings' of Waller." In addition, Tom had pointed remarks to make about a first version of the narrative Waller had written from Susi and Chuma's tale of Livingstone's last days and their journey to the coast with his body. He warned Murray: "[A]ll I can say is that when he turns it into better English as he threatens to do it will be even less like anything Susi, Chuma or my Father could have produced & is thoroughly 'Wallerian' if I may coin a word."[55]

Whatever Murray thought of Tom's "solution" to the question of reading proof, he soon heard from Waller on the subject. Waller, in his turn, insisted that the printer send him the proof directly. He was careful to assure Murray that he did not anticipate a problem with Tom over this issue, but he also wanted to convey how strongly he felt about the matter. The strength of his objections to Tom's reading the final narrative he was producing at the proof stage suggests that Tom had already made his own views apparent to the author of these passages.

I see parcels come for Tom Livingstone days before I get the same material and I have to ask him to allow me to use them. . . . I don't want the proofs to my M.S.S. to go to Livingstone at all. . . . you will have duplicates and this will suffice for all criticism. I say this not with any cross feelings, for Tom is very nice about everything but I am of necessity writing so fast to get the narrative welded together in its several parts that I would much rather it come back from the printers direct to my hands without going elsewhere than to yourself.[56]

Waller's letter to Murray was dated August 3, 1874. He had made the final arrangements about his editorial work with the publisher on July 20. He was only two weeks into his formal work on the book, and he had already grasped the scale of the work before him. Apparently not for the first time he warned the publisher, ". . . you will have too much for 1 vol." Whatever Tom's opinion of the editor of his father's last journals, Murray's judgment that choosing Waller for the task would give them a chance to get the work out on time was borne out. In just under three weeks from the date he accepted the assignment, Waller finished the narrative by Susi and Chuma. In the meantime, two days after Waller's outburst on the subject of Tom's receiving proof before he did, he announced to Murray that Oswell Livingstone "promises to come and help as amenuensis next week."[57] The two brothers continued to take opposite sides.

By August 8, Waller had begun the two other parts of his editorial task: editing the Unyanyembe journal coming from the printer and making sense of Livingstone's field diaries and the loose papers that had accompanied them. At the beginning of September, he complained to Murray that Tom had gone off to Scotland without giving him any corrected proof and that he had deciphered but three of twenty-nine pages of obscure writing. Waller therefore asked his friend the Reverend Charles A. Alington for help. Alington had accompanied Bishop Tozer to Africa in 1863 to take over the original Universities' Mission to the Shire Highlands; there he met both Livingstone and Waller. He had subsequently corresponded with Livingstone and was familiar with his handwriting. Waller urged Murray not to mention these problems to Tom. "Really," he concluded, "it is quite useless to rely on him."[58]

The competing claims of Livingstone's family and the authorized editor of the last journals over control of the first proof presented Murray with a problem that he handled as diplomatically as possible. There still exist proof sheets for the first portion of the book, printed from the Unyanyembe journal, which contain a number of decisions and corrections initialled by Tom Livingstone and first and second "revises" that indicate decisions and corrections made by Waller, along with some initialled by John Murray himself. The pattern suggests that the publisher met this awkward situation by simply sending Waller a separate set of proof while asking the printer to continue to respond to Tom's corrections, supplementing the process to some extent with his own set.[59] As we shall see in the next chapter, on the whole this process worked because Tom dealt with the first set of proof before Waller could begin to look at it and Tom, though he made a number of significant early deci-

Signed photograph of David Livingstone by Thomas Annan of Hamilton and Glasgow, 1857. Perhaps it is the most famous photograph of the missionary explorer; he gave the signed copy reproduced here to the Universities' Mission to Central Africa. The artist J. W. Whymper made an engraving made from this likeness for the frontispiece for Volume I of the *Last Journals*.

sions, did not attack the prose in any systematic way, merely looking for what he saw as egregious material to be excised.

Waller's warning that the material he was working with would require two volumes was heeded by the publisher. By October 19 Waller reported that he had corrected proof for the first volume and planned to be finished with the second within a week. He even allowed himself to pass along some praise at this stage, writing Murray that "Kirk speaks well of the book. I know he considered it almost hopeless before we set to work – this cheers one up a bit."[60] By this time, more sure of himself in the editorial role, Waller was also willing to respond graciously when Agnes Livingstone wrote Murray that she felt "entitled to see the proof of Mr Waller's work." He agreed to share with both Agnes and James Young the proof of the narrative that formed the last part of the book.[61]

When Agnes received her copy of the published volumes of the *Last Journals of David Livingstone* in mid-December 1874, she assured Murray of her appreciation for all Waller's work. "I am perfectly satisfied . . ." she wrote, "& do not think it could have been edited more carefully or more lovingly."[62] Four days later, however, she had discovered that Tom's name was nowhere to be found in the Introduction and she expressed indignation on behalf of the family. She wrote Murray in some dismay, "As Grandpa [Dr. Robert Moffat] says Tom worked hard at correcting proofs, & believed he was giving assistance, tho' Mr Waller says the proof was of no use to him. . . . Why could you Mr Murray allow Tom's name to be omitted when you knew how much work he was doing. I understood that Tom was to edit the large journal and Mr Waller the rest."[63] Agnes's remarks are a comment on the balancing act Murray performed with regard to how much each participant in these events knew what was actually happening with the proof.

From Alexandria in Egypt in January 1875, Tom Livingstone expressed himself more pungently and bitterly on receiving his ten copies of the book. He complimented its appearance, but he objected to the use of some of the illustrations from his father's book *The Zambesi and Its Tributaries*. He then praised the facsimile illustration of the newspaper Livingstone had used to write across when he ran out of paper in 1871, and he liked the portrait of his father at the beginning of the first volume. These preliminaries over, he let loose his pent-up indignation and rage against Waller.

> I have nothing to say as to Mr Waller's not having mentioned me, as that was entirely as he chose, and at his discretion, but he needn't tell my friends that there isn't a single line of mine in the book. As Mr Waller never saw beyond 36 pages or so of the *first* proofs how

does he know? I can point out a few variations in the original that
he had nothing to do with. My agreement with you sir was that
there wasn't anything to be published without my approval & I
could & did excise whatever I chose. I never claimed any "Editorship" in this & Mr Waller needn't howl so loud about his agreements with you. I suppose he has got his £250 & glory; what more
does he want?[64]

Murray, in fact, may well have believed that he emerged relatively
unscathed from a potentially explosive situation. He had managed to
keep each person closely involved in the process of bringing the last
journals to publication sufficiently, if not fully, informed to allow the
project to proceed. The result was a book that he could bring out at the
height of the publishing season. He expressed his own appreciation of
this achievement by presenting Waller with the more aristocratic sum of
250 guineas, instead of the plebian pounds promised in the original
agreement. Since guineas were only an elegant turn of phrase for the
equivalent of one pound and one shilling, the receipt that Waller signed
discreetly recorded in the bottom left corner the sum of £262–
10–0. It was paid December 5, 1874.[65]

Any inclination on the part of Livingstone's family to continue to feel
aggrieved on behalf of Tom tended to dissipate in the first two months
of the new year. By that time it became clear that Tom had been rather
careless in the early stages of the management of his father's papers. The
coastal section of the map Livingstone had drawn of his journey inland
in 1866 could not be found. Waller asked Agnes in October 1874 to check
among her brother's papers for any additional material in her father's
handwriting. She asked her Aunt Janet in Hamilton, one of Livingstone's
sisters, to check on a box of papers Tom had stored with her. Early in
January 1875, after the publication of the book, Janet Livingstone sent
John Murray a note that she had come upon "three sections of maps"
among her nephew's papers. She wrote she was "deeply grieved &
ashamed" that such documents should have gone unnoticed.[66]

In early February, Waller recorded that there had turned up ". . . another 2 pages with maps & important notes one especially about the
Arabs [sic] journey to the North." Agnes became exceedingly embar-
rassed about her brother's neglect: "I have lost heart in the Book now that
I know how doubly careless my brother has been. It made me sick at
heart indeed to hear that more maps had been found. I trusted all to my
brother, & Mr & Mrs Webb can bear witness to how he kept me completely in the dark all along." She now expressed regret that she had not

taken full charge of all the papers from the very first. She defended herself to John Murray, however, saying, ". . . I feel hurt at Mr. Waller's want of confidence in me, by giving me a share of the blame."[67]

Robert Moffat's anger at the omission of his grandson Tom's name from the Introduction of the *Last Journals* did not cool in the same way. He spoke to his friend Bevan Braithwaite, a Quaker and barrister with whom Livingstone corresponded regularly after 1857 and at whose home Mary Moffat Livingstone had often stayed with her children. Braithwaite spoke to Waller on the subject January 4, 1875, the day John Murray first heard from Janet Livingstone about Tom's negligence. Waller refused to change his mind, and noted in his diary on January 12 that Braithwaite had also seen Murray, who raised the same issue with him that day. Waller still refused and, on January 16, sent back proof of a revised Introduction to the printer. At Newstead Abbey on the 18th, Waller wrote, W. F. Webb "pressed me hard to say Tom L. had assisted me but I refused to do so." He showed his amended Introduction to John Murray, who said he "would have the note about Cameron altered still more strongly." Then, on February 3, "I received [a] letter from Murray inclosing notice from Editor of Leisure Hour [James Macaulay, 1817–1902] showing that a paragraph was going in about Tom L's helping me. . . . I have added his name to his sister's and Alington's to prevent an expose in print for it w[oul]d hurt the book." Waller wrote Moffat a letter the next day and gave Murray a revised Introduction on February 16.[68]

Despite the family's disappointments, the *Last Journals* did in fact prove to be a lasting memorial to David Livingstone. It provided the platform for his voice to be heard all across England and Scotland, as though, in Waller's graphic simile, from a balloon over Salisbury Plain. Then and later, his countrymen would point to Livingstone's words as justification for an ever greater British presence in Eastern Africa. Waller as the editor of the *Last Journals* had undertaken to shape this memorial to reflect the role he believed David Livingstone should play in such a process. To the extent that he had to mold the public man to fit the role, Waller contributed in his own right to the making of a Victorian legend.

Tom Livingstone sensed that Waller needed heroes to people his world. He was aware that as the immediacy of his relationship with Livingstone receded, Waller was already engaged in transferring the hero's mantle to the shoulders of another antislavery man, Colonel Charles George Gordon. With considerable bitterness, Tom wrote Murray, ". . . one is gone & there is a new traveller coming, who may be useful to Mr. Waller as my Father was."[69]

NOTES

1. Agnes Livingstone to Murray, Durris [House] n[ea]r Aberdeen, August 8, 1872, JMPA. At Ujiji, December 17, 1871, Livingstone recorded that he had also packed a "large tin box with Manyuema swords and spearheads" to go home with Stanley, and that he was sending home two chronometers, two watches, and "anklets of Nzige and of Manyuema." *The Last Journals of David Livingstone*, 2 vols. edited by Horace Waller (London, 1874), 2: 161 (hereafter, *LJDL*). Having been instructed by Livingstone to deliver the journal to Agnes, Stanley did not give it to her younger brother Oswell, with whom he travelled from Zanzibar. He did then give it to Tom as Agnes's agent.

2. François Bontinck reexamined the conflicting evidence concerning the actual date of Livingstone's death. He disputes both May 1, used by Waller in Livingstone's *Last Journals*—and inscribed on Livingstone's gravestone in Westminster Abbey—and May 4, used by Jacob Wainwright when inscribing the tree at the foot of which the explorer's heart was buried in Africa. He places Livingstone's death on April 28 at sundown. François Bontinck, "La Mort de Livingstone Réexaminée," *Africa: Revista trimestrale di studi e documentazione dell'Istituto Italo-Africano* (Rome) 33, no. 4 (Dicembre 1978): 579-603, esp. 581, 594-98.

3. *LJDL*, 2:339. The impulse to bury Livingstone in Africa was twice defeated. After the men resisted Cameron at Unyanyembe, he alerted Capt. W. F. Prideaux, the acting British consul at Zanzibar, about their impending arrival. The message arrived January 3, 1874, and was telegraphed to London. Meanwhile, Prideaux decided that when the body arrived, he would bury it with due honors. Only the Foreign Office telegram authorizing shipment home prevented him from putting this plan into action. The body left Zanzibar March 11. Capt. Lindeson Brine of *HMS Briton*, to Robert Cooke, January 15 [1874], JMPA. For the date of departure, see Central African Mission Diary, UMCA, USPGA.

4. "They have also two boxes of books with them and say there is another at Ujiji, which the Doctor told them to fetch and take down to the coast with them; so I intend, as the caravan consists of seventy or eighty men, to send part down to the coast at once with the body, and take part to Ujiji, to bring back the said box." Cameron to RGS Secretary, Unyanyembe, October 16, 1873, *PRGS* 18 (1873-1874): 177. For Livingstone's last instructions, see Bontinck, "Mort de Livingstone," esp. 585, 587-89. On the health of Cameron's party, see Cameron to Kirk, Unyanyembe [October 1873]; Dillon to his mother, Unyanyembe, October 8 [extract enclosed, Kirk to Frere, February 16, 1874]; and Murphy to Frere, Zanzibar, March 7 and 10, 1874, Cameron Papers, RGSA.

5. *LJDL*, 2:339. David Livingstone's sister Janet mentioned that among the instruments borrowed by Cameron was her brother's gold chronometer watch. Janet Livingstone to Murray, February 27, 1875, JMPA. Ostensibly defending the African caravan leaders for not resisting Cameron's removal and retention of a number of Livingstone's instruments, Waller made clear his disapproval of Cameron's actions: "It cannot be conceded for a moment that these poor fellows would have been right in forbidding this examination, when we consider the relative position in which natives and English officers must always stand to each other; but it is a source of regret. . . . We could well have wished these instruments safe in England with the small remnant of Livingstone's personal property, which was allowed to be shipped from Zanzibar. *LJDL*, 2:339-40. See below, n. 6.

The issue did not end there. When Cameron returned and presented a report "On his [sic] Journey across Africa, from Bagamoyo to Benguela," April 11, 1876, RGS president Sir Henry Rawlinson complimented him on the "astonishingly numerous, elaborate, and accurate" observations he had brought home. He noted Cameron "had the advantage of using certain instruments which he found in charge of Livingstone's party in their memorable journey to the coast." Rawlinson referred to the matter again in his presidential address May 22, 1876. His remarks suggest that Cameron was asked to supply more information on the subject. Rawlinson said many of the instruments supplied Cameron by the Royal Geographical Society ". . . had been damaged and rendered useless by the accidents of travel on his passage from the seacoast to the interior; and it was therefore most fortunate in the interests of science that . . . he was able to reinforce his surveying apparatus from the Doctor's stores." Cameron had "taken charge" of the chronometer given Livingstone by the Society in 1856, a sextant, and some barometers and boiling point thermometers, and his "obligations to his illustrious predecesor we are thus prepared to acknowledge." *PRGS* 20 (1875-1876): 325, 327, 438-39. After this attempt to lay the matter to rest, it was unfortunate that at the meeting of the British Association at Sheffield in 1879, Cameron was reported as saying that at the time of Livingstone's first cross-continental journey he was ". . . not able to fix his positions with any degree of exactitude [and had] . . . no means of fixing a basis with scientific accuracy." Waller immediately wrote to the *The Times* on August 30 to say that after Livingstone's observations for that journey had been checked at the Cape, the late Lord Ellesmere, then president of the Royal Geographical Society, praised him for "sound geography." *The Times*, September 3, 1879.

The subject was still very much alive when Blaikie wrote his authorized biography of Livingstone, first published by John Murray in 1880. Blaikie's remarks reflected the long-lasting concern of Livingstone's family about Cameron's borrowing of those geographical instruments for his own journey. To them the action diminished the possibility of a full recognition of Livingstone's geographical achievement: "[I]t was not warrantable in the new–comers to take the boxes from them, examine their contents, and carry off a part of them. Nor do we think that Lieutenant Cameron was entitled to take away the instruments with which all Livingstone's observations had been made for a series of seven years, and use them, though only temporarily, for the purposes of his expedition, inasmuch as he thereby made it impossible so to reduce Livingstone's observations as [sic] that correct results should be obtained from them." Blaikie, *Personal Life*, 377–78. For a scholarly assessment of Cameron's work, see James A. Casada, "Verney Lovett Cameron: A Centenary Appreciation," *Geographical Journal* 141, no. 2 (July 1975): 203–15. Cameron did not allude to the matter in his exploration journal or in his published account, *Across Africa* (New York, 1877), 125. I am grateful to Major H. P. Lovett Cameron, who kindly permitted me to obtain photocopies of the entries for the time of Chuma's arrival in October to December 4, 1873, from the microfilm of the journal on deposit at the National Library of Scotland.

In February 1881, Agnes Livingstone's husband, A. L. Bruce, reopened the question on behalf of the family. RGS secretary H. W. Bates replied March 5, 1881, that the Council did not think "any useful purpose" would be served "at this late date" by tabulating and scientifically arranging for publication "Dr L's notes & observations in Central Africa." RGS Letter Books, 1879–1893, RGSA. Waller later supplied "Dr. Livingstone's Rainfall Observations in Central Africa, 1866–71," for the *Report of the Sixty-Fourth Meeting of the British Association . . .* , London, 1894, 352.

6. *LJDL*, 2:339. Tom first became aware of the loss early in May 1874: "I find from a list written at Unyanyembe by Jacob Wainwright that Cameron took two chronometers, 1 aneroid 2 compasses 1 sextant & some other instruments out of my father's box. I suspect a lot of other things too." Tom Livingstone to Murray, Newstead Abbey, May 7, 1874, JMPA. The second loss occurred after the body reached the British consulate. ". . . Then at Zanzibar Lieut. Murphy with the concurrence of Col. [sic] Prideaux, making [sic] a sale of Dr. Livingstone's effects." Janet Livingstone to Murray, February 27, 1875, JMPA.

Murphy reported on what he had done to the RGS president: "All Dr. Livingstone's letters, papers, and the few things that were fit to send home as mementoes of him, I have handed over to Captain Prideaux."

Murphy to Frere, Zanzibar, March 7 and 10, 1874, Cameron Papers, RGSA. In the same letter, Murphy acknowledged that on the way to the coast, after Dillon's suicide, he had sold "one of Dillon's guns, a sporting Snider," to a M. Philippe Broyan, a Swiss at Mpwapawa, "connected with a French or German house at Zanzibar, who has been there for the last six months, driving a very profitable trade in ivory. . . ." On Broyan, see Norman R. Bennett, *Mirambo of Tanzania, 1840(?)-1884* (New York, London, and Toronto), 1971, 72–78.

7. Cameron, *Across Africa*, 125–26, 221. In a letter to the editor of *The Times*, written from "1, Savile-row" [Royal Geographical Society], December 5, 1874, Horace Waller announced that the *Last Journals*, of which he was the editor, would be available to the public in a few days. He therefore wished to clarify a telegram from the Zanzibar consulate published in *The Times* that day, announcing the safe arrival of "Livingstone's Journals." He thought the telegram referred to "many of the rough notes from which the Lett's Diary [Unyanyembe journal] was compiled." *The Times*, December 7, 1874.

8. Diary of Horace Waller, January 28, 1875, Horace Waller Papers, Library of the Yale Divinity School (hereafter WPYDS).

9. *PRGS* 19 (1874–1875): 261. For the most authoritative description to date on the journals, field diaries, and notebooks written by Livingstone, with information about the journal and diaries used by Waller in editing Livingstone's *Last Journals*, see *Livingstone Catalogue*, 272–79, esp. entries for Journal 11 (here called the Unyanyembe journal) and Field Diaries 14–39. Until there is a definitive edition of the *Last Journals*, no detailed correlation of what Waller used can be established. For my analysis, see below, chap. 3, n. 2.

10. Kirk to Murray, February 27, 1874, JMPA. Kirk informed John Murray of the arrival of the official telegram. Kirk to Murray, January 28, 1874, JMPA. Tom Livingstone learned the news on January 26, when the telegram passed through Egypt. Janet Livingstone to Murray, Ulva Cottage, Hamilton [Scotland], February 13, 1874, JMPA. Kirk's sentiments reflected general expectations. Waller had written Livingstone in 1869, "If anything were to happen to your journals where should we all be!!" Waller to Livingstone, December 23, 1869, WPYDS.

11. Agnes Livingstone to Murray, January 4, 1873, JMPA. Judging by Blaikie's biography, which used correspondence Agnes and others lent him and carefully went over this ground again in 1880, Agnes's suspicions about Kirk's inactivity on behalf of her father had not diminished. Blaikie, *Personal Life*, 421–32. Sir Reginald Coupland, still concerned in 1945 with clearing up the "legend of Kirk's lethargy," attributed to Blaikie's book responsibility for continuing the notion that "Kirk had been

guilty of culpable negligence," for "it leaves its readers in little doubt that Kirk failed to do what he ought to have done." Coupland, *Livingstone's Last Journey*, 216. Blaikie clearly was transmitting Agnes's views.

12. Agnes Livingstone to Murray, April 8, 1874, JMPA.

13. Stanley to Agnes Livingstone, Langham Hotel, London, March 18, 1874, Stanley Papers, NLS.

14. Stanley, *How I Found Livingstone*, 1890, lxvi–lxix; *Illustrated London News*, April 25, 1874; *PRGS* 18 (1873–1874): 445–50. Stanley gives the wrong date (April 16) for the Malwa's arrival, *How I Found Livingstone*, lxvi. For the pallbearers' heights, see Augusta Z. Fraser, *Livingstone and Newstead* (London, 1913), 206.

15. April 13, 1874, *PRGS* 18 (1873–1874): 243.

16. *PRGS* 18 (1873–1874): 255.

17. Tom Livingstone to Murray, May 7, 1874, JMPA.

18. The first public notice of Wainwright's diary was made by Arthur Laing at the Royal Geographical Society meeting April 13, 1874. Laing had accompanied Wainwright along with Livingstone's body and papers from Zanzibar to Suez—and thereafter took a more direct route to London. He noted that "Jacob Wainwright writes and speaks English very well, and had kept a full diary from the time of Livingstone's death to the arrival of the body at Zanzibar." *PRGS* 18 (1873–1874): 246. Writing from Zanzibar, Murphy described Laing as a "gentleman in business here. . . . He is a friend of Cameron's and came out here hoping to join the Expedition, but it was too late." An Indian Army officer on half pay, Murphy said he could not afford to go to England. Following the suggestion of Capt. Prideaux, he handed over Livingstone's remains as well as Wainwright's diary to Laing's care. Murphy to Frere, Zanzibar, March 7 and 10, 1874, Cameron Papers, RGSA. Further notice of the diary appeared in *The Times* of April 22 in a letter from the Reverend W. Salter Price: "An enterprising gentleman at Zanzibar, under pretense of wanting to transmit the contents to the family of Dr Livingstone, obtained possession of this valuable document and having made a copy of it for publication, as it appears, in whole or in part, in the Bombay papers, rewarded Jacob with a present of 2 s[hillings]! This circumstance coming to the knowledge of Her Majesty's Acting Consul, he very wisely took the precaution of having the diary sealed up and handed over to Mr. A. Laing for safe transmission to England,—[sic] and by that gentleman it was duly returned to Jacob in my presence." For a discussion of this letter, the circumstances surrounding the diary, and a French translation of the diary from a German version published in 1874 (n. 21 below), see François Bontinck, "Le Diaire de Jacob Wainwright (4 Mai 1873 – 18 Fevrier 1874)," *Africa: Revista trimestrale di studi e documentazione*

dell'Istituto Italo-Africano (Rome) 32–33 (Settembre 1977–Dicembre 1978): 399–435, 603–4. The fate of Wainwright's original English version remains a mystery. Simpson, *Dark Companions*, 101.

19. The African Asylum at Nasik, which existed for twenty years (1854–74), educated some 200 liberated slaves. Despite this relatively small number, as only one of several institutions in India and East Africa which took in slaves rescued by the British East Africa Antislavery Squadron, many Nasik-trained Africans subsequently played a significant role in East African history. Joseph E. Harris, *The African Presence in Asia: Consequences of the East African Slave Trade* (Evanston, 1971), 74–75. Compare A. J. Temu, *British Protestant Missions* (London, 1972), chap. 1, esp. 12–13, and Robert W. Strayer, *The Making of Mission Communities in East Africa* (Albany, 1978), 14–15.

20. Murray to Edward Hutchinson, April 23, 1874. The letter makes clear that Hutchinson initiated these negotiations.

21. Murray to Tom Livingstone, May 7, 1874, JMPA. Wainwright's diary was published in Germany in 1874 as "Tagebuch von Jacob Wainwright uber den Transport von Dr. Livingstone's Leiche 4. Mai 1873–18. Februar 1874," in *Petermann's Mittheilungen* 20: 187–93 (as cited in James A. Casada, *Dr. David Livingstone and Sir Henry Morton Stanley: An Annotated Bibliography* (New York & London, 1976), no. 711 (hereafter, *Livingstone and Stanley Bibliography*).

22. Edward Hutchinson to Murray, May 7, 1874, enclosing a letter from Dr. A. Petermann to Messrs Sampson, Low, Marston & Co., April 28, 1874; Petermann's [?] handwritten copies of Price's letter, published April 22, 1874; and a brief notice in the *Athenaeum* of April 25, 1874, declaring that it was the editor's understanding that Wainwright's diary would not be published until Livingstone's "own narration" was in print, JMPA. Hutchinson believed Petermann's copy of the diary was "fraudulently obtained by [Dr. James] Christie" in Zanzibar. Bontinck, however, has shown that the copy originated with a member of the late Baron von der Decken's party, Richard Brenner, who had become Austrian consul at Aden and was in Zanzibar in January 1874. Bontinck, "Diaire de Jacob Wainwright," 402–3.

23. Murray to Tom Livingstone, May 7, 1874, JMPA. Stanley reproduced the *Herald* dispatch in the preface to the 1874 (1890) edition of *How I Found Livingstone*, lviii–lx. Stanley said that his own interview with Wainwright on the *Malwa* in Southampton corroborated the story of the dispatch, *How I Found Livingstone*, 1890, lxvii. For a detailed account of Wainwright's movements in England, see Bontinck, "Diaire de Jacob Wainwright," esp. 401.

24. Tom Livingstone to Murray, May 9, 1874, JMPA. Stanley to Mur-

ray, May 4, 1874, JMPA. Stanley's letter was stamped as having been received May 7.

25. Edward Hutchinson to Tom Livingstone, June 9, 1874, JMPA. Hutchinson and Murray were allied in various British philanthropic causes; neither would have wanted to act too highhandedly in this matter. Earlier in 1874, for example, Murray had published a little book by Hutchinson entitled *The Slave Trade of East Africa*, the profits of which went to the CMS Special Fund for East Africa. The Special Fund was to help establish freed slave settlements on the East Coast, expected to be needed as a result of the new Zanzibar treaty outlawing the slave trade. Norman R. Bennett, "The Church Missionary Society at Mombasa, 1873-1894," in Jeffrey Butler, ed., *Boston University Papers in African History*, vol. 1 (Boston, 1964): 160-64.

26. Horace Waller, Letter to the Editor, *The Times*, March 31, 1874, dated March 30. See Bontinck, "Mort de Livingstone," 584.

27. Tom Livingstone to Murray, June 10, 1874, JMPA. Hutchinson did not forget the matter entirely, however, for in January 1875 Agnes Livingstone instructed Murray ". . . not to show the Journals to anyone without first getting my consent." She explained that Hutchinson had written her grandfather Robert Moffat, asking to see the original diaries, "especially the one in which Jacob Wainwright made an entry." Agnes clearly stated: "I do not choose that he should see it or any of the others." Since Hutchinson had written Moffat that he did not want " 'the family' " to know of his request, she decided, "I do not trust him one bit." Agnes Livingstone to Murray, January 11, 1875, JMPA.

28. Newspaper clippings for 1872-1875, RGSA. The newspaper may have been the *Daily Telegraph*, May 30, 1874.

29. *The Times*, June 2, 1874. In his letter of condolence to Agnes Livingstone, Stanley had referred to his reservations about Chuma's reliability. Stanley to Agnes Livingstone, March 18, 1874, Stanley Paper, NLS.

30. Tom Livingstone to Murray, June 10, 1874, JMPA.

31. Tom Livingstone to Murray, June 16, 1874, JMPA.

32. The Royal Geographical Society sent a memorial to the government requesting a pension for the members of Livingstone's family, his children and his sisters. A deputation on this subject called upon governmental offices in the week after the funeral; it included Horace Waller, W. F. Webb, and Major-General Sir Thomas Steele. Gladstone's government transferred to Livingstone's children a civil list pension that only recently had been granted him as a roving consul in Central Africa, but at the reduced rate of £200 per year, recommending a grant from the Queen's bounty for their education. Shortly thereafter, in 1874, the gov-

ernment changed hands. Disraeli's incoming government agreed to award a lump sum of £3000, in trust, to the Livingstone family, giving Livingstone's two unmarried sisters a life interest in the fund. Newspaper clippings for 1872–1875, RGSA; Bridges, "Sponsorship," 102–3. For the involvement of Baroness Burdett–Coutts in these efforts, see Burdett–Coutts to Buxton, May 16, 18, 1874, MS. Brit. Emp. s 22/G7, BFASSP, RH. Waller "signed the Treasury Memorandum & became a Trustee for the L[ivingstone] children" on January 20, 1875. He noted in his diary the week before, "We have to hear if the boys will carry out the Drs [sic] written wishes 'the boys to have a good education & the girls all the rest.' " Diary of Horace Waller, January 14, 20, 1875, WPYDS. Agnes wrote Murray, January 13, 1875, asking that he submit to the other trustees her wish—in which she believed her sister concurred—that "in the case of one of my aunts dying that the survivor should have the *whole* of the interest instead of only the half."

33. "Tom's complaint I have today ascertained from Dr Watson to be blood & albumen from the kidneys. . . . My friends took Oswell and him from school in England against my will & put them . . . [in a] miserably ill drained school near Glasgow. . . . He is not to be in cold or damp." Livingstone to W. C. Oswell, March 23, 1865, NMLZ, RH; Livingstone to W. C. Oswell, June 6, 1865, Livingstone Papers, LI 2/1/1, photocopy from NMLZ, NAZ; Livingstone to Kirk, June 8, 1865, in Foskett, *Zambesi Doctors*, 117–18. On Oswell Livingstone's school prizes, see Fraser, *Livingstone and Newstead*, 158; on the concern about his completion of medical training, James Young to Murray, September 28, 1872, JMPA. On the state of Tom's health in 1872 and 1873, Waller to Bates, January 13, 1872, RGSA; Waller to Livingstone, November 25, 1872, and February 17, 1873, WPRH, 2; Agnes Livingstone to Murray, January 1873, JMPA. In mid–March, 1875, Waller learned from F. W. Webb that Tom was dying of Bright's Disease; a few days later, he read of Tom's death in *The Times*. Diary of Horace Waller, March 15 and 18, 1875, WPYDS.

34. Agnes Livingstone to Murray, Ulva Cottage, Hamilton [Scotland] July 30, 1874, JMPA. Agnes loved travelling and enjoyed describing what she saw. Fraser, *Livingstone and Newstead*, 173–74.

35. Cooke to Murray, August 2, 1872, JMPA.

36. *Daily Telegraph*, July 29, 1872. Oswell wrote the letter July 27 from the Royal Geographical Society. His statements were uncompromisingly partisan: "Dr. Kirk is totally unworthy of the accusations which are daily reaching the public, and which can have only one source. . . . Dr. Kirk plainly stated that henceforth it was only left to him to deal with Dr. Livingstone in a purely official capacity, and that the old

friendship between them had been laid aside." Livingstone, in turn, commented to Waller on these events with evident bitterness, "I complained to Kirk against the slaves and Banians. . . . Kirk in high dudgeon asserted that 'I believe niggers in preference to his written statement' and he pumped Oswell full of this idea and others not usually conveyed to a son against his father." Livingstone to Waller, September 2, 1872, WPRH, 1. The language of this letter suggests that Livingstone's information came from Stanley. Compare Stanley to Livingstone, Zanzibar, May 27, 1872, Stanley Papers, NLS. Kirk reported to the Foreign Office May 28, 1872: "Mr. W. O. Livingstone since perusing his father's letters, and after seeing how grossly unjust and ungrateful his behavior, to myself in particular, has been, refused to accompany Mr. Stanley's party or to go to his father. . . ." Printed in *PRGS* 16 (1871–1872): 437. On the same day he wrote to the *Daily Telegraph*, July 27, Oswell also wrote up his official report to RGS president Sir Henry Rawlinson from Waller's vicarage at Leytonstone. Of Kirk he declared, "I found him an invaluable friend, and I cannot sufficiently deplore the circumstances which have lately occurred tending to his prejudice." *PRGS* 16 (1871–1872): 425.

37. Webb to Murray, June 25, 1874.

38. Agnes Livingstone to Murray, June 25, 1874, JMPA. Murray had no objections to Stanley in principle. When Stanley arrived in England August 1, 1872, and sought out Livingstone's publisher, Murray was ready to publish his book. He even offered Stanley the same arrangements he had with Livingstone, which gave the author two thirds of the profits, with an advance of £2000 upon publication. Murray's letter from Scotland authorizing this arrangement was delayed in reaching his partner in London. According to Hall, it was the delay which sent Stanley to Sampson Low "for £1000 down and half the net profits." Murray to Stanley, August 9, 1872; Cooke to Stanley, August 12, 1872, JMPA; Hall, *Stanley*, 214.

39. *Stanley's Dispatches*, xxviii, The joint *New York Herald* – London *Daily Telegraph* Expedition under Stanley was formally announced July 17, 1874. Stanley's plans were common knowledge before that date. On July 2, from London, Major C. B. Euan-Smith wrote William Mackinnon, the Scottish shipping magnate, "You have heard that the Daily Telegraph and the New York Herald are going to send out Stanley to Africa to put down the Slave Trade. . . ." Mackinnon Papers, Library of the School of Oriental and African Studies, London University (hereafter, MP, SOAS). Euan-Smith had acted as Sir Bartle Frere's secretary during the Zanzibar mission in 1872–1873; his correspondence with Mackinnon, who was opening negotiations for sending his ships to Zan-

zibar on a regular basis, began at that time. Compare Hall, *Stanley*, 23–25.

40. Agnes Livingstone to Murray, July 6, 1874, JMPA.

41. *Ibid.* Agnes knew W. Cotton Oswell when she was a little girl in Africa; she knew he was a champion of her father's and that he had helped with the proof of his Zambezi book. When Oswell escorted Agnes home from France—where Livingstone had left her for a year's schooling in 1865—he had told her she should look to him if she ever needed help. Fraser, *Livingstone and Newstead*, 163–65; Oswell, *William Cotton Oswell*, 2: 80–81, 93–94, 95–96, 98–99, 100, 104.

42. Waller to Murray, July 10, 1874, JMPA. How much did Waller want this assignment? He certainly considered it an honor. When Cameron's letter of October 20, 1873, first reached England, giving the bare details as he had learned them from Chuma, Waller had written a letter to the editor of *The Times:* "If this be true, then I say let no lesser hand than a Tennyson's write this chapter of the 'In Memoriam' of Livingstone, and describe how these men cast aside all their deep horror and fear of the dead to bear their dead [master] on towards his own far-off home." *The Times*, February 12, 1874.

43. Agnes Livingstone to Murray, July 16, 1874, JMPA.

44. Oswell, *William Cotton Oswell*, 2:133. John Murray was well acquainted with Oswell as an author. Oswell had sent him an unsolicited manuscript in January 1871, with an offer to provide a dozen stories of African hunting such as the three submitted. Murray returned the manuscript two months later, declining the offer. Oswell to Murray, January 11, 13, 1871, with a note about the returned manuscript on the first letter, JMPA. In 1865, Livingstone used Oswell's services for his Zambezi book to correct proof, to make paragraph divisions, write chapter heads, and edit for clarity. Oswell, *William Cotton Oswell*, 2:81–87. For example, Livingstone wrote Oswell, "I did not like to say my companions had courage & perseverance because some had neither the one nor the other but I put it all on your conscience." Livingstone to Oswell, February 15, 1865, NMLZ, RH. A few weeks later, Livingstone let Murray know he was using Oswell's services, "Oswell does not pretend to be literary – but he has good taste and a great knowledge of African affairs. His help need not interfere with that your [editorial] friend." Livingstone to Murray, March 3, 1865, JMPA.

45. Oswell, *William Cotton Oswell*, 2:133–34. Oswell commented on the "short, curt sentences, full of pith" that so vividly brought Livingstone to mind as he read the *Last Journals*, and yet "how quiet and gentle he had grown in these last journals." On the style of the journals, compare below, chap. 3.

46. Minutes, Council of the Royal Geographical Society, July 13, 1874, RGSA.

47. It is not possible to judge exactly how well Waller knew the languages of Susi (from Shupanga on the Zambezi River) and Chuma (a Yao). Waller did spend three and a half years acquiring some rudiments of the language spoken by the Mang'anja and Yao associated with the Universities' Mission in the Shire Highlands and on the lower Zambezi River. He recorded vocabulary in his African diaries of 1861–64; ten years later he still used it for passages in his diary that were meant for his eyes alone. WPRH, 4–5; Diary of Horace Waller, 1875–76, WPYDS. In 1866, he sent a letter to *Mission Life*, written by Wikatani in Bombay August 13, 1865, and forwarded by Livingstone. To accompany it, Waller included a fairly literal translation, commenting: "[L]et me point out the great feat Wakotani [sic] has accomplished in reducing his own language, phonetically, into English characters. No one at Bombay could help him in this." "Letter from a Native Lad," *Mission Life: A Magazine* 1 (February 1, 1866): 26–30. As noted already, Livingstone referred Yao and Mang' anja vocabulary questions to Waller when preparing *Zambesi and Its Tributaries*. The oldest Webb daughter, Augusta, recollected Waller speaking to Susi and Chuma "in their own African dialect [sic]." Fraser, *Livingstone and Newstead*, 214–15. In taking notes from Susi and Chuma to get information about Livingstone's last days and their journey to the coast, Waller recorded his transliteration of some of their words. "Notes from Susi and Chuma concerning their travels with Dr. Livingstone 1865 to 1874," Notebook no. 24, WPRH, 4 (hereafter, Susi/ Chuma NB).

48. Murray to Waller, July 17, 1874, JMPA. James Young paid to bring Susi and Chuma to England and for some clothing and travel for them. When Stanley hired the young men from Nasik to enter Livingstone's employ in 1872, he offered them the annual salary of 30 East African dollars. Stanley to Murray, May 4, 1874, JMPA. By 1874, the need for porters on the coast opposite Zanzibar had driven up the cost from an average of two and a half dollars to five or even seven and eight dollars per month. Simpson, *Dark Companions*, 115. In 1866, Livingstone engaged Musa from Anjouan in the Comoros Islands for ten dollars per month, and his men for seven. Copy of Agreement, after entry for December 19, 1869, Unyanyembe journal, SNMDL (microfilm NLS, MS. 10734 and hereafter Uj, NLS). Calculating from a letter written by Lt. Murphy, I estimate that the 1874 pound sterling was worth $4.85 East African dollars. The special duty pay of £5 per month given Susi and Chuma in England was relatively generous by East African standards and may have been necessary as an inducement to get the men

to remain there. Murphy to Frere, Zanzibar, March 7, 10, 1874, Cameron Papers, RGSA. By the time Waller transmitted the £40—augmented by donations of £15—to Kirk in England early in 1875, acting Consul Frederick Holmwood had written from Zanzibar that Chuma and Susi had acquired two slaves each. Waller stipulated that they should receive their money only if they were no longer slave holders. Diary of Horace Waller, January 12, 25: February 2, 1875, HWYDS.

49. Agnes Livingstone to Murray, July 22, 1874, JMPA.

50. Tom Livingstone to Murray, July 23, 1874, JMPA.

51. Waller to Murray, July 20, 1874, JMPA.

52. As a young woman, Agnes spent most of her summer holidays with the Young family in Scotland or on their yacht. Fraser, *Livingstone and Newstead*, 173. Yet Tom suggested to John Murray an underlying friction in the relationship: "I met Mr James Young of Kelly coming out of your place on Monday. In case he may wish to do anything for our Family would you please get him to put down any arrangements in *black* and *white* as neither we nor any one else are willing to take his word only. His co–trustees know better now & only too late." Tom Livingstone to Murray, May 7, 1874, JMPA. Compare Waller's diary, January 14, 1875: "The Youngs condemn the ingratitude of the whole [Livingstone] family very much. Mr Young spoke very plainly to Murray about the Aunts"; and Glasgow, February 19, 1875: "Mr Annan of Hamilton . . . said he did not come as the representative of the aunts . . . [but his] nasty violence against Mr Young was fairly outrageous and evidently the mind of the aunts. He held in his hand a paper on which all Mr. Young's gifts were set forth & said that they were done for the public to see and he had never done a single thing for any of the family. . . ." Diary of Horace Waller, WPYDS. Tom in 1874 was therefore most likely reflecting a concern that originated with his aunts over the handling of the trust Livingstone had set up for the money he earned from *Missionary Travels* (see below, chap. 6, n. 2). One source of deep anguish was the great loss of money incurred by Livingstone's decision to build the *Lady Nyassa*, when the government refused to authorize this expense, and by the subsequent loss of the lesser amount for which it was sold when the Bombay bank in which he had placed the money failed. Jeal, *Livingstone*, 272, 349. Annan tried to elicit Waller's aid in getting the government to repay the money Livingstone had expended on the ship—over £5500. Waller told him it was hopeless. Diary of Horace Waller, February 19, 1875, WPYDS. For Livingstone's authorization to his trustees for this expense in 1862, see *Livingstone Catalogue*, 155, no. 1296.

53. James Young to Murray, July 25, 1874, JMPA.

54. Agnes Livingstone to Murray, July 28, 30, and August 1, 1874, JMPA.

55. Tom Livingstone to Murray, July 31, 1874, JMPA.

56. Waller to Murray, August 3, 1874, JMPA. If Waller's temper was kept well in hand in his personal relations with Tom, he vented it to Murray in another quarter: "If you see Mr. Stanford [then working on Livingstone's map], kindly instruct him to render me what assistance he can. I think I was hardly identified in the eyes of his assistants yesterday." Waller to Murray, August 8, 1874, JMPA. Eight years later, when turning down a request that he write a biography of the late UMCA Bishop Edward Steere, Waller wrote bluntly, "Few know what your humble servant . . . had to put up with from Livingstone's relatives when I edited his Last Journals." Waller to Reverend M. Heanley, October 19, 1882, UMCA, A1 (III) Box 1, USPGA.

57. Waller to Murray, August 5, 1874, JMPA. Waller did not originally predict that there was enough material for two volumes. "Mr Webb & Mr Waller calculate that the Journal printed in extenso will not be much more than 400 pages but I doubt it." Tom Livingstone to Murray, Newstead Abbey, June 10, 1874, JMPA.

58. Waller to Murray, September 3, 1874, JMPA. Livingstone to Alington, December 18, 1863; February 3, 18, 1865; May 26, June 20, 1865, photocopies, UWL (originals in NLS).

59. Proof sheets 1–8, 178, 217, and 328, WPRH, 6. Tom made the decision to omit the account of the attack on Baron von der Decken at Brava, placed by Livingstone in the middle of his diary entries for Zanzibar, February – March, 1866. When Waller returned his proof sheets to the publisher, September 2, he noted that he had not yet made any comparisons with "T.L.'s revisions," proof sheet 65, WPRH, 6. When the suppressed passage was published—soon after Waller's papers were placed on deposit in Rhodes House Library, Oxford—it was assumed that the decision to excise this material was made by the editor, Horace Waller. Jack Simmons, "A Suppressed Passage in Livingstone's Last Journals Relating to the Death of Baron von der Decken," *Journal of the Royal African Society* 40, no. 161 (October 1941): 335–46. See also, *Livingstone and Stanley Bibliography*, Item no. 375.

60. Waller to Murray, October 19, 1874, JMPA.

61. Agnes Livingstone to Murray, September 29, October 9, 1874, JMPA.

62. Agnes Livingstone to Murray, December 18, 1874, JMPA.

63. Agnes Livingstone to Murray, December 22, 1874, JMPA.

64. Tom Livingstone to Murray, January 11, 1875, Alexandria, JMPA. Tom also criticized Waller for toning down his "fulminations" against

Cameron for raiding instruments from Livingstone's boxes. Waller had in fact written of this action as a "disaster" and a grave "indiscretion," but John Murray, sensitive to the shifting currents in contemporary geographical circles, may have convinced him that to air these sentiments was unwise. Proof sheets 46–47, WPRH, 6.

65. Copybook of Out-Letters, December 5, 1875, JMPA. Waller also signed for the sum of £40 on behalf of Susi and Chuma.

66. Janet Livingstone to Murray, January 2, 12, 1875, JMPA. When Waller saw the maps discovered by Janet Livingstone, he found one to be "the supposed fountains of Herodotus with also a good part of his last march to Bangweolo [sic]," while another was "Keith Johnston's map which I sent him [which Livingstone] corrected according to his own ideas." In addition, she had turned up some writing identified as "part of the notes kept on the last 7th April." Diary of Horace Waller, January 6, 1875, WPYDS. At a meeting of the Royal Geographical Society the previous December 14, 1874, after a report from Cameron was read, Waller had announced that ". . . he had received that evening *the last portion of Dr. Livingstone's map*—a little slip bearing on his route from the East Coast to Lake Nyassa. It was much stained and travel-worn. . . ." *PRGS* 19 (1874–75): 104, emphasis added. The origin and nature of this little map is puzzling; compare Waller's description of it with his remarks on the map found in Livingstone's Ujiji box sent home by Cameron and opened in late January 1875: "a map . . . beautifully laid down from the coast to . . . Lake Nyassa which we wanted." Diary of Horace Waller, January 28, 1875, WPYDS. Since the map mentioned December 14, 1874, came to light on the night a report was read from Cameron to the Royal Geographical Society, its most likely immediate source was Cameron.

67. Diary of Horace Waller, February 3, 1875, WPYDS; Agnes Livingstone to Murray, February 25, 1875, JMPA. Waller recorded in his diary for January 15, 1875, "Alice [his wife] says that whilst A.L. [Agnes Livingstone] was at Durris [James Young's house near Aberdeen] she delayed going to Hamilton for 10 days and then was in the neighbourhood for 2 days before looking for anything at her aunts." Diary of Horace Waller, WPYDS.

68. On Braithwaite, *Livingstone Catalogue*, 99; Diary of Horace Waller, January 4, 5, 6, 12, 16 18, 21, February 3, 4, 16, 1875, WPYDS. When a two-part review of Livingstone's *Last Journals* appeared in the *Leisure Hour*, it was signed by Edward Whymper. F.R.G.S., and mentioned "Mr. Waller, who speaks from authority and with experience. . . ." Edward Whymper, "Livingstone's Last Journals," *Leisure Hour: A Family Journal of Instruction and Recreation*, nos. 1208–9 (Feb-

ruary 20 and 27, 1875): 124–28, 134–40. I have been unable to locate any copy of the book with an Introduction that contains the alterations to which Waller referred.

69. Tom Livingstone to Murray, January 11, 1875, Alexandria, JMPA. Waller met Gordon in January 1874, just before Gordon left England to take service for the Egyptian khedive. For the next ten years, Waller did view Gordon as the inheritor of Livingstone's antislavery mantle in East Africa. He sent Gordon a strand of Livingstone's hair as a *memento mori*. Gordon acknowledged the gift from the Sudan. Gordon to Waller, Gondokoro, November 20, 1874, WPRH, 2.

§ 3 ₰

The Editorial Plan

The editorial process by which the Unyanyembe journal, the field diaries and loose papers, and Susi and Chuma's narrative were turned into a final coherent, published version in four months was a complex one. Decisions were made by the publisher, by Tom Livingstone, and by Waller. The reasons for some of these decisions are fairly obvious; about others it is possible only to conjecture. Only a full-scale reediting of all the materials, both those available in the summer and fall of 1874 and those which, together, comprise all the extant field notes, will reveal the layers of selection and change represented by the published work— including the decisions made by Livingstone himself as he transcribed his field diaries into the Unyanyembe journal. While such a task lies outside the scope of the present study, it remains an important work of scholarship that needs to be done.[1]

I propose to untangle some of the main strands or themes in Waller's editing of the *Last Journals* and to suggest where possible the ways in which Livingstone was his own first Victorian censor. Such an analysis shows that Waller left his own mark upon the work by stylistic changes, footnotes, editorial additions, and omissions from the materials available to him.[2]

Waller divided his editing task into three parts. The first claim on his attention, because the materials were by far the most elusive, was to prepare a narrative of the period of Livingstone's last illness and the long journey which Livingstone's African servants, his "faithful followers," made to carry his remains to the coast.[3] Waller sought the threads of a connected narrative of Livingstone's last illness and death from Susi and Chuma, who had been living with him in England since the end of May. He drew from them as detailed a description as possible of their steps during those last days and immediately thereafter. Waller was particularly interested in capturing the last days and final moments of Livingstone's life.

Deathbed scenes, a well-established part of Victorian literature, demanded as vivid detail as could be provided. One central problem loomed. Waller needed to overcome the awkwardness of a death without a parting message, for Livingstone had died quite alone. The living, however, wanted a memory to fix the end of Livingstone's life in space and time, some imagery within which to cast a final farewell. Waller's achievement was to establish that wordless death scene in such a way that it conjured up an appropriate image, symbolic of the man's life as well as evocative of the moment when his spirit departed from his body. The scene is described in Livingstone's *Last Journals* in this way:

A candle stuck by its own wax to the top of the box, shed a light sufficient for them to see his form. Dr. Livingstone was kneeling by the side of his bed, his body stretched forward, his head buried in his hands upon the pillow. For a minute they watched him: he did not stir, there was no sign of breathing; then one of them, Matthew, advanced softly to him and placed his hands to his cheeks. It was sufficient; life had been extinct for some time, and the body was almost cold: Livingstone was dead.[4]

But was this enough? Waller seemed unable to let the moment go without further comment. He anticipated that the reader would ask, where are the parting words, the farewell lines to his family and friends; why did he not leave instructions for such an event to ensure the preservation of his notebooks and maps? Waller decided to address the issue directly: "Fair questions, but reader, you have all—every word written, spoken, or implied." As if still unsatisfied himself, however, Waller commented on these circumstances in terms of his own African experiences. "In full recollection of eight deaths in the Zambesi and Shiré districts, not a single parting word or direction in any instance can be recalled. Neither hope nor courage give way as death approaches."[5]

Waller was certain that Livingstone was suffering from malarial fever, though he added in a footnote that Livingstone had recorded a great loss of blood. He chose, however, to emphasize the fever and the drowsiness reported by Livingstone's attendants, for to these symptoms he could assign the dying man's inability "to realize vividly the seriousness of the situation." Still reluctant to allow readers to interpret the scene for themselves, Waller then pointed to the symbolism of the posture in which death overcame the great traveller: "It may be that at the last a flash of conviction for a moment lit up the mind." From this thought, Waller proceeded with a fuller description:

Livingstone had not merely turned himself, he had risen to pray; he still rested on his knees, his hands were clasped under his head: when they approached him he seemed to live. He had not fallen to right or left when he rendered up his spirit to God. Death required no change of limb or position; there was merely the gentle settling forwards of the frame unstrung by pain, for the Traveller's perfect rest had come. Will not time show that the men were scarcely wrong when they thought "he yet speaketh"—aye, perhaps more clearly to us than he could have done by word or pen or any other means![6]

In this way Waller turned the reader's attention again to the figure of Livingstone, kneeling at prayer by his bedside, in an attitude that readily suggested itself as consonant with the man's life and spirit. Having focused the reader on this scene, Waller then asked,

Is it, then, presumptuous to think that the long-used fervent prayer of the wanderer sped forth once more—that the constant supplication became more perfect in weakness, and that from his "loneliness" David Livingstone, with a dying effort, yet again besought Him for whom He [sic] laboured to break down the oppression and woe of the land?[7]

The second capital "H," unconscious error or deliberate assertion, slipped into print. Waller had consecrated Livingstone to the everlasting image of a man beseeching his God to "break down the oppression and woe of the land," the slave trade. It is in the very image of the man at his death that the Livingstone legend was fixed. From a few clues given him by Chuma and Susi, Waller had constructed so vivid an image of Livingstone's death that it marked the memory of Livingstone in the minds of contemporaries and has been used by his biographers ever since. By focusing on the one act which would convey the essence of the man's life, Waller had shaped Livingstone's legacy.

The narrative that followed dramatized the events of Livingstone's death, dwelling on the unswerving dedication of his "faithful followers" intent on taking Livingstone's remains back to the British consulate at Zanzibar. The story of concealing Livingstone's death, the burial of Livingstone's heart and interior organs "in a tin box, which had formerly contained flour," while Jacob Wainwright read the burial service, the exposure of the body to the sun and the painstaking preservation of the flesh and bones that remained, the wrapping of the body in calico,

"Evening. Ilala 29 April, 1873." This engraving was the frontispiece for Volume II of Livingstone's *Last Journals*. Its story is clear: the fatally ill Livingstone must be helped into his hut at Ilala, Chitambo's village, by two of his attendants. The excruciating pain he experienced from any pressure on his back made it difficult for him to travel in any conveyance, even the kitanda shown here. His attendants are drawn, presumably at the editor's behest, as wearing both Arabic and African styles.

"the legs being bent inwards at the knees to shorten the package," the many trials that his carriers faced, including resisting burial at Unyanyembe by Cameron, and their ultimate triumph in reaching Zanzibar eight months later, all lent drama to Livingstone's death that would help fix the legend as a passion play in its own right.[8]

The text of these events occupied only forty-eight out of 706 pages in the original edition, but these were the events that were remembered as the story of Livingstone's last journey—sharing fame only with Stanley's gauche "Dr. Livingstone, I presume."[9] Tom accused Waller of turning Susi and Chuma's tale into a language more Wallerian than Livingstonian. He was right. The issue is whether his father's well-known understated and unadorned style would have been more effective with his Victorian readers. Waller clearly had worked at polishing this section. Sheets of manuscript interspersed with printed proof sheets reveal Waller's hand at work writing and rewriting the death scene. At the proof stage the material was reworked yet again. Waller made some deletions that indicate he was conscious of the need to tighten up his prose. Two such deletions are noteworthy. At one point, Waller thought better of a sentence which immediately followed his description of Livingstone kneeling at his bedside and eliminated the words: "Death surely was not unkind to those who lament him when they reflect upon this scene." He also added, and then deleted again, several sentences of rather purple prose which drew from the last scene of Livingstone at prayer an explicit moral with regard to the future of Africa, with a disastrous metaphor about "he who ploughs Africa for the future harvest of her peace . . ."![10]

Still further examination of the source of this material, the notebook in which Waller had jotted down what Susi and Chuma told him, reveals only a bare sketch of these events. Upon these notes Waller built, omitting some detail, reshaping what he heard as he chose. His object was a compelling narrative as he understood that term. If we look again at the famous death scene and examine it in the light of the notebook, we find: "Dr when he died had on trowsers. The boy said he fell asleep & when he woke he still saw him in this position & got alarmed. He was kneeling on his bed with his head on the pillow."[11]

Compare again the words Waller used to describe Livingstone's deathbed. "Dr. Livingstone was kneeling by the side of his bed, his body stretched forward, his head buried in his hands upon the pillow." On this Waller built: "Livingstone had not merely turned himself, he had risen to pray; he still rested on his knees, his hands were clasped under his head. . . . Is it, then presumptuous to think . . . that David Livingstone, with a dying effort, yet again besought Him for whom He laboured to break down the oppression and woe of the land?"[12] Once we know

Waller's original source, we realize Waller was raising a real question, not a rhetorical one. Waller did presume; he changed the details supplied him to evoke in the reader his own convictions about the dying man.

Waller presumed that Livingstone was praying to his maker at his extreme hour of need, and Waller presumed that Livingstone's prayer must have included a plea that his life's work be completed. Waller insisted that the man in trousers, kneeling on his bed with his head on the pillow, was a man who had risen from his death bed to kneel beside it to pray. Waller presumed in order to ensure that Livingstone's death scene would achieve the drama needed to fix it in memory and to bequeath it to posterity.

The notebook containing Susi and Chuma's story also reveals details that Waller chose not to use. For example: "This day Dr told Susi he was so cold & so he got a cloth out of the bale & put it on him," or "Susi noticed his eyes looking no strong. . . . They made a WC in the corner of the house for him." Some details concerning the state of Livingstone's embalmed remains were suppressed while the basic information in which they were embedded was supplied in a profusion of words. "1 day march – Body smelt very much men could not eat so covered it with tar – in a length of bark" became:

> They found on this first day's journey that some other precautions were necessary to enable the bearers of the mournful burden to keep to their task. Sending to Chitambo's village, they brought thence the cask of tar which they had deposited with the chief, and gave a thick coating to the canvas outside.[13]

Waller did turn into a Wallerian narrative the bare facts given him by Susi and Chuma about the trek to the coast. Another notebook entry read: "One day to Chiwais village. He objected to England and Arab flags & drums but eventually they passed in peace & slept on the other side of a stream. . . ." From Waller's pen—perhaps after further probing of the men as he set about writing—this emerged as a much longer passage in the published journal:

> They now drew near to Chiwaie's town, which they describe as a very strong place, fortified with a stockade and ditch. Shortly before reaching it, some villagers tried to pick a quarrel with them for carrying flags. It was their invariable custom to make the drummer-boy, Majwara, march at their head, whilst the Union Jack and the red colours of Zanzibar were carried in a foremost place in the line. Fortunately, a chief of some importance came up and stopped the

discussion, or there might have been more mischief, for the men were in no temper to lower their flag. . . . Making their settlement close to Chiwaie's. . . .[14]

The narrative is clearly in Waller's voice, with a characteristic choice of rhetoric that takes it far from any direct transmission of what Susi and Chuma may have said. Waller made the narrative his own; he is the storyteller and it is through his eyes that we learn what happened.

The key to Waller's presentation of this narrative was his need to establish the primacy of Susi and Chuma as the leaders of the caravan to the coast. Since Nasik-trained Jacob Wainwright, who had joined the expedition with the men sent up to Livingstone by Stanley in 1872, was the only one among them who could write, he had already figured prominently in the story so far as the general public was concerned. After Livingstone's death, he was inventory taker, reader of the burial service, inscriber of the tree where the tin box was buried, letter writer to the Cameron party, and—as the only African attendant to accompany Livingstone's body to England—pall bearer at Westminster Abbey. He had then travelled around the country in the company of the Reverend Mr. Price of the Church Missionary Society. And Tom, as Waller knew, had at first intended to rely on Jacob Wainwright's diary for the substance of the final narrative.

Waller's own campaign to assure that Susi and Chuma receive the recognition due them began with a protest at the Royal Geographical Society's meeting March 23, 1874. Because some people who heard Cameron's first news of Livingstone's death had raised doubts about believing any story based solely on Chuma's word, Waller was anxious to defend his honesty and honor in particular. Frere, as the RGS president, referred to the fact that Stanley had recently arrived in England and had stated that since as many as twelve "Nassik boys" might have been in Livingstone's caravan, some of them would no doubt be able to supply full particulars of Livingstone's last days. In response to this remark, Waller declared, "Already innuendos [sic] had been thrown out against Chumah [sic]; but he had known him as a boy, and had continually heard about him from the Doctor, who always spoke of him with esteem." Chuma and Susi were loyal attendants who "had been with Livingstone for eight or nine years." "The task that these men had performed," he added, "was truly Herculean." Frere, presiding over the meeting, professed Waller had misunderstood if he thought there was any slight intended against Chuma.[15]

But upon hearing that Jacob Wainwright, one of the Nasik men sent to Livingstone in 1872 by Stanley, was accompanying the body home,

Waller sent a letter to the editor of *The Times*, March 31, 1874. Chuma and Susi, he said, "have a length of service to show out of all proportion to the rest . . . is it too much to say that they remain the greatest African travellers of the present day?" Only a week and a half later, Waller sent another letter to the editor of *The Times*, with contents of a letter he had just received from Chuma, dictated to Capt. L. Brine of *HMS Briton* at Zanzibar. "Thanks to the heroic conduct of these men an enormous mass of geographical information is now in the possession of Dr. Livingstone's family."[16]

After the two arrived, late in May, they visited the Webbs at Newstead Abbey, where they were photographed with their hosts, Tom and Agnes Livingstone, Waller, and some of Livingstone's relics. The eldest Webb daughter remembered Waller forty years later as "a striking looking man . . . with his sun-burnt skin, dark deep-set eyes, eagle face, and long flowing black beard. . . ." Susi and Chuma were twice presented at the Royal Geographical Society, June 1 and 22. On the first occasion Waller was not with them and they remained mute; on the latter occasion Waller led them up to receive bronze medals voted them that day by the RGS council. "Let us never forget," said Frere in his presidential address, "what has been done for geography by the faithful band who restored to us all that it was in their power to bring of our lost friend, and who rescued his priceless writings and maps from destruction." It was an official benediction. There was no bronze medal for Jacob Wainwright.[17]

Once the narrative of Livingstone's death was completed, Waller turned to fixing upon the reader's mind the leadership roles that Susi and Chuma would play thereafter. He had already referred to them as primary actors in the events of Livingstone's last days. Now he told of the clear decision Livingstone's attendants made to entrust these "old hands" with the leadership to the coast:

> Calling the whole party together, Susi and Chumah placed the state of affairs before them, and asked what should be done. They received a reply from those whom Mr. Stanley had engaged for Dr. Livingstone, which was hearty and unanimous. "You," said they, "are old men in travelling and in hardships; you must act as our chiefs, and we will promise to obey whatever you order us to do." From this moment we may look on Susi and Chumah as the Captains of the caravan. To their knowledge of the country, of the tribes through which they were to pass, but, above all, to the sense

of discipline and cohesion which was maintained throughout, their safe return to Zanzibar at the head of their men must, under God's good guidance, be mainly attributed.[18]

There was widespread press coverage of Jacob Wainwright during the spring of 1874. The association of his name in the public's mind with the story of bringing Livingstone's remains back home clearly moved Waller to set forth emphatically that it was Susi and Chuma who were the caravan leaders. Three other, relatively brief narratives—by Jacob Wainwright, Carus Farrar, and Matthew Wellington, Nasik-trained Africans sent to Livingstone by Stanley in 1872—have borne out the essential elements of their story.[19] The significance of their taking over of the caravan leadership, however, may have been even more striking than Waller suggests. According to Waller's narrative, Susi asked Jacob Wainwright to carve an inscription on the tree under which Livingstone's heart was buried, "stating the name of Dr. Livingstone and the date of his death." Twenty years after the publication of the *Last Journals*, the tree and its inscription were visited by an Englishman, who reported that it also contained the words "Yazuza Mniasere Vchopere."[20]

The explanation for these words lies in a letter written by Livingstone to H. M. Stanley late in 1872 and published in the 1874 edition of *How I Found Livingstone*, for which Stanley wrote a memoir of Livingstone as a new introduction. The letter made its way to him courtesy of the American consul at Zanzibar, to whom it had been delivered by Lt. Cecil Murphy on his arrival with the Africans bearing Livingstone's remains. In reporting on his progress and the new recruits supplied by Stanley, Livingstone announced that he had "made Manwa Sera, Chowpereh, and Susi, heads of departments. . . ." Stanley had already listed in the memoir the names of the fifty–seven men he had sent to Livingstone, including "Chowpereh" and "Uredi Manwa Sera (Leader)." Both had accompanied Stanley on his journey to find Livingstone in 1871–1872, and Manua Sera had served as one of his caravan leaders, having previously worked with Speke in 1860–1862. In fact, as Donald Simpson has noted in his path–breaking book *Dark Companions*,

Those who gathered round the camp fires on the evening of the day in October 1873 when Livingstone's body was carried into Unyanyembe included men [counting as well Cameron's expedition] who had been on every significant expedition of the previous fifteen years, and many who had major journeys still ahead of them.[21]

Mpundu Tree at Ilala. Fear that the tree was being attacked by disease led to cutting it down in 1899 and sending the inscribed portion to the Royal Geographical Society. Such was the power of the Livingstone legend shaped by Waller that the memorial erected to replace it included Chuma's name, assumed to be missing.

Section of tree bark carved by Jacob Wainwright at Ilala, Chitambo's village, before restoration. It is just possible to discern as the second two lines: "Yazuza (Susi) Mniasere (Muana Sera) Vchopere (Chowpereh)."

The accumulated experience of the men who accompanied Livingstone during his last year, 1872–1873, therefore, was considerable. In addition, until the time when Jacob inscribed the Mpundu tree—or Mvula tree, as Waller called it after the name of its fruit—at Chitambo's village (Ilala) at Lake Bangweulu, the Africans were organized under three caravan leaders—Susi, Manua Sera, and Chowpereh. Susi and Chuma's story of their "election" as caravan chiefs, therefore, is crucial to the rest of the narrative. Whether or not Waller read Stanley's new 1874 memoir, he certainly did not mention the further words of the tree inscription. It is unlikely that Susi and Chuma brought it to his attention.

Finally, at the time of Livingstone's death, it is likely that only the six new Nasik-trained Africans—including Jacob Wainwright, Carus Farrar and Matthew Wellington, the men who have left memoirs on the subject—were practicing Christians. Certainly Carus Farrar considered Chuma a lapsed Christian:

> Of the nine boys who followed the Dr. on the first outset two only followed his remains to Zanzibar: to wit Ed. Gardiner [Gardner] and Nathaniel Cumba [Mabruki]. These men throughout the journey never associated with us six Christian boys their brothers as they have turned out Mohammedans. Chuma and Suse [sic] in spite of all that the Dr. did for them in getting them English education at Dr. Wilson's school at Bombay have at last turned out Mohammedans also.

Farrar mixes up Susi, the Shupanga man, with Wikatani, the other Yao rescued by Livingstone in the Shire Highlands and sent to Dr. Wilson's school along with Chuma. Susi, however, was a Muslim; he received Christian baptism as David Abdallah Susi only in 1886.[22]

Two conclusions are possible. One is that Susi and Chuma, asserting the length of their ties to Livingstone and their knowledge of a route which would assure them the way to the coast, did successfully assert primary leadership at this stage over the two sets of men who might have challenged them: the several veterans of African travel and the recent, Christian-trained recruits. There can be no doubt that their voices were important ones at the critical juncture of Livingstone's death, especially in the question of what they should decide to do about the body.

The second possibility is that the strongest leaders of both groups—Manua Sera, Chowpereh, and perhaps Mabruki Speke (from men sent to Livingstone by Stanley) and Gardner and Mabruki (two men remnants of the first group of Nasik-trained companions who had travelled with Livingstone since 1866)—joined Susi, Chuma, and Amoda (men whose ties to Livingstone went back to the early 1860s) to form a kind of

leadership cohort. From the point of view of pulling the caravan together and making vital decisions about Livingstone's remains, that kind
of cooperative leadership would have had the greatest strength. To
make Susi and Chuma the uncontested caravan leaders clearly served
Waller's purposes, not the least of which was that he had them with him
to tell the tale as they remembered it. Not surprisingly, between their
recollections and Waller's predilections, they emerge as the dominant
figures in the narrative. Whether or not the scene depicted by Waller—in
which all promised to obey Susi and Chuma—occurred, the result for
readers of the *Last Journals* was the same: a narrative which told what
Waller believed was important and suppressed what he felt could not be
told.[23]

There exists another eyewitness account from the time Chuma—as
the group's advance-runner—arrived at Cameron's camp in Unyanyembe, October 20, 1873, against which Waller's narrative, based solely
on Susi and Chuma's story, can be gauged. Lt. Cecil Murphy, who resigned the Livingstone East-Coast Aid Expedition along with Dr. Dillon
on the arrival of Livingstone's men, accompanied them to the coast and
wrote to Sir Bartle Frere, as the president of the Royal Geographical
Society, describing some of these events from his own perspective.
Murphy does not mention the opening of Livingstone's boxes, a major
point in Waller's account. On the other hand, Murphy does say that
Chuma announced that his party were in need of aid because they were
"nearly naked, and starving." Murphy then describes the arrival of the
rest of the Livingstone caravan, bearing Livingstone's body,

> brought by the savage looking followers of the great traveller, who
> had dressed themselves fantastically in various articles of costume,
> ostrich feathers, &c, picked up from the tribes among whom they
> had wandered. . . .

Murphy agreed these men "deserved great praise," but, he added, once
at Unyanyembe, "a set of orderly followers were for several days converted into a drunk and riotous mob."[24]

According to the *Last Journals*, Cameron asked Livingstone's men "if
they could attach his [Murphy's] party to their march; if so, the men who
acted as carriers should receive 6 dollars a man for their services." Thereafter, Dillon joined them. Problems on the march to the coast were explained by Waller as follows:

> There seem to have been some serious misunderstandings between
> the leaders of Dr. Livingstone's party and Lieut. Murphy soon after
> setting out, which turned mainly on the subject of beginning the

Chuma (left) and Susi, 1874. Arrayed in their own clothing, they are posed against a painted background of rocks and trees that make them appear almost as unnatural as in the photographs in which they wear their heavy, scratchy-looking Victorian woolens and heavy, shiny shoes (compare illustrations in chap. 2). The artist Whymper based a drawing on this photo for Volume II of the *Last Journals*, one of fourteen full-page illustrations in that volume.

day's march. The former, trained in the old discipline of their master, laid stress on the necessity of very early rising to avoid the heat of the day, and perhaps pointed out more bluntly than pleasantly that if the Englishmen wanted to improve their health, they had better do so too. However, to a certain extent, this was avoided by the two companies pleasing themselves.

The extent to which Waller may have been understating the clash may be gauged from Murphy's version of it. If Susi and Chuma viewed Murphy as joining their caravan with their permission, in his view:

The men behaved well considering they are natives of Africa, and I was indeed surprised to find them so tractable, though requiring at the same time a good deal of tact in their management, as they did not at first quite recognise my right to command them.

Indeed, when Murphy and Cameron met again briefly after Dr. Dillon committed suicide, Cameron supplied Murphy with the following authorization, dated December 4, 1873, and signed "Actg [sic] Consul Central Africa."

My Dear Murphy
    Would you be kind enough to take charge of the Livingstone caravan to the coast, as I place no confidence whatever in Susa [sic], in fact if rumours are true which have reached me about him he is an arrant rogue.

Livingstone's men seemed unaware of this document, but Murphy may have used it in dealing with the disposition of Livingstone's possessions once he reached Zanzibar.[25]
    Finally, according to the narrative in the Last Journals, when it seemed clear that news of their travelling with Livingstone's body might lead to trouble in the villages between Unyanyembe and the coast, the men removed the old bark wrappings, wrapped the body as though a bale of cotton, and used a ruse to let it be known that the body in its bark wrapping was on its way back Unyanyembe.

A consultation now became necessary. . . . A plan was quickly hit upon. . . . They feigned that they had abandoned their task, having changed their minds. . . .
    Susi and Chuma went into the wood and stripped off a fresh length of bark . . . in this the remains, conveniently prepared as

to length, were placed, the whole being surrounded with calico.
. . . They next proceeded to gather a faggot of mapira-stalks, cutting them in lengths of six feet or so, and swathing them round with
cloth to imitate a dead body. . . .

Once they were a distance from the village, they dismantled the false
burden and scattered the parts and wrappings.[26]
Murphy, in writing Frere, takes the entire credit for this plan:

I may mention that . . . it being considered impossible to travel
through Ugogo openly with a dead body, I had to commit a pious
fraud. Taking the corpse out of the bark case, I had the latter borne
away in state. . . . The bearers went away with the case into the
thick jungle and there deposited it, returning secretly at night. . . .
Meanwhile the body was taken into a tent and secretly enveloped
in cloth and matting to give it the appearance of an ordinary load of
cloth. . . .[27]

However the plan was arrived at—and in Waller's version a careful passive voice is used to relate that part—Murphy claimed responsibility for
it, while Susi and Chuma supplied Waller with a greater grasp of the
details that made it work.

Because Waller had been exploring the story of these last days with
Susi and Chuma for a month and a half before he accepted the editorship of the *Last Journals*, he was able to produce a first version of the
narrative during the first ten days he was officially at work. Once that
draft was done, he wryly compared himself to "the man who plays the
fiddle, the drum, and the flute all at once." While he revised the draft of
the narrative, he also had to turn to the proof sheets of the Unyanyembe
journal that were coming from the printer, and he had to begin work on
deciphering the field diaries. As he described it, he was faced with "dri-
blets of proof from Clowes, pumping Susi and Chuma and working with
a magnifying glass at the pocket books!"[28]

The publisher must have written back urging Waller to finish the narrative first, without delay, for Waller's reply was to promise to concen-
trate on it. He asked only that the printer send him proof sheets of Livingstone's first journey to Lake Bangweulu—which he reached July 18,
1868: "to render the road taken by the men on their way back a ship-
shape account, because they so often say I shall find the country described in his journal as no doubt it is."[29]

It might be argued that an editor's goal should be that of an invisible
presence, behind the scenes, organizing and selecting material to make

its contents clear to the reader— neutral, self-effacing, low-keyed. Such an editor would have served Livingstone and his narrative effectively by allowing the reader the opportunity to judge the man and his words without any intermediary. From the very beginning these were not Waller's goals. On the basis of the editorial decisions he made, we understand the extent to which he believed he had unique contributions to make to help the reader understand Livingstone's last journals, his field notes, and his miscellaneous jottings. Waller's contribution was different from that which Livingstone's son Tom, his rescuer Stanley, or his old friend William Cotton Oswell might have made in editing the *Last Journals*. Waller created a distinctive flavor, through small word changes, changes in sentence structure, editorial additions, an editorial reworking of Livingstone's last moments of life, and his narrative of the men's final journey to the coast.

To begin with, both the Unyanyembe journal and the field diaries that were brought back with Livingstone's body were written in a simple run-on style with little formal punctuation beyond the use of dashes. Livingstone tended to omit pronoun subjects and to rely on simple sentences or compound sentences joined by conjunctions. Only occasionally did Livingstone use internal descriptive or qualifying clauses. As editor, Waller uniformly joined short declarative sentences to form longer ones. One example will make his editorial method clear. It is drawn from the entries for May 5, 1866.[30]

UNYANYEMBE JOURNAL	EDITED *LAST JOURNALS*
At Nyamba a village where we spent the night of the 5th was a doctor and rain maker– She presented a basket of "Siroko" or as they call it in India "Mung" and a fowl– She is tall & well made with fine limbs and feet she was profusely tatooed all over– Even hips and buttocks had their elaborate markings– No shame is felt is exposing these parts.	At Nyamba, a village where we spent the night of the 5th, was a doctoress and rain-maker, who presented a large basket of siroko, or, as they call it in India, "mung," and a fowl. She is tall and well made, with fine limbs and feet, and was profusely tattooed all over; even her hips and buttocks had their elaborate markings: no shame is felt in exposing these parts.

An examination of early proof sheets stored with Waller's papers at Rhodes House Library suggests that when the Unyanyembe journal was placed in the printer's hands by the publisher, some general directions must have been given about interpreting dashes in the original manuscript as punctuation marks: periods, commas, and even semicolons. Someone at the publisher's, perhaps John Murray himself, was the most likely person to have done so. No license was given to add or change words, however, and the first proof sheets give evidence of the editorial work of adding articles and subject pronouns and creating paragraphs. A light editorial hand, by deduction Tom Livingstone's, made some of these changes before Waller set to making uniform decisions throughout. The stage at which Waller became aware that Tom had done little to change the earliest proof sheets by way of punctuation and sentence construction and making African names uniform can be dated to his letter to Murray September 3, 1874. He noted, "I shall not finish off the portion on which I was at first engaged till I can fetch all up to the same standard of correction because I find now that I have seen some of the Journal several alterations will have to be made."[31] The example above is typical of such uniform application of grammatical style: primarily running together short sentences by means of semicolons and colons.

Originally, all dates were printed in a uniform style, including month, day, and year. Later, Waller decided to retain the year only for the first date in each chapter and the first date of every month. The only exceptions made were to repeat the full date when several pages intervened between dated entries. The net result of this decision is to make it slightly more difficult to locate what is happening when the book is used for reference. A more significant problem was created for scholars when some manuscript dates were simply eliminated and passages run together in such a way that it becomes difficult to match dates between the original and published versions. Some of these decisions may have arisen because overlapping sources were available, but in the end the decision appears to have been made on the basis of the appearance of the finished volumes. Waller's primary concern appears to have been less the exact reproduction of the journals, in terms of dating all the events described, than the overall impact of the work in establishing Livingstone's reputation and enshrining his work to end the slave trade in East Africa.

Waller had a fairly careful editorial eye. He imposed uniformity on the spelling and accent marks of African names, which varied considerably in Livingstone's manuscript. A chief called "Kimsusa" was variously rendered as "Kimasusa," "Msusa," and "Kiemasusa" in the original passages and first proof sheets for October 5, 6, 7, and 8, 1866. These first proof sheets suggest that such differences went undetected by Tom Livingstone; they were later caught by Waller for the final version.[32]

Waller worked out a system of accents for the *e* in the last and sometimes penultimate syllables, and he decided to place a tilde accent over the *n* preceding *g*. Livingstone did not ordinarily use such accents, nor had he adopted them for *The Zambesi and Its Tributaries*. On the other hand, Waller also knew from their correspondence over that book that Livingstone was concerned about the proper spelling of African names and places.[33] Similarly, just as Livingstone had referred botanical questions to John Kirk when writing his Zambezi book, so Waller took advantage of Kirk's presence in England in 1874 to send him proof sheets of this sort to check.[34]

On the basis of Tom Livingstone's initialled instructions, his handwriting, and his characteristic editorial marks, we find clear evidence of his editorial presence on at least the first third of the proof sheets for the Unyanyembe journal. His editorial impact is an erratic one, however, at times hard at work supplying articles and pronouns and changing some internal sentence punctuation, at other times appearing only in occasional *x* marks indicating passages he wanted deleted. In two instances, for example, Tom marked for deletion entire paragraphs describing a chief with a secondary syphilitic infection of the skin. Waller then restored part of these passages, omitting only the direct references to the sores in question and a passage about the chief's wives, some of whom had been infected by him. In the first instance, Waller rephrased the identification of the sores to "a loathsome disease derived direct from the Arabs." In the second passage, he deleted only the sentences in which the chief "leaned on the bosom of one of his women" and told Livingstone that five of his wives had "taken the complaint," while six more "now present were most assiduous in their attentions to him . . . apparently not conscious that their own fine light-brown skins may have received the seeds of contagion."[35] Both Tom Livingstone and Horace Waller were indicating by their editorial decisions what they believed to be appropriate levels of censorship for the sensibilities of Victorian readers. Tom's reactions were more censorious or quicker to condemn whole passages without trying to save part of their content. Waller, though equally sensitive to his readership, was more willing to take the time to prune in order to save the plant. That the two men had different notions about what constituted appropriate material in travel literature is also possible.

Before presenting a systematic analysis of the categories of omissions made in translating the manuscript materials into the published book, I will examine Waller's editorial additions in explanatory footnotes and expanded editorial comment. Footnotes appear on ninety-four of the 706 text pages of the first edition, of which forty-two were signed "—

Ed." How or why this distinction was made is not entirely clear, since all the footnotes, both signed and unsigned, were a mixture of information, opinion, and Waller's comments.

The footnotes range from an explanation of words like *dhow* and *tsetse* to explanations of Livingstone's references to his previous journeys, especially the Zambezi trip, for it had taken him to territory he visited again on his last journey. From Waller's point of view, the signed footnotes may have contained his personal voice, more self-consciously dispensing information drawn from his own African experiences or other sources. In such notes he comments upon the differences between the Yao or "Achawa" and the Mang'anja peoples, tells the reader of Livingstone's ability to fall asleep at short notice, and asserts unequivocally that Livingstone used the Church of England services in Africa "at all times."[36] The tone of such footnotes is that of the shared reminiscences of an intimate friend. Waller comments on the behavior of African vultures as experienced by "the sportsman." In another place, he allows himself to remark on Livingstone's description of a chief's gesture of unbelief, the pulling down of the underlid of the right eye:

> It seems almost too ridiculous to believe that we have here the exact equivalent of the schoolboy's demonstrative 'Do you see any green in my eye?' nevertheless it looks wonderfully like it![37]

The editorial notes, interspersed within the text between journal entries, are also expressed in an informal, conversational tone. Such notes helped the editor make the necessary transitions to the next entry in the journal where changes of direction of thought occur without any warning. By means of these textual notes Waller gained some flexibility in a narrative that is otherwise cast in rigid journal form. He supplied eighty-six such editorial notes within the text of the two volumes. His remarks ranged from one-liners such as "Here is an entry concerning the tribe living far to the East,"[38] to comments that extended to over a page in length. The last "editorial note" is the forty-eight-page narrative which ends the book, covering the time from Livingstone's last journal entry in April 1873 to the arrival of his body in Zanzibar at the beginning of 1874.

Addressing the reader directly in his editorial notes, Waller offers personal details about Livingstone that help form a bond of intimacy between editor and reader. In this way, Waller dispenses freely his personal opinions throughout Livingstone's *Last Journals*. For example, Waller stops the reader before the entry for January 1867 in which Livingstone, recording the loss of his medicine chest, makes the comment,

"I felt as if I had now received the sentence of death, like poor Bishop Mackenzie." Waller prepared the reader to appreciate this remark:

We now come to a disaster which cannot be exaggerated in importance . . . it is hardly too much to believe that his constitution from this time was steadily sapped by the effects of fever-poison. . . . In his allusion to Bishop Mackenzie's death, we have only a further confirmation . . . the traveller in Africa goes—not with his life in his hand, but in some luckless box, put in the charge of careless servants. Bishop Mackenzie had all his drugs destroyed by the upsetting of a canoe. . . .

It cannot be too strongly urged on explorers that they should divide their more important medicines in such a way that a *total loss* . . . impossible. Three or four cannisters containing some calomel, Dover's powder, colocynth, and, above all a supply of quinine, can be distributed in different packages. . . .[39]

Waller wanted the reader not only to savor the full meaning of Livingstone's comment at this dramatic moment, but also to take heed of his own lecture on the subject. It is a right that he asserts, based on his own experiences in Africa, believing that his own words were sufficiently important that they might be interjected into this important moment in the narrative. Waller shares with the reader his own distress at the workings of fate and at the lack of proper precautions on the part of seasoned and unexperienced African travellers alike, laying themselves open to the disasters wreaked by "careless servants."

Yet if the reader follows the next passage carefully, there was more than "carelessness" involved. Livingstone had hired two Yao, who had become "free men" when their masters were killed. By their early conduct he judged them trustworthy; yet they not only deserted, they also planned and executed a major theft of dishes, powder, flour, tools, guns, and cartridges, along with his medicine chest. The ordinary carrier of the chest was very careful of his load because, in addition to cloth, it contained his own clothing and beads. One of the thieves offered to exchange loads with the medicine-bearer in a show of cooperation. Livingstone's own comment was that being sold into slavery early in life was not useful for learning to be honest and honorable: "they gave way to temptation which their good conduct had led us to put in their way." Waller's emphasis upon the long-range nature of this disaster, taking place as it did early in 1867, was not misplaced. Yet, by directing the reader to this aspect of the affair and framing it in the generalized context of "careless servants," he seems deliberately to have tried to deflect the reader from dwelling upon the calculated dishonesty of men in whom Livingstone had too readily put trust.

At a later time, in connection with an entry for July 1867, Waller commented from personal experience about Livingstone's description of a "poor old woman and child" among some captive slaves. Livingstone referred to a three-year-old boy who understood that he was being sold away from his mother and was therefore crying bitterly, clinging to her. Livingstone's point was that the woman was being sold for one fathom of cloth and her child for two fathoms. Waller added:

> The above is an episode of every-day occurrence in the wake of the slave-dealer. "Two fathoms," mentioned as the price of the boy's life—the more valuable of the two, means four yards of unbleached calico, which is a universal article of barter throughout Africa: the mother bought for two yards. The reader must not think that there are no lower prices; in the famines which succeed the slave-dealer's raids, boys and girls are at times to be purchased by the dealer for a few handfuls of maize.

Here a comparison with the Unyanyembe journal shows Waller making a deliberate decision to avoid what had been Livingstone's uncertainty about whether the woman was the boy's mother or grandmother. Waller's object was to sustain the power of the dramatic scene by paring it down to essentials, and he did not hesitate to eliminate details from Livingstone's journal to achieve this effect.[40]

In another instance, Waller introduced excerpts from a letter Livingstone had written to him concerning his African companion Wikatani. As a lad, Wikatani had been released by Livingstone in Waller's presence from a slave gang being led through the Shire hills. Wikatani was the young man whom Stanley, to Waller's great discomfort, had called a "deserter" in his newspaper account of Livingstone's travels. Waller now used his position as editor to tell his version of what had happened, conscious of giving these events their final shape. The consciousness of that power frames all his decisions.

He was ever full of information to share. He had taken Susi and Chuma to visit the warehouse of a great bead merchant in London in order to reconstruct the many kinds and colors of beads Livingstone carried for barter. He also shared with the reader the scorn Livingstone felt about "arm-chair geographers," aiming his remarks at W. D. Cooley. Without naming him, Waller referred to Cooley's most recent "arm-chair" criticism of Livingstone's work, published after the funeral at

Westminster Abbey, by calling it the work of an "addled geographical egg" whose pages would find few readers.[41]

There are twice as many editorial notes as footnotes in the second volume of the *Last Journals*, reversing the distribution found in the first volume. Together, one or the other kind of editorial comment appears every three or four pages. While the total effect is actually unobtrusive, the editor's presence is clearly felt. The sum of the additions is to emphasize that Horace Waller was an intimate friend of David Livingstone, that they shared African experiences, and that the editor was, accordingly, a qualified spokesman for Livingstone's views on Africa and the slave trade.

In sum, Waller's editorial contribution necessarily filtered out some of the special character of the author of these journals and field notes. From altered sentence structure to small word changes to editorial additions, it remains to be seen how these filters contributed to a pointed selection process by which consistent omissions separated the human, flesh and blood Livingstone from his Victorian readers and, in consequence, from history.[42]

One clear result of Waller's editing of Livingstone's *Last Journals* was to fix in the public memory the legendary, saintly figure first presented to the world by Stanley in 1872. Peeling back the hagiographic layers, I have sought to understand in more depth Livingstone the man, Livingstone the missionary, Livingstone the traveller, and Livingstone the antislavery crusader. In the process, however, the impact of Waller's Livingstone on his contemporaries is important in its own right. Livingstone's life became symbolic of the inextricable links that entangled Victorian philanthropy with Victorian imperialism in the last quarter of the nineteenth century. The mythic proportions of Livingstone's legacy made it more powerful and more compelling and ultimately more useful for the imperialist ends to which it was turned.

NOTES

1. Donald H. Simpson, Librarian and Director of Studies of the Royal Commonwealth Society, London, and Professor Roy C. Bridges, University of Aberdeen, have discussed this undertaking and Bridges has made some initial studies for it. Personal communication, D. H. Simpson.

2. My inspection—using NLS microfilm copies of the manuscripts on deposit at the Scottish National Memorial to David Livingstone (here-

after, SNMDL)—suggests Field Diaries 27 through 32 were used by Waller. I agree with the compiler of the *Livingstone Catalogue* that Waller did not use various daily entries in Field Diary 33; this is puzzling, since it was one of three journals Stanley gave Livingstone for his use and presumably came home with his body. Of the fragments listed in the *Livingstone Catalogue* as Field Diaries 34 - 39, I conclude Waller used at least Field Diaries 35, 37 (see remarks below), and 39. Of the separately listed Notebooks 15 through 18, the dates of which refer to the period of the last journey, a comparison of entries in the *Last Journals* suggests Waller used No. 17 but not No. 15. On No. 16 I have arrived at no conclusion, and I have not seen the twelve-page fragment listed as No. 18.

According to the *Livingstone Catalogue*, Field Diary 37 covers the period August 18, 1870 to August 10, 1871. It consists of "notes written on scraps of paper, printed books, and newspapers (some made up into a notebook now dismembered and incomplete) paginated with Roman numerals. 156pp." Several loose sheet marked "Dr. Livingstone's diary C. A. Alington" are to be found among proof sheets in the Waller Papers, Rhodes House. These are numbered 9–20 (internally numbered by Livingstone in capitalized Roman numerals *CXIV-CXXI*). The part transcribed by Alington covered April 25 - 28, 1871, and included a number of notes that followed these dates, WPRH, 6. Agnes Livingstone transcribed loose sheets dated August 17 [sic], 1870 - March 11, 1871, see proof marked "1st revise 251-286," WPRH, 8.

Exactly which of the field diaries made up the package of fourteen pocket-books that Cameron sent to England is still uncertain. Waller described them as: ". . . 14 memorandum books, 1 on the Zambesi & the rest from leaving London to far on in his last travels." Diary of Horace Waller, January 28, 1875, WPYDS. Thirteen were most likely Field Diaries 14 - 26, which cover the period of August 4, 1865 - February 25, 1871, written up by Livingstone in his Unyanyembe journal and left behind at Ujiji when he and Stanley left it December 27, 1871. There is not enough evidence from Waller's description of the fourteenth "pocket-book"—"on the Zambesi"—or in the *Livingstone Catalogue* for me to hazard a guess about its identity.

3. The men hired to carry supplies in caravans from the east coast were called porters (Swahili: *pagazi*), attendants, and servants. Some were *askari* (soldiers, or armed) or, for Livingstone, Indian marines. Some were women—like Halima, who married Amoda, and Ntaoeka, who married Chuma—hired especially for cooking tasks and sometimes attached by caravan men in the interior. Depending on caravan needs, African attendants acted as cooks, personal servants, interpreters, and guides; they were also cow herders, boatmen, or underbrush clearers.

Some remained with the caravan for an entire trip; others deserted and were replaced or temporarily supplemented along the way where possible. As Donald Simpson has shown in *Dark Companions*, the success of a European expedition might turn on the leadership qualities of these African companions. Many were accomplished travellers, well-known for hiring out their services to Europeans who needed guides. Most Englishmen who engaged in African exploration or took an interest in it at home were members of the upper or upper-middle classes (Livingstone was a notable exception). To such Englishmen, their African companions, even when known as noted travellers in their own right, were simply servants, and that is what they were called. (Augusta Webb's account of the distress felt by a luncheon party at eating at the same table with Jacob Wainwright well illustrates the point. Fraser, *Livingstone and Newstead*, chap. 25, esp. 224–25.)

In the case of the men who travelled longest with Livingstone, and those who joined him in 1872 for his last year, it was common for contemporaries to recognize the value of their services by calling them "faithful followers" or "faithful attendants." H. A. C. Cairns has called the concept of the faithful porter "somewhat mythical," suggesting it

> . . . implied a division of function between the leadership qualities of intelligence and organization and the secondary qualities of muscle and brawn, possessors of which obeyed orders and implemented the plans of others. . . . Praise for faithful followers was implicitly praise of whites who had elicited such fidelity.

Cairns, *Prelude to Imperialism*, 40. Sir Bartle Frere's presidential address at the RGS on June 22, 1874, can be placed in this context, especially his reference to Livingstone's "negro followers" who, "by contact with him, felt their own natures raised to deeds of faithfulness and heroism. . . ." *PRGS* 18 (1873–74): 511. See similar remarks by Frere, January 30, 1874, opening the new African Section at the Society of Arts. *Journal of the Society of Arts* 22:203 (hereafter, *JSA*). Compare Simpson, *Dark Companions*, esp. chs. 1, 6, 7, 8, and Glossary, 199–200.

4. *LJDL*, 2:308.
5. *LJDL*, 2:309.
6. *LJDL*, 2:310–11.
7. *LJDL*, 2:311.
8. *LJDL*, 2:316–46.
9. Whether Stanley actually said these words or not is less important than that he announced them to the world. They appeared first in the *New York Herald*, July 15, 1872. Bennett, *Stanley's Dispatches*, 52. As

Jeal notes, Stanley ". . . tried to imagine what an upper–class English-man would have said and done in the same situation. . . . The very people he had attempted to impress later found his formal greeting a ludicrous parody. If ever there had been an excuse for effusive behavior, surely this had been it." Jeal, *Livingstone*, 343.

10. Manuscript sheets *xxvi–xxvii* and proof sheet 30, WPRH, 6. One reviewer of Livingstone's first book, *Missionary Travels*, said, ". . . it is to the credit of this generation which loves 'style' so much, and is so great-ly influenced by literary graces, that work *so entirely devoid of both* should, nevertheless, have attained so remarkable a popularity." [Mar-garet Oliphant], "The Missionary Explorer," *Blackwood's Edinburgh Magazine*, 83 (April 1858): 394, emphasis added. Author identification: *Wellesley Index to Victorian Periodicals*, vol. 1.

11. Susi/Chuma NB, WPRH, 6. Simpson used this notebook as the basis of his narrative of these events, *Dark Companions*, 93–99. Compare Roy C. Bridges, "The Problem of Livingstone's Last Journey," in *David Livingstone and Africa* (Proceedings of a Seminar held on the occasion of the Centenary of the Death of David Livingstone at the Centre of African Studies, University of Edinburgh, May 4 and 5, 1973), 175 n. 4. Bridges adds, "Of course, this need not necessarily imply that Living-stone was not engaged in prayer at the time of his death," but he also notes how biographers, including recent ones like Tim Jeal, elaborated further on this image. Compare Jeal, *Livingstone*, 366. Harry Johnston, an explorer, botanist, linguist, and government official—and a man who liked to see himself as an iconoclast—wrote in the early 1890s, "It has pleased many of Livingstone's commentators and biographers to sur-mise that he died in prayer . . . It is an idea which is pleasing to the fancy . . . I do not think it is consistent with actuality." Harry H. John-ston, *Livingstone and the Exploration of Central Africa* (London, 1891), 355.

12. *LJDL*, 2:311.

13. *LJDL*, 2:319. Waller also suppressed Susi and Chuma's recollec-tion that Dr. Dillon "was for taking it [Livingstone's body] down." The details of Dillon's suicide were fairly gruesome and it is not surprising that Waller chose not to include them. From what they saw, the men concluded: "He had sat down & put the string on his foot & muzzle to forehead – fell back . . . 3 balls in 1 cartridge –balls passed through tent." They then noted, "Murphy saw blood from the door & would not go in sent Chuma in who collected bones of skull helped by little dog who brought pieces & laid them down." Susi/Chuma NB, WPRH, 6.

14. Susi/Chuma NB, WPRH, 6; *LJDL*, 2:330.

15. *PRGS* 18 (1873–74): 222; Waller's sensitivity to the report of Stan-

ley's remarks at the March 23 meeting stemmed from his knowledge that there were misgivings about Chuma's faithfulness as a servant. The first reports of Livingstone's death, which had reached England in January, had been skeptically received by people who had been in correspondence with Livingstone and knew of Chuma's temptation to leave Livingstone in 1866 when Wikatani separated from him and of the temporary desertion of Susi and Chuma for six months in 1868. Writing John Murray from Hamilton in Scotland, February 13, 1874, Livingstone's sister Janet cited both instances as reasons why she still hoped Cameron's news would prove false. Janet Livingstone to Murray, February 13, 1874, JMPA. Similarly, in his letter of condolence to Agnes upon his return to England, Stanley said that at first he too "was almost sure that Chumah's story was false, because Chumah had once before deserted your father in his hour of need. . . ." Lack of fidelity was thus interpreted as cowardly desertion and dishonesty, not a problem of leadership (see n. 3 above). Stanley to Agnes Livingstone, March 18, 1874, Stanley Papers, NLS. Yet Waller, who also knew these facts, was unwilling to dismiss Chuma so readily. He had known him as a boy rescued from a slave gang in the Shire Highlands. Therefore, as early as January 30, Waller suggested that Chuma should be brought to England and referred to "the thorough truthfulness and honesty of this young man." He added that Agnes Livingstone "desired him to say how sincerely she hoped this would be done. . . ." JSA 22:210.

16. *The Times*, March 31 and April 10, 1874. Capt. Brine was employed in the British navy's antislave trade patrol of the East African coast. He had met Livingstone once at the home of Robert Cooke. Brine to Cooke, January 15 [1874], JMPA. Chuma's letter was quite explicit about his and Susi's motives for writing Waller: "I do not know what work to do. . . . Susi . . . give his compliments to Mr. Waller, and to Dr. Livingstone's son, and now he is in Zanzibar and will wait for a letter. If you have any business in Africa, let us know. We want to go in Africa again where Dr. Livingstone died." *The Times*, April 10, 1874.

17. Fraser, *Livingstone and Newstead*, 214; PRGS 18 (1873–1874): 495, 511. See also, Simpson, *Dark Companions*, 100–3. On the Livingstone silver commemorative medals struck by the Royal Geographical Society, see Isobel Pridmore and Donald H. Simpson, "Faithful to the End," *Numismatic Circular*, 78:192–96.

18. *LJDL*, 2:313.

19. Bontinck, "Diaire de Jacob Wainwright"; H. B. Thomas, "The Death of Dr Livingstone: Carus Farrar's Narrative," *Uganda Journal* 14 (1950): 115–28; T. W. W. Crawford, "Account of the Life of Matthew Wellington in His Own Words, and of the Death of David Livingstone

and the Journey to the Coast," Part 2 of "David Livingstone: Two Accounts of His Death and Transportation of His Body to the Coast," *Northern Rhodesia Journal* (now *Zambia Journal*) 6 (1965): 99–102. Wellington's account was not taken down until 1911 and may reflect what he had learned or been told since as well as direct recollections. Not all details, of course, are common to all versions.

20. *LJDL*, 2:313. E. J. Glave to Alfred Sharpe, September 8, 1894, cited in Simpson, *Dark Companions*, 96, 212 n. 19. The portion of the tree trunk with the inscription was sent to the Royal Geographical Society in 1899, where it remains; its arrival was reported in *The Times*, April 26, 1900, and a photograph of the inscription appeared in *The Graphic*, May 5, 1900. A memorial erected on the site in 1902, however, included Chuma's name "from an assumption that the first A of YA-ZUZA was the end of another, missing word." Donald H. Simpson, "The Part taken by Africans in the European Exploration of East and Central Africa," in *The Exploration of Africa in the Eighteenth and Nineteenth Centuries* (Proceedings of a Seminar held at the Centre of African Studies, University of Edinburgh, December 3 and 4, 1971), 100.

21. Stanley, *How I Found Livingstone*, 1874, 1890, *lxx, liii*; Simpson, *Dark Companions*, 189, 192–93 (Chowpereh), 195 (Manua Sera). Half of the men listed by Simpson in his "Who's Who of Africans" were on Livingstone's last journey. Simpson, 191–98.

22. H. B. Thomas, "Carus Farrar's Narrative," 120. Matthew Wellington also referred to Christian–Muslim tensions between new recruits and old hands, ascribing the desire to bury Livingstone immediately to the latter (which would have included Susi and probably Chuma). Crawford, "Matthew Wellington," 101.

23. On the question of motives for bringing Livingstone's body and possessions back to the coast, see an excellent discussion by Bontinck, "Mort de Livingstone," 589–94. Bontinck also questions the notion that Susi and Chuma were the sole leaders of the return caravan. Bontinck, "Mort de Livingstone," 600 n. 54.

24. Murphy to Frere, Zanzibar, March 7, 10, 1874, Cameron Papers, RGSA. Waller also made explicit reference in the narrative to four bales of cloth that Livingstone had stored with the Arabs of Unyanyembe, ". . . and these were immediately forthcoming for the march down." *LJDL*, 2:340. Concerned about critics who said that but for finding Cameron's party at Unyanyembe the returning caravan "would have been brought to a standstill," Waller added an editorial footnote for August 18, 1872, asking the reader to note particularly that Livingstone had left "goods" there at the time of his departure. *LJDL*, 2:230. Yet, in his letter to Frere, cited above, Murphy wrote, "From each man's pay has been

deducted his share of the price of some cloth I had to buy for them at their request, to get them food near Unyanyembe. Cameron had given them ample to live on down to the coast, but it nearly all went in drinking at Unyanyembe. . . ."

On a minor detail, Murphy remembered Chuma arriving at Unyanyembe with four men; Chuma told Waller he went with three. *LJDL*, 2:337. On the exact location of Livingstone's death, the 1874 end map of the *Last Journals* places Chitambo's village at approximately East Longitude 30°. Cameron, Murphy, and Holmwood all estimated it a little more to the west. Compare: Cameron, *Across Africa*, 125; "He finally succumbed to his illness at about East Longitude 27° ¼ and South Latitude 12°," Murphy to Frere, March 7, 10, 1874; and "I fancy the spot where Livingstone died is about 11.25° S and 27° E." Holmwood to Frere, March 12, 1874, *PRGS* 18 (1873–1874): 246.

25. *LJDL*, 2:340–41; Murphy to Frere, March 7 and 10, 1874, Cameron Papers, RGSA. Murphy sent Frere a "true copy" of Cameron's authorization. Cameron's signature as "Actg Consul" is puzzling, as are its contents. At this time Cameron possibly assumed that Livingstone's roving consulship in East Africa fell to him as the leader of the relief expedition; he does not seem to have pursued the idea any further. Murphy himself was probably the source of the "rumors," since the document was aimed at aiding him assert authority over Susi. When Cameron returned to England in 1876, he gave Waller "a vile account of Murphy," which Waller believed ". . . corroborates C[huma] & S[usi] about his being a thief and everything else bad." Diary of Horace Waller, May 12, 1875, WPYDS.

26. *LJDL*, 2:341–42.

27. Murphy to Frere, March 7 and 10, 1874, Cameron Papers, RGSA.

28. Waller to Murray, August 3, 1874, JMPA.

29. Waller to Murray, August 5, 1874, JMPA. The section in question came toward the end of *LJDL*, 1:301–30, the greater part of chap. 12, covering June 1 – September 1, 1868.

30. Uj, NLS; *LJDL*, 1:34. The effect of Waller's imposition of longer, more densely punctuated sentences upon the *Last Journals* may be gauged against the style of *The Zambesi and Its Tributaries*. For the latter, Murray had supplied a "literary friend" whose stylistic changes Livingstone accepted with fair grace, though not entirely without grumbling. Livingstone to Murray, February 24, March 3, 1865, JMPA, and Livingstone to W. C. Oswell, March 23, 1865, Livingstone Papers, NMLZ, RH.

John Murray gave Livingstone's first book, *Missionary Travels*, a similar editorial review in 1857. In his first experience with the publishing world, Livingstone repeatedly raised cries of authorial pain whenever his prose was called "obscure." After three weeks of seeing his writing changed in March 1857, Livingstone wrote his publisher: "Now my good friend I can not think you have noticed the process of emasculation for which I fear you have been paying – the liberties he has taken are most unwarrantable and I cannot really undertake to father them. I am willing to submit my style uncouth though it be to Mr Elwin or any friend you like and if it is not clearer more forceable [sic] and more popular than anything this man can give I shall then confess I am wrong. My letters written to the Geographical & Missionary societies are popular. Why must you pay for diluting what I say into namby pambyism. Excuse me, but you must give this man leave to quit. I really cannot afford to appear as he would make me." Livingstone to Murray, March 22 [1857], JMPA. As to whether Livingstone was a good judge of his own style, see n. 10, above.

31. Waller to Murray, September 3, 1874, JMPA.

32. See, for example, proof sheets 77–78, WPRH, 7.

33. Several fragments among Waller's papers indicate the concern Livingstone exhibited about proper spelling. WPRH, 1. See also above, chap. 1, n. 24.

34. For example, *Clarias Capensis* was Livingstone's *Clavas Capensis*. *LJDL* 1:183 and proof sheet 114, WPRH, 7.

35. Proof sheets 72–74, September 24–25, 1866, WPRH, 7; *LJDL*, 1:113.

36. *LJDL*, 1:53, 169, 222. In these signed footnotes, Waller explained—from information he gleaned from Susi and Chuma—what otherwise might have puzzled readers. For example, he assured the reader that Livingstone's porter James was only killed, not eaten, by the Manyema; he gave information about Livingstone's cook Halima, who accompanied his body to Zanzibar; and he explained a reference made by Livingstone to a tale by Daniel Defoe. *LJDL*, 2:44, 193, 282. For a suggestion why Livingstone had the Defoe character of Captain Singleton in mind, see George Birdwood, "Last Journals of David Livingstone," *Academy*, no. 145 n.s. (February 13, 1875): 160.

37. *LJDL*, 1:182; 2:190.

38. *LJDL*, 1:218.

39. *LJDL*, 1:176–77. Modern analysis suggests that Livingstone's death was due to his long-standing problem of severe bleeding hemorrhoids, which weakened his resistance to bouts of fever. Bridges, "Problem of Livingstone's Last Journey," in *David Livingstone and Africa*, 165; Cecil Northcott, *David Livingstone: His Triumph, Decline and Fall* (Philadelphia, 1973), 106–7.

40. *LJDL*, 1:222; July 28, 1867, on proof sheet 138, WPRH, 7.

41. *LJDL*, 1:109–10, 180–81; 2:63. Cooley's pamphlet was entitled *Dr. Livingstone and the Royal Geographical Society* (London, 1874). On Cooley, see Roy C. Bridges, "W. D. Cooley, The RGS and African Geography in the Nineteenth Century," *Geographical Journal* 142 (March and July, 1976): 27–47, 274–86. Under journal date May 21 [1872], Waller deleted: "Cooley penned a pretentious pamphlet, modestly styled 'INNER AFRICA LAID OPEN', and not only had no doubts, but in his virulent style seemed to 'cuss and swear promiskus' at anyone else who dared to doubt. The publication was only Paddy's nate way of holding round his hat." Proof sheet 7, WPRH, 8. Considering these deletions, it is ironic to find one reviewer (a member of the Royal Geographical Society, Bombay Geographical Society, and Royal Asiatic Society) defending Cooley with a comment more critical of Waller than of Livingstone: ". . . where Livingstone has *unwittingly* done palpable injustice, as in his criticism of Mr. Cooley's account of the hydrography of the Chambeze, Mr. Waller has simply cast an insult at the victim of Livingstone's *inadvertence*, and passed on." The reviewer further scorned Waller's role as editor, "He has virtually left Livingstone's notes just as he found them—a jungle, without sign-posts or tracks. . . ." Birdwood, "Last Journals," *Academy*, no. 145, n.s. (February 13, 1875): 160, emphasis added.

42. There were many small word changes, usually from a rather simple to a more elaborate or elegant form of the word, versions that Waller obviously considered more "literary." For example, *there* in the Unyanyembe journal (June 16, 1867) became *thither*; *makes up* (June 17–19, 1867) was replaced with *comprises*; and the sentences: "Their side of the village was all burned. Three goats were burned" (July 24, 1867) turned into: "Their side of the village was all consumed, and three goats perished in the flames." Uj, NLS; *LJDL*, 1:215, 216, 221.

§ 4 ⧟

Major Editorial Decisions

Either John Murray or his partner Robert Cooke is the most likely person to have made the initial decisions with regard to printing the Unyanyembe journal.[1] Instructions at the back of the journal told the printer to delete various passages and to typeset separately as an appendix Livingstone's observations about rainfall and altitudes and a "Note on Christian Missions." The passages marked for omission at this stage were, in order: 1865 and 1866 dispatches from Livingstone to Lord Stanley at the Foreign Office; reflections on "God's concern with individuals and hence disapproval of slavery"; comments on the transfer of physical vitality; private memoranda—so labelled—on Prince Albert, John S. Moffat, missionaries of the Kololo Mission, Thomas Baines, the Universities' Mission, and Richard Thornton; an 1872 Dispatch to Lord Granville at the Foreign Office; and Livingstone's summary of the contents of his journal.[2]

Waller early eliminated an 1869 Dispatch to Lord Stanley, two 1869 letters to the sultans of Zanzibar and Johanna, an 1866 memorandum regarding the wages Livingstone had agreed to pay the Comoran island men, the rest of Livingstone's Foreign Office dispatches for 1870 and 1871, and two dispatches to John Kirk in 1871.[3] Waller was undoubtedly pleased to agree with Murray that including the Foreign Office dispatches would only duplicate the narrative unnecessarily, since that elimination also got rid of the unpleasant semiofficial letters of complaint that Livingstone had written Kirk in 1871. He quickly decided to have the printer reset the "Note on Missions," however, and reintroduced it into the text under the date July 10, 1872.[4]

In the extant manuscript journal, the pages about Prince Albert, John S. Moffat, and the first part of the Kololo mission have been torn out. Since the Instructions to the Printer at the back of the journal, dated July 16, 1874, included these pages, this drastic excision must have occurred after the initial printing of the journal. Just when the offending pages were pulled out is impossible to tell, but it is safe to surmise that the act of tearing pages out of the journal could have been done only by its owners, the Livingstone family. Whoever decided to remove them so irrevocably not only wished them to remain unpublished but was anxious that no one else should read them.[5]

The character of the passages torn out also suggests why the Livingstone family might want them expunged. In the first memorandum, Livingstone had hard words to say against the late Prince Consort. It was not a moment to bring down upon themselves the ill will of Queen Victoria. Her Majesty's Government had only recently decided to pay life pensions to the Livingstone children and to give his sisters a life interest in a family trust fund. As for the second memorandum, making public Livingstone's cutting remarks about his own brother-in-law, now employed with the colonial administration in South Africa, may simply have seemed distasteful. He was the brother of Tom and Agnes's mother and, whatever their feelings, the passage must haved distressed their grandfather, Robert Moffat. The page torn from the third memorandum, on the Kololo Mission, left a passage without any names attached. The fact that the unnamed missionary so assaulted by Livingstone was Roger Price, now married to Robert Moffat's daughter Bessie, offers further evidence that the pages torn out reflected immediate family concerns. Knowing such private memoranda existed may have been an added spur to Tom and Agnes to check Waller's editing and to see the proof.

The nature of the missing passages is clear enough from their brief description in a table of contents Livingstone had written on the final pages of the journal: "Prince Albert [:] the Portuguese rights [in East Africa] tenderly cared for [and] the native rights ignored – [and the] contrast presented by good Lord Palmerston";[6] "[my financing of the missionary work of] John Moffat a mistake[:] missionaries [are] but men and not always very honest ones";[7] "Of two Makololo [Kololo] missionaries [sent by the London Missionary Society:] Helmore & Price – one [was] a good man [and] the other a born fool."[8]

The passage on physical vitality is a curious one, labelled by Livingstone: "Paragraph left out of vol. printed." The reference is to *The Zambesi and Its Tributaries*. At first there seems no reason to pause to examine the passage in any detail, but in fact the ideas involved illuminate both Livingstone's notions and the assumptions he shared with contemporaries. Livingstone's remarks reflect both personal observations and reading and discussion with others; they reveal his view of physiological causality. He mused about the transfer of actual, physical energy—what he called "vital force"—from one person to another. He maintained as fact that if a young child slept with an elderly person for a period of time,

"the younger loses, and the older gains in vital force; and the child becoming sickly and old looking can only be restored to blooming condition by being allowed to sleep alone in its crib." He then wrote that the
"like happens when old men marry young wives (well known to the
harsh physicians who tried to prolong the life of King David)." Continuing this thought, Livingstone noted, "[W]here Portuguese officers [on
the Zambezi] had black wives a transference of colour as well as of
vitality takes [sic] place. They became decidedly darker than any of us.
This was particularly marked in one whom we had an opportunity of
observing for eight years."

Livingstone discussed these ideas with Professor (later Sir Richard)
Owen, with whom he had studied comparative anatomy and physiology
in London at the Hunterian Museum in 1840. Owen was superintendent
of the British Museum (Natural History) from 1856 to 1883. Livingstone
sent him various animals from the Zambezi and, in 1864–1865, consulted
him on natural history in connection with the publication of the Zambezi
book. Owen suggested that married couples, too, might become "assim-
ilated in features," speculating that the cause lay in the "fact" that when
pregnant, the woman carried "the blood of a being only half her own
circulating through every part of her system. . . ."[9]

On this line of thought, Livingstone mused further in his journal, that
there was also a "peculiar odour which want of cleanliness developes
[sic] in some Africans" which Arab men took on when living with African women in the interior. He concluded, "In connection with this subject I observed that my Zambesians who were taken to India with the
African odour strongly developed – lost it entirely in the course of a year
and acquired the peculiar mousy smell of East Indians." Livingstone
viewed his thoughts on this subject as serious science. His attitude is clear
from an exchange he had with his friend W. C. Oswell in the course of
correcting proof for his Zambezi book in 1865. Livingstone's comments
on the suppressed paragraph are especially revealing if "C." represents
Robert Cooke, John Murray's cousin and partner. At first Livingstone
wrote Oswell on February 18, "You had better send the part about old
bachelors marrying young wives to Owen, and then you will see what he
says about it. C. is one of them. The wretched fellow may think I am
personal, and not anxious for the good of the Commonwealth alone." On
April 15, apparently after the publisher expressed doubt about including
the paragraph, Livingstone wrote Oswell: ". . . I confess that I have full
confidence in your judgment and none at all in C.'s. It was rather stupid
in me not to see you tolerated the "Transference" par. . . ." Three
weeks later, these considerations still on his mind, Livingstone wrote
Oswell: "When speaking of the natives being men with every attribute of

human kind, will it do to say that not only are the mixtures of races "fertile" but they readily coalesce, as in the case of the transference of colour already mentioned? In that of vitality, shall we mention the strength imparted by black nurses?"[10]

This twice-suppressed passage on physical vitality therefore provides us with an extraordinary opportunity to probe some of Livingstone's assumptions, attitudes, and beliefs. From youth, he was an enthusiastic reader of science and took a keen interest in every kind of scientific information. Because he was trained in physiology and anatomy in the 1830s, his views on scientific and physiological facts continued to reflect what he had learned during this period. We can only speculate on why this passage was censored and twice removed before publication. Did the publisher with, in the second instance, the agreement of the editor, set aside the passage because it seemed to them beyond the pale of good taste? Was it in some other way offensive? Since Livingstone discussed his views about the exchange of bodily "vitality" or skin color with Professor Owen, who indulged in similar speculation, it is more likely that the topic itself was being censored rather than that there was any disagreement with Livingstone's opinions. If Livingstone and Owen do reflect contemporary opinion on physiological causality rather than personal idiosyncrasy, the entire passage takes on an interest in its own right from a historical perspective.

The views Livingstone expressed in this passage about the transference of bodily vitality, skin color, and body odor are certainly consistent with his stated opinions about Africans, Arabs, and slaves. Two beliefs are paramount: physiological changes may have external causes and physiology undergirds character.[11] These beliefs explain comments Livingstone repeatedly made about the inferiority of "half-castes," a term he used for dark-skinned Arabs and light-skinned Africans. They also explain why, when he began to encounter problems with his attendants at the beginning of his last journey, Livingstone commented on their skin color: "A few of the Nassick boys have the slave spirit pretty strongly; it goes deepest in those who have the darkest skins."[12]

Such views convinced Livingstone that the enslavement of Africans—taking them out of their native environment and subjecting them to different cultures, that of the Arab slaver or the English liberator—irrevocably destroyed their original upright character. Livingstone was not unique in holding such opinions. They were common to contemporaries who made fun of West Africans who "imitated" English ways, and they were central to European and American notions of the virtues of being "pure bred," whether the quality referred to domesticated animals or "legitimate" first sons and heirs. Livingstone, however, explicitly extended the idea of "bloodlines" to the transfer of physiological phenomena by virtue of ongoing physical contact. Livingstone had introduced himself to the English public in his first book of *Missionary Travels* as the descendent of a long line of Scottish farmers, proud of a grandfather who "could give particulars of the lives of his ancestors for six generations." From the beginning of his travels, Livingstone praised those he met in the interior of Africa whom he believed to have "pure African blood," sharing the contemporary hostility, on both sides of the Atlantic, to any kind of miscegenation—an attitude which often masked a fascination with the subject.[13]

Furthermore, Livingstone was interested in various aspects of sexuality that he encountered. Twice censoring the passage on the transference of human vitality is all the more puzzling when we discover that neither publisher nor editor saw the need to delete Livingstone's observations about marriage patterns and sexual relations he encountered in Africa. We find these remarks in volume 1 of the *Last Journals*, for the year 1866:

> 16th June.— . . . The cattle of Africa are . . . only partially tamed; they never give their milk without the presence of the calf. . . . The women adjacent to Mozambique partake a little of the wild animal's nature, for, like most members of the inferior races of animals, they refuse all intercourse with their husbands when enceinte and they continue this for about three years afterwards, or until the child is weaned. . . . I was told, on most respectable authority, that many fine young native men marry one wife and live happily with her till this period; nothing will then induce her to continue to cohabit with him, and, as the separation is to continue for three years, the man is almost compelled to take up another wife: this was mentioned to me as one of the great evils of society. The same absurdity prevails on the West Coast, and there it is said that the men acquiesce from ideas of purity.[14]

This published passage raises many questions. Who were the informants who called this custom "one of the great evils of society"—were they Arabs, Africans, or Portuguese? We must presume they were male. What is particularly striking is that neither Livingstone nor his editor or publisher saw anything offensive—merely an observation of facts—in alluding to African women as having a nature like that of "wild animals" or "inferior" animals because they spaced their children by the only contraceptive method readily available to them, abstinence. It would have been necessary to be far more circumspect if he had made such remarks about English women, though the notion that women were closer to nature and more animal-like than men in their reproductive function coexisted in Victorian England with the idea that English women had more passive, nonsexual natures than animal-like, lustful men.[15] In this passage, Livingstone focused entirely upon the husband's sexual deprivation, concluding that his only recourse on being deprived of his wife's sexual services for three years was to take another "wife." Livingstone's final remark emphasized his views: not only was a long sexual abstinence between married partners absurd, but strange indeed was the society where husbands agreed to it, even for the reason assigned.

Further light is shed on this passage when we look at the proof sheets. The paragraph appears among the earliest numbered sets. From a study of the editorial marks which Tom Livingstone made, a comparison with the kind of editorial decisions and marks Waller made, and a knowledge of the "history" of the proof sets from Waller's letters to the publisher, I conclude that the editorial changes made for this passage were Tom's work. He exchanged the phrase "when enceinte," for his father's original phrase, "after pregnancy is established." He transformed his father's phrase "they continue to avoid the male" into "they continue this," and Tom's "till this period" replaced Livingstone's "live happily with her till she becomes pregnant." Livingstone finished the passage by saying he had learned that West African men acquiesced in abstinence because of ideas of "cleanness and uncleanness." Tom replaced the phrase with the word "purity."[16]

Aside from the euphemisms and vaguer phraseology Tom introduced into this passage, the change that may significantly distort Livingstone's meaning lies in the use of the word *purity*. His father's original phrase, "from ideas of cleanness and uncleanness," conveyed what he had learned to be the motivation and, together with the word *acquiesce*, hints at his surprise that such ideas were strong enough to regulate male sexuality. The term *purity* detracts from the nuances of the original phrase and introduces the contemporary Victorian meaning of "single sexual standard," which may or may not be what Livingstone had in mind. The point is, of course, that in suppressing the original words, Tom made editorial changes that have obscured Livingstone's information and have even hidden the value judgments implied in his word choice.

An inspection of Livingstone's Field Diary 16, for May 30, 1866, a manuscript that Waller certainly saw only after the publication of the *Last Journals*, reveals a relevant passage that Livingstone did not include when later writing up his large (Unyanyembe) journal from these daily notes. What he wrote that day bears on his reflections under the journal date of June 16, quoted above: "As many women are seen in the family

way and have some children at the breast and another about 3 years old
at the knee the stupid way of women retiring for 3 years from the husband cannot be in vogue among Makonde & Metabwe [sic].[17] Here, as in
the first passage cited on this subject, Livingstone expressed his own reaction, using the words *absurdity* and *stupid*, with regard to wives imposing sexual abstinence on husbands. His reaction may be gauged in
the light of his own marital history. During the first six years of his own
marriage, from 1845 to 1851, he fathered five children (the fourth dying
in infancy) and impregnated his wife again in 1858, during the only other
period in which they spent any time together.[18] Aside from examining
his own conduct, it is only from his comments on African marital behavior that we can gather Livingstone's personal views on these matters.

The private memoranda marked for omission were each labelled
"Private Memo" by Livingstone, both in the places where they appear in
his journal and in his table of contents. His instructions to his daughter
Agnes had been quite explicit: "Mr. Stanley leaves. I commit to his care
my journal sealed with five seals: the impressions on them are of an
American gold coin, anna [an Indian coin], and half anna, and cake of
paint with royal arms. Positively not to be opened."[19] These memoranda
were primarily elaborate defenses, rationales for his past behavior. In
each case, Livingstone's mind was circling round and round incidents or
events in which his actions had been publicly criticized. His remarks do
not constitute any reassessment of his own responsibility; instead, they
are vehement and unforgiving diatribes against his critics, reaffirming
the correctness of his own behavior and the culpability of others for
these past misfortunes. Livingstone's determination to exonerate himself
reveals at best his lack of the power of empathy or the impulse to charity.
In some instances, he actually borders on misrepresenting what occurred. He attributed to his accusers the same bitter singleness of vision
that he himself demonstrated.[20]

Waller, clear in his own mind about Livingstone's greatness of character and achievements, would see in these passages the intemperance of a
fevered mind, too ill to throw off such musings and too disordered to be
held accountable for them. Yet similar preoccupations haunted Livingstone even after Stanley's medicines and supplies left him better able to
resist fevers, and at their worst such rantings only represented what was
characteristic of his thinking, though in a much exaggerated form. In his
field diary for September 1872, for example, which Waller had available
to him, Livingstone looked back on his life in Africa with many regrets;
he had regrets about the actions or failures of others and his own failure
to grasp more effectively the rewards available to him for the benefit of
his family. He repeats a familiar tale of regret that he had not taken up

Lord Palmerston when he sent someone to Newstead Abbey in 1865 to inquire what the government might do for him, to ask perhaps for some pension that would bring secure provision for his family. He regrets that he had not asked Sir Bartle Frere, then the Governor of Bombay, for the Zanzibar consulate for himself that same year: "I had the offer of a consulate on the coast of Africa of much higher grade than Kirk now holds [Kirk was still vice consul at this writing] but declined it from not thinking enough of my own need and from not remembering that I could have got unlimited leave while the donor Sir Bartle Frere lived in power. I was too short sighted for my own interests. . . ."[21]

At the same time, Livingstone continued to dwell on the loss of his supplies earlier in his travels; he had been duped by Arab agents from Zanzibar who in turn were financed by British Indian subjects (Banians). He brooded over the excuses offered by the Muslim carriers, who told him that Kirk had ordered them to force him back to the coast. Stanley's critical comments about the laxness of Kirk's efforts to send him relief had made him fix on Kirk as the culprit, rather than on the Arabs. He then thought endlessly about the turning back of his son Oswell, as well as of the Royal Geographical Society's Search and Relief Expedition, once they heard the news of Stanley's rescue. With such thoughts gnawing at him, Livingstone imagined the worst of possible scenarios:

[N]ow I see that Dr Kirk had no sort of compunction in trying to supersede me. . . . The eagerness with which he recommended that I should retire & leave the rest to other travellers. The strong urgings to the S[earch] & R[elief] Expedition to resign & go home and the culpable negligence of placing all my supplies in Banian hands & there leaving them, tell a tale. If Dr Kirk had never got the offer of the leadership of the Sources of the Nile he would not have had the additional strain put on his moral nature which the prospect of superseding me after he had assured his two prerequisites – a salary & position to fall back upon for which he at first declined.[22]

The notion that Kirk was eager to become his rival for geographical fame—as had been the case with Speke and Burton—led Livingstone to dredge up his recollections of past incidents that suggested such motives had operated from the beginning. Writing Waller at this time, Livingstone referred to returning from the Zambezi Expedition to find a map of Kirk's "blazoned on the walls [of the Royal Geographical Society] though it was essentially a copy of mine." Later in the same letter Livingstone again harped upon this theme: "I recommended Kirk for the lead-

ership of this Expedition and he refused it unless he had a good salary
and an office to fall back on afterwards as Speke & Grant did on their
commissions. It was only after this that I consented to take it myself and
unsalaried. . . ."[23]

Except for the brief interlude with Stanley in 1871–1872, Livingstone
was in Africa without European companionship for seven years, from
March 1866 to his death at the end of April 1873. He had chosen to work
during his last journey as he had during his first transcontinental cross-
ing, as the sole authority of the expedition. He needed to consult no one.
His will, depending upon the circumstances he met, would not only be
supreme but could be exercised without his having to explain what he
chose to do to companions whose views might differ from his. Many of
the unpleasant complications of his Zambezi Expedition, which ended
in his being recalled, involved his relationship with other Europeans,
several of whom were members of his own expedition. Livingstone had
not wanted for offers to join him on his last journey, but he had firmly
decided that—except for his own son Robert, whom he thought of taking before he learned of his death in the American Civil War—he would
go alone.[24]

In Africa, Livingstone's mind was occupied with a wide range of concerns and responsibilities: geographical pursuit of the sources of the
Nile; increasing acquaintance with the Arab slave trade of the interior;
daily problems of obtaining food and African guides; keeping his African servants in order and, at the beginning of the trip, the Indian marines
and Comoran porters—as well as various beasts of burden; his health
and that of his party; diary writing; astronomical observations; map-
making; and dispatch and letter writing. Yet, long stretches of time presented themselves, during which his mind returned repeatedly, like a
tongue to an aching tooth, to the events of the past. Without companions
who did not present some language or cultural barrier, Livingstone held
internal discourses; from these came the passages he labelled "Private
Memoranda." If they represent a brain at fever pitch, as Waller saw it, it
was still a brain that returned to sources of pain in the irrational hope that
contemplation would yield reassurance.

Waller's goal as editor of these *Last Journals* was not to portray a
disappointed man, or even a flawed and complicated man, but a simple,
great man whose prophetic vision was still to be realized. Like Livingstone, Waller believed that only through great public fame—recognition
of geographical tasks brilliantly executed and acclaim for philanthropic
goals still incomplete—would Livingstone's plans for Africa receive a
proper hearing. Livingstone took very seriously the need to maintain
British influence in Africa, "to carry out the great work of civilization

which Providence in its wisdom has entrusted to our nation."[25] Waller's self-defined editorial task was to ensure that Livingstone's last recorded words should contribute to contemporary concern for Africa's future and inspire an audience still untouched by the urgency of this cause.

Following instructions, the printer typeset separately all the astronomical readings in the Unyanyembe journal. Waller raised the subject with John Murray early in October when he received the proof for this appendix; he recommended to the publisher that they not be published with the book. "In their present condition," he reasoned, "they will be left unread by the general reader and picked to pieces by every tyro in Geography."[26] Waller reminded Murray that Livingstone specifically advised that no astronomical readings be placed at the disposal of the Royal Geographical Society until they were checked for correctness by Sir Thomas Maclear, astronomer at the Royal Observatory at Cape Town and an old friend of Livingstone's. Waller further pointed out that there were additional astronomical readings in the field diaries for the period after Stanley left with the Unyanyembe journal, ". . . which it will take a very long time to set in order and which must be added, or the extracts from the large journal will be only a fragment." The editor won his argument and referred to this delayed publication in his Introduction, indicating that the map prepared for the book should also be taken as tentative until these observations had been verified.[27]

Waller was not eager to omit material from the *Last Journals*. Some days later, he wrote Murray greatly concerned. With the return to him of the "marble-covered" copybooks—field diaries which had been at the printer's since early August with instructions for omission of some "private jottings" only—". . . some of the very best matter has been omitted, and of a nature which needed no restriction on my part."[28] Because he was working quickly, Waller had not read the diaries carefully before marking them for the printer. He therefore had not noticed, without careful comparison with the manuscript original, that material he had not intended to leave out had been omitted. Keenly aware of the publisher's deadline (once he discovered what had happened), he sought "to make a separate chapter of the omitted part."[29]

Because Waller was a conscientious editor, concerned about inadvertent omissions, we are safe in assuming that the deliberate omissions tell us clearly the nature of his editorial goals. To analyze these omissions, it is necessary to discover the way in which Livingstone acted as his own first censor. A comparison of his field diaries from 1866 to 1871 (material not available to Waller during the editorial process) with the Unyanyembe journal—on which the published version for these years is based—reveals how much vivid detail Livingstone suppressed in writ-

Waller's preliminary sketch of a slave gang for Livingstone's *Last Journals*. He wrote "some legs" under the bent-legged figure yoked to the slave stick at the left and "coming down a steep hill" below the line of marchers on the right to indicate to the artist who would draw the engraving what he intended. (Compare with the finished illustration on p. 150.)

ing up the version he intended for the public. We look in vain in the *Last Journals* for numerous details found in these diaries: people listening "with intense eagerness" to his playing an accordian (April 11 and 23, 1866); carrying along a coffee mill, until he sent it to be stored at Ujiji (September 9, 1867); quick cures of the fevers suffered by his attendants by means of pills of his own formulation, followed by their rapid relapses (April 11 and 24, November 28, 1866); or the various grievances to which he gave voice regarding the behavior of his attendants, particularly those from the Church Missionary Society's Nasik Asylum (March 1, 1867).[30]

Livingstone not only left such material out of his journal, but he also provided self-censorship in matters of Victorian euphemisms. On this score he had already had two manuscripts subjected to the hand of a "literary friend" of his publisher. He had learned what words, such as *urine*, were unacceptable, and he had become self-conscious about following this standard. In his field diary for May 18, 1866, he wrote, "A child could not go behind the house to make water unless her grandmother stood near her and watched so she was not stolen." In the Unyanyembe journal, under the date May 18, 1866, we find: "Observing that a child would not go a few yards for necessary purposes unless grandmother stood in sight."[31]

The field diaries are also far more graphic, both in the words used and the small drawings provided, about the scenes of horror Livingstone encountered along depopulated slaving routes into the interior: "A slave tied to a tree dead & putrid & greatly eaten by the Hyaenas." Accompanying these words, Livingstone had sketched a genderless skeleton, a haunting vision simply not conveyed in the words of the journal and published version: "It was wearisome to see the skulls and bones scattered about everywhere."[32]

Livingstone was also his own first censor in omitting his real disappointments in human relationships. He did not write up in his big journal the notes he jotted down in his field diary for January 1867, describing how he had found Chuma secretly hoarding two bags of meal some hours after Livingstone had announced that he had no food left for himself. Chuma, like Wikatani, had been only nine or ten when rescued by Livingstone from a slave gang in the Shire Highlands in July 1861. Livingstone had taken him to Bombay in 1864 and had left him and Wikatani in the care of Scottish missionary Dr. John Wilson. Chuma and Wikatani were baptized by Wilson in December 1865 and left for Africa again with Livingstone the next month. At the time of the incident Livingstone recorded in his field diary, Wikatani had already left the Doctor to remain with relatives at Mponda's at Lake Malawi; Chuma had opted to stay with Livingstone.

"Slavers Revenging their Losses." This engraving is the second of six full-page illustrations in Volume I of Livingstone's *Last Journals*. Based on Waller's preliminary sketch, it appears next to a description of forced marches required by a scarcity of food in June 1866 after the party left the banks of the Ruvuma River and headed south to Chief Mataka's village. It was a trying time for Livingstone: the last of his animals were dying, there was growing bitterness with his Indian marines, and—not least—every day they met these terrible scenes of slave devastation.

Chuma, now perhaps fifteen years old, acted in a way that left Livingstone feeling betrayed, much as a parent might. Livingstone chose to confront him on the issue: "I went into the hut assigned & found my boy munching cakes he had made. . . . He took up his two bags crammed full of meal & was walking off when I asked him if he knew that I was in actual want. . . . He blushed if a black man can blush & said he 'did not know . . . till this morning.' It was 7 AM when I told him & this was now 2 PM without his offering any."[33] Chuma then offered Livingstone some of his meal; and Livingstone paid him for it in beads. The result, Livingstone noted in his field diary with grim satisfaction, was that Chuma used his beads to buy elephant meat and suffered from a bout of diarrhea.

Livingstone's choices in self-censorship are important. On the one hand, they represent the ways in which Livingstone wished his activities and the events of his travels to be seen by others. Since he wrote up his Unyanyembe journal at long intervals, he often knew the outcome of some of the day to day problems that plagued him as he jotted daily notes in his field diary. If we compare those daily field notes with his finished journal, we understand how Livingstone decided to present his activities. Except for scattered overlapping entries in field diaries available to him, Waller did not have this window into Livingstone's thinking.

The comparison does demonstrate, however, that many of Waller's editorial choices were consonant with Livingstone's views about what was proper to reveal to the public. For example, both men wished to shield from public censure the actions of Livingstone's closest followers, like Chuma and Susi. Livingstone might condemn their behavior from time to time—including their temporary desertions—but he also forgave them; and they remained with him to the end. In Chuma's case, of course, except for a year and a half in India, he had grown up in Livingstone's company. In his field diary for August 14, 1866, Livingstone wrote, "Obliged to supplant Wekatani [sic] & Chuma in the cooking department on account of inveterate carelessness – and always losing my things. They allowed the Shupanga men [Susi and Amoda] to consume my sugar and last night left a basin outside to be stolen. I am sorry to part with them thus but they evidently prefer the favour of these two thieves to mine. . . ."[34]

Though conscious of some constraints, Livingstone was far more willing to expose the shortcomings of the Africans educated at Nasik than Waller would be. Waller was aware of the contemporary humanitarian politics surrounding these issues. For example, one reason Waller chose to be discreet involved the activities of Sir Bartle Frere, who had led the mission to Zanzibar to obtain a new slave trade treaty in 1872–1873 and presided at the Royal Geographical Society in 1874. As he edited Living-stone's *Last Journals*, Waller was aware that the Church Missionary Society, urged on by Frere, was making efforts to send Nasik-trained Africans to East Africa to establish a new freed slave settlement. When he was in East Africa in 1873, Frere had investigated the possibilities for this project and had given it his blessing. To publicize the need for this new missionary venture, he had written about it in three "open letters" to the Archbishop of Canterbury. John Murray published the letters as a book in the spring of 1874, soon after Livingstone's funeral.[35]

Frere's recommendations were based on his knowledge of the Nasik Asylum near Bombay, whose pupils he had recommended to Living-stone in 1865. Both he and all those interested in the project—and especially the Church Missionary Society which was raising money for it—were interested in what Livingstone reported in his *Last Journals* about his Nasik-trained attendants. Frere had written in his little book, ". . . doubtless we shall find, among his letters and notes, some details of their conduct." To Frere the participation of the Nasik-trained men in helping to bring down Livingstone's remains proved "the excellent results of Christian and industrial training on average African children" and their usefulness to African missions.[36] Livingstone had always urged more missionary work in East and Central Africa. Had he known about this venture, he too, it might be argued, would have chosen to play down for publication his more critical views about the training at Nasik and the use of liberated Africans as missionary agents.

The situation was doubly difficult. While Waller understood that any denunciation by Livingstone of Nasik training would be impolitic, he was also concerned to counter what he viewed as the "overexposure" in England of the Nasik-trained Jacob Wainwright at the expense of Susi and Chuma. Such problems circumscribed Waller's hand more than they would have affected Livingstone in publishing his journals. But to Waller, not Livingstone, fell the task. Waller decided to suppress passages whose airing he believed would be inappropriate in terms of the philanthropic diplomacy of the day. He also omitted "private jottings," as he would have called them, that showed Livingstone at his worst. These might take the form of paragraphs, phrases, or adjectives. The next chapter examines these categories of omissions. The reader must judge whether, taken together, they significantly changed the substance of the *Last Journals*, or only their tone.

Although Livingstone inevitably would have made some different choices about what to put before the public in these last journals, Waller did make his editorial decisions fully conscious of the burden of choice. He might be guilty of interjecting his own, more florid style when he spoke in his editorial voice and when he made stylistic changes, but he was generally careful about presenting to posterity as many details as possible about Livingstone's last travels. He was conscious of a duty to ensure that Livingstone's fame was in no way diminished by what was published and that, taken as a whole, the journals would ensure the lasting image of Livingstone the gentle missionary, Livingstone the great-hearted antislave trade crusader. In this task, Waller acted with complete self-confidence, based on all the beliefs he knew he shared with Livingstone as well as the goal they shared for the future of Africa: to end the slave trade by the exertion of British influence.

NOTES

1. The instructions to the printer concerning which pages to omit and which to set separately as an appendix appear on the last page of the Unyanyembe journal and are dated 16/7/74, the day before Murray made Waller a formal offer of editorship. The initials at the end, above the date, are possibly "WCKle." In 1976, Donald Simpson was kind enough to share with me some notes he had prepared on "Livingstone's Journal 1866-1872: Preliminary Appraisal" for the David Livingstone Documentation Project of the National Library of Scotland. He noted that Livingstone irregularly made entries in his large or Unyanyembe journal from his field diaries, usually writing up the journal at periods when he was delayed at any one spot. An entry in Livingstone's Field Diary 34, dated March 1870, indicates that the large journal had been left at Ujiji in July 1869; he could not write it up until his return there in October 1871, shortly before Stanley arrived. Livingstone finished bringing his entries up to date after Stanley had joined him, for he allowed Stanley to help him make a copy of his long dispatch to the Earl of Clarendon at the Foreign Office, dated November 1, 1871. No doubt Stanley was glad to oblige Livingstone; doing so provided him with information he sought about Livingstone's travels.

In 1979, the Livingstone Documentation Project produced the *Livingstone Catalogue* (see chap. 1, n. 1). The value of this catalogue goes far beyond a simple listing of Livingstone manuscripts. The notation of geographical location at the time each letter was written by Livingstone, for example, provides a chronological check list of his whereabouts, while information provided on his correspondents, alphabetically arranged, and brief summaries of each letter, grouped chronologically, provide the best reference available for simple facts connected with Livingstone. The meticulousness of the compiler and thoughtful plan of presentation make this catalogue and its supplement a model of scholarship. The large or Unyanyembe journal is listed as Journal 11, "28 Jan. 1866 – 5 Mar. 1872. 763 pp. (numbered 1–769; 621–6 have been torn out). 315 x 195. Brown leather binding, with brass lock. Lett's Perpetual Diary. SNMDL (microfilm NLS, MS. 10734)." *Livingstone Catalogue*, 273. (In citing this catalogue, I conform to its dating style.) The field diaries which cover the period are numbered 21 through 39. *Livingstone Catalogue*, 275–77. The catalogue compiler also indicates that for the *Last Journals of David Livingstone* Waller used Field Diary 28 (7 Jul. – 1 Dec. 1872); Field Diary 31 (16 Apr. – 1 Jun. 1872); and Field Diary 32 (1 Jun. – 12 Jul. 1872), as well as portions of Field Diary 37. Waller used a page of Field Diary 37, part of which had been made up of old newspapers and ink Livingstone produced on the spot, to illustrate the traveller's ingenuity. *LJDL*, 2:facing 114. For my analysis of which manuscripts Waller used, see chap. 3, n. 2.

2. Uj, fol. 9–12, 131–43, 171–72, 201–2, 621–44, 737–69, NLS. Folio numbers on the microfilm copy of the Unyanyembe journal sometimes prove difficult to follow; here and in n. 3 below I rely primarily on Instructions to the Printer, noted above, and Simpson, "Livingstone's Journal 1866–1872: Preliminary Appraisal."

3. Uj, fol. 493–5, 535–99, 737–69, NLS.

4. *LJDL*, 2:209–12. Waller edited the reset passage to delete a disparaging reference to an "English sailor" on the Zambezi and to remove Livingstone's final comment: "Burton's silly dictum that Moslems would be better missionaries than Christians, because they would allow polygamy, is equivalent to saying that they would catch more birds, inasmuch as they would put salt on their tails. Moslem zeal is NIL." Proof sheet 22, WPRH, 7.

5. Uj, NLS, Instructions to the Printer. As Simpson notes, "The bitter tone of what remains indicates why these pages were removed." "Livingstone's Journal 1866–1872: Preliminary Appraisal."

6. Uj, fol. 759, NLS. Livingstone believed that his problems with the Portuguese in the Zambezi region during the period of his expedition could have been avoided had Prince Albert not intervened in the late 1850s to ensure that the Foreign Office placed good relations with Portugal above expanding the British role there. Jeal, *Livingstone*, 314–15. Jeal also argues that in refusing to become Patron of the Oxford and Cambridge Mission, Prince Albert was making a hostile statement concerning Livingstone. Jeal, *Livingstone*, 277.

7. Uj, fol. 759, NLS. Livingstone was annoyed that while he was sup-

porting John Moffat's missionary work among the Ndebele from 1859 to 1865, Moffat reentered the employ of the London Missionary Society. To Livingstone it seemed an attempt to draw two salaries for one job. For a summary of the letter he wrote Moffat on the subject, see *Livingstone Catalogue*, 170, no. 1637.

8. Uj, fol. 759, NLS. The Kololo Mission, 1858–1860, was initiated by the London Missionary Society in response to Livingstone's direct encouragement. Largely because of fever, but also as a result of ill treatment by the Kololo, the Rev. Holloway Helmore, his wife Anne, and two of their four children died, as did Mrs. Isabella Price and her infant daughter. Only Roger Price and two Helmore children survived. In the public outcry that followed, Livingstone felt himself undeservedly blamed and in turn blamed Price's behavior toward the Kololo (based on what Sekeletu told him at Linyanti in August 1860) for the disaster. See Jeal, *Livingstone*, 175–94. The reference to this disaster in *The Zambesi and Its Tributaries* not only did not mention Price by name but referred only briefly to the nature of "the burial place where poor Helmore and seven others were laid." *Zambesi and Its Tributaries*, 314. My 1866 American edition (New York: Harper & Brothers) of *The Zambesi and Its Tributaries* does not have the reference to "five Europeans" cited by Jeal, *Livingstone*, 182. At one point, Jeal mistakenly refers to the death of "five out of a total of seven children" with the Helmore-Price mission. All other sources indicate there were four Helmore children and the Price baby in addition to the two couples. Livingstone's remark also does not tally with the numbers involved. Jeal, *Livingstone*, 177. Compare: Norman R. Bennett and Marguerite Ylvisaker, eds., *The Central African Journal of Lovell J. Procter, 1860–1864*, African Studies Center, Boston University (Boston, 1971), 6–7; Reginald J. Campbell, *Livingstone*, 1930; reprint, Westport, Conn., 1972), 208–9.

The contents of the other suppressed passages accused the artist Thomas Baines (Zambezi Expedition) with being "a thief and moral idiot," Bishop Mackenzie's UMCA mission of "Nil teaching," UMCA Bishop Tozer of propagating a Portuguese scandal, and geologist Richard Thornton (Zambezi Expedition) of drunkenness, debauchery, and laziness. For Livingstone's tangled relations with these men, see Wallis, *Thomas Baines of King's Lynn*, 140–228; Chadwick, *Mackenzie's Grave*; *The Zambezi Papers of Richard Thornton*, 2 vols., edited by Edward C. Tabler, Robins Series, no. 4 (London, 1963); and Jeal, *Livingstone*, chaps. 14–18.

9. Uj, fol. 201–2, NLS. For a brief biographical note on Professor Owen and a list of Livingstone's letters to him, see *Livingstone Cata-*

logue, 196–97. From the Zambezi, Livingstone arranged to send Owen a "new mud-fish," which Kirk had identified, an elephant, a small black ant, and a larva-depositing fly.

10. Uj, fol. 201–2, NLS. Oswell, *William Cotton Oswell*, 2:83–86.

11. It is not obvious how much Livingstone owed his views to his physiology courses in the late 1830s in Edinburgh and in 1840 in London with Professor Owen and the extent to which they were idiosyncratically his. The precise contributions of female and male to reproduction were not clearly understood in this period, and the inheritance of acquired characteristics was still stressed. Discussions of the importance of body odor and "vital force" were part of the medical literature of Livingstone's day. In 1828, for example, George Man Burrows (1771–1846), M.D. St. Andrews, the owner of a private insane asylum, wrote in his *Commentaries on Insanity*: "The odour of perspirable matter is often very strong and peculiar; and in some adults it is very offensive. . . . [William] Humboldt remarks, that the difference of odour is so striking in some climates, that the Indians of Peru can distinguish by it, even in the night, a European, an American Indian, or a negro, from each other." In 1843, John Barlow (1799–1869), a clergyman and secretary of the Royal Institution, wrote in *Man's Power over Himself to Prevent or Control Insanity* of ". . . the two great forces which manifest themselves in the phaenomena [sic] of man's nature. The VITAL FORCE by virtue of which he is an animal—and the INTELLECTUAL FORCE by virtue of which he is something more." Vieda Skultans, *Madness and Morals: Ideas on Insanity in the Nineteenth Century* (London, 1975), 78, 161.

In his first book, *Missionary Travels*, Livingstone had offered similar reflections concerning anatomy and physiology. For example, he discussed instances when he believed "maternal instinct" in a grandmother or father, upon the death of the actual mother, had made it possible for them to suckle a new-born baby. That this might happen, it seemed to him, was not unreasonable ". . . as anatomists declare the structure of both male and female breasts to be identical." *Missionary Travels*, 126–27. For an earlier comment by Livingstone on "vital force," dating to January 2, 1852, see *David Livingstone: Family Letters, 1841–1856*, 2 vols., edited by Isaac Schapera (London, 1959), 2:164–65.

The related question of insanity also interested Livingstone. In Field Diary 31, fol. 18, in a passage Waller asked the printer not to set, Livingstone mused on the insanity of Dr. Buckland, the Dean of Westminster, the circumstances of which had been related to him by his friend Professor Owen. His remarks hint at matters he otherwise did not write about: "It must be a sore affliction to be bereft of ones [sic] reason and the more so if the insanity takes the form of uttering thoughts which in a sound state we drive from us as impure." Field Diary 31 (16 Apr. - 1 Jun 1872) SNMDL (photocopy NLS, MS. 10731).

12. *LJDL*, 1:13.

13. *Missionary Travels*, 128. See also: "To my eye the dark colour is much more agreeable than the tawny hue of the half-caste. . . ." *Missionary Travels*, 186. To set Livingstone in his Victorian context, see Christine Bolt, *Victorian Attitudes to Race* (London, 1971), 22-23, 109-56; Cairns, *Prelude to Imperialism*, chap. 2, esp. 53-63; and Philip Curtin, *The Image of Africa: British Ideas and Action, 1780-1850* (New York, 1964), esp. chap. 15.

14. *LJDL*, 1:51-52.

15. Another explanation is that what occurred in Africa was considered *sui generis* and therefore unrelated to the world inhabited by ordinary Victorians. For the importance of spacing births for survival in hunting-gathering societies, see Marjorie Shostak, *Nisa: The Life and Words of a !Kung Woman* (New York, 1981), 66-68, 217-18, 375-76. For a discussion of the contradictions between "conjugal duty and maternal duty" in early modern Europe, see Jean-Louis Flandrin, *Families in Former Times: Kinship, Household and Sexuality*, translated by Richard Southern (Cambridge, 1979), 206-12, and Steven Ozment, *When Fathers Ruled: Family Life in Reformation Europe* (Cambridge, 1983), 118-21. For a discussion of the traditional use of maternal nursing to achieve natural birth control in Livingstone's day and later, see Angus McLaren, *Birth Control in Nineteenth-Century England* (New York, 1978), 67, 125, and 203. The Victorian view of women as having passive sexual natures beyond the maternal "instinct" is usually discussed in connection with the work of the venereologist William Acton, *Prostitution, Considered in Its Moral, Social, and Sanitary Aspects* . . . (London, 1857, 1870). For a review and analysis of Victorian views, see F. Barry Smith, "Sexuality in Britain, 1800-1900: Some Suggested Revisions," in Martha Vicinus, ed., *A Widening Sphere: Changing Roles of Victorian Women* (Bloomington, 1977), 182-98.

16. First proof sheets 37-38, WPRH, 6. On the use by Tom of the word *purity*, it should be noted that when these volumes were published in 1874 the campaign for the repeal of the Contagious Diseases Acts had recently been launched by Josephine Butler and the Ladies' National Association. In their notions of "social purity," they would have applauded the idea of a single sexual standard that Livingstone called unreasonable in the African context. On the social purity campaign against prostitution and the "wife's right to demand of her husband periods of abstinence," see McLaren, *Birth Control*, 198-99. On the ideological implications for women of the repeal campaign and the "rescue work" of

the mid 1870s, see Judith R. Walkowitz, *Prostitution and Victorian Society: Women, Class, and the State* (New York, 1980), esp. Introduction and chaps. 5-6.

17. Field Diary 16 (14 May - 30 June 1866), SNMDL (photocopy NLS, MS. 10721). Livingstone's descriptions of African women in all of his writing deserve detailed study. He closely observed the daily life of African women, took an interest in social attitudes between men and women, recorded customs with regard to pregnancies and birthing (for example, *Missionary Travels*, 126-31), and took note of women chiefs, women rain dancers, and women's community and individual activities. A number of these observations on Livingstone's last journey exist only in his field diaries. Livingstone left some of them out when writing up the Unyanyembe journal, and Waller edited out a few. For example, Waller deleted Livingstone's journal description of women's work in the Manyema villages, which would have fallen between *LJDL*, 2:57 and 58. See proof sheet 303, WPRH, 8. Livingstone did not include in the Unyanyembe journal the note he made on two rainmakers in his field diary for December 28, 1866: "Two women were performing a rain dance when we arrived with their faces smeared with pipe clay. When the rain came down they ran about caricolling [sic] all over the place in triumph." Field Diary 20 (26 Dec. 1866 - 1 Mar. 1867), SNMDL (photocopy NLS, MS. 10725). On women rainmakers and spirit mediums in the interlacustrine and Nyamwezi areas north of locations where Livingstone mentions them, see Iris Berger, "Rebels or Status-Seekers? Women as Spirit Mediums in East Africa," in Nancy J. Hafkin and Edna G. Bay, eds., *Women in Africa: Studies in Social and Economic Change* (Stanford, 1976), 157-81.

18. Jeal, *Livingstone*, 75, 111-12. On the last occasion, Livingstone was upset because the pregnancy, discovered on the voyage to Cape Town in 1858, deprived him of his wife's help on the Zambezi Expedition. Livingstone did not wish the situation to be known widely. Jeal speculates that Livingstone's annoyance stemmed from embarrassment: he feared he would be thought a fool for having made his wife pregnant at this time. Jeal, *Livingstone*, 197. Since Livingstone did not customarily put private thoughts about his or others' sexuality into diaries or letters, only from such reflections on sexual questions regarding Africans and remarks like that in n. 11, above, is it possible to glimpse his views.

19. LJDL, 2:173. Stanley clearly supplied the American gold coin and Livingstone must have had the small Indian coins from his last visit. But what was a "cake of paint with royal arms"?

20. Jeal suggests this analysis of Livingstone's sentiments by focusing on the Linyanti Mission. Jeal, *Livingstone*, 175-84. My judgment is based

on a knowledge of the primary sources dealing with the Oxford and Cambridge (Universities') Mission.

21. Field Diary 28 (between September 9 and 22, 1872), SNMDL (photocopy NLS, MS. 10728).

22. *Ibid.* Livingstone may have been thinking of Murchison's letter to him of January 5, 1865, asking him his wishes about renewing African exploration. Murchison wrote, "If you do not like to undertake *the purely geographical work*, I am of opinion that no one, after yourself, is so fitted to carry it out as Dr. Kirk." Blaikie, *Personal Life*, 349. See also, chap. 1, n. 50.

23. Livingstone to Waller, East of Tanganyika, September 2, 1872, WPRH, 1.

24. Writing to C. A. Alington May 26, 1865, Livingstone declared: "We cannot always follow our own inclinations. . . . I should have liked your company I think, and this I cannot say of anyone else who has offered." Photocopy, A347, UWL (original, NLS).

25. Field Diary 28 (September 9, 1872).

26. Waller to Murray, Brighton, October 8, 1874, JMPA. No more was done with this appendix material. Waller carefully kept the proof in anticipation of later publication, but the solution to the geographical puzzle Livingstone had sought to unlock came from others. Livingstone's laborious, painstaking observations, whatever their merits or the light they would shed on his travels, have lain there ever since. For an unsuccessful attempt by the Livingstone family to get this material properly prepared and published, see above, chap. 2, n. 5.

27. *LJDL*, 1:*vi*. If Waller had known the problem of subsequent publication, would he have argued so forcefully for postponement?

28. Waller to Murray, October 12, 1874, JMPA.

29. Waller to Murray, October 19, 1974, JMPA. The adjective Waller used, "marbled-covered" copybooks coincides best with the "mottled paper cover" description of Field Diaries 31–33 in *Livingstone Catalogue, 276* (SNMDL, photocopies NLS, MSS. 10731-3). These form a series "given to Livingstone by Stanley." Inspection of the arrangement of material in both volumes of the *Last Journals* suggests that Waller's solution was to place the material he was concerned not to leave out in vol. 1, chap. 12, 323–32 and chap. 13, 333–45. Although written up in 1872, the notes were generally dated to the second half of 1868. I am indebted to Donald Simpson for this suggestion.

30. Contemporaries, Livingstone included, referred to the young men of Nasik as the "Nassick boys." Those who accompanied Livingstone from 1866 grew to adulthood in Africa, yet they continued to be called "boys" throughout. Similarly, when Halima and Ntaoeka join Liv-

ingstone later in his journey, they were mature women; yet he and others frequently referred to them as "girls." On the Nasik Asylum, see Strayer, *Mission Communities in East Africa*, 14–15; Simpson, *Dark Companions*, 54; and below, chap. 5, n. 23.

31. Livingstone learned about the editorial objections to his use of the word *urine* in connection with the publication of his first book. Livingstone to Murray, n.d. [1857], JMPA.

32. September 4, 1866, Field Diary 17 (1 Jul. – 5 Sep. 1866), SNMDL (photocopy NLS, MS. 10722); *LJDL*, 1:97–98 (under the date September 8, 1866).

33. January 13, 1867, Field Diary 20 (26 Dec. 1866 – 1 Mar. 1867) SNMDL (photocopy NLS, MS. 10725).

34. Field Diary 17. Under August 14, 1866, in the Unyanyembe journal (censored by Livingstone) and the published book, there is only a brief allusion to Livingstone's energies being "sorely taxed" by his Indian bearers (marines). *LJDL*, 1:92. Waller was well acquainted with the sugar incident from a letter he had received. Livingstone to Waller, November 3, 1866 (received in 1868), WPRH, 1.

35. Sir [Henry] Bartle [Edward] Frere, *Eastern Africa as a Field for Missionary Labour: Four Letters to the Archbishop of Canterbury* (London, 1874).

36. *Ibid.*, 111–12.

§ 5 §

Categories of Omissions

When editing the proof of Livingstone's *Last Journals* or marking Livingstone's field diaries for the printer, Waller designated for omission primarily those comments which concerned Livingstone's relationships with other people, more rarely his geographical musings, but nowhere his theoretical concerns about "regenerating" Africa. Livingstone's relations with his own attendants were, of course, a very sensitive subject in Waller's view, but so were a number of Livingstone's comments: about other explorers; other government officials; the Foreign Office; and his appreciation of the Arab ivory and slave merchants with whom he travelled for many years in Central Africa. Lastly, Waller exhibited some not surprising Victorian reluctance to discuss in graphic detail subjects which involved or implied sexuality. The issue raised by these categories of omissions is an evaluation of the total effect of such editing on whether the edited volumes fully convey Livingstone's actual thoughts on his last journey.

Livingstone's reputation for turning African attendants and porters into "faithfuls" began with his early association with the Kololo. Their chief had placed a party of twenty-seven men at his disposal as porters for his trip to the West Coast of Africa in 1853–1855. In his *Missionary Travels*, published in 1857, Livingstone emphasized that his decision not to sail home from Luanda, Angola, in 1854 reflected his commitment to return these "faithful" attendants to their homeland in the interior. As he put it, he had "found the tribes near the Portuguese settlement [Angola] so very unfriendly, that it would be altogether impossible for my men to return alone."[1]

Livingstone's biographer Tim Jeal has pointed out that Livingstone's real concern when he reached Luanda was that he now knew that the path to the West Coast would not be a useful one for European "legitimate" commerce. He anxiously turned his attention, therefore, to the critical need to examine the path between the mid-continent Kololo base at Linyanti and the East Coast, in the hope of finding another route that would prove practical for development by the British. Jeal's point is that Livingstone may well have felt an obligation to return with the Kololo to their homeland, as he had promised, but that—for the goal he had set himself—he also found it strategically useful to do so. When he subsequently reached the East Coast and no longer found it so convenient to lead the Kololo back to Linyanti, Livingstone simply left those who had accompanied him to await his return for some years.[2] Nonetheless, much was made of Livingstone's selfless dedication to keeping his word to the Kololo, as well as to their devotion and loyalty to him. From the perspective of people in England, Livingstone's choice not to turn homeward at Angola in a ship at hand and awaiting him, but instead to plunge again into the relatively uncharted paths of Southern Africa to keep his promise to the Kololo to take them home was the stuff of honor, courage, and heroism.

When Livingstone returned to the Kololo chief at Linyanti in November 1855, the chief again equipped him with a party of 114 Kololo for his journey to the East Coast. Livingstone promised to bring them back within a year. Actually, he did not return to Linyanti until 1860. Livingstone left his Kololo attendants at Tete in Mozambique from 1856 until his return there from England in 1858 at the head of a new Zambezi Expedition. Thereafter, except for the few Kololo who joined his expedition, they remained at Tete until 1860, when Livingstone led thirty of them home. By this time another thirty had died of small pox and about two dozen expressed no desire to return to their homeland. A further thirty who accompanied Livingstone back from Linyanti deserted on the way to Tete.[3]

Livingstone had spoken at length in public about these "faithful" attendants and of his commitment to return to Africa to take them home once more to Linyanti, as he had promised Chief Sekeletu. Later, when writing the narrative of his Zambezi Expedition—a book jointly authored with his brother Charles[4]—Livingstone carefully and formally reiterated the sentiments he himself had first announced: "Feeling in honour bound to return with those who had been the faithful companions of Dr. Livingstone in 1856, . . . the requisite steps were taken to convey them to their homes."[5] As Cairns notes, the quality of "faithfulness" became the chief virtue of Livingstone's Kololo attendants and the "faithfuls" achieved great popularity. Livingstone, in turn, by appearing to be the model of a Christian gentleman doing his duty to his heathen followers, gained renown as a great leader of Africans. Livingstone's claim that he had refused the easy water route home in order to return the Kololo to their homes had "moved the heart of the British public."[6]

The concept of the "faithful" servant not only carried implicit praise for the master but also conveyed the picture of complaisant obedience. In nineteenth-century East and Central Africa, however, throughout the period when British caravans made their way into the interior, the explorers, missionaries, traders, and consuls who wrote of their travels alluded to the use or threat of physical force and arms to achieve obedience from their African porters and servants. Threat of force or resort to it was used to stop porters from disputes over the relative weights of their loads, to punish attendants caught plundering the people among whom the caravan passed, to act as a warning to other porters if one were caught stealing caravan supplies, or simply to push on weary men who preferred to stop and rest.

The personal style of the leader of the caravan accounted for different methods of handling bearers, and there came to be a set of opposites against which travellers were measured. H. M. Stanley, in reporting in 1872 on his "finding" of Livingstone and subsequently in his newspaper reporting and book on his Central African expedition of 1874–1878, set before the public a clear picture of the hot-tempered, harsh methods he used to keep a caravan going. A comparison between his practices and a gentler style of managing Africans came to be referred to, in the words of a member of the Church Missionary Society in 1891, as "the Livingstone way and the Stanley way." By this definition, the Livingstone way was a style that made minimum use of both flogging or threats to shoot anyone; the Livingstone way was the "slow and conciliatory way." Stanley, by contrast, had proven himself quick to resort to both flogging and his pistols to keep his exceptionally large caravans in order and his methods came under considerable public criticism in Britain for what one indignant observer later characterized as a "system of exploration by warfare."[7]

Waller was aware of such factors in 1874. If his object was to preserve and protect Livingstone's fame as the missionary explorer *par excellence* in order to use that fame as the basis for an antislavery crusade in East Africa—as he believed Livingstone would have wished him to do—it was necessary to suppress the full story of Livingstone's tribulations with those who served him on his last journey. For this reason, and others discussed below, Waller completely deleted Livingstone's account of flogging a Nasik-trained attendant, Andrew Powell, who decided to leave the party and remain behind at Chief Mataka's on the way to Lake Malawi. Livingstone wrote up the episode in his Unyanyembe journal for September 4, 1866:

> The sepoys introduced the practice of remaining behind till sent for. This had been followed by the Nassick boys when they have been offended or baulked in any way – one – Andrew sulked be-

cause he got a blanket & bag only a few pounds more to his load than he liked – as it was a second offense—gave him twelve cuts with a ratan and told him that he might leave us and go to his own people as he had come to do but if he remained he must do what he was told. He preferred to go and I was glad to get rid of him. Mataka's place has great attractions for them as they get plenty to eat there & had [sic] nothing to do. It is questionable if slave boys, however educated, will ever except in rare exceptions go to a tribe and work as missionaries for the good of their tribe. They cling for support to their liberators. They might be useful as assistants to a mission but only if led with a tight rein.[8]

In his field diary, in which the incident was initially noted, Livingstone also said of Andrew that he "made a great outcry but it will have a good effect." From the vantage of hindsight, however, in writing up the Unyanyembe journal, this optimistic comment was eliminated, for according to Livingstone's next note on the subject, "Andrew left rather than carry the lightest load of the party. . . ."[9] The caning had only convinced Andrew that he should leave Livingstone's caravan.

By the time this incident had occurred, only five months into his journey inland on his way to Lake Malawi, Livingstone had already lost one "Nassick boy," Richard, in June (death from "fever") and another, Reuben, had elected to remain at Chief Mataka's in July, subsequently accompanying the Indian marines who left Livingstone to go back to Zanzibar. Reuben's fate was not recorded in the *Last Journals*, nor did Waller allow further details concerning Reuben's decision to remain behind at Mataka's to be published with Livingstone's journal entries for July 14–28, 1866. He edited out Livingstone's summary of what happened and his thoughts on the subject: "He [Reuben] carried a small ammunition case. When opened about 250 or more ball cartridges had been extracted . . . he was strongly suspected as the thief. . . . The day after we left Mataka, Reuben feeling that his character was gone resolved to return & stay with Mataka – gave a packet of cartridges to a man to carry his load back to a village & there sat till we sent for him. A happy riddance."[10]

Livingstone's capacity to keep "faithful followers" was, therefore, more modest than the legend initially established with regard to the Kololo and confirmed in the public's mind by the journey his attendants had taken to bring his body to the East Coast in 1873–1874. He had dismissed the Indians of the Bombay Marine Battalion, eleven sepoys and their *naik* (corporal), only four months into his journey inland. Their *havildar* (sergeant) alone had asked to remain with Livingstone, and he died a short time later. All the men Livingstone had hired from Anjouan (then called Johanna), an island in the Comoros, deserted after seven months. Of the nine young men trained at Nasik who first entered Africa with Livingstone in 1866, after the loss or departure of Richard Isenberg, Reuben Smith, and Andrew Powell within the first four months on the mainland, three more deserted and one was killed. One of these, Albert Baraka, ran away at the end of August 1867 to join Tippu Tip—Hamed bin Muhammed—a great Arab trader in Central Africa who gained his wealth from trading ivory and slaves and used it to buy clove plantations on Zanzibar.[11] Two others, the Gallas Simon Price and Abraham Pereira, left him in June 1870, and James Rutton was killed at Bambarre in Manyema country in 1871. Two of the deserters had a history of stealing from loads and taking African women as captives, in emulation of the Arab traders with whom Livingstone travelled from 1867. Of the original nine, therefore, only two Nasik-trained men, Edward Gardner and Mabruki (a.k.a. Nathaniel Cumba), remained with Livingstone to the end.[12]

Livingstone's success rate was higher with the four attendants he had taken with him to India from Africa in 1864: the two Yao, Chuma and Wikatani—rescued by him from slavers in 1861—and the two men from the village of Shupanga on the Zambezi River, Susi and Amoda—who aided him in sailing the *Lady Nyassa* from Zanzibar to Bombay. Three of these four remained with him to the end of his life: Chuma, Susi, and Amoda. The fourth, Wikatani, left him to remain with relatives at Mponda's, just south of Lake Malawi, in 1866.

In light of this history, it is not surprising to find evidence of Waller's editorial pen in passages that dealt pejoratively with Livingstone's Indian and African followers. Typical of Livingstone's complaints against his sepoys was a Unyanyembe journal entry for June 3, 1866. The previous day's entry made clear to the reader that Livingstone believed these men had vitiated his animal experiment by overloading the animals and wantonly wounding them. They had even beaten the camel to death with the butts of their muskets. Livingstone also believed that the Indians had conspired to desert him by offering money to the party's guide to lead them back to the East Coast. In the passage for June 3, censored from the published version, Livingstone declared, "I have sometimes thought of going back disarming half & sending them back so." He weighed his options, "This might be disapproved by the military authorities in India. On the other hand in going back armed they may use their arms among the Makonde and bring disgrace on the English name. If I had known their language it might have been different. . . . I had however ready translaters in the Nassick boys."[13]

Livingstone's anxiety about the Anglo-Indian Government's opinion of any action he might take to disarm the marines before sending them

Tippu Tip (Hamed bin Muhammed), a Swahili-Arab trader. He personally dominated the partially Islamized forest region of Manyema west of
Lake Tanganyika, a control imposed and sustained by slave armies organized to pursue the ivory trade. He sent armed agents to raid for slaves to
serve as porters and guards and to commandeer the food to feed them.
Livingstone's attendant Albert Baraka, one his first party of Nasik-trained
companions, deserted him in August 1867 to join Tippu Tip.

back was substantial, and in the end he did not do so. He was also concerned about how his actions toward them would be regarded by the British public as well as by colonial authorities. When he wrote up their official dismissal in his journal, in a passage published under the date July 15, 1866, he very carefully noted, "It is likely that some sympathizers will take their part, but I strove to make them useful." Again he weighed the case, "They had but poor and scanty fare along the way, but all of us suffered alike. They made themselves thoroughly disliked by their foul talk and abuse. . . . I felt inclined to force them on, but it would have been acting from revenge, and to pay them out, so I forbore."[14]

Despite omission of Livingstone's harshest accusations, his words convinced his readers (who were ready to share his convictions) that the sepoys were a bad lot. The burden of the charges Livingstone lodged against them had in fact already appeared piecemeal in letters published in the beginning years of his expedition, not long after these events took place. Livingstone had written to most of his correspondents about his Indian marines, charging them with sabotaging his animal experiment and conspiring to turn him back or to desert him, taking along the Nasik men and leaving him stranded. He also complained that after all the animals died and he assigned the sepoys duties as carriers, they had dawdled on the path, slowing down the expedition's progress. He became enraged when, instead of carrying their assigned loads, they found local women to carry them at Livingstone's expense, either directly charging him for payment or stealing goods to do so.[15]

What Livingstone never comprehended about his relations with the Indian marines was the fact that they had volunteered to act as a defense unit, equipped with muskets, and had never anticipated acting in any other capacity. This interpretation is suggested by the fact that when Livingstone enlisted them in Bombay, he found it necessary to promise them explicitly that their luggage would be carried for them, apparently referring to the beasts of burden he intended to take along as an experiment. When these animals were killed off by the tsetse fly, which had always been a possible outcome of the experiment (whatever ill-treatment was given them by the Indians), Livingstone calmly reversed what they understood as an official promise regarding to their working conditions and ordered them to become porters, luggage carriers. On June 18, 1866, Livingstone announced, "If they behave [well] then they will get fatigue pay for doing fatigue duty; if ill, nothing but their pay."[16]

Within a month of this significant change of status, the marines had threatened both the life of their *havildar*, whose authority over them was not sufficient to meet the new situation, and the life of one of the young

Nasik men, who had threatened to reveal their pilfering. By this time, Livingstone declared that he was ashamed of them because they "were such a disreputable looking lot." As he put it quite graphically, "[A]ll wore the sulky dogged look of people going where they were forced but hated to go. This hang-dog expression of countenance was so conspicuous that I many a time have heard the country people remark, 'These are the slaves of the party.' "[17] It rings true as an accurate description of their misery. In expecting these Indian recruits from the Bombay marines to act as African porters, Livingstone asked more of them than they were prepared, or had ever expected, to perform.

Having thus concluded that these malingerers would ruin his expedition if he kept them much longer, Livingstone arranged to send them home with the next Arab trader going to the East Coast. Livingstone censored from the Unyanyembe journal the bitter comment he entered in his field diary for June 20, 1866: "It is hard to feel charitably towards the sepoys whose game or aim seems to have been to detach first the Nassick boys then the Johanna [Comoran] men and of course leave me alone to perish." Under this date, he also wrote: "Ramnack [a sepoy] thinking it was Simon Price who had reported him told him if he saw him in the jungle he would shoot him. . . . He has threatened to shoot Simon three times." A month later, his thoughts still dwelling on this matter, Livingstone wrote in his field diary, "I suspect the havildar had been afraid of them all along."[18] In other words, Livingstone saw the cause of the sepoys' misbehavior in their leader's lack of authority over them, rather than in any actions—or failures of leadership—of his own.

In presenting Livingstone's case against the sepoys, Waller suppressed some of the more graphic language Livingstone used in the Unyanyembe journal to condemn them. Livingstone accused the sepoys, for example, of excelling only at ". . . eating and vomiting. The climate gives a keen appetite and unrestrained indulgence then results in emesis." Livingstone never speculated on whether the change of terrain and climate had, in fact, temporarily affected their digestive systems. When Livingstone wrote in his journal that he despaired of their. ". . . filthy habits soiling all about the huts instead of going afield," he did not consider whether these were their normal habits or the result of suffering so severe a diarrhea that it overcame them before they could get far from their huts.[19] If Livingstone's relations with the sepoys were strained, indeed overwrought, it must also be remembered that he never learned to speak their language and he never tried to understand their customs.[20] If in his ready condemnation of the sepoys Livingstone was guilty of ethnocentricity—ascribing their behavior in Africa to their lack of proper military (and Christian) training, rather than to their different culture—he based his responses on assumptions fully shared by contemporaries at home. The terrible excesses of the "sepoy mutiny," as the British called it, had occurred only two decades before, in 1857. The legacy of that bloody and brutal episode made it easy for the British to expect the worst from Indians, even those trained by English officers. Waller saw no need to soften any but the grossest accusations against the sepoys in editing Livingstone's *Last Journals*.

More important to the image of Livingstone as the gentle, heroic missionary traveller were his relations with his various African attendants. When, a few months after the sepoys left him, his Comoran porters deserted him as well, the world still agreed with Livingstone that the fault lay not in the abilities of their leader but in the laziness, cowardice, and untrustworthiness of the men who betrayed him. Livingstone's account of the desertion of the Anjouan men, motivated by fear of the warlike tribes that were reported to lie ahead in their path, and his subsequent comments about their tendency to steal his goods were both given a full airing in the published work. The men had already earned a bad public repute, having been found out to be fabricators of a false tale of Livingstone's murder when they arrived back at Zanzibar early in 1867.[21]

Livingstone's dealings with the young African men trained at the missionary school at Nasik in India and brought back with him to Africa in 1866 involved far more serious decisions at the proof stage of the editing process. Livingstone's relations with these young men were important because they represented the hope of the contemporary mission efforts for the African evangelization of Africa, especially those efforts begun by Sir Bartle Frere on his visit to the East Coast of Africa in the early months of 1873. Because their actions were such an integral part of Livingstone's travels, Waller's deletions were specifically focused on the most biting and vituperative comments about these Christian-trained freed African slaves. Waller suppressed passages which showed that Livingstone flogged them, threatened to shoot them, and docked their pay in his efforts to deal with behavior he scorned as careless, idle, and outright thieving, as well as passages in which Livingstone accused them of emulating the Arab slavers and taking African women as captives for themselves.[22]

The young men of Nasik had been rescued as children by British cruisers which stopped and searched Arab dhows in East African waters and in the Indian Ocean. Not only had they experienced the wrench of separation from home and kin, but they also knew the alienation of being orphans in a strange land where it was necessary to adapt to both their Indian surroundings and their English missionary guardians. Those who accompanied Livingstone to Africa in 1866 found themselves "at home" under the supervision of a fairly kind but absolutely single-minded European who expected them, because of their Christian training at Nasik, to be natural missionaries to their fellow Africans and to subordinate themselves entirely to his not always comprehensible purposes.[23] They had volunteered to accompany Livingstone to Africa, but they could hardly have expected the hardships, hunger, danger, and human misery they experienced on this expedition. Those who grew to maturity in Africa with Livingstone also lived in the company of Arab traders and their slaves from 1867 to 1872, when lack of supplies made it impossible for him to hire porters and guides of his own. On September 1, 1867, for example, Livingstone complained, "Two of the Nassick boys remained behind. They take advantage of our being with Arabs to skulk, and pretend to being overladen, and say, 'The English are said to be good, but they are not so.' They carry about one third of a slave's load. One of them was offended because his very light load was increased by three pounds of beads."[24]

Against this background must be gauged the behavior, the peccadilloes, the sexual liaisons, and even the resort to using guns of the first group of Nasik-trained Africans who accompanied Livingstone. Livingstone, who generally disliked opposition from any source and tended to grow intolerant of most people with whom he had to work closely, attributed every deviation from the norm of his expectations of Christian-trained youth to their slave origins or, in a few cases, to their mixed parentage. As already noted, the term "half-caste" was used by Livingstone—as it was generally used in his time and by his contemporaries—as a term of opprobrium. For Livingstone this notion seemed to have an important explanatory power: the products of mixed unions necessarily inherited "the bad without the good qualities of both parents." At first he called the lighter skinned Gallas among the Nasik "the most intelligent and hard working." Before these two Gallas, Simon and Abraham, had deserted in 1870, the story had changed. Simon became a "sly half-caste . . . obstinate as a mule" on one occasion, while he fled from danger "with characteristic timidity" on another. When Simon killed two Babema, he became "a nuisance for stealing, lying, uncleanness and every wickedness."[25]

Within two months of their arrival in East Africa, Livingstone had formulated a view of these young men that did not change: "Sneaking deception is so dear to these Nassick boys, I suspect they have been sold out of their countries for crimes." The misconduct that occasioned this condemnation was the overloading of the animals of the expedition. When one Nasik youth was reproved by Livingstone, he "shouted out his determination to do nothing, and growled out in addition about the crime I had been guilty of in bringing them into this wild country." Intent upon his own ends, Livingstone did not stop to examine this behavior as an expression of the pain, anger, and despair felt by a young African who found himself estranged in his own land. Instead, Livingstone resorted to force. He "applied a stick vigorously to a part of his body where no bones are likely to be broken, till he came to his senses." Livingstone then noted, "On the first application he said, 'You may take your gun and shoot me; I'll do nothing.' This showed me that a gentle chastisement would not do, and I gave it him in earnest, till he was satisfied he had made a mistake in ringleading." When Livingstone recorded this event in his field diary, he indicated that he had applied the stick to the young man's "bottom." Writing it up in the Unyanyembe journal, he gave it the circumlocution. The field diary reveals that the lad in question was Albert Baraka, who later would be involved in the loss of Livingstone's medicine chest and still later would desert to Tippu Tip.[26]

Nasik-trained Mabruki, however, was one of two of this original group to survive to the end of Livingstone's life and thus to become another acclaimed "faithful." In his case, Waller eliminated passages that showed him in a poor light. For example, Livingstone's comment of July 1866, deleted by Waller on the proof sheet, was: "A Nassick boy, called Mabruki, came up with the havildar, . . . his load reduced to a very small bulk. He had either stolen the cloths it contained, eight or nine, and one fathom of calico, or allowed the sepoys to do it while he remained out of sight."[27]

By February 8, 1867, not quite eleven months into his journey, Livingstone wrote (and Waller omitted) that he now needed to threaten his Nasik African attendants in order to overcome their fears of rumored "Mazitu" ahead, the same kind of rumor that had caused the Comoran men to desert. Livingstone's explanation for their fears was now set: "those who have been slaves generally cringe till 'the end of the chapter.'" A week later, he referred to the young Nasik-trained Africans as "wretched cringing slavelings" or "crawling slavelings." Waller's reaction of surprise upon first encountering these epithets in the proof sheets of the Unyanyembe journal led him to write in the margin: "fever here evidently." Waller substituted "boys" for the last cited phrase in the sentence: ". . . it is immense conceit in mere crawling slavelings to equal themselves to me."[28] From time to time thereafter, Livingstone explicitly blamed the quality of the training given these young men at the Church Missionary establishment at Nasik. He began this line of complaint as early as July 15, 1866, in another passage that Waller censored: "The Nassick system seems to convey to their minds an extravagant idea of the value of their labour." By December 12, 1871, Livingstone's remarks on this subject were caustic: "Those I had were not men, nor yet slaves. Hybrids between bond and free, so petted and coddled as to think the English feared them."[29]

Livingstone's relationship with Chuma and Susi, whom he took with him to India in 1864 (Livingstone's "most faithful followers" Waller had dubbed them in the public press in March 1874), was at times as bad as any he had with the Nasik-trained Africans. Not surprisingly, Waller was convinced that to parade their transgressions on the last journey would serve no purpose, since in the end they became the sturdy shoulders on which Livingstone, literally and metaphorically, came to rest.[30] Waller repeatedly pointed out to the British public that these men had been with Livingstone longer than any of his other attendants. Chuma was a young boy when Livingstone (and Waller) liberated him from a slave gang and cut off his chains in 1861. Susi was much older, already a Zambezi river man, when he—and Amoda—went to work for Livingstone at Shupanga in 1863, to help put together the pieces of the *Lady Nyassa* and to sail her to Bombay a year later.

Perhaps the lowest ebb of Livingstone's confidence in these men who became his "most faithful followers" came during his long stay at Kazembe's in 1868. When he was at last able to leave, Livingstone found Chuma and Susi, along with the remaining Nasik Africans, unwilling to follow him on what must have seemed to them heartless, fruitless adventures. To Livingstone's bitter dismay, both men (Chuma was perhaps sixteen by then) had begun to enjoy the charms of women and *bhang*— the Indian term for marijuana, also called Indian hemp or cannabis. To these temptations Livingstone attributed their new assertion of independence:

Susi, for no confessed reason but he has got a black woman who feeds him. Chuma for the same reason. . . . Came with his eyes shot out by *bange* [sic]. . . . "He could not leave Susi," . . . and Abraham had brought up some old grievance as a justification for his absconding. James said, ". . . He was tired of working." Abraham apologized and was forgiven. Susi stood like a mule. I put my hand on his arm. . . . He seized my hand, and refused to let it go. When he did I fired a pistol at him, but missed. There being no law or magistrate higher than myself, I would not be thwarted if I could help it. The fact is, they are all tired. . . . They would like me to remain here and pay them for smoking the *bange*, and deck their prostitutes with the beads which I give regularly for their food.[31]

All that reached publication in the *Last Journals* of this incident was: "13th April.—On preparing to start this morning my people refused to go: the fact is, they are all tired, and Mohamad's opposition encourages them." In November 1868, upon his return to Kazembe's after successfully finding Lake Bangweulu, Livingstone felt more conciliatory. "Have taken all the runaways back again," he wrote, "After trying the independent life they will behave better." Livingstone dismissed the episode with, "I have faults myself."[32]

It was not the end of the desertions, however. In the Unyanyembe journal for June 16, 1870, Livingstone confessed with some rancor, "The Nassick pupils now lived with the slave women whose husbands were away on trade, and got plenty to eat. . . . They did nothing for me, but seeing I was at their mercy in Manyema . . . they acted like the Irish helps in America. The want of a chain to confine them emboldens them. . . ."[33] The passage reveals a Livingstone who accepted the contemporary British and American stereotype of Irish emigrants and a bitter man who could not resist the temptation to condemn the Nasik Africans for their slave past. Ten days later, June 26, 1870, only Chuma, Susi, and Gardner accompanied Livingstone in his attempt to leave Manyema and head northwest to find the Lualaba River. When Livingstone threatened his other attendants with the combined wrath of the sultan and British consul at Zanzibar, Simon had mocked him: "Give me a bit of paper, to tell that I am a very bad boy."

Forced within ten days to turn back because of extremely painful "irritable-eating" ulcers on his feet, Livingstone now complained that Chuma, Abraham, and Gardner took part in an Arab assault on Manyema people. Gardner returned with a woman he had captured; Abraham brought back two fowls and some tobacco he had stolen; Chuma came "caricolling [sic] in front of the party like a spaniel running 20 yards or so on one side then making as if discharging his gun and then mimicking shooting which he is too cowardly to do actually anywhere." Livingstone lashed out at them; he had assumed that "Christian boys from Nassick who had been trained for years there and were confirmed by Bishop Harding did not need to be told not to murder." By this time Simon had, by his own report, already killed two men. Livingstone confronted Chuma as the least vicious of the group, "What a fool you make yourself – What would Waller & Dr. Wilson think if they saw you capering there as I have?" When Chuma pointed out that the English at Bishop Mackenzie's station in the Shire Highlands had gone to fight the Ajawa [Yao], Livingstone replied, "Yes to make slaves free but you want to make free people slaves."[34]

Waller deleted this despairing passage. Not only did it shed unfavorable light on two "faithfuls," Chuma and Gardner, but it also reopened an old controversy regarding the fighting engaged in by the missionaries of the Universities' Mission to Central Africa early in the 1860s. A member himself of that missionary party, Waller was acutely aware how sensitive an issue the matter still was for all those who had backed the mission and regretted its removal to Zanzibar. He could take advantage of being editor of Livingstone's *Last Journals* to expunge the inflammatory reference. Similarly, Waller eliminated information offensive to his English readers that Livingstone's own attendants, liberated slaves, were guilty of capturing women and goats of their own.[35]

The painful ulcers on his feet kept Livingstone in Bambarre between July 1870 and February 1871. On October 19, 1870, the Nasik men who had deserted him in June—Simon and Abraham—announced, through Chuma, that they (like Baraka, who joined Tippu Tip in August 1867) were going to accompany the Arab traders who were now moving on. Part of this episode reached the published version under that date, including, "They think that no punishment will reach them whatever they do: they are freemen, and need not work or do anything but beg. 'English,' they call themselves, and the Arabs fear them, though the eagerness with which they engaged in slave-hunting showed them to be genuine niggers." Not only is this one of the relatively rare occasions on which Livingstone used the term *niggers*, it is the only time Waller allowed such sentiments to escape deletion.

However, Waller did cut out the final sentences of this passage: "To lie without compunction seems to be one of their Indian acquisitions. Abram said, "That I told him to beg!" And Simon said that I had spoken to him only once, and he would have gone, or intended to go, till I took the gun from him. . . . The gun would have been used to steal from the Manyema, as it was when we came back here to bully them for four fowls." Three months later, on January 16, 1871, Livingstone not only despaired of making his Nasik attendants do as he wished, he also gave up hope of ever being able to mete out any appropriate punishment. "My Nassickers," he wrote, in sentences Waller deleted, "cooly assert they did not desert. After this it will be impossible to take the ringleaders, but [sic] some will believe them, as for instance, Mr. Tozer and Co." By February 16, a month later, when Livingstone finally left Manyema, he wrote, "Simon and Ibram [sic] were bundled out of the camp, and impudently followed me: when they came up, I told them to be off, *or I would certainly shoot them.* Waller deleted the italicized words.[36]

Other types of editorial censorship also followed a general pattern. They involved a mixture of language or topics Waller, Tom Livingstone, and the publisher John Murray considered impolitic or inappropriate for publication by the dignified firm of John Murray. In the category of "impolitic" fell a mixed bag of criticisms that Livingstone lodged against such governmental and influential entities as the Foreign Office or the Royal Geographical Society. Both had contributed financially to Livingstone's travels. Both government figures and the president of the Royal Geographical Society aided the effort to obtain for Livingstone's children a governmental subsidy for their education and a pension. Prominent men in the government and the Royal Geographical Society had also arranged for Livingstone's state funeral and thus the enhancement of his posthumous fame.

Equally impolitic to publish were Livingstone's acerbic, throw-away comments about other British explorers, such as Sir Samuel Baker, Sir Richard Burton, and John Hanning Speke, his contemporary rivals for the glory of solving Africa's geographical puzzles. Livingstone's caviling comments on the Portuguese explorers who preceded him in exploring Southern Africa were also politically sensitive. Waller was cautious, too, about Livingstone's remarks concerning his relationships with the Arab ivory and slave merchants with whom he travelled and resided between 1867 and 1872. Without means of his own, Livingstone came to rely on the hospitality and good will of these Muslims, all of whom engaged in some level of slave trading. The contradiction implied by this particular connection seemed worrisome enough to Waller to take some care about how it would appear to Livingstone's readers.

In terms of Livingstone's relations with the Foreign Office, the primary focus of his rancor lay with the nature of the arrangements made for his last journey. Not only had Foreign Office officials not provided him initially with a fund to draw upon for supplies, but they had mishandled the details of his consulship. Livingstone considered the way he was treated so grossly unjust and mean-spirited that his recollection irked him more and more the longer he ruminated on it during his long, enforced stay in Manyema country in 1870. At this time his health and fortunes were at a low ebb, and only Arab friendship provided him with any succor. "I have no letter from the Foreign Office," he wrote in his journal at Bambarre for October 25, 1870, after commenting, "In this journey I have endeavoured to follow with unswerving fidelity the line of duty. . . . All the hardship, hunger, and toil were met with the full conviction that I was right in persevering to make a complete work of the exploration of the sources of the Nile." Waller deleted the comment about awaiting a letter from the Foreign Office and the further remarks that accompanied it:

The last I had was a piece of the most exuberant impertinence that ever left the Foreign or any other office. I was to have no claim for any services rendered, no position when my work was done. . . . the effusion of supernumerary under Secretary [sic] Murray. I expect only the same treatment that Murray would claim for himself—the offer of other work, or of being provided with another office. The slave-trade on the West Coast having ceased, he ought to have resigned, but he thought to earn his salary by unjustly stopping mine.[37]

Before setting out for his last journey, Livingstone had received £500 and the honorary rank of Consul. The official letter conveying this information, signed by Lord John Russell but drafted by the "supernumerary" undersecretary Mr. Murray, had stated for the record that Livingstone was not eligible for a consular salary or a consular pension. As Tim Jeal remarks, in his biography of Livingstone, the tone of the document was both "chilling" and "dismissive." Livingstone understood the conditions of his appointment, but he did not like to be treated as an inferior underling to be reminded of his manners. In fact, as Jeal notes, Russell had not meant to treat him so; but by the time it was decided to recognize his most recent African explorations, on June 19, 1873 (by granting him a Civil List pension of £300), he was already dead.

Livingstone ended the deleted passage of October 25, 1870, with a passing reference to another of his bugbears. "The only annoyances I have suffered were from this . . . ," he wrote, "and from a letter of busy-body instructions from the Royal Geographical Society." The society, under Murchison's guidance, offered him £500 toward his expenses on his last journey, on the understanding that he would search for the Nile sources. He thought it exceedingly highhanded for a committee to issue him formal "instructions" about taking careful astronomical observations. He viewed their treatment as patronizing, considering his long connection with the society. His dismay was compounded by a formal request that he be prepared on his return to supply them with all his calculations and personal notes.

Livingstone's comments on his fellow British explorers, his predecessors and rivals who also worked to find the solution to the geographical puzzle of the Nile sources, were not generous ones. They were excised, some in the first instance by Tom Livingstone and then, more systematically, by Waller. Whether from caution or chagrin, Tom was especially sensitive to his father's gratuitous criticisms of other famous men. In at least one case, Tom and Waller disagreed about the propriety of allowing to stand a critical remark concerning Speke. Tom marked it for deletion; Waller countered this instruction to the printer by writing *stet* next to it. Yet it does not appear in the published version. In the offending sentence, under the date August 1, 1867, Livingstone noted, "In calling the Lake discovered by Mr. Baker the 'Luta Nsige,' Speke must have been misled by his interpreter, for both are foreign words." Tom also deleted from June 16, 1868, a dismissive reference to Speke's claim that African chiefs walked in an imitation of lions. Livingstone had observed, "[T]hat animal has a cat-like movement, and the back hangs loosely."

Judging from the editorial markings, I believe Tom Livingstone was also responsible for removing some November 19, 1968 musings by Livingstone: "Burton was given the name of "stingy white man," and he speaks as if this name indicated fear; the fear, so far as I can glean from his own account, was all on his side. He sheepishly complied with every demand made by the natives, and revenged himself by making mouths at them, in pedantic verbiage, in his journal." On the other hand, it was Waller who deleted a critical passage under the date October 4, 1870. Livingstone's remarks here would have sounded like sour grapes within a short time, when Stanley confirmed the accuracy of Speke's claims for Lake Victoria as the source of the Nile: "When Speke saw that his little river out of the Victoria Nyanza would not account for the Nile. . . ." Finally, May 21, 1872, in a context that made clear he was in fact criticizing all his competitors by claiming his own humility, Livingstone wrote: "I wish I had some of the assurance possessed by Baker, Cooley, and others." Waller not only deleted that sentence, but also the passage that followed it, in which Livingstone specifically heaped scorn on the claims of these men to having solved the Nile question.[38]

Tom, aware of the sensitive nature of his father's denunciations of Prince Albert for protecting Portuguese claims in Central Africa, deleted a passage, dated May 7, 1868, which was critical of the Portuguese explorer Dr. Lacerda. At Kazembe's, commenting on earlier visits to him by Portuguese explorers, Livingstone had described Lacerda as ". . . the only visitor of any scientific attainments, and he was fifty miles wrong in latitude alone." Farther on in the proof sheets, under the date November 8, 1868, Tom again marked for elimination two very long passages. In these Livingstone denigrated Portuguese knowledge of Central Africa as "a delusion," and called the ". . . good Vicount de Sa's maps, which were lately sent to the different Governments of Europe, . . . simply pretentions." In this excised passage, Livingstone went on to castigate the English armchair geographers William D. Cooley and James MacQueen for taking the Portuguese claims so seriously.[39]

Editorial censorship fell on other assertions that might have passed muster in informal conversation, but seemed inappropriate fixed in print. Among these were scathing references to Islam Livingstone made from time to time. For instance, Livingstone wrote, "The cholera came along the seashore from Mecca, but this year it came inland and made great havoc. . . . Letters from Mecca told of its coming from that focus of filth, but the rest of the world must do nothing, for political economy says we must not interfere." Part of a longer passage, marked for elimination because it dealt with the rebellion of the remaining Nasik men, also contained a slightly different version of Livingstone's relations with Arab traders in Manyema territory from that which appears in the published book. The passage is a retrospect, written in August 1870, about the events of June and July. Livingstone related that he, Susi, Chuma, and Gardner started in search of the Lualaba River by accompanying

> . . . three deputies from the head Arabs and their slaves; but they hated me, and tried to get away from me. I, however, kept up, and on the fourth day passed through nine villages destroyed by the worthies, who did not wish me to see more of their work. Then met with Muhamad Bogharib and Joseph coming back from Kasongo's. I slept at a village a little way from them, and was met in the morning with the news that a man of the party which eschewed my company had been stabbed by night in revenge for the slaughter of relatives and burning of nine villages.

The unchanged spelling of "Muhamad" and "Kasongo's" here—words which Waller consistently changed to "Mohamad" and "Kasonga's"— suggests that the passage was censored by Tom Livingstone before Waller could mark his standard alterations. A comparison with vol. 2 of the *Last Journals* reveals a different version of this story under the date "July, 1870." The published account eliminates Livingstone's attempt to keep pace with the Arab party. Instead, it implies that Livingstone just happened to be "sleeping quietly here," when "some trading Arabs camped at Nasangwa's, and at dead of night one was pinned to the earth by a spear, no doubt . . . in revenge for relations slain. . . ."[40]

Waller felt no admiration for Bishop Tozer of the Universities' Mission to Central Africa and was keenly aware that Livingstone had sent thunderbolts against Tozer in his Zambezi book for relocating the UMCA mission at Zanzibar in 1864. Yet Waller saw fit to remove Livingstone's critical references to him in the *Last Journals*, aware of the fact that Tozer's successor, Bishop Edward Steere, now planned to reenter the once-deserted field near Lake Malawi. Waller did not think it was the time to rake up old antagonisms. Livingstone had written, "Bishop Tozer, curiously enough, follows the policy of Bishop Mackenzie, which he so formally repudiated; rearing boys from captives of men-of-war, and writing to India that to teach the young thus obtained is the great secret of Mission-work. He does not know that the especial instruction of the young has been advocated and acted on for the last thirty years in Africa, India, South Seas, and elsewhere." A reference to the former British consul at Zanzibar, Colonel Lewis Pelly, whom Waller had come to know at the Royal Geographical Society, was similarly deleted: "I am anxious not to appear as if reflecting on others, as Colonel Pelly, . . . but it is his policy that has allowed the Zanzibar slave-trade to go on."[41]

To some extent, as Agnes and Tom Livingstone suspected might happen, Waller's personal editorial hand, as distinct from that of any other editor sensitive to the philanthropic politics of the day, can be discerned in muting allusions to Livingstone's grievances against John Kirk. Since these centered on Livingstone's suspicions that Kirk had not been as diligent as he might have been to keep Livingstone adequately supplied from the coast—thus failing to help him achieve his geographical goals—Waller's editorial pen hovered over Livingstone's remarks about the "Banian slaves" hired as porters to carry supplies to him from Zanzibar. His first deletions, for February 1871, had the effect of leaving the reader with Livingstone's praise of Kirk for getting out any caravan during the cholera years and with the impression that any problems that arose were due entirely to the mischief perpetrated by these Muslim slaves in using up the supplies entrusted to them for their own purposes.[42]

An Indian merchant, Ludda Damji—an agent of Jairam Sewji, the Zanzibar customs collector whose wealth had made him moneylender to the sultan—had organized these men into a caravan in 1869 to take supplies for Livingstone. They took over a year and a half to make a trip of ordinarily a few months' duration. Livingstone quickly discovered that they had malingered along the way, sold his goods, and lost all his letters but one. At this point, still grateful to Kirk for his efforts, Livingstone wrote: "Great havoc was made by cholera, and in the midst of it, my friend exerted himself greatly to get men off to me with goods." The only adverse comment Waller deleted here was, "When they [the caravan leaders] came to Ujiji, Shereef, the headman, stopped with four, and is now feasting and drinking on my goods, though he knows me to be here." Once ten of these men reached Livingstone, they refused to accompany him northward, "struck work for higher wages," and "swore" that the consul, meaning Kirk, had "told them not to go forward, but to force me back. . . ." In the published version, this passage is followed by: "But for Mohamad [sic] Bogharib and fear of pistol-shot they would gain their own and their Banian masters' end to baffle me completely. . . ." Waller had deleted from the proof sheet: "Muhamad

Ludda Damji, 1860, photograph by James A. Grant. Damji was an agent for Jairam Sewji, for many years the customs collector at Zanzibar. These Indian money lenders to Arab, Indian, and European merchants became millionaires. Livingstone purchased his trade goods in Zanzibar from Sewji's firm in January 1866 and only later realized his implication in the slave trade. In fact, there was no way to untangle the Swahili credit and trade system from purchases of or raiding for slaves, which were aspects of trading arrangements in the interior.

swore that he would kill them if they contended with me, and they gave in. . . ."[43]

In the spring and early summer of 1871, these "Banian slaves," as Livingstone called them, travelled with him through Manyema and remained a source of complaint. Livingstone wrote his first protest to Kirk about them in June 1871 and two far more sharply worded complaints while Stanley was with him, one an official consular report and the other a direct letter to Kirk. Before he was relieved by Stanley, Livingstone recorded on July 4, 1871, his sense of frustration with his current attendants. In a paragraph that Waller deleted, Livingstone told of being advised by an Arab with whom he was travelling that these caravan men were spreading the story among the Manyema that Livingstone's real aim was not to enslave them or buy their ivory, but to kill them. Livingstone lamented his sense of isolation among his African companions, despite long years together: "Susi and Chuma . . . hear it all, but never tell me. This has been the course all the liberated slaves have adopted ever since I had them. Though they saw stealing and plundering of my goods, they would never reveal it to me, and even denied knowledge of it, though partaking of the plunder. It is not now open refusal by the Banians I have to contend against, it is secret slander and villainy, and no one on whom I can rely.[44]

As already noted, Waller's personal warning system was also at work to censor highly critical remarks Livingstone made about the first UMCA missionary party in the Shire Highlands and to delete any story in which Waller himself was the butt of criticism or where the point was made at his expense. In this respect, however, Tom also acted upon his own understanding of what was sensitive, for it was he who crossed out a sentence of this kind from the proof of his father's journal for July 14–28, 1866. It followed Livingstone's comment: "I shall never cease bitterly to lament the abandonment of the Magomero mission." The passage had continued, "Any . . . [other] society would have prized the advantages there with delight, while this O.C.M. [Oxford, Cambridge Mission] affair let them slip through sheer want of pluck." A few pages later, part of Livingstone's summing up was allowed to stand: "The silly abandonment of all the advantages of the Shire route by the Bishop's successor I shall ever bitterly deplore, but all will come right some day. . . ." His explicit criticism of the Universities' Mission, however, was again removed: "No other society would have acted so blindly to obvious facilities." The name of Bishop Tozer, Mackenzie's immediate successor was deleted here, and Waller's editorial note, preceding this passage, makes reference only to Bishop Steere, who now planned to open a way to reoccupy the district.[45]

Despite the need to censor critical remarks about so many people, it must have come as a surprise to Waller to find it necessary to do so on his own behalf. Livingstone's astringent comments about the ineffectiveness of Waller's medical treatment of the Africans at the UMCA mission station must have inflicted pain, since Waller was quite proud of the medical lore he had acquired from reading and from working with the physician Charles Meller, who was attached to Livingstone's party at various times. Waller had put together the medicine chest for E. D. Young's expedition in 1867, and he had even published an article on African fevers. Yet here, in Livingstone's journal, was the doctor's dismissive censure of Waller's efforts to help heal the Africans' chronic ulcerated sores: "Treated or maltreated at Bishop Mackenzie's Mission by irritating salves they became frightful sloughs, and often caused death. I had nothing to do with the treatment, but saw Dr. Meller applying red precipitate to one on a Makololo! . . . I recommended the missionaries to give support by quinine, but never saw it given. Mr. Waller sent me some of the salve. His own people laughed, and said Waller told us lies about that. It never cured us, though he said it would."[46]

Finally, Waller marked for omission references that any Victorian publisher would have expected to be expunged by the editor of Livingstone's *Last Journals*. These offending words included specific mention of body parts (testicles became "tenderest parts") or reference to the prevalence of syphilis: "Syphilitic skin diseases are common among Manyema; large scabs on face and body, even among children. The Arabs increase them by impure intercourse. Filthy talkers all. White leprosy is also common." Both identification of Livingstone's painful hemorrhoids and the gorier details were left out, as was a description of the same problem as suffered by Sir Roderick Murchison: "He himself when a soldier spoiled his saddles by frequent discharges from the piles, but would never submit to an operation, and he is now eighty years old."[47]

Is it possible, then, to sum up what was kept back from the reading public as a result of Waller's having been chosen as the editor of Livingstone's *Last Journals*? Waller set out to ensure that these journals would not present a picture of Livingstone at his worst, an intolerant man, bitingly critical of all who did not fall in with his own plans and all whose activities made difficulties for him and seemed thereby, in small things and large, to be obstructing his own great work. Waller did understand the toll that African travel took on Livingstone, at the level of deprivation and fever-induced weakness that shadowed him from the time of the loss of his medicine case early in 1867. During these years, Waller had also received the letters which explained Livingstone's frustrations with his attendants, his problems with supplies, and his geographical speculations about the fountainheads of the Nile. Even more important, Waller knew the man, had spent long hours with him in Africa, and understood how fiercely committed he was to the goal he defined as regenerating the continent and its people. For Waller that shared goal, couched in terms of eradicating the evil of the trade in slaves, made it possible for him to perform these editorial tasks with a clear eye to their ultimate purpose. Waller wished to turn Livingstone's *Last Journals* and Livingstone into the living legend whose name would have the power to energize and recommit the British nation to intervention in Africa in the name of humanitarian Christianity.

Waller's aim was not to give the world a picture of a great man with human failings. That view of Livingstone might have emerged if he had written up his own journals for publication; yet we know from his previous books that Livingstone was aware of the need to curb his pen. Those who seek in Waller's edition of Livingstone's *Last Journals* firsthand information about the Africa Livingstone observed, however, receive that image through the partially distorting lens of Waller's editorial eyes. The overall filter does not blur out of recognition what Livingstone observed and recorded; but in various parts and in various ways—as the last two chapters demonstrate—it does prevent the reader from grasping some of the details that might shape our understanding of what happened on this last journey. Some kinds of information are missing. For example, an adequate understanding of Livingstone's dealings with the African, Indian, and Comoran porters and attendants who formed his work force—and who gradually dwindled to a tiny few until reinforced in 1872—is obscured by the partial picture presented in this published version. Both Tom Livingstone and Horace Waller eliminated details about Livingstone's comments, interactions, and relationships which provide clues to how his actions and requirements may have been interpreted by those men, especially those he condemned as most uncooperative. A work of reconstruction has begun as scholars begin to turn to Livingstone's original field diaries; but a detailed analysis of all the suppressions, those initiated by Livingstone as well as his editors, is an essential agenda for future scholarship.[48]

NOTES

1. *Missionary Travels*, 391.
2. Jeal, *Livingstone*, 141.
3. *Ibid.*, 230.

4. "Livingstone wrote this book by substantially revising, adding to, and subtracting from a narrative written by Charles Livingstone in the first half of 1864. . . ." *Livingstone Catalogue*, 268. Using Charles Livingstone's papers, Gary W. Clendennen has prepared a study of the joint authorship of *Zambesi and Its Tributaries*. For the need to reassess the participation of Charles Livingstone in the Zambezi Expedition, see V. L. Bosazza, "The Hero's Brother – Charles Livingstone," in *David Livingstone and Africa*, 105–11, discussion, 112–13.

5. *Zambesi and Its Tributaries*, 173.

6. Cairns, *Prelude to Imperialism*, 40. These views are discussed above, chap. 3, n. 3; compare Jeal, *Livingstone*, 141.

7. Cairns, *Prelude to Imperialism*, 42. The last phrase is Henry M. Hyndman's—the founder of the British Social Democrats—who criticized Stanley in 1878 for his method of exploration. Cairns, *Prelude to Imperialism*, 44. Stanley was aware of the contrast between his methods of keeping a caravan together and those of Livingstone. His 1874–78 expedition into Central Africa was a very large one by the standards of the day. By August 1876, after over forty desertions, his caravan still numbered 132 porters. At that point, having just crossed Lake Tanganyika, he was angered by the desertion of his protégé Kalulu (who had travelled with Stanley in England and the United States and had attended school in England for eighteen months at Stanley's expense). Having sneered in print in 1872 at the desertion of Livingstone by Wikatani ("one of the 'nice honorable fellows' of Mr. Waller"), Stanley did not allow it to happen to him. Kalulu was caught and he and other deserters were given punishments meant to discourage them and others from leaving. Stanley claimed that his action put an end to further "misconduct and faithlessness," but he does not indicate the severity of his punishments. At this point, he reflected—in possibly the only negative words he ever published about him—that Livingstone's failure to take adequate measures with regard to his men was his undoing: he ". . . lost at least six years of time, and finally his life, by permitting his people to desert. . . . The consequence of this excessive mildness was that he was left at last [when they met] with only seven men, out of nearly seventy. . . . His noble character has won from us a tribute of affection and respect, but it has had no lasting good effect on the African." Stanley asserted that his was not brutal treatment but the meting out of "pure, simple justice between man and man." Henry M. Stanley, *Through the Dark Continent, or the Sources of the Nile around the Great Lakes of Equatorial Africa and Down the Livingstone River to the Atlantic Ocean*, 2 vols. (1878; reprint, New York, 1969), 2:67. In editing the *Last*

Journals, Waller tried to keep to a minimum the descriptions of the desertions Livingstone experienced.

8. Waller added Livingstone's journal entry for September 4, 1866, in an abbreviated form, to the previous entry and the date was eliminated entirely. *LJDL*, 2:95.

9. Field Diary 17.

10. Livingstone had already exercised censorship when writing the Unyanyembe journal from his field diary for July 29, 1866, the day after his departure from Mataka's. According to his daily notes, "Andrew & Reuben two Nassick boys remained behind and we have to send for them. The boy Reuben . . . always lagged behind and enabled the sepoys to steal. . . . Andrew came up with two men I sent for him. Says a pain in his chest was the cause . . . Reuben still behind. Sent 3 men for him. Says he is going to stop with Mataka. Sent for the musket a Govt one." Field Diary 17; compare Simpson, *Dark Companions*, 60. Just over one month later, September 4, 1866, the scene with Andrew occurred.

11. Cooper, *Plantation Slavery on the East Coast of Africa*, 67–68, 144. Livingstone wrote Baraka off: "He tried perseveringly to get others to run away with him; [in January] lost the medicine-box, six table-cloths, and all our tools by giving his load off to a county lad while he went to collect mushrooms: he will probably return to Zanzibar, and be a slave to the Arab slaves after being a perpetual nuisance to us for upwards of a year." Livingstone set down Baraka's motives in leaving him for Tippu Tip as "putting his intention of begging among the Arab slaves into operation." *LJDL*, 1:228. Many years later, Tippu Tip recollected this event for Heinrich Brode, who recorded his memoirs (originally published in 1902–3 in the *Mitteilungen des Seminars fur Orientalische Sprachen*). Tippu Tip recalled meeting David Livingstone "who had *given me one of his servants* and a letter to take to the coast." Emphasis added. Tippu Tip then noted, "By the way, this man whom Livingstone gave . . . (me) [sic] is still alive today." He also recollected delivering Livingstone's letter to Kirk. Tippu Tip, *Maisha ya Hamed bin Muhammed el Murjebi yaani Tippu Tip*, text with translation by W. H. Whitely, East African Literature Bureau, Kampala, Nairobi, and Dar es Salaam, 1966; reprinted, 1974. First published as *Supplement to the East Africa Swahili Committee Journal* 28–29 (1958–59).

Stanley provided a vivid picture of Tippu Tip's immense following of 700 dependents whom he met in Central Africa in November 1876. There were Arabs and Africans, young men "ranging from ten to eighteen years of age, being trained . . . as gun-bearers, house servants, cooks, carpenters, house builders, blacksmiths, and leaders of trading parties." The women of his and his followers' households were ". . . all purchased with ivory, guns, cloths, or beads." Stanley, *Through the Dark Continent*, 2:129–30. While in England, Susi told Waller that "Tipo Tipo" received his nickname because on one occasion he stood over the spoils of a defeated enemy and declared, "Now I am Tipo Tipo," or "gatherer together of wealth." See *LJDL*, 1:230, Ed. note. According to Tippu Tip, however, ". . . the name Tip Tip [sic] had been given me by the locals who had fled . . . they said . . . this man's guns went 'tiptip,' in a manner too terrible to listen to." Tippu Tip, *Maisha*, 29.

12. Identifying and tracing the fate of the original Nasik-trained attendants is facilitated by Simpson, *Dark Companions*, chaps. 6–8.

13. At first, when his expectations of the sepoys were still high, Livingstone tried communicating with them directly, using "a few words of Hindustani picked out of a book in Roman characters." Rozina Visram, "Livingstone and India," in *David Livingstone and Africa*, 152. In his Unyanyembe journal, Livingstone continued the passage quoted: "Must go forward for I have to send some forty miles for food and am wearing out my other men while the sepoys sit and talk. It seems certain that they gave Ali eight Rupees to take them back to the coast without ever asking leave to go." June 3, 1866, Uj, NLS; compare *LJDL*, 1:45 and proof sheet 34, WPRH, 7. The first proof sheets for this date show that Tom Livingstone eliminated the passage. Waller also wished to play down the affair. In the Unyanyembe journal for June 2, 1866, for example, Livingstone had noted, "I suspect the sepoys." The published version, *LJDL*, 1:44, ends with these words; Waller deleted what followed: "This suspicion is supported by my lighting on one of them belabouring a camel with a thick stick and next day the beast was unable to move from inflammation on the hip if not from blows on the trochant [sic] major. This had I not seen & shouted to the fellow I should have set down to natural causes." These two sentences had been allowed to stand by Tom Livingstone when correcting his copy of first proof. See first proof, 33, signed by T. S. Livingstone and stamped as returned to the publisher "31 August 74," WPRH, 6.

14. *LJDL*, 1:76.

15. "They have gone on employing people to carry their things – one came up with a woman carrying his muskets & belts – He had promised the woman three cubits in my name – I paid it because she was a woman." July 15, 1866, Uj, NLS; compare *LJDL*, 1:75.

16. When Livingstone asked the Indians of the Marine Battalion at Bombay for volunteers in October 1865, twenty came forward but then

hesitated and drew back. Thereafter, ". . . 14 volunteered *after hearing that we had carriage provided for their luggage.*" September 20 and October 5, 1865, Field Diary 14, SNMDL (photocopy, NLS, MS. 10719), emphasis added. The sepoys were on loan from the British Indian government at Bombay, which continued to be responsible for their regular pay. The bracketed word *well* appears to have been added at the proof stage in response to a query from the printer's proof reader; compare proof sheet 39, WPRH, 6, and *LJDL*, 1:54.

    17. *LJDL*, 1:75, under date July 15, 1866,

    18. For June 20, 1866, Field Diary 16; compare Simpson, *Dark Companions*, 58. For July 23, see Field Diary 17; compare July 15, 1866, *LJDL*, 1:75-76.

    19. Uj, May 20; June 18, 1866, NLS.

    20. Rozina Visram first pointed out the need to reassess Livingstone's relations with his Indian attendants in "David Livingstone and India," M.A. thesis, University of Edinburgh, 1973. The author generously allowed me to consult her copy of this thesis. Compare Bennett, "David Livingstone," in Rotberg, *Africa and Its Explorers*, 46.

    21. Part of the editorial history of Livingstone's *Last Journals* includes the placement of Livingstone's later reflections on this desertion, in the published version, at the actual time of the Comorans' departure. The field diary for the dates in question—not available to Waller at the time of his editing—makes clear that Livingstone transposed the dramatic story describing Musa's desertion from September 29, 1866, when he had written it up in his field diary, to September 26, 1866, the actual date of their departure, in his Unyanyembe journal. This account included the dramatic description of the way "Musa's eyes STOOD OUT" when listening to stories about the dangerous Mazitu (Ngoni) just ahead of them. Livingstone allowed to remain under the date September 29 his suspicions that the Comorans were inveterate thieves and that their leader, Musa, knew about their depredations and even shared with his men the "dainties" they bought with their plunder. He was certain that Musa ". . . could have stopped it had he chosen." Tom Livingstone (using his initials) instructed the printer on the first galley proof to place these reflections under September 26, to accompany the account of the desertion. Compare: September 26 and 29, 1866 in Field Diary 18, SNMDL (photocopy NLS, MS. 10723); Uj, NLS; proof sheet 74, WPRH, 6; and *LJDL*, 1:114-16.

    22. With regard to the Nasik youths, a survey of the material marked for deletion on the proof sheets among Waller's papers at Rhodes House, WPRH, 6-8, shows editorial deletions or significant changes as follows:

proof sheet(s)

28	May 9, 1866;	141	Sep. 1, 1867;
51	Jul. 14–28, 1866;	144–45	Sep. 24–25, 1867;
63	Sep. 4, 1866;	178	Apr. 13, 1868;
117–19	Feb. 8, 13, 16, 18, 1867;	248–49	June 26, 1870;
122	Feb. 26, 1867;	300, 302	Aug. 24, 1870;
127	Apr. 29, 1867;	306	Oct. 8, 1870.
136	Jul. 10, 1867 (date eliminated);		

23. In 1867, at a meeting of the Royal Geographical Society, a letter from the Reverend W. Salter Price, head of the Church Missionary Society mission at Nasik, described them as ". . . nine African Christian lads . . . without exception intelligent youths, about twenty years of age. . . ." At the same meeting, a Mr. D. J. Kennelly commented that some of the young men educated at the "industrial mission" at Nasik had been enslaved originally in the Somali country. *PRGS* 12 (1867–1868): 23, 25. There were two Gallas among the first group of Nasik who accompanied Livingstone. The African Asylum at Nasik received both female and male children from among the slaves liberated by the British cruisers. The Anglo-Indian government at Bombay contributed a subsidy to this Church of England charity. The program of instruction included English history, European geography, English grammar, arithmetic, and Bible studies. The girls were trained in sewing and cooking to prepare them to become domestic servants; the boys were trained in carpentry and masonry. Some 200 liberated African children may have attended between 1854 and 1874. Harris, *African Presence in Asia*, 74–76.

24. Uj, NLS; deleted from proof sheet 141, WPRH, 7; compare *LJDL*, 1:228. Livingstone recorded Tippu Tip's generosity to him when they met July 9, 1867: "He presented a goat, a piece of white calico, and four big bunches of beads, also a bag of Holcus sorghum, and apologised because it was so little." *LJDL*, 1:222. Tippu Tip recalled Livingstone's plight and the help he supplied:

> He and the ten members of his party had almost been killed and a number of the locals came with him. Some of my men brought him to camp. . . . he had neither goods nor rations. Said bin Ali and I took him (in). He wanted guides to take him to Lake Mweru. He went and came back again, anxious now to visit Runda-Cazembe's. We gave him guides to take him there. . . . We sent word to . . .

one of my father's relatives . . . Mohamed bin Sali en Nabhani
. . . that one Livingstone would be arriving and that he was to
respect him and not give him any trouble.

Then Livingstone required guides to take him to other places
and wherever he wanted to go he sent him.

Tippu Tip, *Maisha*, 29.

25. *LJDL*, 1:16 (April 4, 1866) and 1:13 (March 26, 1866); editorially
29, deleted, Uj, February 26 and April 1867, and June 18, 1870, NLS. On
"half-castes," see also, above, pp. 141–42.

26. Uj, May 9, 1866, NLS; editorially deleted, proof sheet 28, WPRH,
6. For the word change made by Livingstone, see May 9, 1866, Field
Diary 15, SNMDL (photocopy, NLS, MS. 10720). On Baraka, see *LJDL*,
1:117 (January 20, 1867); proof sheet 141, passage deleted under September 1, 1867, together with handwritten marginal note, WPRH, 6; and
LJDL, 1:228–29. Compare: "They were of the lowest or criminal class in
Africa." Uj, NLS, August 24, 1870, deleted editorially. "Ringleading" as a
threat to the expedition appears in the published version of the *Last
Journals;* it was a term Livingstone used when he feared that some action
by one of his African companions would set off a chain reaction among
the rest of his followers. His aim was to reduce the effectiveness of those
who set a bad example. See: "I gave beads to all but the ringleaders,"
LJDL, 2:57 (August 24, 1870).

27. On "first" proof sheet 51, Tom Livingstone changed the word
order but allowed the passage to stand. Waller deleted the entire passage
on "second" proof sheet 51, WPRH, 6. Compare *LJDL*, 1:75, under July
15, 1866 (Waller eliminated the July 17 date, where these words first
appeared).

28. Proof sheets 117 (February 8, 1867); 118 (February 13, 1867); and
119 (February 16, 1867), WPRH, 7. Compare *LJDL*, 1:190–92.

29. Proof sheets 53 (July 15, 1866) and 326 (December 12, 1870),
WPRH, 6 and 8; compare *LJDL*, 2:87 and Field Diary 37, section marked
"LXX–LXXV" (10 - 30 Dec. 1870), SNMDL (photocopy NLS, MS.
10703), fol. 24–26. In a letter marked "Private," January 24, 1872, Living-
stone complained about the training given Africans at the Nasik Asylum
of the Church Missionary Society to Dr. John Wilson, the Scottish Free
Kirk missionary in Bombay, the minister who sheltered Wikatani and
Chuma in 1864–1865:

All their desires in Africa were to get back to live in idleness at
Nassick. . . . On the desertion of the Johanna [Anjouan] men

they did pretty fairly because I employed the country people to do
my work; but on coming in contact with Arab slaves [sic] they
turned back to their youthful habits of lying, stealing and every
vice . . . All shewed [sic] eagerness to engage uninvited in slave
hunting. (Simon was no carpenter; Abraham no blacksmith). . . . if
you can inform the Bombay Government privately and propose a
ship anchored in a healthy spot as a school where real bona fide
work would be taught it would be a benefit to the community.
Taught to cook – wash – sew – all the jobs sailors can do and discipline enforced these poor unfortunates would prove a blessing. At
present the teachers fear them. They dread their desertion and
bringing an ill name on Nassick School. . . .

Livingstone Papers, MS. 7792, NLS.
    30. Proof sheets, WPRH, 6-7, with editorial deletions from the Unyan-
yembe journal concerning Chuma and Susi are as follows:

22	Apr. 25, 1866;	208	Nov. 1, 1868;
77	Oct. 4, 1866;	274	Jul. 4, 1871
178	Apr. 13, 1868;		

    31. April 13, 1868, proof sheet 178, WPRH, 6; *LJDL*, 1:286–87. Waller
also deleted from April 15, 1868, proof sheet 178: "James, a Nindi," as the
culprit who spread the rumor that no one would be paid; and the sentence: "Abraham must have promised to run away, too, for Susi began
and built a 'big house' for him."
    32. *LJDL*, 1:346.
    33. Editorially deleted, *LJDL*, 2:45. The reference to slave chains in
1870 should be noted in light of the comment in England when Stanley
reported in 1872 that Livingstone had asked him to send slave chains, to
aid him against future "slaves" who might try to drive him back to the
coast, see above, chap. 2. Compare Livingstone's contemptuous attitude
toward the Irish implied in his comment on W. D. Cooley above, chap.
3, n. 41.
    34. Proof sheet 300, written retrospectively in August 1870 concern-
ing the events that took place in June, WPRH, 8; and Uj, July 6, 1870,
NLS.
    35. Proof sheet 302, WPRH, 8, deleted from a passage which appears
under the date August 24, 1870, *LJDL*, 2:57.
    36. *LJDL*, 2:71; proof sheet 265, WPRH, 8. From the proof sheet it is
evident that Waller initially intended to cross out the first sentence and
Abram's name; he then changed his mind and marked the entire passage
for deletion. Proof sheets 328 (January 16, 1871) and 331 (February 16,

1871), WPRH, 8; *LJDL*, 2:95, 100; Field Diary 37, section marked "LXXVI" (16 Jan. 1871), JMPA (photocopy, NLS, MS. 10717), and "LXXVII–CI" (24 Jan.–22 Mar. 1871), MS. 10703, fol. 27–35, NLS. Elsewhere, it is not clear whether Livingstone complained on February 17, 1873, of an African attendant from his first or second Nasik group. See: proof sheets 69–70, WPRH, 8; and *LJDL*, 2:277.

37. October 25, 1870, Uj, NLS; proof sheets 310–11, WPRH, 8; *LJDL*, 2:72–73; see also Jeal, *Livingstone*, 287, 288–89.

38. Proof sheets 138 (August 1, 1867); 189 (June 16, 1868); 217 (November 19, 1868); 261 (October 4, 1870); and page proof for vol. 2:188 (May 21, 1872), WPRH, 6–7. Compare *LJDL*, 1:224, 305 (June 15, 1868; June 16 date deleted), 348; and 2:65, 188.

39. Proof sheets 183 (May 7, 1868) and 211–12 (November 8, 1868), WPRH, 6; *LJDL*, 1:294 (under May 6, 1868), 340. On Cooley, see above, chap. 3, n. 41. Livingstone never forgave MacQueen for assigning the priority of discovery to Portuguese explorers when reviewing Livingstone's geographical work in Southern Africa. See "Notes on the Geography of Central Africa from the Researches of Livingstone, Monteiro, Graça and Others," *Journal of the Royal Geographical Society* 26 (1856): 109–30.

40. Proof sheet 330 (on Islam) and 300 (on accompanying Arabs), WPRH, 8; *LJDL*, 2:98 (would have been the last entry for January 28, 1871) and 2:45. The Arab trader was Muhammed bin Gharib; on him, see Bennett, "David Livingstone," in Rotberg, *Africa and Its Explorers*, 56.

41. On Tozer, see proof sheet 262, WPRH, 7; *LJDL*, 2:68 (October 10, 1870). On Pelly, see proof sheet 62, WPRH, 6; *LJDL*, 1:93 (August 24, 1866).

42. In 1882, when J. Scott Keltie was commissioned to write an article on Livingstone for the *Encyclopedia Britannica*, he wrote Waller for comment. Waller agreed to help him and when he received proof, ". . . toned down the expression relative to Dr. Kirk and the men he sent. He did his best but the men were slaves. . . ." Waller to Keltie, Twywell, March 16 and (letter cited) April 1, 1882, RGSA. Since most caravans from the East Coast into the interior were composed at least in part of hired slaves, Waller's justification for the behavior of this particular group explains nothing. See Wright, "East Africa, 1870–1905," esp. 552.

43. *LJDL*, 2:98–100; proof sheets 330–31, WPRH, 8. Under February 11, 1871, there appears both in the proof sheet and published version: "Another hunting quelled by Mohammad and me." Agnes Livingstone had deciphered and transcribed her father's hard-to-read writing across old printed paper for the dates August 17, 1870, to May 11, 1871. In her

script, the word *hunting* is clearly legible as *mutiny*. If this error crept in at the printers, neither printer's proof reader nor Waller stopped to check the odd wording. Agnes Livingstone's manuscript, WPRH, 8. Tippu Tip said he and other Arab merchants were reluctant to deal with Jairam Sewji, but that the sultan urged him to do so. Tippu Tip, *Maisha*, 33. See also Wright, "East Africa, 1870-1905," 548, and Cooper, *Plantation Slavery on the East Coast of Africa*, 140.

44. Proof sheet 274, WPRH, 8; *LJDL*, 2:130.

45. See July 14-28 and September 13, 1866, proof sheets 55, 67, WPRH, 6; *LJDL*, 1:81, 101. On the omission of Tozer's name, see *LJDL*, 1:100-1; and editorial note, 1:99-100.

46. Proof sheet 55, WPRH, 6; *LJDL*, 1:81 (July 14-28, 1866). For Waller's editorial report on Steere, *LJDL*, 1:100. On the salve used by Meller and Waller, proof sheet 207, WPRH, 6; *LJDL*, 1:333 (October 11, 1868).

47. On testicles and social diseases, see proof sheet 326, WPRH, 8; *LJDL*, 2:87 (December 12, 1870). Proof sheet 304, WPRH, 8; *LJDL*, 2:61 (August 25, 1870, after a comment on the tape-worm). On Murchison's suffering from hemorrhoids, see proof sheet 270, WPRH, 7; *LJDL*, 2: 125 (May 18, 1871). Compare Bridges, "Problem of Livingstone's Last Journey," *David Livingstone and Africa*, 165.

48. Donald Simpson's use of the diaries for *Dark Companions* is a case in point. Andrew Roberts at the School of Oriental and African Studies (University of London) made a brief study of comparisons between the field diaries, the Unyanyembe journal, and the published version in connection with his own work, which he kindly shared with me. He notes field diary information that does not appear in the *Last Journals*, such as the following: a comment made around December 1, 1872, calling Kirk's description of Lake Bangweulu "a sally of audacious ignorance"; a comment dating to December 4, 1867, noting that chief Kazembe ". . . is always succeeded by a brother or in cases a sister's son"; and further comments in January 1868, discussing the practice of successors in Kazembe to build a new town. Personal Communication. See Andrew D. Roberts, "Livingstone's Value to the Historians of African Societies," in *David Livingstone and Africa*, 49-67. See also chap. 3, n. 1.

§ 6 &

The Livingstone Legend

On November 2, 1874, Waller completed and dated his Introduction. In the early part of December, John Murray officially published *The Last Journals of David Livingstone, in Central Africa, from 1865 to his Death.* Also printed on the title page were the words: "Continued by a Narrative of His Last Moments and Sufferings, obtained from His Faithful Servants Chuma and Susi, by Horace Waller, F.R.G.S., Rector of Twywell, Northampton." Though never the record-breaking best seller that *Missionary Travels* had been in 1857, the *Last Journals*, in two volumes, proved to be a solid, long-running success.

The initial print order was relatively high for nineteenth-century travel books, but essentially a good estimate by the publisher of the audience available for the book; 10,000 sets of two volumes were ordered, of which 7,500 were to be bound. By June 1875, the major reviews of the book had appeared and over 7,000 of the bound sets had been sold. In addition, 65 sets had been delivered to the journals as review copies, and 109 sets were distributed as presentation copies. Thereafter, the publisher annually ordered more of the printed sets bound. In the next five years, ending in June 1880, a total of 748 additional sets had been sold, the last eight for nineteen shillings. At this point the publisher reduced the price for the two-volume set from the original twenty-eight shillings to fifteen shillings. Through the 1880s, 1,670 copies were sold at the new lower price; and through the 1890s, a further 177 sets were sold. Horace Waller died in February 1896; by June that year, over 9,550 copies of the *Last Journals* had been sold.[1]

The publisher's first accounting with the executors of Livingstone's estate, in November 1875, augmented the author's initial share of the profits (two thirds of the net profits) with the sale of rights to American, German, and French editions. The total, including interest on the money for foreign rights, came to over £3,300. A small but steady sale continued, from a half dozen to two and a half dozen sets each year, new sets

Rev. Horace Waller, c. 1890. Having shared missionary and antislavery experiences with Livingstone in Central Africa and having edited his *Last Journals*, Waller continued to play a key role in humanitarian, commercial, and proimperialist ventures. Just as he shaped the Livingstone legend to tell a simple tale, so he continued to present a simple view of national duty. As he wrote in April 1871, in the *Antislavery Reporter*: "Let but the word be spoken by such a nation as our own, and the present curse of this great evil shall be, by God's blessing and by the power entrusted to us, done away with at once."

being bound as necessary from time to time. The last order to bind copies occurred in 1914; and on February 1, 1920, the price was actually raised to eighteen shillings. The last fifteen copies were sold in 1923. The book remained in print, therefore, for just under fifty years. This long record of sales exceeded most travel books published in the nineteenth century and was greatly outdistanced only by Livingstone's own *Missionary Travels*, which sold 30,000 copies of its guinea (twenty-one-shilling) edition.

On March 20, 1875, John Murray asked Waller if he would be able to cut the length of Livingstone's Zambezi book by one third. When Waller agreed on April 6 to cut it by 200 pages, Murray offered him fifty guineas for the work. As a result, Waller became editorially connected with a reissued two-volume cheap edition (seven shillings and six pence each volume) of Livingstone's first and second travel books. Down into the twentieth century, as the publisher continued to print orders of all three of Livingstone's books of African travel, Horace Waller was editorially connected with two of them. By the late 1880s and early 1890s, orders for the cheap edition of the first two books were placed by school authorities, and Livingstone's life and work became part of the learned culture of the mass educational experience of late Victorian England.[2]

As we have seen, Waller sought to imbue the *Last Journals* with his view of Livingstone as, first and foremost, a missionary for whom exploration was but the means of accomplishing his larger goal, the dedication of England to ending the slave trade in Central Africa. We can now ask whether those who read these edited pages reacted to its underlying message as Waller hoped they would. Late twentieth-century historians agree that Livingstone's last journey left an enduring mark on his time. The African historian Norman Bennett calls Livingstone's last journey "the most important single expedition undertaken by a European in nineteenth-century Africa." In his opinion, "[I]ts effects upon future European reactions to involvement with Africa were paramount." "He wrote to persuade others to come to redeem Africa, either through commerce or Christianity," and, he adds, "Livingstone's impact on the course of history in Africa was immense." Specifically, however, Livingstone's significance lay in "the impact his character and way of life made in Europe."[3]

This emphasis on the importance to subsequent history of Livingstone's life and work, as presented in his three African travel books and recorded in the pages of contemporary newpapers, periodicals, and books about him, makes the fundamental point. It was not just what Livingstone wrote, it was the life he led, as revealed in his writings, that caught the popular imagination. If the enduring image of that life was shaped by his books, the legend of the heroic missionary explorer was imprinted on the public consciousness by the *Last Journals* as much as by the life itself. Waller had carefully fixed the picture of a gentle but determined missionary, exploring Africa to expose to the conscience of the world its brutal trade in slaves. That was the image that came to mind when Dr. Livingstone's name was invoked by the generation that would be responsible for British imperial expansion in Eastern and Central Africa. This chapter looks briefly at the public reception of the *Last Journals* immediately after its publication to gauge contemporary opinion about the Livingstone legend.

Just as in 1856 Livingstone became a national hero marked for fame and controversy, so in 1874 he became a national legend about whom extensive popular writing and scholarship have continued ever since. A century after that initial burst of popular acclaim, the anthropologist Max Gluckman undertook to comment on the issues involved when anyone wrote about Livingstone. He observed that Livingstone himself understood how easy it was, by "a selection of cases of either kind" concerning people's character, to make them appear "as excessively good or uncommonly bad." He took the quotation from words Livingstone wrote about the Kololo people with whom he had a number of encounters. Gluckman turned this quotation into a discussion of Livingstone's failings in his dealings with the Kololo and some historians' failure to note the full story of that relationship, concerned as it was with what the Kololo expected from Livingstone, and failed to get. He used the example to plead for a better understanding of what Africans wanted or planned or expected in situations in which they dealt with Europeans.

This issue of perspective is a critical one. Gluckman pressed it because he was calling on scholars to understand on its own terms the African world through which Livingstone travelled. It is equally necessary to apply these standards of analysis when looking closely, as this book does, at the human failings of a particular man at a particular time in history. From our late twentieth-century vantage point, many of Livingstone's views make him look like a nineteenth-century racist. At the same time, it is easy to identify nineteenth-century racists of a more blatant and pernicious kind, beside whom Livingstone and his opinions represent a call for better understanding of Africans on their own terms. He was a man of his time as well as a man who made a unique contribution to his era, and some of the illustrations in the previous chapters have sought to demonstrate this point. When we examine closely what Livingstone thought, we can draw clear distinctions between his views and the more vicious racist thinking of his day. Similarly, it has been necessary to dwell on the ragged edges of Livingstone's character and his less laudatory actions and words to understand better what was left out of his *Last Journals*. For that reason, the reader should remember Gluckman's refinement for historians of Livingstone's warning, that anyone can be shown to be "excessively good or uncommonly bad," depending on "a selection of cases of either kind."

Just as Bennett expressed it in his more recent assessment, Gluckman believed Livingstone "undoubtedly made known Central Africa to the world, as no other explorer had done." As a scholar, Gluckman rejected the legend of the saintly missionary because he studied the all too fallible Livingstone in his dealings with the Kololo. Similarly, modern biographers point out the many mistakes Livingstone made on his last journey. In a way that proved fatal to the success of his travels, he erred as a cartographer in mapping new territory. He also made mistakes in planning his supplies, organizing his animals, dealing with his Indian marines, and underestimating the toll the long, hard journey would have on his companions. These were mistakes of judgment. He suffered too from mistakes made because of circumstances beyond his control: clouds made star readings impossible; instruments became damaged; accidents of travel perpetuated the misunderstanding of the geography of Lake Bangweulu; and fever and serious ill-health drove him to travel with Arab traders who, though generous, thwarted his plans.

At the same time, deep in the heart of Africa, Livingstone read and reread his Bible and brooded on Herodotus and became obsessively convinced that he would find, in the region of Lake Bangweulu, the fountainheads of the Nile. Only faintly did his own skeptical Scot's mind warn him that he might be discovering instead a major source for the Congo. In a similar way, in his isolation, he became suspicious that his former companion Kirk was no longer intent on supporting him from Zanzibar. When Waller discovered these thoughts and others that surprised (perhaps shocked) him, and certainly made him uncomfortable, he put it down to "fever"; and there is something to be said for the view that Livingstone's thoughts and actions after January 1867 owe much to a steadily deteriorating physical condition. Far earlier in his travels, however, Livingstone had demonstrated a doggedness of will to follow his own line that was not facilitated by any diplomacy of leadership among Europeans or tact among his African companions. Altogether, his was a lonely and frustrating odyssey. As Gluckman acknowledged, however, a "mystique" was built up around Livingstone which made him a hero in Europe and, thereby, allowed him " 'to alter the whole European conception of Africa and Africans'." That "mystique" drew its inspiration and final form from the way Waller handled the issues of human error and judgment in Livingstone's *Last Journals*.[4]

The same issue of perspective is involved in the ways in which readers of Livingstone's *Last Journals* grasped the message so carefully honed for them. Among the first notices to appear was one in *The Saturday Review* for December 19, 1874. The *Saturday Review* had a circulation of 20,000 in 1870, and has been characterized as "far above all political-literary Reviews of the time, both in terms of quality of writing, and importance as an organ of opinion. Readers were middle to upper class, highly educated, of both liberal and conservative opinions . . . with some preponderance of the latter." The review in this journal, therefore, was an important one. The writer declared that Waller, as editor, merited "great praise" for his "labour of love" in putting together what were "at best . . . the raw materials of a book of travels. . . ." The reviewer pointed out, with mild astonishment, that the traveller remained "warm in his admiration of the unsophisticated native," despite "frequent helplessness owing to the desertion of his servants and the bad faith of the Arab traders. . . ." There was praise for the "fidelity of the native servants" who carried the body to the coast and the concluding comment that it was ". . . impossible to put it down without a new sense of the moral grandeur of Livingstone's character. . . ." Even in the somewhat hastily constructed review, which appeared within the week of the book's publication, the writer gives the impression that Waller had succeeded in the task he set himself. He had conveyed, as he had intended, the gentleness, the sincerity, and the heroic moral stature of the man he so admired.[5]

Since the preoccupations of the holiday season followed the publication of the book, we do not find the next important notice until two and half weeks later, January 7, 1875, in *The Times*. Waller noted it with pleasure in his diary: "The Times reviews the Journals very nicely today – much to my comfort. 4½ columns and complimentary." Waller's success in conveying exactly the portrait he had aimed to create is evident by the nature of the praise awarded to him as editor and to Livingstone as the great humanitarian of his age. The reviewer accepted the cumulative impression, conveyed by the Introduction, the editorial comments, and the illustration of the newspaper-and-bark-ink diary pages deciphered by Agnes Livingstone and C. A. Alington, that every recoverable word of the great traveller's account had been faithfully reproduced. "Mr. Waller's notes and comments as well as his narrative of the closing scene of the traveller's life and of the return journey are worthy of the subject and of his friendship for Livingstone; nor have we anything but praise for the way in which he has exerted his most difficult task, for he no doubt considered that he was bound to print every word in the Journals as they stood."

The volumes, *The Times* reviewer continued, were "deeply interest-ing . . . indeed, the most valuable memoranda of travel ever seen of late years. . . ." There was no mistaking the "legacy of Livingstone to his country." "Greater than all his achievements [in geography] . . . must be counted the creation of a deep feeling of sympathy for some of the races [of Africa] . . . as well as their sufferings . . . and . . . the horror of . . . what he termed 'the great open sore of the world'—slav-ery and the slave trade." The reviewer recorded the impression made on the reader of "the simple, faithful, and noble character of the traveller, who never once pulled a trigger in anger on a human being, who re-proached himself for temper because he once chastised unruly servants with a rod, and who by mere force of gentleness exercised a sort of charm over the cruel savages in whose wilds he fearlessly wandered." The "sweetness and serenity of Livingstone's character" was matched by the "moving . . . account of the faithful service rendered by the 'benighted heathens' to the master after death whom they so honoured in his life."

The reviewer captured in a description of the book's cover both the way the illustration aptly rendered the heart of the story about the great traveller as found within these volumes and also the way readers were sure to respond to it. "The exhausted wanderer is represented to us borne through a mournful marsh. The rain is falling in torrents; the cur-rent sways the half-submerged rushes; water-plants rise above the tur-bid stream; in front, buried up to the neck in water, a stalwart negro, with a bale as big as his body on his head, breasts the flood; another follows with the water nearly to his lips. On the shoulders of the faithful Susi the traveller is seated, with his legs projecting in front, his hands resting on the neck of his bearer, and his body sustained in equilibrium behind by another of his faithful attendants, whose head and arms only appear above the surface. His servants, carrying his arms and baggage, follow in single file. There is a whole history within the four corners of that little sketch, and those who read the Journals—and who will not who can!—will soon learn its moral for themselves."[6]

In the first months of 1875, two major reviews appeared in an influen-tial quarterly and in a serious monthly magazine. They present a marked contrast with each other; each reviewer had a clear agenda in writing his review, related to his professional concerns. Professor (later Sir) Richard Owen, Livingstone's instructor in comparative anatomy and his lifelong friend and consultant, wrote an unsigned review for the *Quarterly Re-view*. Like the book itself, this journal was published by John Murray, and on the whole a favorable review would be expected in its pages. However, it was also a journal of conservative religious opinion and Livingstone was, despite his relationship to Anglicans as missionaries, very much a nonconformist. These considerations may have led to the choice of Owen to write a review that would be primarily concerned with Livingstone the scientist. The *Quarterly Review* had a circulation of about 8,000 in 1870 and "was usually mentioned before all other quarterlies in the contemporary press notices." Because its rate for advertisements was higher than its rivals, it is thought to have had "the largest circulation among the quarterlies of the day. . . . A political, literary and philosophical organ, it appealed to the educated upper and middle class, predominantly those with Tory political views."[7]

In contrast, the review in *Macmillan's Magazine*, is signed. Sir Samuel Baker conveys clearly in this article his concerns as an African explorer, his own views of Africa and Africans—views Livingstone explicitly rejected in his *Last Journals*—and his essentially imperialist prescription for mending the ills of the slave trade. *Macmillan's Magazine* also had a circulation of approximately 8,000, and like the *Quarterly Review*, it cost the relatively high price of six shillings. The readership of both journals, however, was higher than their circulation figures, since both were available at Mudie's lending library. In addition, Baker's review was reprinted in *Littell's Living Age* and the *Eclectic Magazine*. *Macmillan's Magazine* was as "an organ of opinion"; its readers had a superior education, were "middle to upper class, Broad Church or even agnostic in religious matters, [and] politically predominantly Liberal."[8] The contrast presented by Owen in the *Quarterly Review* and Baker in *Macmillan's Magazine*, is not only one of the personality and professional interests of the writers but also, very likely, one of quite different political and religious readerships. They provide a good way to compare how different circles of contemporary opinion might interpret the Livingstone legend embodied in his *Last Journals*.

Both Owen and Baker specifically complimented Waller for his excellent editorial work. Baker, however, immediately pointed out some fundamental problems geographers and explorers in the field would have with the book. Although filled with geographical information of all kinds, he noted, the *Last Journals* lacked an index and would be more difficult to use as a reference. In addition, as an explorer accustomed to poring over maps for practical purposes, Baker complained that the editor had not offered "some explanation of the system adopted in editing." He pointed out a number of discrepancies in the spelling of a village and two nearby rivers located near the site of Livingstone's death, citing the different versions that appeared on the large, fold-out, end-paper map of volume 1 and in Livingstone's last journal entries as reproduced as facsimile pages of illustration in volume 2.

In chapter 3, I discussed Waller's editorial decision to impose uniformity of spelling upon the many variants that appeared within Livingstone's Unyanyembe journal and between it and the field diaries and scraps of papers he had available to him. As Baker noted, uniformity was crucial to "future explorers who [might] depend on Livingstone's map for their guide." Waller had been sensitive to the problem and insisted that the map carry a warning that Livingstone had addressed to him in a letter in 1873: "No dependence is to be placed on the Map except as to the general features of the country and rivers till my observations are recalculated at the Cape."

The problem of typographical errors for unfamiliar names was a universal one, illustrated by the fact that in reproducing the spellings he complained about, Baker did not catch the fact that one of the names on the facsimile page to which he referred was misspelled in his own review article. Baker's observations were pertinent, however, for in the autograph version of the original journal reproduced in the book, the spellings were "Muanzabamba," "Lukolu," and "Molilamo," while on the end-paper map they were rendered as "Muanazambamba's," "Molikolu R.," and "Lilimala R." In addition, in the entry in vol. 2 under April 19, 1873, "Muanzambamba," was used, while it appears as "Moanzambamba," in the entry for April 20, and both versions were different from the original autograph manuscript. They are closer in spelling to the end-paper map, but are alternate versions of that spelling as well.[9] At the very least, such problems indicated the stress under which Waller and other proof readers were working during the last days of publishing the book.

Of these two reviewers, the scientist Owen was by far the more receptive to Waller's underlying message concerning the evangelical significance of Livingstone's life and work. Though his long career in science (which would be capped, in 1884, with a knighthood) gave Owen a real appreciation of Livingstone's geographical researches and scientific contributions, he was moved to open his remarks with a tribute to Livingstone the missionary and antislave trade crusader. For that tribute, he quotes directly from Waller's introduction:

He was, first and last, the Christian missionary; next, or rather an inseparable part of the Gospel message of freedom, was (in the words of his friend and Editor) "a sincere trust that slavery, 'the great open sore of the world,' as he called it, might, under God's good guidance, receive healing at his hands." His persevering and enthusiastic labours in the cause of geographical science were always subordinate to those higher aims, prompted by "a fervent hope that others would follow him after he had removed those difficulties which are comprised in a profound ignorance of the physical features of a new country."[10]

Samuel White Baker, in contrast, read Livingstone's *Last Journals* as the fitting tribute to the "greatest among African travellers [who] . . . has infused a new spirit into African exploration; and by his high example . . . has stimulated others to follow upon the same course, which will eventually result in the opening of that hitherto mysterious region."[11] Baker read the *Last Journals* with a keen professional eye as to its geographical content. He not only had explored for the sources of the Nile in the early 1860s, but he also had spent the previous four years in the employ of the Egyptian khedive, extending his equatorial domain southward toward Lake Victoria. His own book, *Ismailia, A Narrative of the Expedition to Central Africa for the Suppression of the Slave Trade*, identified his activities with a great Egyptian antislavery effort, and not just with an extension of Egyptian territory. Baker's claims were received with skepticism in some quarters, judging by a review of his book that appeared in the *Edinburgh Review* the month before.

Like the *Quarterly Review*, the *Edinburgh Review* was one of the few quarterlies of this period with a long history, having begun to publish early in the century. "In the contemporary press, the *Edinburgh* was usually mentioned second after the *Quarterly*." Also like the *Quarterly*, it was priced at six shillings an issue. Its circulation, about 7,000, was augmented by its availability for middle-class readers at Mudie's. It was well-known for paying its contributors "handsomely," and its readers were at the upper reaches of society, "the educated upper and upper middle classes, with some predominance of Whig-Liberals."[12] According to the *Edinburgh* reviewer, Baker's "military expedition," which consisted of hundreds of men, was led by a commander who "assures us that it was undertaken for the extirpation of that nefarious traffic in slaves, which he had discovered in his travels . . . to be the great bar to the civilisation of Central Africa. This object is put forth on his title-page, professed in the first chapter of the book, and paraded, if we may use the expression, on page after page throughout these volumes. It was against the slave trade and the slave trade alone, that Baker's expedition . . . was planned. . . ." Baker's emphasis on this point led the reviewer to protest: "that a tried traveller . . . a man who had already spent years in those regions of Central Africa where the slave trade is indigenous . . . should be so credulous as to suppose that even the Khedive would be ready to organize such an expedition for philanthropy alone, quite passes our belief. . . ."[13]

Baker, however, knew the value of explaining in antislavery terms his efforts to extend Egypt's domain on the Upper Nile. His earliest interest in African exploration led him to seek, unsuccessfully, to join Livingstone's Zambezi Expedition in 1858.[14] Thereafter, he used his independent wealth to establish himself as a bona fide explorer searching for the Nile sources. After he was knighted for his "discovery" and naming of Lake Albert, he gained entry to the circle around the Prince of Wales and accompanied him to the opening ceremonies of the Suez Canal in 1869. Baker's introduction to Khedive Ismail by the heir to the English throne gave him a special position which he happily turned to good use. Ismail offered him the title of "Pasha" and the large sum of £10,000 a year to establish and govern Egypt's Equatorial Province and extend its southern boundaries to the lake region of Central Africa. Baker's instructions included the placing of steamers on the lakes and setting up a chain of trading stations "on the system adopted by the Hudson Bay Company."[15] Baker wrote about his years of service, from 1869 to 1873, in *Ismailia*, published in the fall of 1874. He flatly declared that he had crushed the slave trade in the Sudan and had extended Egypt's boundaries to the equator; he had, in fact, done neither.[16] As one biographer suggests, "The greatest impact of Baker's mission . . . was felt . . . in Britain itself. The very scale of the expedition aroused philanthropic, economic, and strategic interest in the southern Sudan."[17]

As a successful publicist of his own activities, Baker paid to Livingstone, the African explorer, a tribute which was both sympathetic and eloquent about the hardships and frustrations of African travel. Baker's experiences in Central Africa and the Sudan gave him cause to admire Livingstone's courage and accomplishments. Like the writers in the *Saturday Review* and *The Times*, he praised Waller for "the great labour of love in editing and publishing" Livingstone's last journals. He also responded specifically to Waller's graphic imagery of Livingstone kneeling by his bed, "apparently in prayer," at the time of his death. Baker then traced for the reader the geographical route Livingstone had followed, pointing out the critical points of geographical controversy which the missionary explorer's remarkable travels had filled in or still left open.

Baker was generous in his tribute to the hero whose exploits had first inspired him to think of African travel:

Having carefully read every word of his long diary, we feel that we have been his companion throughout his seven years of difficulty; we have shared his emotions, his troubles, disappointments, and the short joys that so seldom came, until we almost see him die. Closing the book in sorrow, it becomes impossible to criticize now that he is dead. His geographical opinions may or may not be accepted upon all points, but there can be only one opinion concerning the man: he was the greatest of all explorers of this century; *he was one of a noble army of martyrs who have devoted their lives to the holy cause of freedom, and he had laid down his life as a sacrifice upon a wild and unknown path, upon which he has printed the first footsteps of civilization.*

Livingstone has given the grand impulse to African exploration; *it was he who first directed public attention to the miseries and horrors of the East African slave trade, which he had persistently exposed throughout his life.*[18]

Baker's words, especially those I have italicized for emphasis, were an eloquent comment on the vision of martyrdom implicit in Waller's shaping of the *Last Journals*—through patient endurance and indomitable will to sainthood. Even Baker, most assured about his view of Livingstone as primarily a great African explorer, felt compelled to pay tribute to him as the great East African antislavery crusader.

Baker's writings, however, had made clear his low opinion of Africans, whom he considered to be innately susceptible to idleness and savagery, incapable to raising themselves from their lowly estate unless "specially governed and forced to industry." Livingstone's more pungent views of Baker's opinions had been edited out of his *Last Journals*. In reviewing Livingstone's comments on Africans, which we now know had also been censored, Baker followed his predilections and seized upon any description he felt he could make bear out his own point of view. He thus proclaimed, "Throughout these pages the reader will observe that the negro is painted in his true character. Although Livingstone never loses an opportunity of doing justice to the race when praise is due, he produces so many pictures of their brutality and natural love of homicide and savagedom, that the greatest friend of the black must stand aghast."[19]

Baker conflated the incidents Livingstone recounted, ignoring (perhaps not seeing) the differences between circumstances involving Africans, Arabs, slavers, or enslaved. Of his eight examples of African brutality, their "natural love of homicide and savagedom," three referred to Livingstone's dealings with Africans and five to the treatment of African slaves by Arab merchants. The first case, in fact, involved an unusual exchange of gunfire on the Rovuma River in 1862, during Livingstone's previous Zambezi expedition; the second was a rather general reference to what Baker called, from his own experiences "the usual African troubles . . . his men mutinous," and the third entailed the only instance of desertion by Africans temporarily hired by Livingstone to act as porters. The other five "illustrations" of Baker's point all refer to the abandonment by Arab slavers of Africans too weak from hunger to continue marching in slave gangs.[20]

One can wonder what Baker would have made of the material Waller suppressed. To him, the point was that Africans, *as a racial category*, represented human degradation, the only answer to which was to establish firm "civilized" governments over tribes "that, if left to themselves, will simply revel in brutality." These governments might be those of Christian countries like England or France, or they might even be the more sophisticated Muslim governments of Egypt or the sultan of Zanzibar. In Baker's view, the issue was one of an organized political order versus anarchy. He saw no contradiction in the extensive use of force to crush the slave trade in the cause of fostering the pacific concerns of legitimate commerce. Like Livingstone and other Europeans of his day, he failed to see the functional links between licit and illicit trade.[21]

In contrast, Professor Owen in the *Quarterly Review*, after acknowledging Livingstone as a great humanitarian, set out to share with his readers a clear assessment of the scientific contributions made by Livingstone on his last journey. He briefly described Livingstone's geological, mineralogical, botanical, and zoological contributions to Victorian knowledge. The sheer range of Livingstone's scientific observations over the country he travelled, unknown as it still was to European science, made the reader appreciate his journey as an awesome achievement.[22]

As for Livingstone's ethnographical observations during his seven years' journey, both Owen and Baker understood the importance of stressing how Livingstone's portrayal of life in the interior of Africa might be read for the purpose of future relations between Great Britain and Africa. Baker was characteristically forceful in pressing his views. He declared, "At the same time that we condemn the slave-traders, it must be acknowledged that the brutal Manyuema [sic] deserve no better fate than that of slavery; it appears impossible to transact legitimate business with such savage people." He then concluded, to his own satisfaction, ". . . the whole story of seven years' travel is a repetition of barbarity such as should dispel forever the idea that the African race is naturally docile and ready to welcome the pioneers of civilization."[23]

Owen was not without his own particular brand of Victorian stereotypes about the people of Africa. When Livingstone had described the characteristics of the Waiyau (Yao), he noted that by European standards they uniformly had rather small feet and hands. Professor Owen quoted Livingstone on the subject and noted, succinctly, that the small

Statue of David Livingstone, Victoria Falls. In the heart of the continent, where his hopes for a continuous waterway into the interior were dashed by this great natural wonder, stands this statue as an embodiment of the Livingstone legend. The missionary explorer, wearing peaked cap and rifle, feet firmly planted, eyes gazing forever beyond the horizon, seeking new peoples, new lands, and new pathways, firm, determined, serious, and dedicated. He symbolizes the nineteenth-century faith in the efficacy of self-help, hard work, and progress: Decide on your goal and never swerve from it; God is on your side.

size of these features represented "essentially a character of inferiority. Our evolutionists point to it as common to negroes and apes, more especially as regards the hands."[24] Earlier in his review, this Victorian scientist also remarked, in passing: "The negro is the African form of man, call him as you please, species or variety. . . ."[25] In 1875, such a reference would have reminded many readers of the rather violent controversy that erupted in 1863 over the question of "The Negro's Place in Nature." That year, Dr. James Hunt had dismayed his audience at the Newcastle meeting of the British Association for the Advancement of Science by asserting that the "Negro" was a separate species of human being, half way between the ape and "European man." Hunt had gone on to say, ". . . the Negro becomes more humanized when in his natural subordination to the European than under any other circumstances." "European civilisation," he concluded, "is not suited to the Negro's requirements or character."[26]

Hunt's remarks coincided with his leaving the Ethnological Society to form his own Anthropological Society of London in 1863, attracting to it men like the explorers Winwoode Reade and Richard Burton. The latter's low opinion of "the African character" had been published in 1860 in *The Lake Regions of Central Africa*.[27] This mid-century controversy, which owed some of its edge to the fact that it occurred during the American Civil War, was a matter of great discussion when, in 1864, Livingstone had returned to England from the Zambezi. In writing *The Zambesi and Its Tributaries*, Livingstone felt the need to address the question early in the book:

> We must smile at the heaps of nonsense which have been written about the negro intellect. . . . A complaint as to the poverty of the language is often only a sure proof of the scanty attainments of the complainant. . . . Quite as sensible, if not more pertinent answers will usually be given by Africans to those who know their language, as are obtained from our uneducated poor; . . . a couple of centuries back the ancestors of common people in England . . . were as unenlightened as the Africans are now. . . .[28]

The issue was significant for humanitarians who believed they had a mission to save souls, free slaves, and bring Africans into contact with European civilization. Livingstone returned to the question later in the Zambezi book, asserting, "[W]e do not believe in any incapacity of the African in either mind or heart." He was quite explicit: "In reference to the status of Africans among the nations of the earth, we have seen nothing to justify the notion that they are of a different "breed" or "species" from the most civilized." He believed Africans of the nineteenth century suffered from the same backwardness experienced by any people cut off from the mainstream of civilization. His comparison was with the Irish Catholics pushed to the western edges of their country by the influx of Protestants settled in Ireland by the English government in the seventeenth century. "Centuries of barbarism have had the same deteriorating effects on Africans as . . . on certain of the Irish who were driven, some generations back, to the hills in Ulster and Conaught. . . . This degradation, however, would hardly be given as a reason for holding any race in bondage."[29]

In his review of the *Last Journals*, Baker focused on one remark by Livingstone, "Educated free blacks from a distance are to be avoided: they are expensive, and are too much of gentlemen for your work." In context, Livingstone was reflecting on his experiences in Central Africa with the Universities' Mission as well as on the Nasik trained Africans on his last journey. In Livingstone's eyes, being "too much of gentlemen" carried the implication that free blacks considered themselves "too fine" to do the hard work necessary for missionary labor; in fact, it also meant that Livingstone found them unwilling to obey directions to the letter, to do what they were told without independent and contrary thoughts of their own. Baker, with his own agenda for imposing a strong authority over African peoples, seized upon Livingstone's remark, calling it "a serious warning." For Baker, "if the black when freed and educated is useless . . . to perform his part as missionary to his ignorant brethren in Africa, from whence he himself was liberated, he must be decidedly useless in any other position." With a gravity laced with irony, Baker concluded, "Upon such a question Livingstone is the highest authority, and his unfavourable opinion throws a dark shade upon the prospects of native improvement."[30]

Livingstone had held a different view in 1865, when he started his last journey and he may have inspired a new direction of mission work in East Africa as a result. While staying with Sir Bartle Frere, then governor at Bombay, he discussed alternatives to keeping liberated slaves in India, suggesting that freed slave settlements on the East Coast of Africa might become centers of missionary proselytization. When Frere visited East Africa in 1873, to seek a new antislave trade treaty with the sultan of Zanzibar, he investigated the possibility of such a settlement near Mombasa on behalf of the Church Missionary Society, which managed the Nasik asylum near Bombay.[31] As a result, as he edited the *Last Journals*, Waller was aware that the first CMS settlement for freed slaves was being established at what would be called Freretown. In 1875, the Reverend W. Salter Price, previously in charge of the Sharanpur Christian

Village and orphan asylum at Nasik, was transferred to East Africa to organize the settlement, bringing with him a hundred and fifty of his "Bombay Africans." The object was a training school for African Christian teachers, evangelists, and pastors. By the early 1890s, 921 slaves liberated by the British antislavery squadron had been assigned to the mission, most of them being settled at Freretown.[32]

Livingstone's later reflections and Baker's views about the impossibility of Africans' assuming positions of leadership and responsibility in Africa were symptomatic of a gradual shift in European expectations that became evident by the 1880s. As one of its recent historians has shown, the CMS freed slave settlements of Freretown and Rabai near Mombasa reflected that shift. They were initially established at the "tail end of the 'conversionist' thrust of mid-nineteenth century missionary thinking," which was "positive in its assessment of African capacities for absorbing western civilization and looked forward with optimism to the creation . . . of a self-supporting, self-governing and self-propagating African church."[33]

By the beginning of the 1880s, however, a new paternalism emerged, consonant with Baker's openly racist view that Africans required an external authority to tell them what to do and how to do it. Underlying this change was a new European expansionist spirit, which emphasized the need for direct European involvement in Africa and was accompanied by "a racially defined and pessimistic paternalism." In fact, the freed slave communities on the Mombasa coast developed, as would the British colony in Kenya in the twentieth century, a "caste-like character" in the relationship between two groups, the Bombay Africans and freed slaves on the one hand and the European missionaries on the other, and their "political rights, social roles, economic functions and cultural possibilities were defined essentially on the basis of race."[34] In the 1860s, Livingstone had called for African agency by which to spread the evangelical message into the interior; by the 1880s, African "agents" for Christianity, who viewed themselves as co-workers, found they were looked upon by their European colleagues as merely instruments of policy, not policy makers. The extremist racial anthropology of the 1860s had shifted from displaying a view forcefully rejected by humanitarian agencies to generating an implicit, pseudoscientific permissiveness within mission circles for a cultural arrogance and condescending paternalism consonant with a new imperial era.

The reviews of Livingstone's *Last Journals* by Baker and Owen concluded in characteristically different ways. Having described in some detail the major events of Livingstone's journey, Owen fashioned his final remarks on Waller's carefully worked out death scene, word for word.[35] His meaning was clear: he could not find the words to present this scene in any more telling way. Baker, so very recently returned from his years of employment by Egypt, was concerned with the political fate of East Africa and particularly with the role Great Britain might play there. He therefore offered specific observations about Africa's future:

> Oriental governments may not be immaculate, but they are far superior to that petty negro chiefs, whose only aim in life is to war against and enslave their neighbours. The sultan of Zanzibar is too weak to follow the example of the khedive of Egypt, and annex the country south of the equator to the territory of Uganda (M'tesa), but *should an arrangement be made with a greater power*, he might with assistance effect this object, and become responsible to his supporter for the good government of his territory and the total suppression of the slave trade.
>
> *By such means only can legitimate commerce be established and the slave trade be totally suppressed.* It is simply necessary to read with attention the journals of the lamented Livingstone to be convinced of the utter impossibility of improving the savage tribes of Central Africa by other means than the *strong hand of paternal government*. Humanitarians of a fanatical school, who are not true philanthropists, may object to the blood that must of necessity be shed in a war of annexation; that blood is but a drop in the ocean to the torrents that annually flow in the internecine wars that accompany the slave trade of Central Africa. By annexation those torrents must cease, and when the government is established there will be a foundation for future progress; but *without that government it is idle to preach against the slave trade, or to hope for permanent improvement*.[36]

Baker accepted Livingstone's—and Waller's—underlying message, that the "regeneration" of Africa required help from outside, and translated it into his own imperialist vision. This kind of transmutation was a harbinger of the way others would use the Livingstone legend in the next quarter century.

Just as Baker and Owen brought their own preoccupations and preconceptions to the reading of Livingstone's *Last Journals*, others would find in the Livingstone legend it contained special resonances they, too, could build upon. Two long review articles also appeared in the serious quarterlies devoted primarily to religious subjects, the *British Quarterly Review* and the *London Quarterly Review*. Each journal had a circulation of some 2,000, was priced at six shillings an issue, and could be borrowed at Mudie's. The *British Quarterly Review* "appealed to the educated portions of the Congregationalist and Baptist denominations, mainly Liberal in politics." The *London Quarterly Review* "was the organ of the Methodists, who were the largest of the Dissenting sects. It was read by the educated middle class members and ministers of the denomination, politically tending to conservatism."[37] The denominations of the readers of the two journals made up seventy percent of nonconforming Protestants in the mid-1870s. Politically speaking, these nonconformists were part of Gladstone's new Liberal coalition of 1868, defeated by Disraeli's Conservative party in 1874.

The *British Quarterly* reviewer dwelt at length on the English preeminence in African exploration, in world trade, in colonization, and in the struggle against the slave trade. Considering the book under review, the writer was strangely emphatic in describing as "dull, monotonous, and unprogressive" the nature of the climate and terrain of Africa, as well as "the character, the habits, and the life of the people" of that continent. The implications of these remarks were then stated as clearly as any member of the Anthropological Society might have put it in the previous decade: to develop their "latent powers," Africa and Africans needed "the impulse of a strong civilisation from without. . . ." Africans were "children." Missionaries like Livingstone might express "a very high sense of their capacity, and their moral openness to the influences of Christianity and civilisation," but African development was in an "infantile stage" of human progress and needed "for the present the continual 'episcopacy' of the European."[38]

The *British Quarterly* reviewer then expanded on the import of Livingstone's death in Africa. "The men who drop with their work half done *bequeath a great inspiration as their legacy*." "Such lives as Livingstone's," he continued, "are always germinant. . . . He did more by dying *in* Africa and *for* Africa, than he could possibly have accomplished had he been spared to return in triumph. . . . his death had bequeathed the work of African exploration and civilisation as *a sacred legacy to his country*. . . . The life which Livingstone offered for the salvation of Africa, like a greater life, is a pledge and a prophecy of its redemption." Livingstone was only the last of a long line of English explorers of Africa who "claim[ed] Africa as the field of English culture and civilising Christianising energy. England, too," the writer continued, "has always held the foremost place among the nations which are now happily combined in the endeavour to close 'the open sore of the world'—the African slave trade." To this was added, "And it is right that it should be so. England is the great colonist of the modern world."[39] The reviewer referred at length to Baker's recent experiences in Africa and juxtaposed the approaches of the two travellers:

> Commerce first, the missionary after, is Sir S. Baker's formula. The missionary first, and commerce after, is the formula of those who have lived among the African people. They are emphatically a race to be won by loving personal influence. . . . Compare the results of such work . . . on the African character, with the fruits of brilliant martial expeditions . . . compare the bloody march to Gondokoro, with the 'death scene' in Livingstone's 'Last Journals,' and the heroic march to the coast, and you have a fair key to what the two methods are likely to accomplish for the regeneration of the African race."[40]

The writer in the *London Quarterly Review* addressed the book more closely. The review dwelt at great length on Livingstone's terrible physical ailments once he had lost his medicine chest: bouts of Africa fever, pneumonia which made it impossible for him to walk, irritable eating ulcers on his feet, loss of appetite, violent diarrhea, problems with his bowels, chronic dysentery, and haemorrhagic discharges. The reader felt awe that the Doctor, "wearied, worn, but still courageous," could have lasted the seven years of his journey. By April 1873, "pale, bloodless, and weak from bleeding profusely," Livingstone felt it was too painful even to be carried. Waller's description of the death scene, quoted at length by the reviewer, came almost as a blessed release of the weary frame, and Waller's imagery captured that final sense of calm: "In the attitude of prayer he passed away." Susi and Chuma "were appointed chiefs," resisted Cameron's suggestion to bury the body at Unyanyembe, could not resist his taking over Livingstone's instruments, and at last handed over "their dead master to his own countrymen." "It was a worthy sequel to the history of a great traveller, and is an evidence of the respect and affection with which he ever inspired those with whom he was brought into association."[41]

After the story of this martyrdom, the *London Quarterly* reviewer focused on Livingstone's evidence that the greatest hindrance to his work was the slave trade. This review, like the one in the *British Quarterly*, quoted at length from the passage describing the massacre of the Manyema market women, but added as well Livingstone's despair on meeting slaves in heavy yokes, slaves tied by the neck to trees and left to die, the scattered skulls and bones of those who had died, and the special slaves' disease of "broken-heartedness."

The *London Quarterly* writer emphasized Livingstone's "intense religiousness. . . . He was not a mere scientific geographer. There was a noble spiritual purpose ever animating his soul and leading him out to the great work of his life." The reviewer noted Livingstone's careful observance of the Sabbath and cited his remarks each New Year's Day and birthday, rededicating his spirit to the divine purpose. Livingstone's report that he had read the Bible four times in Manyema country was quoted as proof of "intense religiousness." Finally, the legend shines forth: "Livingstone, by his unshaken fortitude, his unwavering determination, his lofty purpose, and his deep religiousness has gathered about his name a high honour. . . . Through his efforts the slave trade has received a heavy blow, and right jealously will British people see to it that the treaties which have been entered into shall be kept."[42]

Livingstone's *Last Journals* were published by Harper & Brothers in New York in 1875 and carefully reviewed in *Appleton's Journal*, the *Canadian Monthly and National Review*, and in *Harper's Magazine*. For my purposes, a more important analysis was written two years later, in 1877, in the *North American Review*, published in Boston. The writer was Laurence Oliphant, a major journalist and sometime private secretary to Lord Elgin on diplomatic missions to Washington and China. He included the *Last Journals* in a long review article on "African Explorers." His other texts were the travel books of Speke, Grant, Cameron, and the American Charles Chaillé-Long and the letters of H. M. Stanley to the *New York Herald* since 1874. Oliphant surveyed the results of geographical discovery in Africa over the previous twenty-five years. The "large blank space marked 'unexplored' " on the maps of Equatorial Africa of his youth had all given way; the great geographical puzzles of the Africa continent were solved. He intended, therefore, to award two laurels for the greatest achievements. To Speke went the prize for discovering Victoria Nyanza, for it had proven to be, as he had claimed, the source of the Nile. To Livingstone went the other prize, for contributing the greatest extent of geographical knowledge on the interior of Africa by his three great journeys. In Oliphant's words:

With Livingstone's last journals fresh in the memory of our readers, we need not recapitulate his discoveries. . . . To him belongs the honor of having first crossed Africa between the tropics. . . . He first revealed to us the majestic [Victoria] falls of the Zambesi, showed our missionaries the way to the unknown lakes of Shire and Nyassa and is still the sole explorer of that singular lacustrine region through which the Congo flows, rising in Lake Bangweolo [sic], and so through Lake Moero [sic], till it joins the other branch which

Statue of David Livingstone, Royal Geographical Society, 1953. Erected on the north wall of the building in Kensington Gore just as the British Empire in Africa and elsewhere was beginning to come apart. The stance is more informal; the cloth coat rests easily over the arm and the walking stick replaces a rifle. The peaked cap and determined look remain: it is the composed and unshakable stance that created British achievements in the past, whether in exploration, proselytization, empire-building, or commerce. The message is simple: Only emulate heroes of this stamp and the nation will maintain its place in the world.

flows through the Lake Kassali of Cameron. It may be said of Livingstone, that no man ever contributed so large an unknown portion of the earth's surface to the cause of geography, while *his unvarying benevolence and gentleness have left him a reputation among the savage tribes of Africa as remarkable as that which he has achieved among his own countrymen for undaunted courage and indomitable perseverance.*[43]

There, in cameo, was the Livingstone legend. All the reviewers came away from reading the *Last Journals* with a sense of the remarkable achievements of a remarkable man, a Victorian hero, a gentle missionary, and a martyr to the cause of antislavery. The particular features of the book carefully constructed by Waller, the transitional notes, the explanations, the death scene, and the stirring journey to the coast with Livingstone's body, all emerge as a backdrop to the profile of an extraordinary life lived among extraordinary scenes and dedicated to a great humanitarian cause.

What remains to be seen is how Livingstone's countrymen used that legend. Before we look at its impact on the two decades of imperialist expansion that followed his death, we must focus on the ideas of the Livingstone's legacy that inform and energize his legend into a vehicle for empire in Africa. The seeds were clearly there in the reception of the *Last Journals*, whether the reader was politically Liberal or Conservative, an Anglican or a nonconformist, an explorer or a scientist. No message is heard if it falls on deaf ears. If the Livingstone legend helped release British energies and direct them to East Africa, there were actors ready to play their parts. Implicit in Livingstone's conviction that Great Britain had a role to play in "opening up" Africa to new influences was a link between humanitarian causes and practical concerns of British trade and British diplomacy. The activities that were designed specifically to honor Livingstone's memory in Central Africa would develop a vitality of their own and produce a ripple effect on the interest and commitment of others to help them continue. Waller would play yet another part in the chain of actions that led the British more deeply into an involvement with East and Central Africa. This was the kind of intervention that Livingstone, much earlier, came to believe was Africa's only chance for social, economic, and spiritual progress. Played out to its logical end, therefore, the British antislavery impulse led to empire.

Notes

1. "Dr. Livingstone's Last Journals," Ledger Journals, 1: fol. 395–96 (1874 Dec. 30 – 1885 June 30); 2: fol. 278 (1886 June 30 – 1891 June 30); 3: fol. 366 (1893 June 30 – 1899 June 30); CIH: fol. 322 (1901 June 29 – 1913 Apr. 30); and R: fol. 4 (1914 Apr. 30 – 1929 Apr. 26), JMPA. The last sales entry was December 31, 1923. The final entry was dated April 26, 1929, and involved a permission fee paid by J. M. Dent & Son for publishing extracts in an anthology on "African Exploration." The first page of entries has "T. S. Livingstone £20 – –" with a circle around the sum and the words "to come out" written alongside, Ledger Journal 1: fol. 395. Apparently Tom Livingstone was initially to receive payment for his services on the manuscript and proof. From the beginning, Waller expected the sales of the book to be far better and was severely disappointed. After four weeks, he noted in his diary, "The book sells slowly." Eight months later, he was still dissatisfied: "They have barely sold 7,500 copies." Diary of Horace Waller, January 12, September 10, 1875, WPYDS.

2. Two account sheets, dated Glasgow, Nov. 1 and 2, 1875, indicated that the publishers paid to the Trustees of Dr. Livingstone's estate the sums of £87/18/10 as final profits on the cheap abridged edition of *Missionary Travels* (first published in 1861) and £3,314/4/8 for the *Last Journals*, only £1,885/2/5 representing direct two thirds profit due the author.

On the best-selling character of *Missionary Travels*, see Altick, *The English Common Reader*, 388. Of the 4,603 new books published in England in 1874, 244, or 5.3 percent, were classified "Voyages and Travels" by the Publishers' Circular reports, *Journal of the Statistical Society* 38 (1875): 91. This category accounted for five to six percent of new books each year in the last decades of the century. The best-selling *Missionary Travels* earned its author upwards of £8,500. *The Zambesi and Its Tributaries*, published in 1865, proved to be the least successful of Livingstone's works in terms of sales. John Murray was probably not surprised by its reception. He initially ordered only 5,000 bound copies in 1865, and though he had only 212 copies left by June 1866, he printed no more. He sold his last twenty copies of this edition of the book in 1879. It earned less than £740 for Livingstone in its first year. By arranging for the printing of a new cheap, abridged edition of the Zambezi book as vol. 2 of a set with *Missionary Travels*, in 1875 Murray was capitalizing on whatever new readership was stimulated by the publication of the *Last Journals*. Ledger Journals, "Livingstone's . . . South Africa" through "Third Edition" fol. 422 (1857–58); "South Africa abridged," fol.

166 (1861-67); " 'South Africa' abridged," fol. 305 (1872-76); "Livingstone's Zambezi," fol. 357 (1865-79); "Livingstone's First and Second Visits 2 vols." fol. 306 (1876-82) and fol. 203-4 (1883-92); fol. 321 (1901-9); fol. 344 (1910-16); "Livingstone's First Expedition to Africa," fol. 290 (1899-1904); fol. 269 (1913-1924), JMPA. The last folio notes the book was now "Mr. M's property."

3. Bennett, "David Livingstone," in Rotberg, *Africa and Its Explorers,* 46, 57, 59.

4. Max Gluckman, "As Men Are Everywhere Else," *African Social Research: Journal of the Institute for Social Research, University of Zambia* (formerly *Rhodes-Livingstone Journal*) 20 (1956): 68-73. The essay is a review of Frank Debenham, *The Way to Ilala: David Livingstone's Pilgrimage* (London, 1955) and Jack Simmons, *Livingstone and Africa* (London, 1955). The quote cited by Gluckman is a remark by Simmons.

5. Alvar Éllegard, "The Readership of the Periodical Press in Mid-Victorian Britain: 2. Directory," *Victorian Periodicals Newsletter,* no. 13 (September 1971): 9, 10-11. "Livingstone's Last Journals," *The Saturday Review* 38, no. 999 (December 19, 1874): 801-2.

6. Diary of Horace Waller, January 7, 1875, WPYDS; *The Times,* January 7, 1875, 7. The original cover illustration reproduced the engraving which appeared in vol. 2, between 268 and 269. The review had some negative aspects. It commented on the dubious nature of Livingstone's proposed solution to the problem of the Nile sources (the fountains of Herodotus); and referred to comments by Livingstone that might "provoke ridicule" were it not for the "reverence which marks every serious line he wrote." The reviewer also pointed out (by implication suggesting that the editor had ignored them) there were "apparent contradictions in statements which seem very precise"—for example, about the existence of cannibalism—which "would probably have been explained by the writer if he had been spared to put his notes into shape. . . ." *The Times,* January 7, 1875, 7.

Five weeks later, Waller noted an unfavorable review by a weekly magazine: "An infamous review of Livingstone's Journals in the Academy today abusing me in the most transparent style - signed by Birdwood." Diary of Horace Waller, February 13, 1875, WPYDS. What Waller had read was: "These Journals are the best work that we have ever had from Livingstone's pen, but it is impossible to condemn too severely the careless, vulgar, and ignorant way in which Mr. Waller has edited them. Nothing can exceed the bad taste of his preface, and of the remarks, within brackets, which he constantly obtrudes between the paragraphs of Livingstone's diary." Waller's offences were the "utter want of delicacy" in publishing Livingstone's private prayers ("those hallowed utterances of the deepest feelings of his nature"); his failure in making clear why Livingstone undertook this journey, what he wished to accomplish by his different "excursions," and how his discoveries fit into those of other geographers. Birdwood was also incensed that, "Mr. Waller throughout the two volumes entirely ignores the name of Sir Roderick Murchison." Birdwood's wrath did not extend to Livingstone, however: "These journals are a most interesting contribution to our knowledge of Inner Africa." But the illustrations were "very poor"; "the likeness of Livingstone trashy and theatrical"; and the map "already obsolete" due to Cameron's "recovery of Livingstone's route map from the coast to Nyassa. . . ." Yet it is worth noting that Birdwood found the "narrative of Livingstone's last sufferings and death, and of the transport of his body to Zanzibar . . . admirably elaborated by Mr. Waller. He tells [it] in fitting language. . . ." The reviewer was clearly a geographer in the thick of contemporary controversies, as Waller noted in his reference to the writer's "transparent style." George Birdwood, "Last Journals of David Livingstone," *Academy* 7 n.s., no. 145 (February 13, 1875): 159-61.

The truism that what reviewers take from a book is what they bring to a book was also borne out by an appreciative and lengthy review in *Mission Life*, a journal whose editor knew Waller in the context of his missionary work in Central Africa. In contrast to writer in *The Times*, for example, who made a point of noting, "In the Journals before us there is scarcely a trace of missionary exertion—none of missionary success," the writer in *Mission Life* reported that "no village is visited without an endeavour (often successful) to interest its chief and inhabitants in the great truths of the Christian faith." "Livingstone's Last Journals," *Mission Life: An Illustrated Magazine of Home and Foreign Church Work* 6 n.s. (1875): 242.

7. Éllegard, "Readership of the Periodical Press," 13–14. [Richard Owen], "Last Journals of David Livingstone," *Quarterly Review* 138 (1875): 498–528 (hereafter, Owen, *Quarterly*). That Owen was the author of the article was confirmed by Virginia Murray, Archivist at John Murray, Publisher, personal communication.

8. Sam[uel] W. Baker, "The Last Journals of David Livingstone," *Macmillan's Magazine* 31 (1874–1875): 281–92 (hereafter, Baker, *Macmillan's*); Éllegard, "Readership of the periodical press," 18–19; Altick, *The English Common Reader*, 359. Baker's review appeared in *Littell's Living Age* 124 (1875): 617–27, and *Eclectic Magazine* 53 (1875): 181ff. See *Livingstone and Stanley Bibliography*, 51. Both periodicals re-

printed articles of general interest to a wide audience. *Macmillan's Magazine* had also published articles by Baker on "Savage Warfare," and "Slavery and the Slave Trade," in January and July 1874.

9. *LJDL*, 2:298-99 (facsimile pages), 297-98 (text entries, April 19-20, 1873). Compare: "Molilamo" (*LJDL*, 2:303) and "Mulilamo" (*LJDL*, 2:305, 307). The latter spelling represents editorial haste. The "Editor's Note" that accompanied the first appearance of this name explained: "The name Molilamo is allowed to stand, but in Dr. Livingstone's map we find it Lulimala, and the men confirm this pronunciation. —Ed." Baker ignored the fact that Waller understood the problem.

10. Owen, *Quarterly*, 498.

11. Baker, *Macmillan's*, 281.

12. Éllegard, "Readership of the Periodical Press," 13. *Whig* in this context is understood to mean the old aristocratic or landed interest of the new Liberal party.

13. [G. W. Dasent], "The Heart of Africa and the Slave Trade," *Edinburgh Review* 141 (January 1875): 211, 242. Author identification: *Wellesley Index of Victorian Periodicals*, vol. 2. Sir George Webbe Dasent (1817-1896) was a scholar of Old Norse and associate editor of *The Times* until he accepted a job in the civil service in 1870; he was a brother-in-law of John Delane, the editor. He also reviewed the letters of *Colonel Gordon in Central Africa*, ed. G. Birkbeck Hill, in October 1881, for the *Edinburgh Review*. He is characterized by the *Dictionary of National Biography*, as a "well-known figure in London society." *DNB* 22, *Supplement*, 536-37. Modern scholars have credited Khedive Ismail with more sincerity with regard to fighting the slave trade than believed to be the case by many nineteenth-century British observers. See: Peter M. Holt, *A Modern History of the Sudan: From the Funj Sultanate to the Present Day* (London, 1961); Robert O. Collins, "Samuel White Baker: Prospero in Purgatory," in Rotberg, *Africa and Its Explorers*, 163-64.

14. Hall, *Lovers on the Nile*, 14.

15. Collins, "Samuel White Baker," in Rotberg, *Africa and Its Explorers*, 164.

16. Hall, *Lovers on the Nile*, 181ff. and 202; Collins, "Samuel White Baker," in Rotberg, *Africa and Its Explorers*, 170-71.

17. Collins, "Samuel White Baker," in Rotberg, *Africa and Its Explorers*, 172.

18. Baker, *Macmillan's*, 291, emphasis added.

19. *Ibid.*, 283.

20. *Ibid.*, 283-84.

21. *Ibid.*, 292. See Introduction, n. 14, above.

22. Owen, *Quarterly*, 500–17, *passim*. For a modern assessment, see D. J. Siddle, "David Livingstone: Mid-Victorian Field Scientist," in *David Livingstone and Africa*, 87–99.

23. Baker, *Macmillan's*, 287–88.

24. Owen, *Quarterly*, 517.

25. *Ibid.*, 515.

26. James Hunt, "On the Negro's Place in Nature," *Memoirs of the Anthropological Society of London* 1 (1863–1864): 1–64. According to the West African traveller Winwood Reade, the audience at Hunt's lecture stirred uncomfortably as he first delivered these views, and finally broke out in undignified hisses. W. Winwood Reade, *Savage Africa* (London, 1864), 509n. On Hunt and his society, see Douglas A. Lorimer, *Colour, Class and the Victorians: English Attitudes to the Negro in the Mid-Nineteenth Century* (New York, 1978), chap. 7; Charles H. Lyons, *To Wash an Aethiop White: British Ideas About Black African Educability, 1530–1960* (New York, 1975), chap. 4; and John W. Burrow, *Evolution and Society. A Study in Victorian Social Theory* (Cambridge, 1966), 118–35.

27. Hunt's views may have been reinforced by Burton's. Burton referred to the "rudimental mind" of Africans, who had neither progressed nor retrograded, demonstrating their "apparent incapacity for improvement." Richard Burton, *The Lake Regions of Central Africa*, 2 vols. (London, 1860), 2:324–25, 337. Burton presents a paradox. He was a fine Oriental linguist and ethnographer who appreciated Arabs and despised Africans. Of the latter, he wrote, "In intellect the East African is sterile and incult, apparently unprogressive and unfit for change." Quoted by Caroline Oliver, "Richard Burton: The African Years," in Rotberg, *Africa and Its Explorers*, 86.

28. *Zambesi and Its Tributaries*, 77–78. For Livingstone's views on Africa and evolutionary progress, see below, chap. 7.

29. *Ibid.*, 624–25. For examples of missionary and Anti-Slavery Society editorials challenging the validity of the views expressed by Hunt and his new "anthropologists," see the *Church Missionary Intelligencer* 1, n.s. (1865): 193, and the *Anti-Slavery Reporter*, September 16, 1867, 208. Compare Livingstone's other comments about the Irish, chap. 3, n. 41, and p. 173 above.

30. Baker, *Macmillan's*, 290.

31. Oliver, *The Missionary Factor*, 19–25; see below, chap. 8. The 1871 Select Committee of the House of Commons on the Slave Trade on the East Coast of Africa raised the question of using Zanzibar or some mainland location as a depot for adult slaves liberated by the East Coast antislavery squadron. Waller gave evidence, stating that Dr. Kirk had

recently written him to suggest that "a station might be found on the mainland near to Zanzibar, where Europeans could live in perfect health, and where, if it were necessary, liberated slaves could be sent to be kept under safe supervision." The CMS lay secretary Edward Hutchinson declared that his society had been investigating the question for four years and at that time favored a freed slave settlement, especially for educating children, on the Seychelles Islands. "Extracts from Evidence Taken before the Select Committee of the House of Commons," Appendix in G. L. Sullivan, *Dhow Chasing in Zanzibar Waters and on the East Coast of Africa* (1873; reprint, London, 1968), 297–380. Waller's statement was made in answer to Q. 974; for Hutchinson's evidence, see Q. 1337, Sullivan, *Dhow Chasing*, 375, 317. On the 1871 Committee, see Coupland, *Exploitation of East Africa*, 165–67. Baroness Angela Burdett-Coutts, who befriended Livingstone in 1856 on his return from Africa, contributed £1,000 to the Church Missionary Society in November 1872 to help launch a special appeal aimed at establishing a freed slave settlement on the coast opposite Zanzibar. Eugene Stock, *The History of the Church Missionary Society*, 3 vols. (London, 1899), 3:76.

32. Harris, *African Presence in Asia*, 75–76; Temu, *British Protestant Missions*, 12–13; Bennett, "Church Missionary Society at Mombasa," in Butler, *Papers in African History*, vol. 1, 162–66; and Strayer, *Making of Mission Communities in East Africa*, 14–15.

33. Strayer, *Making of Mission Communities in East Africa*, 8.

34. *Ibid.*, 9, 15, and chap. 2; see Temu, *British Protestant Missions*, chap. 4.

35. Owen, *Quarterly*, 528.

36. Baker, *Macmillan's*, 292, emphasis throughout added.

37. Ellegård, "Readership of the Periodical Press," 15–17. Statistics kept by these denominations for 1875 indicate a membership of 358,062 for the Wesleyan Methodists; 263,729 for the Baptists; and 366,090 for the Congregationalists, making a total of 987,881 out of a total of 1,417,790, or 70 percent of all nonconforming Protestants. The Church of England kept no comparable statistics. At the time of the church attendance census of 1851, however, it recorded a slight majority over nonconforming sects. Owen Chadwick, *The Victorian Church, Part 2* (New York, 1970), 221, 227.

38. "Livingstone's 'Last Journals,' " *British Quarterly Review* 61 (January and April 1875): 398–401.

39. *Ibid.*, 397–99, emphasis added, except for the words *in* and *for*.

40. *Ibid.*, 417, 419–20. A number of remarks—Tom Livingstone's name had been omitted from the Introduction credits; praise was due "Moffat and Livingstone" and the London Missionary Society; Stanley's

sentiments to Livingstone were "tender and almost filial"; and Livingstone's boxes should not have been opened on their way home—suggest the reviewer had some inside knowledge of the Livingstones and Moffats. This seems confirmed by a letter from Dr. Robert Moffat to Murray, May 12, 1875, asking for another copy of the *Last Journals* because he had lent his to the "reviewer in the British Quarterly." JMPA.

   41. "*The Last Journals of David Livingstone. . . .*" London *Quarterly Review* 44 (April and July 1875): 40–52.

   42. *Ibid.*, 56–60, 61.

   43. "Livingstone's Last Journey," *Appleton's Journal* 13 (1875): 97–102, 129–34, 161–65, 193–97; "Livingstone's *Last Journals,*" *Canadian Monthly and National Review* 7 (1875): 254–63; and "The *Last Journals* of David Livingstone," *Harper's Magazine* 50 (1874–75): 544–58. See *Livingstone and Stanley Bibliography*, 50. Laurence Oliphant, "African Explorers," *North American Review* 124 (1877): 401–2, emphasis added.

§ 7 &

David Livingstone and Africa: The Legacy

The legend of David Livingstone's life and work, fixed in public memory by his death, interment in Westminster Abbey, and the publication of his *Last Journals*, left a three-part legacy culminating in the creation of a British Empire in East and Central Africa. First, and most compelling, was his exposure of the prevalence and cruelty of the East African slave trade. Second was his vision of Christian missions committed to the material well-being as well as the spiritual regeneration of Africans. Third was his belief that the production of raw materials in great demand in the world market—such as cotton—and the introduction of mechanization—technological advances such as improved sugar mills and steamships—would stimulate sufficient legitimate commerce to drive out the slave trade. This economic revolution, as Livingstone envisioned it, would occur when Africans were persuaded that they would prosper by keeping their labor power at home to make use of improved systems of processing (milling) food and other resources, sending these products into the world market by means of mechanized transportation. Livingstone aimed at a double assault on African poverty and spiritual "ignorance." His message was simple: raise African living standards by bringing Africa within the worldwide system of British trade and African hearts will open to the message of Christian salvation.[1]

Any of the three parts of Livingstone's legacy might be the focus of the energies of any of a number of groups, with the expectation that the realization of one facilitated the achievement of the others. In addition, each part of the legacy implied a reliance on the British flag to sustain it over a long time. The renewed commitment of British officials and philanthropic circles to the suppression of the slave trade of East and Central Africa, for example, required increasing British intervention. By the late 1880s, the belief that British leadership was critical to end the slave trade underlay an insistence on a British presence in specific East and Central African areas against the claims of other European nations. Similarly, where no strong African ruler existed, the missionaries found themselves with questions of civil jurisdiction and secular punishments for Africans who operated under mission authority. Such missionaries became, in effect, rival chiefs, while remaining British subjects who felt justified in calling for the protection of consuls and metropolitan governments to sustain them.

British investment in steamships, telegraph lines, road building, and railroad schemes carried the same kind of assumption. Those who initiated these ventures believed they were entitled to government encouragement, for they saw their efforts as mutually beneficial to the African and British economies.[2] Once such British investment existed in a specific region of East or Central Africa—such as the Malawi–Tanganyika area supplied by the African Lakes Company or the Lake Victoria–Uganda region, the concern of the Imperial British East Africa Company—it was anticipated that British governments would protect such enterprise from being brought under the control of any other European power through negotiations at conference tables. In the event— as the Imperial British East Africa Company would learn in the early 1890s—there was a gap between the expectation of government subsidies by capitalists who viewed their investments as nationalist-inspired philanthropy and the attitude of governments, which weighed pleas for monetary help against their own assessment of national priorities and the interests of British tax payers. Public opinion could be rallied, however, to assert where national duty lay in terms of British trade, the slave trade, and missionaries. As we shall see, these popular expressions of a British mission in Africa would follow, to a significant degree, the ideas first publicized by Livingstone and, after his death, identified with his name.

This chapter reviews the formulation of Livingstone's theories about Africa and African development. It traces the growing conviction on Livingstone's part that to open African hearts to the message of Christian salvation it was necessary to help Africans develop economically. He desired a new era of civilization in Africa; his measure of "civilization" was the world he had left behind in Great Britain. It was a world characterized by advanced agricultural techniques, technology, and industrial development.

The next two chapters will highlight the operation of Livingstone's legacy in the two decades following his death and the publication of his *Last Journals*. They focus on Horace Waller as a conduit for the Livingstone legend, for he was uniquely equipped for this task as a knowledgeable and respected figure in his own right in Victorian philanthropic circles. Invoking Livingstone—whether for fighting the slave trade, founding new missions, introducing legitimate commerce, setting steamships upon the interior lakes, or building new roads—made a cause worthy, whatever its merits. Maintaining these particular memorials to Livingstone in East and Central Africa then became further justification for British imperialism.

Livingstone's memory acted as a moral imperative for a national mission. To turn away from this national duty, to allow Livingstone's legacy to be lost, would constitute rejection of Britain's role as the upholder of serious ethical ideals in world politics, and in particular its century-long commitment to end the slave trade everywhere in the world. Within twenty years of Livingstone's death, his name would be synonymous with the imperial cause in East and Central Africa. This equation was constructed on a series of mistaken assumptions. First, European contact promised mutual benefit and prosperity to Africans and Europeans. Second, ending the slave trade would, automatically, redirect African economies into "legitimate" trade. Third, legitimate commerce would automatically end domestic slavery. Fourth, trade in raw materials and industrial goods would create stable economies in Africa. Fifth, material well-being would foster the widespread adoption of Christianity. Sixth, a Christianized, economically developed Africa would operate as an equal in international exchanges. Livingstone had fewer illusions about the difficulties that existed in realizing his goals for Africa than most of those who invoked his "legacy." The assumptions implied by his recommendations were rarely questioned. No effective propaganda for national action is ever complicated by qualifying clauses. Those who sought to honor Livingstone by carrying forward his work in Africa found it enough to invoke his name to convince potential backers that their plans were part of a great, ongoing moral crusade.[3]

Ultimately, the Livingstone legend was used to call into being a new kind of British Empire. As Tim Jeal notes, the prevailing image of empire in Great Britain at the time of Livingstone's death was of white settlement colonies. Direct British Indian rule had been established only fifteen years before, in 1858, when a major revolt among Indian troops led the crown to dismiss the East India Company, which had exercised supervision over a large part of the subcontinent for a century. The comparatively recent demise of that chartered trading company as a ruler of foreign territory may provide the reason why, over the next two decades, so many British observers of the African scene entertained the idea that royally chartered companies in Africa could provide a means of exerting British influence without formal colonies. In the early 1870s, "empire" was still viewed as synonymous with the British settlement colonies: Canada, New Zealand, the Australian colonies, and Cape Colony and Natal in South Africa. Jeal concludes: "Events in Africa between 1874 and 1894 forced a reassessment of what the Empire really was. The addition of new African colonies, peopled not by whites but by blacks, changed the whole balance of the Empire and inevitably altered the way people in Britain viewed it. This new view was significantly influenced by Livingstone's ideas and those of his missionary successors."[4]

Jeal further suggests that sentiments by Joseph Chamberlain after the annexation of Uganda in 1894, referring to Britain's "manifest destiny" to be "a great civilizing power," were but the latter-day echo of Livingstone's 1858 instructions to the members of his Zambezi Expedition: "We come among them as members of a superior race and servants of a Government that desires to elevate the more degraded portions of the human family . . . to become harbingers of peace to a hitherto distracted and trodden down race."[5]

Between 1858 and 1894, many in Britain expressed similar views. Livingstone's acceptance of the inferiority of Africans was, in fact, the product of a long history of fallacies about racial difference.[6] Livingstone's attitudes were significant because of his belief that cultural differences did not preclude either the spiritual or material rebirth or "regeneration" of Africa on a higher level of human development. He treated his government-sponsored expedition to the Zambezi as an official endorsement of this position. By 1894, Chamberlain's imperial vision diverged from Livingstone's in a fundamental way. Livingstone fully expected Africans, once brought within the worldwide networks of British trade and introduced to Christianity, would develop as autonomous agents. He envisioned white settlement colonies in highland locations, spurring African economic development and spiritual enlightenment; but he hardly saw Africa, as Chamberlain did, as a vast agricultural estate whose ownership and management should be under formal British control. For Livingstone, British influence in Africa meant ending the export trade in slaves, developing indigenous material wealth, fostering new varieties of legitimate commerce, and introducing the gospel. He envisioned British settlements, lay and missionary, as models of conduct, industry, and religious salvation. Despite his knowledge of Boer treatment of Africans in South Africa—and his antipathy to Baker's push southward toward Uganda on behalf of Egypt—Livingstone never seems to have anticipated fully the potential exploitation of Africans that might arise from other white rule, certainly not from British rule.

Roland Oliver, in a pioneering study of this subject in 1952, points out that Livingstone's claim in the 1840s, that it was the duty of missionaries to introduce "the arts and sciences of civilisation" as a means of spiritual regeneration, was not part of the prevailing evangelical tradition. He notes that Livingstone's proposition that a missionary "should consciously aim at the indirect results, and press on into unexplored regions" was "quite startling." In the course of his travels, Oliver states, Livingstone concluded that "the chief hindrance to the Gospel lay not so much in the refractory wills of individuals as in the great social evils of African society, in the poverty which bound it to material ambitions, [and] in the ignorance which surrounded it with fear. . . ." Both poverty and fear led to the clash of tribal groups, competing for human and nutritional resources. Livingstone believed this situation created social isolation, and that in turn prevented cultural diffusion. Trade would be the solution. Livingstone's remedy was the Zambezi Expedition, the purpose of which was to bring to Africa "the impact of civilised and Christian society as a whole." According to Oliver, the consequences of Livingstone's analysis on reshaping the nineteenth-century missionary world were nothing short of revolutionary.[7]

Livingstone's ideas were by no means original. His theories gained prominence as a source of inspiration to others because of his persistence in bringing them forward at a time that proved receptive to them. The timing was a critical factor in capturing the attention of the public, as a brief summary of the development of his ideas reveals. Livingstone's opinions were developed in the 1830s, within the framework of the successful British abolitionist movement; they were shaped within an evolutionist expectation of linear progress that prevailed during this period. Part of this notion of progress was the optimistic expectation of what might be achieved by applying science to the "arts of life."[8]

The Emancipation Act of 1833 was not seen by its most active supporters as the end of the antislavery movement. The internal logic of the antislavery position, as Harold Temperley has emphasized, carried the concerns of abolitionists beyond national or imperial borders: "If slavery were morally wrong, as they and a large segment of the British public were now convinced it was, then the nationality of the slaveholder became a matter of secondary importance as compared with the obligation to act."[9] At the time of the World Anti-Slavery Convention held in London in 1840, estimates were assembled for the extent of slavery that continued to exist: in the United States (2,750,000); Texas (25,000); Brazil (2,500,000); Spanish colonies (600,000); French colonies (30,000); Dutch colonies (70,000); and Danish and Swedish colonies (30,000). These figures did not include the several millions more in the British East Indies and the areas under French, Dutch, and Portuguese control in Asia and Africa, much less those independent societies in the Middle and Far East and Africa.[10] This view of the world as the reformer's stage remained important through the century. During the first years of the Civil War in the United States, 1861–1863, opinions diverged widely among the anti-slavery ranks in Great Britain about the appropriate strategy to follow, preventing a concerted pressure on the government—the economic and social predilections of which were Southern—to aid the Northern cause. By 1864–1865, however, sufficient unity was achieved to ensure that no official move could be made to recognize the Confederacy.[11] One of the marks of a revived British and Foreign Anti-Slavery Society from the late 1860s was its ability to stir public agitation and pressure the government to take an active role once more to end the slave trade in Egypt and East and Central Africa.

British antislavery advocates in the late 1830s, conscious that it was critical not to rest upon their laurels, created new societies to serve new purposes, among them the British and Foreign Anti-Slavery Society and the African Civilization Society. The latter was organized in 1840 by Thomas Fowell Buxton, William Wilberforce's successor as public spokesman for the abolition movement. Buxton published two books dealing with the slave trade: *The African Slave Trade* (1839) and *The Remedy: Being a Sequel to the African Slave Trade* (1840). He argued that despite the efforts of the British government to patrol the West and South African coasts, the African slave trade continued to grow. Buxton's remedy was to teach Africans, in particular African chiefs, to exploit their natural resources by encouraging more extensive agriculture for both home consumption and foreign export, with the emphasis on legitimate trade.

Buxton was a publicist. Underlying the logic of his remedy lay misconceptions regarding the role of chiefs in African society as well as various patterns of cultivation in Africa. Nor, as Philip Curtin notes about other British observers from the late eighteenth century into the nineteenth century, did he consider "the relationship between shifting cultivation and land tenure—and the influence of both on African concepts of real and personal property."[12] The failure to understand the basic structures in African societies, already mentioned in the case of slavery, persisted throughout the century and framed a great deal of cross-cultural misapprehension on the part of Europeans, who usually assumed they could transfer the concepts of their own world into the African scene. To the extent that Europeans understood that fundamental differences existed in the arrangements of African cultures, they sought to bring them into conformity with European concepts, structures, and ideals.[13] Africans were to be "reborn" in a European image.

Buxton proposed a strategy reminiscent of early commercial ventures to India and the New World, updated in the light of recent British technology: trading posts, steamships to carry goods on African rivers, and European participation for keeping the peace and setting up model agricultural farms. In sum, in Temperley's words: "Under British tutelage—but not, he was careful to add, under British dominion—the Africans would be raised from their existing state of poverty and barbarism to one of prosperity and enlightenment."[14] The role of the British government in Buxton's plans was to negotiate with African chiefs treaties that would ensure they would end the slave trade and keep the peace. Thereafter, it would be left to private individuals to build the trading posts, set up the experimental farms, and "use all the means that experience may point out, for a profitable and successful employment of British skill and capital in the African continent."[15] In this way, the British spirit of enterprise, which had linked so much of the world with British commerce in the early modern era, could be left to work out the mutually beneficial goals of enlightened self-interest. The strategy that had worked under mercantilism could be adapted to the new philosophies of utilitarianism, free trade, and the application of science to the "arts of life."

During the late 1830s, David Livingstone was in London completing his medical and theological training under the aegis of the London Missionary Society. Having changed his proposed field of labor from China to South Africa in July 1839, he was receptive to learning about the problems involved in introducing Christianity into Africa. He attended a great public meeting held at Exeter Hall, June 1, 1840, the purpose of which was to launch the African Civilization Society.[16] The society, which Temperley points out was "the most aristocratic of all British antislavery bodies," was presided over by Albert, the Prince Consort, and included among its honorary vice presidents an imposing roster of archbishops and bishops, dukes, marquises, and earls. Prince Albert chaired the public meeting that June, and Buxton presented his "remedy" for ending the African slave trade by "civilizing" Africa.

The government's Niger Expedition of 1841–1842, which took shape as a result of these pressures, was well-equipped with specially constructed steamships and a staff of experienced naval officers, scientists (two botanists, a geologist, a mineralogist, and a zoologist), and missionaries. Because a third of the Europeans with the expedition died in Africa, the larger proportion of them within the first two months, public dismay replaced public enthusiasm and the Niger Expedition was recalled.[17] Curtin comments that "Buxton's plan was little more than a pulling together of . . . the dominant strands, from the mass of older suggestions."[18] For Livingstone, Buxton's ideas were new and compelling.

The scope and goals of the expedition made a lasting impression upon him. His own plans for his Zambezi Expedition in 1858 followed several of Buxton's ideas and many of the features of the Niger Expedition.

Buxton's 1840 vision remained with Livingstone over the next twenty years; it merged with other contemporary views about social and economic change that appealed to him. Livingstone's early years as a piecer and a spinner in a Scottish cotton mill, his youthful reading in contemporary science, and his formal scientific and medical training gave him a profound sense of participating in the great phenomena that marked his generation. The application of science to industry and the great advances of technology were personal experiences that fed his imagination.

Livingstone's first decade among the Bantu and Boer in the missionary world of Southern Africa led him to appreciate how Buxton's ideas about African agriculture and the use of technology might bring about fundamental social change. Introducing British manufactures to Africans along regularized trade routes, beginning with the guns and cloth they already appreciated, would create incentives for change in African ways of life. He fixed his hopes upon the Africans in the interior; they had relatively little contact as yet with the slave trade, and to him they seemed ready to learn about ways they might develop their plant and mineral resources on a scale suitable for a world export trade. Machines, whether sugar mills or light steamships, possessed the "civilizing" power to transform the lives of all who came into contact with them. They would make "unprogressive" tribal customs obsolete and enable Africans in the interior to refuse to take part in the slave trade just beginning to encroach upon them. The introduction of mechanized milling and processing machinery would help Africans achieve the surpluses that would be necessary for entry into worldwide trade. Light steamships on African rivers would bring better communication with the coasts to facilitate that legitimate trade; and their presence on inland lakes would block the water transport used by Arab and African slavers.[19]

Livingstone's ideas can similarly be understood in the intellectual context of Adam Smith and the social theorists of the Scottish enlightenment. This line of intellectual thought appeared in the writings of William Wilberforce, the great abolitionist. According to his 1807 publication, *A Letter on the Abolition of the Slave Trade*, it was "incontrovertible . . . that the arts and sciences, knowledge, and civilization, have never yet been found to be a native growth of any country; but that they have been communicated from one nation to another, from the more to the less civilized."[20] In their defense of this theory of cultural diffusion, abolitionists like Wilberforce sought to make a distinction between the slave trade, which "degraded," and "legitimate" trade, which carried civilization. By the 1830s, "legitimate" trade came to be understood as a means of weaning African rulers away from the slave trade by putting "their slaves to work at agricultural production for export." It was used in this sense by men like Macgregor Laird, who took an expedition to the Niger in the mid-1830s, and this definition came into prominence when Thomas Fowell Buxton popularized it early in the 1840s.[21] Livingstone would base his own analysis of African economic development on the same definition. Like the abolitionists, classical economists, and Utilitarians of his day, he believed the free operation of economic self-interest would bring the greatest benefit to the greatest number. In addition, for Livingstone the most beneficial form of "legitimate" trade was free trade. He was an early enthusiast of this principle and must have seen its achievement by Britain by mid-century as another sign of human progress, as did men like Richard Cobden and John Bright.

The Wilberforce–Macgregor Laird–Buxton definition of "legitimate" trade employed by Livingstone left vague the process by which use of slave labor for agriculture by African chiefs would encourage its transformation into free labor once the emphasis of trade shifted from human to natural resources. In practice, the process did not occur. Just as slave labor continued to be used in the American South to produce for a world market until political forces brought the system to an end, so the use of slaves acquired by purchase or raiding continued to characterize the Arab-Swahili commercial system developing in East Africa even as Livingstone sought its demise. The middle decades of the nineteenth century saw the expansion of clove plantations on Zanzibar and Pemba and cereal and coconut plantations on the East Coast in areas like Mombasa and Malindi, producing for an Indian Ocean and world market while connected by way of Zanzibar to a dhow and caravan trading network to the interior as far as Manyema and Lake Malawi. This plantation and trading economy was based increasingly on use of slave labor: as cultivators, porters, soldiers, concubines, and export commodities. The European expectation, on which Livingstone based his own plans for African development, linked the growth of an economy based on the exchange of goods with material progress, "civilization," and the spread of a free labor system. In the East African realities of the nineteenth century, such an expectation proved to be ideological wishful thinking. In this connection, Livingstone accepted the contemporary view that human beings advance by stages from the lowest rungs of savagery and barbarism to the highest levels of commercial and industrial development. Social progress, therefore, "was stimulated by vigorous economic and cultural intercourse among the various developing societies."[22]

Livingstone accepted the prevailing assumption that Africa, as part of the non-Western world, represented an earlier stage in human progress, "frozen, as it were," to use Philip Curtin's metaphor, "while the European world advanced . . . a kind of living museum of human cultures." This idea has been put another way by Maxine Berg: British scientists in this period viewed small-scale societies of Africa and the Pacific as "fossil" evidence of early stages of development that contemporary British society must have experienced. The enormous gap between the material achievements of early and later "stages of development" seemed to confirm the contemporary belief that industrial capitalism represented the apex toward which all progress was tending.[23] For missionaries like Livingstone and humanitarians in general, this concept of unilinear, progressive development made it imperative to ask why Africans had "stagnated" and how they were to be set moving again, "regenerated," on the path of development. The racists of the nineteenth century used this analysis to emphasize the "backwardness" of non-Western peoples, but they were divided over whether they believed this situation remediable or irremediable.[24]

On his long trek across Southern Africa (1853–1856), Livingstone began to formulate in specific terms his answers to these questions. He was aided in his travels through Angola to the West Coast by a group of Kololo (called by him Makololo), sent by their elders to open a trade route to the west.[25] By the time he reached the capital, Luanda, in 1855, he realized he must look instead to the East Coast to find a major waterway inland. He recrossed eastward to the area occupied by the Kololo, today the southwestern part of Zambia, and decided that a likely spot to start new efforts might be on the Upper Zambezi River. In his journal for June 10, 1855, he described the demands for cloth that the women of the Lunda, themselves without clothes, made on behalf of their little children, who were naked and cold. "If trade could be extended to them," he wrote, "they would be stimulated to industry in raising wherewithal to buy clothing." He noted the "abundance of ground nuts," which he thought could be processed into oil for sale. He believed he had found the right place for new work:

A most eligible site for a commercial and missionary settlement would be the right bank of the Leeba [local name for the Zambezi] near the confluence . . . of the Kabompo [a tributary of the Zambezi, in western Zambia]. . . . There would [be] water carriage over extensive territories, and ultimately the result would be glorious for Africa. I pray God that the good men and true of our benevolent England may be inclined to look to this desirable point. It surely is of as great importance as any in the Niger.[26]

Just about this time, Livingstone revealed the shape his thoughts were taking as he considered future prospects in Africa. The "best" Africans he had encountered, the Kololo, left him with no illusions about the difficulties that lay ahead for Christian conversion: "people [who] are inured to bloodshed and murder, and care for no god except being bewitched, desire of fame by killing people of other tribes, praise for valour when that is exercised only on the flying and defenseless." Yet he saw his goal as "working for such people," because he would be taking part in "that great forward movement which God is carrying on for the renovation of the world." Strikingly, while Berg notes that in this very period "the social reformer found his kinfolk among the missionaries to Africa and Asia, and among the scientists who encouraged them," Livingstone identified himself as a fellow worker in the great cause of "progress": "The great thing in working for such people is to remember that we are forwarding that great movement which God is carrying on for the renovation of the world. We are part of [the] machinery he employs, but not exclusive parts, for all who are engaged in ameliorating the condition of our race are fellow workers, co-operators with God—sanitary reformers & clergy of all sorts, the soldiers of Sebastapol [sic] and the sailors on the coast of Africa, inventors of telegraphs and steam engines, promoters of emigration and of prison reform."[27]

When Livingstone was about to leave the Kololo to continue eastward in his search for an all-water route from their homeland in the interior to a coast, his thoughts turned again to how commerce might be used as a supplement to the work of Christianity in Africa. "Commerce is spreading its ramifications in all directions," he wrote, "and friendly intercourse will be sure to follow in its wake. This [receptiveness] commerce effects readily, but sullen isolation gives way to good will and the feeling of mutual dependence by the influence of the gospel alone."[28]

Livingstone was concerned about finding the means which would enable Africans to develop products beyond ivory for trade with the outside world. He turned to the prospects of food processing, which would convert their agricultural products into a surplus for home use and export. At the end of May 1853, at Linyanti, Livingstone noted that though the Kololo cultivated sugar cane, they obtained its juices only by chewing the stalks. When in Angola in September 1853, he visited a "sugar manufactory" belonging to a Portuguese woman who employed her many slaves to work it. When he described this experience in *Mis-*

sionary Travels, he commented that "far from being in a flourishing condition," Donna Anna da Sousa's slave–run sugar mill contrasted unfavorably with "the free-labour establishments of Mauritius which I have since seen, where, with not a tenth of the number of hands, or such good soil, a man of colour had, in one year, cleared 5000*l*. by a single crop."[29] In November 1855, on taking leave of Sekeletu once more on his way to the East Coast, Livingstone accepted fifteen large ivory tusks and the commission to buy for him a number of items, including "small sugar rollers, for expressing juice (of sugar cane)."[30]

Once Livingstone was en route back to England in 1856, he had sufficiently formulated his plans to write about them in a tone of assurance and authority to Sir Roderick Murchison, the president of the Royal Geographical Society, who had written to welcome him home as a famous man. Livingstone began to realize that his journey across Africa had earned for him a new credibility for what he wished to say. He responded to Murchison with the theme he would develop further, predicting that "the future of the African Continent will be one of great importance to England in the way of producing the raw materials of her manufactures as well as an extensive market for the articles of her industry. . . ."[31]

From the time he emerged on the East Coast of Africa in 1856, eager to pursue the use of the Zambezi River as "God's highway into the interior," to the mid-1860s, when he put the Zambezi Expedition behind him, Livingstone continued to ponder this problem, sharing with his closest correspondents the ideas he hoped would provide the practical answers to African economic development. He extolled Africa's immense, untapped resources, raw materials of value to England as her industrial economy expanded. By helping Africans develop their natural assets, Britain would enable them to pay for English manufactures. This portrayal of Africa as the next "New World" or "India" did not originate with Livingstone, but his serious tone, his mixture of commerce and piety, and the timing of his appeal, in the late 1850s and again in the mid-1870s, made *his* the vision that the next generation of imperialists would take as their text.[32]

In his letter to Murchison on his way home, Livingstone mentioned that he had "an order from Sekeletu to purchase a sugar mill. . . ."[33] He used this example of an African demand for British machinery—a demand he had suggested—when addressing the Manchester Chamber of Commerce the next year, and the story was reported in the *Manchester Guardian*. When he told his tale in Dublin, at the meeting of the British Association for the Advancement of Science, the daughter of the Irish Anglican Archbishop, Richard Whately, promised to raise money toward the considerable cost of an up-to-date model of a sugar mill. She and her friends were successful, and Livingstone purchased a mill in 1858 from the Glasgow firm of Mirrlees and Tait. It was worked by means of cattle "harnessed to hugh levers under a roof" which turned as the cattle moved. This model was described by its manufacturer as "a big advance on any of the sugar mills operating" in Natal. While being carried on the Zambezi Expedition's first steam launch, the *MaRobert*, part of the mill, the boiler tubes and tools, went overboard and were not recovered. When Livingstone found he would not be able to transport the sugar mill to Sekeletu by an all-water route, he ordered that it be erected in the Portuguese town of Tete, in February 1859. He reported to Miss Whately that "he had put up a beautiful sugar mill to show the natives what could be done by machinery." When George Rae, the expedition's engineer, wrote home, he mentioned that he had set up a small sugar mill, a stationary steam engine, and a saw mill brought from Glasgow "to the great delight of the natives." Livingstone noted in his journal that the experiment with the sugar mill had been "successful," but that there was a "great want" of sugar cane at that time; a year later he ordered the machine dismantled and stored. He did obtain enough milled sugar, however, to send a sampling to the Hookers at the Royal Botanical Gardens at Kew.[34]

More important than sugar mills to commercial and manufacturing circles, and to the government of the day, was Livingstone's insistence that he had found in Central Africa another major cotton-growing area. Tensions in the second half of the 1850s in the United States, where the South had produced Lancashire's cotton since the late eighteenth century, left the British anxious about future supplies. As concern mounted, Livingstone devoted his best-selling first book, *Missionary Travels* (1857), to the exposition of his ideas about African development, and in particular about the possibilities for growing cotton in the interior to supplement the supply from America. The peoples of the interior were the key to African spiritual and material regeneration:

> On the latter my chief hopes at present rest. All of them, however, are willing and anxious to engage in trade, and, while eager for this, none have ever been encouraged to cultivate the raw materials of commerce. Their country is well adapted for cotton; and I venture to entertain the hope that by distributing seeds of better kinds than that which is found indigenous, and stimulating the natives to cultivate it by affording them the certainty of a market for all they may produce, we may engender a feeling of mutual dependence between them and ourselves. I have a two-fold object in view, and

"Manufacture of Sugar at Katipo, making the panellas, or pots, to contain it," painted by Thomas Baines, 1859. Several sugar mills were already in operation by the Portuguese in the Tete area when Livingstone imported an up-to-date model from Glasgow. Teaching Africans how to process raw produce for export was the heart of Livingstone's plan to bring Africa into the world market system.

believe that, by guiding our missionary labours so as to benefit our own country, we shall thereby more effectually and permanently benefit the heathen. . . . We ought to encourage the Africans to cultivate for our markets, as the most effectual means, next to the Gospel, of their elevation.[35]

Significantly, Livingstone ended his book by harkening back to Buxton's great experiment of the early 1840s that had so moved his imagination. He recalled and reaffirmed its purpose: "the great Niger expedition; one invaluable benefit it conferred was the dissemination of the knowledge of English love of commerce and English hatred of slavery, and it therefore was no failure."[36] Livingstone's Zambezi Expedition, 1858–1864, embodied his conviction that he could do what others had failed to do. He could bring to fruition in East and Central Africa the plans Buxton had put forward two decades earlier for West Africa.

Livingstone spent his time in England between 1856 and 1858 preaching his new convictions. He addressed the men of the Universities of Oxford and Cambridge to persuade them to follow in his footsteps, to open up Africa to Christianity and civilization. He concentrated his efforts, however, on men of commerce, to convince them that Africa could provide them with a great new field for economic development. He had brought back to England samples of seeds, roots, and plant life, prepared to substantiate his arguments that the interior of the continent was ripe for commercial investment and industrial missions. He emphasized to the cotton merchants of Manchester an image of Central Africa as a potential supplier of cotton grown by free African labor. They assured him that they welcomed alternative sources of supply to replace their reliance on the slave-worked plantations of the American South. Here was an opportunity to strike a double blow against slavery and the slave trade.

When Livingstone returned to Central Africa in 1858, he went with a commission as Her Majesty's Consul at Quilimane for the Eastern Coast and the Independent Districts in the Interior, and he led a government-sponsored expedition. Livingstone had been successful. With support from Sir Roderick Murchison, the Manchester Chamber of Commerce, and the British Association—all of whom had been convinced that large quantities of cotton could be grown cheaply on the Batoka plateau of the Kololo—he had been able to get the Foreign Office to sponsor an official Expedition to the Zambezi. The government could not afford to pass up an opportunity to discover a new cotton-growing region, and the financing of such expeditions of scientific and commercial exploration

"Working a coal seam near Tete, lower Zambezi," painted by Thomas Baines, 1859. Livingstone was interested in exploring the coal resources of the Tete area and set his geologist Richard Thornton to drill a shaft into such a seam.

in West Africa had a long history. Even more evident was the fact that the objects and plans of this expedition to East Africa bore a conscious resemblance to Buxton's Niger Expedition.

The Zambezi Expedition took with it a light steam launch; and the members of the party included a botanist, a geologist, an artist, another clergyman (his brother Charles), and a naval officer. The scientific and commercial elements, therefore, were prominent. Livingstone planned to explore the Zambezi River, confidently expecting to sail over any rapids he might encounter. His instructions to his officers anticipated the establishment of an agricultural station on the Batoka plateau, which had impressed him on his way to the East Coast. Livingstone's letter of instructions to his "economic" botanist, Dr. John Kirk, made his goals clear:

The main object of the Expedition to which you are appointed Economic botanist and medical officer is to extend the knowledge already attained of the Geography and mineral and agricultural resources of Eastern and Central Africa, to improve our acquaintance with the inhabitants and to engage them to apply their energies to industrial pursuits and to the cultivation of their lands with a view to the production of raw materials to be exported to England in return for British manufactures. And it may be hoped that by encouraging the natives to occupy themselves in the development of the resources of their country, a considerable advance may by made towards the extinction of the slave trade, as the natives will not be long in discovering that the former will eventually become a more certain source of profit than the latter.[37]

The instructions continued. The expedition officers would call on influential chiefs to "invite them to turn the attention of their people to the cultivation of cotton by giving them a supply of better seed." Chiefs were to be encouraged to exchange their ivory and cotton for "the manufactures of Europe" so that they would "give up their warlike and predatory habits, and substitute the more peaceable pursuits of agriculture and commerce." Kirk was to write reports on the resources of the Tete area (Portuguese territory) and, especially, "the plant called Buaze . . . and other fibrous substances . . . for transmission home to the Foreign Office." He was to seek out "dye stuffs, gums and medicinal substances" and discover whether they existed "in quantities sufficient to warrant commercial enterprise . . . [to] aid in the great work of supplanting the odious traffic in slaves."

Livingstone's initial plan was to direct the expedition to the Batoka plateau to establish "a depot at some eligible spot beyond the confluence of the Kafue and the Zambesi." There, "after obtaining the consent of any natives who may lay claim to the soil," the expedition was to "set up an iron house to serve as a central station." Once established on a relatively high location, to ensure the health of the party, they would select

> . . . another small spot at a lower level [which] may be planted with cotton and sugar cane and given in charge to the headman of any village adjacent in order to induce the natives to take an interest in the result. . . . moral influence . . . may be exerted on the mind of the natives by a well regulated and orderly household of Europeans setting an example of consistent moral conduct to all who may congregate round the settlement, treating the people with kindness and relieving their wants, teaching them to make experiments in agriculture, explaining to them the more simple arts, imparting to them religious instruction as far as they are capable of receiving it and inculcating peace and good will to each other.[38]

The Zambezi Expedition arrived at the East Coast of Africa in June 1858. By late November, Livingstone found the Caborabassa rapids above Tete impassable. In January 1859, he explored the Shire River, navigated it, and "discovered" and named the Murchison Cataracts which prevented navigation to the Upper Shire. He heard about the existence of highlands and a great lake to the north. Early in March, aware that his original plans were now seriously endangered, he redirected his hopes toward the Shire Highlands. He wrote the Duke of Argyll that "an English colony ought to be attempted in the interior. You threw out this idea once when I called upon you, and since then the scheme has grown daily in importance."[39]

These thoughts had been maturing in Livingstone's mind for some time. The week before he left England, in February 1858, he had revealed the tenor of his thinking to Adam Sedgwick, professor of geology at Cambridge. His objects, he confessed, "have something more in them than meets the eye. They are not merely exploratory, for I go with the intention of benefiting both the African & my own countrymen. . . . but what I tell to none but such as you in whom I have confidence is this. I hope it may result in an English colony in the healthy highlands of central Africa. (I have told it only to the Duke of Argyll.) I believe the [Batoka] highlands are healthy. The wild vine flourishes there. Europeans with a speedy transit of the coast would collect and transmit the produce to the sea and in the course of time, say when my head is low, free labour on the African soil might render slave labour, which is notoriously dear labour, quite unprofitable."[40]

The only change of plan between 1858 and 1859 was the location of the highlands to which he directed British attention. The Caborabassa rapids shifted his focus from the Batoka plateau to the Shire Highlands, where the Mang'anja lived. His notion of a European settlement in healthy uplands remained the same, and his conviction—based on his hopes rather than on any understanding of the economic forces at work —that free labor would always prove more profitable than slave labor undergirded his desire to bring in those who would show by example the fruits that might be gained from the use of their own free labor. On August 4, 1859, he confessed in his journal,

> I have a very strong desire to commence a system of colonisation of the honest poor; I would give £2000 or £3000 for the purpose. . . . Colonisation from a country such as ours ought to be one of hope, and not of despair . . . the performance of an imperative duty to our blood, our country, our religion, and to humankind. . . . It is a monstrous evil that all our healthy, handy, blooming daughters of England have not a fair chance at least to become the centres of domestic affections. The state of society, which precludes so many of them from occupying the position which Englishwomen are so well calculated to adorn, gives rise to enormous evils in the opposite sex—evils and wrongs which we dare not even name,—[sic] and national colonisation is almost the only remedy. Englishwomen are, in general, the most beautiful in the world, and yet our national emigration has often, by selecting the female emigrants from workhouses, sent forth the ugliest *huzzies* in creation to be the mothers—the model mothers—of new empires.[41] Here, as in other cases, State necessities have led to the ill-formed and ill-informed being preferred to the well-formed and well-inclined honest poor, as if the worst as well as the better qualities of mankind did not often run in the blood.[42]

This passage provides us with clear guidance into Livingstone's private thoughts on the question of empire. He stressed the benefits that would accrue to the colonizing country and its inhabitants and focused on the "honest poor," which included his own family. His brothers John and Charles had both emigrated, leaving behind their two unmarried sisters. Livingstone records genuine regret that women like his sisters were deprived of the chance for motherhood. He blamed their lost opportunity to establish domestic hearths in the colonies on state policies that chose instead to send out workhouse "hussies" on rate-aided emigration schemes to populate the empire. Livingstone was disappointed in his hope that his parents and sisters would follow his brothers' example and emigrate to America. He faulted state policy for not encouraging them, and respectable working class people like them, to do so. The contempt he expressed for workhouse women, "ill-formed and ill-informed," conveyed his conviction they would pass on a tainted inheritance and recalls his views on "vitality."[43] His veiled allusion to sexual frustration among male colonists unable to find wives among the "healthy, handy, blooming daughters" of the "honest poor" also brings to mind his concern for the frustration of African husbands whose wives insisted on sexual abstinence when breast-feeding.

To understand what Livingstone believed would be the benefits that Africans would derive from the presence among them of the British, and particularly the Scottish, working classes, we must refer to his journal, written four years earlier while with the Kololo. At that time, he made comparisons between the poor of Africa and those of England and Scotland, about whom he claimed "intimate knowledge." He praised the latter's "disinterested kindness," their "very admirable amount of kindly feeling towards each other," which led to their aiding those in need. He deplored the absence of this moral quality among the people he had seen in Africa: "A poor person who has no relatives will seldom be supplied with water in illness, and when death ensues will certainly be dragged out to be devoured by hyaenas, instead of being buried." His call in 1859–1860 for the settlement of the British "honest poor" in Central Africa reveals his theory of raising the moral standard among Africans by arranging closer contact for them with those qualities he esteemed among the poor he had known in Scotland. He wrote in his journal for October 23, 1855: "The poor manufacturing classes are also remarkable for great independance [sic] of feeling. There are of course many exceptions to this, but these are decidedly not so numerous among them as among the classes immediately above them, & among whom bribery and other forms of venality flourishes [sic]. The astonishing efforts they make for the support of relatives . . . I have often witnessed in Scotland with patriotic pride. I have never seen anything like [it] among the heathen." He added, "There is little manliness, and no gallantry. . . . Nor have they any of that respect for law and order which are found among our own poorer classes."[44]

In contrast with many other emigration enthusiasts in Great Britain between the 1830s and 1860s, therefore, Livingstone did not advocate sending out the middle classes, whom—as depicted in this passage—he considered venal at best, while the "honest," industrial poor, with whose virtues he personally identified, were left to suffer at home.[45] Livingstone actively advanced his colonization schemes for East Central Africa in 1859 and 1860. He wrote James Aspinall Turner, a cotton manufacturer of Manchester, in March 1859, that "colonization will bring the slave trade to an end." In November, he shared this opinion with his friend Thomas Maclear, the Astronomer Royal at the Cape: "I am becoming every day more decidedly convinced that English colonisation is an essential ingredient for our large success. . . . In this new region of highlands no end of good could be effected in developing the trade in cotton and discouraging that in slaves. . . ."[46] According to Blaikie, Livingstone recorded in his journal late in 1859 that he had written James Young that he was ready to sponsor, anonymously, twenty or thirty poor families with £2,000 to come out as an experiment. He urged him to consult cotton merchants Thom of Chorley and Turner of Manchester, Lord Shaftesbury, and the Scottish Duke of Argyll. "Much is done for the blackguard poor. Let us remember our own class. . . ."[47]

Livingstone believed he had found a solution for Africa that also provided a remedy for evils that existed in Great Britain. On December 1, 1859, he wrote in his journal that he wished: "to make Africa North of Lat. 15° South a blessing to Africans and Englishmen. The sons of the soil need not be torn from their homes in order to contribute to the wealth of the world. There is room for them where they are, and they may be led to produce their quota, and a large one, to the circulating wealth of the world. There is room and to spare for English immigrants to settle on and work the virgin soil of the still untilled land of Ham. As the African need not be torn from his country and enslaved, no more need the English poor be crowded together in unwholesome dens, debarred from breathing the pure air of Heaven. There is room for all in the wide and glorious domains of the Lord, the king of all the Earth."[48]

When Livingstone corresponded with Sir Roderick Murchison in August and November 1859, he maintained that an English colony was the only way of eluding the Portuguese grip on the area.[49] The following March, he sought the support of Sir George Grey, the Governor of the Cape Colony, to pressure the Portuguese to open the Zambezi River to free trade. His rationale for urging this policy was that it would facilitate placing English settlers in the highlands of the Zambezi region where they might develop cotton cultivation. He was pursuing his belief that cotton grown by free labor would prove more profitable than cotton grown by slave labor, but he nowhere tried to work out the logic of his assumptions. Nonetheless, Livingstone had moved beyond Buxton's idea of trading posts. He hoped his words had finally been heeded when he learned that the Oxford and Cambridge Mission to Central Africa had been organized; he expressed his anticipation that the mission "might be accompanied by a small colony."[50]

Livingstone's enthusiastic descriptions of the Shire Highlands had indeed drawn the focus of the newly recruited Oxford and Cambridge Mission to Central Africa. Hearing of their intentions, Livingstone wrote James Young that the colonization plans he had asked Young to undertake for him could wait upon the realization of their plans for an industrial mission. Early in 1860, however, he decided to put a small steamship on Lake Malawi, to be financed out of his own "book-money" if the government did not agree to pay for it. He was confident that this embodiment of Western technology, by establishing an "English" presence on the lake, would serve as a warning to discourage the slower Arab dhows and Africans canoes used in carrying slaves across it. He clearly had in mind some analogy to the blockade maintained by British cruisers patrolling the East Coast for slaving ships, but he never spelled out clearly whether he envisioned offensive action by his steamship.[51]

Although Livingstone continued to describe to his correspondents his plans for agriculture and small-scale industrial development with good transportation links to the outside world, he had been advised by Murchison that it was difficult to raise an adequate response in England: "Your colonisation scheme does not meet with supporters, it being thought that you must have much more hold on the country before you attract Scotch families to emigrate and settle there, and then die off, or become a burden to you and all concerned. . . ."[52] Livingstone urged the Foreign Office, in October 1859, to give him a steamer for the lake and "sappers" to help him construct a road around Murchison Cataracts. He emphasized the area's vast cotton-growing potential and stressed the role that the "legitimate" trader might play in putting down the slave trade.

With this introduction to the idea, Livingstone pressed the claims of the Shire Highlands as a location for "a small body of Colonists, with their religious and mercantile institutions, industriously developing the resources of the country. . . ."[53] Although Livingstone did not receive an official reply from the Foreign Office until early 1861, he had been warned by Murchison's comments that his hopes for formal authorization of his schemes would not be entertained. The new Foreign Secretary, Lord John Russell, informed him that plans for colonization were "premature" and not to expect the Treasury to pay for a steamship for Lake Malawi. Lord Palmerston had been quite clear to his Foreign Secretary: "I am very unwilling to embark on new schemes of British possessions. Dr L's information is valuable, but he must not be allowed to tempt us to form colonies only to be reached by forcing steamers up cataracts."[54]

By 1864, a number of critics challenged Livingstone for being overly optimistic in his assessment of the Malawi region and the Zambezi, in terms of its potential for cotton cultivation and his insistence that there were easy water routes inland. He was neither the first nor the last traveller to voice extravagant claims for Africa's potential for economic development, but Livingstone's widespread, popular fame in the late fifties as both a missionary and an explorer lent special weight to his words.[55] His acclaim and the enthusiasm aroused by his first reports, caused the failure of the Zambezi Expedition to engulf him in a wave of bitter criticism. The fact that Livingstone regained a great public following during his last journey, first from the false reports of his death in 1867 and then in the sensational publicity emanating from his meeting with Stanley in 1871, enhanced the formation of the Livingstone legend. His renewed appeal as a national hero strengthened the power of his words—as Waller had predicted—and in consequence the power of his legacy, after death, to move his countrymen to action.

In the end, Livingstone failed to place on Lake Malawi the small steamship he had financed for himself out of his book profits. When he sailed from Africa to India in it in 1864, the events of the previous half-dozen years had modified his views on the nature of colonization for Central Africa. His earlier vision of independent Africans learning from small numbers of British settlers how to develop their agriculture to link it with worldwide trade had been lost. It had been a vision of an agricultural economy bolstered by small-scale industry; it was the Scotland Livingstone remembered from his childhood. He now concluded: "The idea of a colony in Africa, as the term colony is usually understood, cannot be entertained. English races cannot compete in manual labour of any kind with the natives, but they can take a leading part in managing the land, improving the quality, in creating the quantity and extending the varieties of the productions of the soil; and by taking a lead too in trade, and in all public matters, the Englishman would be an unmixed advantage to everyone below and around him, for he would fill a place which is now practically vacant."[56]

As Jeal suggests, Livingstone's contribution to British concepts of empire was his mature reflection upon the kind of role colonial regimes in the tropics might play. He recognized that the highlands could not accommodate the kind of colonization represented by Canada, Australia, New Zealand, or even the Cape Colony, where temperate climates allowed more extensive European settlement than, he finally decided,

David Livingstone, 1864. This is an older Livingstone, filled with the disappointments of his Zambezi Expedition and the loss of his wife Mary on the Zambezi in 1862. The familiar hair line has receded somewhat and the side hairs have turned gray, but the mustache is as bushy as before. But the eyebrows look more knitted over the piercing eyes, making him seem less lean and vigorous and more stern and careworn than seven years before.

would be possible in an area like the Zambezi–Lake Malawi region. However, Livingstone was more certain than ever that there existed a real need for British knowledge and experience in crucial areas of African life, and that the British were uniquely equipped to "take a lead" in land management, trade, "and in all public matters." In the end, therefore, it was a paternalistic vision, one that would blend in well with later Victorian imperialist sentiments in humanitarian circles, providing justification for those who believed that both British commerce and British rule were, by definition, worthy causes.

To argue that Livingstone's legacy could be invoked as permission to colonize is not to argue that it was permission to exploit. Livingstone believed in the material and spiritual superiority of British Christians but he also insisted that preeminence was a privilege that brought responsibilities to aid others less favored. The Europeans who eventually took over and governed African colonies, however, were less likely to be philosopher kings than insistent taskmasters who looked upon Africans who disagreed with them as childish (savage), undisciplined (uncivilized), and disorderly (rebellious). Paternalism looks for gratitude—in the shape of loyalty—and is continually surprised by its absence.

In his editing of Livingstone's *Last Journals*, Horace Waller sought to make David Livingstone's name symbolic of a British commitment to African development in the name of antislavery. To mention Livingstone was to evoke the horrors of the slave trade and a British duty to strike it down by whatever means would prove effective. Waller strove to make Livingstone's memory one which would strike a response that would touch the public conscience and make it more receptive to new schemes of African involvement, whether to introduce Christianity, commerce, or the material aspects of European "civilization." Although it is difficult to gauge his success, there has been general agreement among historians that Livingstone's life and death were critical in shaping history in Africa for the remainder of the century. One historian speaks cogently for the rest:

Livingstone's impact on the course of history in Africa was immense, perhaps greater than that of any other individual of the nineteenth century. It [stemmed from] . . . the impact his character and way of life made in Europe. He became a popular hero, the missionary and explorer par excellence, who brought knowledge of hitherto unknown regions and people to an ever-increasing circle of individuals. The circumstances of Livingstone's death and his burial in Westminster Abbey confirmed the impact and

brought even more people into contact with Africa. With this stim-
ulation, missionary societies were able to raise the extra financial
resources for new ventures into Africa, while those with secular
and humanitarian ambitions were also able to take advantage of
the new tide of interest. The final partition of Africa began about a
decade after Livingstone's death, a decade of intense European
effort in all parts of the continent. The speed of this process destroying the independent existence of most regions of Africa owed
much to the publicity coming from his dramatic career.[57]

The effect created by the narrative of Livingstone's death on the climate of opinion in humanitarian circles and beyond them is captured by
Roland Oliver:

A hundred pulpits took up the tale of the missionary-explorer who
had died on his knees, invoking in his solitude 'Heaven's rich blessing' upon everyone who would help 'to heal this open sore of the
world.' A revolution was set in motion which was to bring a new
kind of missionary into Africa and a new and more numerous class
of subscribers on the societies' lists. In missionary circles the talk
was . . . of Africans 'suffering' and 'neglected'. Soon it would be
of 'open doors' and 'untouched millions'. The *Daily Telegraph* . . . expressed the wider national sentiment and that of the
average subscriber in its obituary article: 'The work of England for
Africa must henceforth begin in earnest where Livingstone left it
off'.[58]

NOTES

1. In the next chapter, the primary examples of this part of Livingstone's legacy will be drawn from schemes to place steamships on lakes
and to build telegraphs, roads, and railways. This chapter demonstrates
that Livingstone also had in mind machines to aid the work of processing
raw materials for export. Although Livingstone sought to convince the
readers of *Missionary Travels* that Africans were quick to understand
"questions affecting their worldly affairs," including the varieties of soils
necessary for their crops, he also believed that scientific agriculture
developed by Europeans could teach them a great deal about the arts of
cultivation. On his Zambezi Expedition, Livingstone took along various
kinds of seeds, including cotton seed, to experiment with soils; and on his

advice the first party of the Universities' Mission to Central Africa brought with them English seeds and English agriculturalists. In preparation for becoming the mission's lay superintendent, Waller "received elementary instruction in the cultivation and management of cotton." Chadwick, *Mackenzie's Grave*, 17.

2. British investment in railway building in the 1860s had "swept five continents . . . [and] reached from Bavaria and Rumania to Egypt and Turkey. At the same time, [rail]roads were being built with English and European funds in India, Japan, Russia, and South America." Dolores Greenberg, *Financiers and Railroads, 1869–1889* (Newark, Del., London, and Toronto, 1980), 41. From the mid-1870s, Cameron's efforts to popularize the idea of European commercial investment in Central Africa led to his (erroneous) description in the 1891 edition of *Men of the Time*, as "being the *first* to point out practical means of civilising Africa by the formation of Chartered Companies, the construction of railways, and placing steamers on the great lakes and rivers." Emphasis added. For example, see Lt. V. Lovett Cameron, "Colonisation of Central Africa," *Proceedings of the Royal Colonial Institute* 7 (June 1876): 274–96 (hereafter, *PRCI*). Enthusiasts described in most glowing terms the "civilizing" potential of roads, telegraph, and railroads in Africa. In the last quarter of the nineteenth century, the Society of Arts, an organization dedicated to promoting industrial arts, manufactures, improvements in agriculture, and the development of trade, had a membership of 3,000 to 4,000, largely composed of merchants and businessmen, many in overseas trade. At this society, in 1879, it was predicted that railways

> . . . would . . . inspire the [African] native with a respect for the mighty power of science [and] . . . teach him . . . how far he is "behind the times." It would cause him, in his wonderment and awe, to forget the petty disputes with his neighbor, and thus act as a general peace-maker; . . . it would . . . promote him to be an industrious cultivator of the soil of his country. It would above all put an end to that abominable traffic in human flesh by substituting legitimate trade.

J. Conyers Morrell, "On the Advantage of Railway Communication in Africa As Compared with Any Other Mode of Transport," *Journal of the Society of Arts* 27 (1879): 482 (hereafter, *JSA*). For equally enthusiastic predictions about the introduction of the telegraph in Africa, compare Sir Rutherford Alcock, *PRGS* 21 (1877): 620, 621–22, and Donald Currie, the president of the Castle Line to South Africa, who presented:

"Thoughts upon the Present and Future of South Africa, and Central and Eastern Africa, *PRCI* 8 (1877): 388. As chap. 8 will show, just at this time Currie was joining William Mackinnon to consider obtaining a vast commercial concession in East Africa from the sultan of Zanzibar.

3. The explorer Joseph Thomson attempted to challenge these assumptions. In 1886, he scoffed at schemes for making Central Africa into a "Second India." He questioned the prevailing view about the quality of African soils, the commercial exploitability of African raw materials and products, the availability of African labor for European plantations, the feasibility of building railroads, and the healthiness of even parts of Africa for Europeans and their families. He attacked the role of Christian missionaries, suggesting they had attempted too much too quickly, in contrast with Islam, which used simpler methods, had fewer expectations, and had more to offer Africans (reflecting Thomson's low estimation of the latter). Yet he also wrote ". . . though a road [between Lakes Tanganyika and Malawi, for example] will never pay its promoters in cash, . . . the influence which the formation of it will exercise upon the natives, is productive of advantages by no means inconsiderable." Joseph Thomson, *To the Central African Lakes and Back: The Narrative of the R.G.S.'s Central African Expedition, 1879-80*, 2 vols. (London, 1881) 2:291. Yet Thomson later criticized the British government for refusing to expand its empire to safeguard the achievements of British explorers, merchants, and missionaries. He blamed "Downing Street" for preventing officials on the spot from advancing British claims inland, betraying "the trust reposed in it" to act "under all circumstances for the honour and advancement of the Empire." "In chartered companies alone," he concluded, "is there any hope for the development of British influence and civilisation in Africa." Joseph Thomson, "Downing Street *versus* Chartered Companies in Africa," *Fortnightly Review* 46 n.s. (August 1889): 176, 177, 185. For his critical views of grand African schemes, see *To the Central African Lakes and Back*, 2:287-88; "East Central Africa, and Its Commercial Outlook," *Scottish Geographical Magazine* 2 (1886): 65-78 (hereafter, *SGM*); "Note on the African Tribes of the British Empire," *Journal of the Anthropological Institute* 16 (June 1, 1886): 182-86 (hereafter, *JAI*); and "Mohammedanism in Central Africa," *Contemporary Review* 50 (December 1886): 876-83. For a recent assessment, see Robert I. Rotberg, *Joseph Thomson and the Exploration of Africa* (London, 1971): 227-32, 256-58; and Rotberg, "Joseph Thomson: Energy, Humanism, and Imperialism," in Rotberg, *Africa and Its Explorers*, 295-320, esp. 311-14.

4. Jeal, *Livingstone*, 382. The idea of the British Empire as primarily a federation of white settlement colonies, in which India was the excep-

tion that proved the rule, did not vanish quickly. In 1883, J. R. Seeley's *Expansion of England* presented such an image, and 80,000 copies of his book were sold in the first two years of publication. John Gross, "Editor's Introduction," in John R. Seeley, *The Expansion of England* (Chicago and London, 1971), *xii.* Jeal also notes the unpopularity of Disraeli's 1876 Royal Titles Bill, which sought to add *Empress of India* to Queen Victoria's other royal titles. He suggests that the opposition to this bill drew on the fact that India ". . . was not a white-settled territory and was therefore considered alien. . . ." Jeal, *Livingstone*, 382. Other historians, however, suggest that opposition to the bill lay more in its implied constitutional threat, identifying an imperial title with the authoritarian regimes of Russia, France under Napoleon III, and the new, aggressive German Empire. Colin C. Eldridge, *England's Mission: The Imperial Idea in the Age of Gladstone and Disraeli, 1868–1880* (London and Basingstoke, 1973), 213–14; Richard Koebner and Helmut Dan Schmidt, *Imperialism: The Story and Significance of a Political Word, 1840–1960* (Cambridge, 1964), 117–24. The charge that the imposition of imperial rule over non-white peoples led to autocracy at home figured in anti-imperialist critiques at the end of the century. For the argument, see John A. Hobson, *Imperialism: A Study*, 1902; reprint with introduction by Philip Siegelman (Ann Arbor, 1965), 145–52.

    5. Quoted by Jeal, *Livingstone*, 382.

    6. Curtin, *Image of Africa*, esp. chaps. 2, 15–17.

    7. Oliver, *Missionary Factor*, 10–11. Oliver notes that in writing *East Africa as a Field for Missionary Labours* in 1874, Frere addressed the need in Africa to counteract ". . . the action of cold materialism which, teaching selfishness as the highest wisdom, isolates every man from his neighbour . . . an effectual obstacle to anything like permanent civilisation." Oliver, *Missionary Factor*, 11, n. 1.

    8. The link between science and technology was a persistent theme in Britain by the 1820s among men interested in economic advancement. Charles Babbage, the inventor of the calculating machine, pointed to the increasing application to industry of the chemical sciences and predicted that his new "science of calculation" would become "continually more necessary at each step of our progress and . . . must ultimately govern the whole of the applications of science to the arts of life." This quotation, from Babbage's *On the Economy of Machinery and Manufactures* (London, 1832), is cited in Maxine Berg, *The Machinery Question and the Making of Political Economy, 1815–1848* (Cambridge, 1980; reprint, 1982), 189. Babbage's book went through three editions in its first year of publication. Livingstone's interest in science was intense from childhood. He also saw what science could achieve in the life and work

of James Young, whom he met at Anderson's College in Glasgow in 1836 and dubbed "Sir Paraffin" because he made a fortune from his chemical discoveries and patents, including distilling oil from shale. *Missionary Travels*, 5; Campbell, *Livingstone*, 31 and n. 13; Jeal, *Livingstone*, 17.

9. Temperley, *British Anti-Slavery, xii.*

10. *Ibid.*

11. *Ibid.*, 248–57. A revealing glimpse into British attitudes toward the American Civil War is found in a letter from the Scottish industrialist James Young to David Livingstone, Limefield, West Calder, Midlothian, February 28, 1862:

> The North thought to get us into the mess and make a quarrel with us an excuse for settling matters with the South so that they might say it was England that broke up the United States [and] then after settling with the South . . . settling with us. But old Pam was too bate [sic] for them; instead of making it a matter of diplomacy as they expected, he broke down all their fine schemes by the plain statement "the men within 7 days or war." This they scarcely believed at first, but three or four days after came the news that ten thousand men were ordered to Canada and part were already on the way. This changed the tune and Jonathan felt himself in a fix and [all] he can do now is to swear eternal vengeance; and everyone here is thankful we are out of the mess.

Livingstone Papers, MS. 7876, fol. 13–14, NLS. Punctuation added to clarify meaning.

12. Curtin, *Image of Africa*, 218. For the scientific aims and cultural blindness of the exploration that preceded the Niger Expedition, see Curtin, *Image of Africa*, 198–226.

13. *Ibid.*, esp. 259–86.

14. Temperley, *British Anti-Slavery*, 53.

15. Quoted in Temperley, *British Anti-Slavery*, 53–54.

16. Jeal, *Livingstone*, 22–23.

17. Curtin, *Image of Africa*, 303–5; Temperley, *British Anti-Slavery*, 57–61.

18. Curtin, *Image of Africa*, 302. For half a century before Livingstone's Zambezi Expedition, there existed a tradition of exploring West Africa in the interests of science and commerce. The African Association, founded in 1788, sponsored African exploration; and the Royal Geographical Society, with which it merged in 1831, carried on that tradition. After the Napoleonic War, the British Colonial Office and the Admiralty sought accurate geographical information in the interests of

African coastal trade; they sponsored scientific and commercial investigations staffed by military men and scientists. The Navy and the Foreign Office, concerned with monitoring antislave trade treaties, needed an accurate knowledge of the coasts to prevent slave ships from escaping. Curtin demonstrates how Buxton's Niger Expedition, despite its failure, stimulated both official and private efforts to explore West Africa and discover its commercial potential. A Parliamentary Select Committee in 1842 actually ". . . recommended a more active British role in West Africa to exploit existing commercial openings." Thus Livingstone's Zambezi Expedition in 1858 was only one of several government-sponsored expeditions to explore for possible commercial advantages—though the first in East Africa. The medical investigation of quinine as a prophylactic against malarial fevers was an integral part of these forward moves; its successful use on the Niger in 1854 was hailed for making it possible for Europeans to live in Africa. Livingstone followed these developments with interest and developed his own version of quinine pills, his "rowsers," by the late 1850s. For details of this history, see Curtin, *Image of Africa*, 15–17, 157–58, 165–76, 199–200, 310–17, 344–57.

19. Berg, *Machinery Question*, 140. In the United States, where the question of transportation on the major rivers and great lakes early captured attention, steamboats started to compete with sailing ships from the 1820s, but by 1850 they still represented only a third of the tonnage on the Great Lakes. Susan Previant Lee and Peter Passell, *A New Economic View of American History* (New York and London), 1979, 76–77. As Livingstone discovered on his Zambezi Expedition, steam-powered ships encountered serious problems with river currents, the frequent need for fueling (in Livingstone's case, chopping down timber), and a heavy demand on space for fuel, especially coal, reducing cargo carrying capacity. Livingstone's enthusiasm for the potential speed of steam power in contrast with the sailing vessels used by Arabs and the canoes used by Africans, however, was part of his appreciation of science and technology as evidence of the superiority of the European world, the material advances of which he identified with the enlightenment of Christianity. These views became the commonplace expressions of enthusiasts after Livingstone's death. For example, in 1876, Sir Henry C. Rawlinson, as RGS president, declared: "There . . . [is] no reason why there should not be two or three steamers on each of the four African lakes; and if that were accomplished and centres of civilising tendency on the highlands, the conquest of Africa in the spirit of Christian zeal and civilisation would not only be begun, but half over." *PRGS* 20 (1876): 454. Roland Oliver notes that placing steamers on inland waterways figured ". . . in the plans of all five of the British missionary societies

which were about to assault the interior of Eastern Africa [in the years after Livingstone's death], and was to be an actual condition of the large benefactions . . . responsible for setting two of them in motion." Oliver, *Missionary Factor*, 27–28.

20. Quoted in Curtin, *Image of Africa*, 252.

21. *Ibid.*, 254–55, 428–29.

22. Lyons, *To Wash an Aethiop White*, 63. Archbishop Richard Whately of Ireland "postulated a series of gradations between the highest and the lowest state of human society. He compared the conditions of those on the lowest rungs of this ladder to 'as low a state as some tribes with which we are acquainted.' " These tribes, he wrote, were incapable of any improvements by their own unassisted efforts. *Introductory Lectures in Political Economy* (London, 1831), cited in Berg, *Machinery Question*, 138. For an analysis of African economic realities and the use of slave labor, see A. E. Atmore, "Africa on the Eve of Partition," in Oliver and Sanderson, *The Cambridge History of Africa*, vol. 6, 70–77; Wright, "East Africa, 1870–1905," in *The Cambridge History of Africa*, vol. 6, 540–60; and Cooper, *Plantation Slavery on the East Coast of Africa*, chaps. 1–4.

23. Curtin, *Image of Africa*, 63; Berg, *Machinery Question*, 142. In addition, in the working out of these ideas, there arose "a definite analogy, current in the work of social reformers, between the savage and the poor and unemployed." In Britain, this meant the themes of "social disease and urban degeneracy endemic to industrialism." In the West Indies and Africa, "Policy makers and reviewers in the late 1830s and 1840s were demanding instruction in agriculture and the mechanical arts for the African natives . . . an adequate education for an inferior people." Berg, *Machinery Question*, 143–44. Compare Curtin, *Image of Africa*, 427.

24. See above, chap. 6, for Hunt and the new Anthropological Society of London in the 1860s. According to Hunt, Africans were incapable of unilinear progress toward European "civilization," and he called on science to affirm these "facts." In the middle of the American Civil War, Hunt was providing a justification for slavery: only by close contact with Europeans would Africans achieve any measure of civilization, although European higher culture would ever remain beyond their reach. See Hunt, "On the Negro's Place in Nature," *passim.* Even though John Crawfurd, president of the rival Ethnological Society of London during the 1860s, did not accept Hunt's polygenesis, he agreed that Africans must be inferior: despite contact with Europe on the West Coast and Arabs and Hindus on the East Coast, they had failed to develop their opportunities to "improve." *Transactions of the Ethnological Society of*

London 4, n.s. (1865): 213-14, 221. On racism between 1830 and 1860, see Curtin, *Image of Africa*, 363-87.

25. "Livingstone's great march to the west was as much an African as a European venture . . . largely managed by two Kololo . . . and . . . equipped by Sekeletu with cattle, as gifts for chiefs, and ivory for sale to the Portuguese." Roberts, *History of Zambia*, 131.

26. *Livingstone's African Journal, 1853-1856*, 2:256.

27. Berg, *Machinery Question*, 143. Livingstone also observed bluntly: "Their smoking the Cannabis sativa perpetually is much against any clear thought on any subject beyond the earth." *Livingstone's African Journal, 1853-1856*, 2:243.

28. October 1, 1855, *Livingstone's African Journal, 1853-1856*, 2:304.

29. *Missionary Travels*, 207, 398.

30. *Livingstone's African Journal, 1853-1856*, 1:160-61; 2:332. At this point in the journal, there is a reproduction of Livingstone's drawing of Donna Anna's sugar mill.

31. *ZEDL*, 1: *xviii*.

32. "Economists . . . had a great deal to say about primitive economies, but their emphasis was on the contrast with industrialised societies and not on the development of those cultures in themselves." Berg, *Machinery Question*, 136.

33. *ZEDL*, 1: *xx*.

34. See A. McMartin, "Sekeletu's Sugar Mill," *Geographical Journal* 139, no. 1 (February 1973): 96-103, esp. 97, 99. He makes the point that several sugar mills were already in operation by the Portuguese in the Tete area. McMartin, *Sekeletu's Sugar Mill*, 100. Interest in better sugar refining was a British Board of Trade concern by the 1830s, when the Board asked Andrew Ure, a chemist interested in applying science to industrial needs, to undertake a series of experiments in the refining of sugar. Andrew Ure, *The Philosophy of Manufactures* (London, 1835), Preface, *vi*. Livingstone's interest in sugar mills may have reflected his awareness that Natal was launching experiments in sugar production in the 1850s. According to Leonard Thompson, "With the help of a few immigrants who had experience of sugar production in the West Indies and Mauritius, a sugar industry was established with cane from Mauritius and milling machinery from England." Natal coastal planters, with help from the Natal Legislative Council and the British Government in India, brought in Indian immigrants under five-year labor contracts, creating the large Indian community in Natal. Leonard Thompson, "Co-Operation and Conflict: the Zulu Kingdom and Natal," in Monica Wilson and Leonard Thompson, eds. *The Oxford History of South Africa*, vol. 1: *South Africa to 1870* (Oxford, 1969), 381, 389.

35. *Missionary Travels*, 675. James Young was an enthusiastic supporter of Livingstone's hopes that Central Africa would supply Britain's cotton needs. He wrote to Livingstone early in 1862, "The want of cotton is now being severely felt but that is all for our good. We will now have many cotton fields and I think if you was [sic] at home you would do as much for Africa as where you are. I am on the Chemical Jury of the International Exhibition. I will lose no opportunity to talk about African cotton fields when among the men of power." Young to Livingstone, February 28, 1862, Livingstone Papers, MS. 7876, fol. 13–14, NLS. Punctuation added to clarify his meaning.

36. *Missionary Travels*, 679.

37. Livingstone to Kirk, At sea off Madeira, March 18, 1858, *ZEDL*, 2:420. For the relationship between exploration, commercial development, and empire in the United States, see William H. Goetzmann, *Exploration and Empire: The Explorer and the Scientist in the Winning of the West* (New York, 1966). For a provocative comparison, see Richard A. Van Orman, *The Explorers: Nineteenth Century Expeditions in Africa and the American West* (Albuquerque, 1984).

38. *ZEDL*, 2:421–22. Before leaving England, Livingstone asked Dr. Joseph Hooker (Kew), Professor Richard Owen (British Museum), and Sir Roderick Murchison (RGS) to compose detailed Instructions on Botany and Zoology for Kirk and on Geology for Richard Thornton, the mining geologist of the expedition. These instructions, like those directed to the other members of the expedition, emphasized the need for these scientists to be alert to the commercial value of their duties. Hooker specifically noted that the recent, successful "introduction of tea, coffee, indigo, oats" to India had followed scientific investigations of this sort. Owen wanted Kirk to investigate the natural history of the tsetse fly because it was "a barrier to progress by means of oxen and horses." Similarly, Kirk was to learn about the elephants of the region because of the commercial value of ivory. *ZEDL*, 425–28. Murchison directed the geologist to gather evidence of the quality, *quantity*, and "accessibility" of metallic ores, limestone, or coal, and the mineralogical context of the "silicified fossil wood . . . brought home by Dr. Livingstone. . . ." *ZEDL*, 429–30. Livingstone asked his brother Charles to undertake meteorological observations and to purchase "as much buaze as can be procured, with a view to developing the trade in that article, and also whatever cotton may be offered for sale." He also asked Charles Livingstone to photograph the different tribes they met for Ethnological purposes, enjoining him to avoid the "ugly" and choose "the better class of natives who are believed to be characteristic of the race." Livingstone suggested photographing "men, women and children" in groups, "re-

markable trees, plants, grain or fruits and animals," and the scenery around Tete. *ZEDL*, 431–32. Since photography was a relatively new technological device, and perhaps not always reliable, Livingstone took along Thomas Baines as "Artist and Storekeeper" to provide "faithful representations" of wild animals and birds, plant specimens, fossils, reptiles, and "average specimens of the different tribes we may meet . . . for the purposes of Ethnology. . . ." He received similar instructions to choose the "comlier countenances." *ZEDL*, 434–35.

39. Livingstone to Duke of Argyll, March 5, 1859. *Livingstone Catalogue*, 91.

40. I have added some internal punctuation, especially to the last sentence to make its meaning clear. The letter was dated February 6, 1858. See Livingstone Papers, LI 2/1/1, fol. 43–46, NAZ. The text of this letter was printed as "Dr. Livingstone on Slave Labour" in the *Anti-Slavery Reporter*, July and August, 1891, 190–91.

41. Emphasis supplied. In 1872, questions raised about the validity of Livingstone's letters to the *New York Herald* cited use of the word *hussies* in connection with a description of the physical charms of Manyema women. Livingstone had not generally used colorful language of this sort to his correspondents or in his published writings. Coupland, *Livingstone's Last Journey*, 171; Jeal, *Livingstone*, 346; Hall, *Stanley*, 215.

42. Blaikie, *Personal Life*, 261. Wallis's edition of the *Zambezi Expedition of David Livingstone* suggests that the first sentence of this passage was entered under August 4, 1859, labelled "Private," and that the rest is from another section called "Private thoughts" set down sometime before October 21, 1859. Blaikie changed some punctuation and capitalization. *ZEDL*, 2:120, 126–27. Livingstone had also written: "As soon as children begin to be felt an incumbrance and what were properly in ancient times Old Testament blessings are no longer welcomed, parents ought to provide for removal to parts of this wide world where every accession is an addition of strength, and every member of the household feels, in his inmost heart, the more the merrier." *ZEDL*, 2:126. His thoughts may be set against his own choices and the separations which they created in his family life. His mother-in-law had made clear to him in 1851 that his first inclinations to keep his wife and children with him wherever he went would be condemned by others. "O Livingstone," she had written, ". . . will you again expose her & them in those sickly regions on an *exploring* expedition? All the world will condemn the *cruelty* of the thing. . . ." Mrs. Robert Moffat to Livingstone, n.d. (probably April 1851), in *Livingstone's "Private Journals," 1851–1853*, 70–71.

43. Livingstone must have been aware that young women in work-

houses were generally unwed mothers unable to support themselves and their children. Their sins of the flesh and their dependence upon state charity evidently made them "ugly" in his eyes, in comparison with the beauty of "honest" poor women. Schemes for the state supported emigration of paupers dated to the Colonial Office of the 1820s, when R. J. Wilmot-Horton proposed that Irish parishes mortgage their poor-rates to pay for sending their paupers to Canada. See Klaus E. Knorr, *British Colonial Theories, 1570–1850* (1944; reprint, London, 1963), 311–13. The Poor Law Commissioners of 1834 favored this form of state-aided emigration; nearly 24,000 workhouse paupers were sent out between 1834 and 1853. Compare: R. N. Ghosh, "The Colonization Controversy: R. J. Wilmot-Horton and the Classical Economists," in Allan G. L. Shaw, ed., *Great Britain and the Colonies 1815–1865* (London, 1970), 110–31; Sidney Webb and Beatrice Webb, *English Poor Law Policy* (English Local Government series, vol. 10, 1910; reprint, London, 1963), 141. On Livingstone's expectations that his parents would emigrate, see Campbell, *Livingstone*, 30.

44. *Livingstone's African Journal, 1853–1856*, 2:319–20. In this passage, Livingstone noted that he disliked behavior that appeared to be "begging in the most abject manner, though they may have no need of any assistance." Compare his contemptuous use of the term *begging* when referring to Baraka's desertion to Tippu Tip, above, chap. 5, n. 11.

45. For the theorists and colonial reformers who advocated middle-class emigration from England after 1830, see Knorr, *British Colonial Theories*, 269–315. Edward Gibbon Wakefield and those who adopted his views of "systematic colonization" stressed the need for finding new lands in which to invest the surplus capital and surplus labor they believed were endemic in Britain in this era. Knorr, *British Colonial Theories*, 294–315. Although Caroline Chisholm concerned herself with emigration to Australia of working-class women and families in the 1840s and 1850s, a Female Middle Class Emigration Society was established in 1862. Margaret Kiddle, *Caroline Chisholm* (Melbourne, 1950); A. James Hammerton, "Feminism and Female Emigration, 1861–1886," in Vicinus, *A Widening Sphere* (see chap. 4, above, n. 15), 56; A. James Hammerton, *Emigrant Gentlewomen: Genteel Poverty and Female Emigration, 1830–1919* (London, 1979).

46. Livingstone to James Aspinall Turner, March 9, 1859, as noted in *Livingstone Catalogue*, 234; Livingstone to Sir Thomas Maclear, November 3, 1859, quoted in Blaikie, *Personal Life*, 262, and dated by means of *Livingstone Catalogue*, 159. In this letter Livingstone reiterated the distinction he felt—in the predominant ideology in which he

grew up—between the deserving and undeserving poor: "My heart yearns over our home poor . . . fighting hard to keep body and soul together! . . . Most of what is done for the poor has especial reference to the blackguard poor."

47. Blaikie, *Personal Life*, 263. There is no record of this letter in the *Livingstone Catalogue*.

48. *ZEDL*, 1:136–37.

49. *Ibid.*, 1:222–23, dated by means of *Livingstone Catalogue*, 178. Portuguese officials in Central Africa, alert to the possible consequences of Livingstone's government-sponsored expedition, set up regulations for trade and navigation of the Zambezi. Bridglal Pachai, "The Zambezi Expedition 1858–1864: New Highways for Old," in Pachai, *Livingstone*, 33–34.

50. Livingstone to Sir George Grey, March 25, 1860, *Livingstone Catalogue*, 130; Livingstone to Charles Murray Hay (Commander of the Garrison, Mauritius, and Livingstone's host on the island during his one stay there), November 26, 1860, *Livingstone Catalogue*, 133–34.

51. Jeal suggests Livingstone wished to place an "armed steamer" on the Upper Shire River and Lake Malawi, but I have not found any indication that Livingstone was suggesting more than an "English presence" to patrol the lake and deter Arab dhows from using it. *Livingstone*, 221.

52. Blaikie, *Private Life*, 268–69; 272–73; 288 (Murchison quote).

53. Livingstone to Lord Malmesbury (Foreign Secretary), October 15, 1859, "copy" in *ZEDL*, 2:332–35, 343–45.

54. Quoted in Jeal, *Livingstone*, 222.

55. When the young Scotsman James Stewart wrote to Livingstone that he was coming to Africa to confer with him, Livingstone interpreted the request to Murchison (November 25, 1861) as: "A Dr. Stewart is sent out by the Free Church of Scotland to confer with me about a Scotch colony. You will guess my answer." Blaikie, *Personal Life*, 289. Stewart was investigating the prospects for a mission and the cotton-growing potential of the region; he went home bitterly disappointed, believing that Livingstone had made exaggerated claims about both. Since Stewart's trip had been supported by the Cotton Supply Association of Manchester, he made a formal report to them on this subject. Pachai, "The Zambesi Expedition," in Pachai, *Livingstone*, 44–45. By 1893, Malawi exported 400 pounds of cotton; by 1918, the cotton industry was the largest in the country, controlled mainly by African cultivators. Pachai, "The Zambesi Expedition," 55–56.

56. Blaikie, *Personal Life*, 332. Compare: "The general model that missionaries had in mind for the [freed slave] settlements seems to have

been that of an idealized, rural, pre-industrial England in which the church played an important social as well as religious role. . . . These images of an 'earlier and happier England' were common in Anglican circles during the second half of the nineteenth century. . . ." Strayer, *Making of Mission Communities in East Africa*, 18.

57. Bennett, "David Livingstone," in Rotberg, *Africa and Its Explorers*, 59–60.

58. Oliver, *Missionary Factor*, 34–35.

§ 8 ⅋

Horace Waller and Livingstone's Legacy: The First Decade

After editing Livingstone's *Last Journals*, Horace Waller spent the remainder of his life committed to the propagation of Livingstone's ideas, contributing in significant ways to major British initiatives in East Africa over the next two decades. As a knowledgeable Africanist, he was sought for his views by those involved in suppressing the slave trade, planning missions, and considering new means of transport and commercial enterprises in Central and East Africa. Between 1874 and 1884, these efforts created a fundamental British humanitarian stake in the ensuing European scramble for empire in Africa.

The enterprises directly inspired by Livingstone included: the African exploration of Cameron and Stanley; Colonel Gordon's antislavery efforts in the Sudan; Scottish missions in the vicinity of Lake Malawi; a renewed mainland focus by the Universities' Mission to Central Africa; missions on Lake Tanganyika and in Buganda by the London Missionary Society and the Church Missionary Society; and a Livingstonia Trading Company to serve the missions in the Malawi region. As Roland Oliver notes, this proliferation of activities created a group of officials at the Foreign Office "well versed in the affairs of Central Africa," while a "small but informed public" watched these events with careful attention, becoming "in time a powerful influence in the affairs of East Africa. . . ." This latter group included such men as: "Church dignitaries, lay committee-men of the missionary organizations, members of the Anti-Slavery Society, explorers, scientists, and, above all, business men with philanthropic interests, who believed in the doctrine of 'legitimate trade', . . . prepared in its interest to risk capital which could have been more gainfully employed elsewhere."[1]

Waller decided that Colonel Charles George Gordon was the man to assume Livingstone's mantle in Africa. Waller and Gordon met in January 1874. By May that year, at the annual public meeting of the British and Foreign Anti-Slavery Society, Waller announced that just at the time he heard of Livingstone's death, he met the man "in whom lives the same identical determination and philanthropic force which acted as the mainspring of Livingstone's life." This man was "Colonel Gordon . . . [who] went away to the heart of Africa with a devotion no less than Livingstone's to take up this cause of the abolition of slavery. . . ."[2]

In 1874, Egypt's Khedive Ismail employed Gordon to replace Sir Samuel Baker, who for four years had tried to extend Egyptian power south on the Upper Nile into the interlacustrine region around Lake Victoria. To gain British approval for this territorial expansion, Ismail asked Baker and then Gordon to attempt to suppress the slave trade in that area. Gordon, aware that Waller was a member of the Committee of the British and Foreign Anti-Slavery Society, wrote him in despair about what he viewed as the unrealistic notions of British antislavery critics. He accused them—and Waller—of maintaining a double standard of conduct. His critics warned him against using force, he said, while Waller reported to him enthusiastically about the wild threats E. D. Young made about running down any Arab slaving dhow he might meet on Lake Malawi. At this early stage of their acquaintance, Gordon had not distinguished between the pacifist views of the Quakers prominent in the leadership ranks of the Anti-Slavery Society and Waller's more bellicose opinions.[3]

Gordon's allusions to E. D. Young concerned a major Scottish effort to found a mission in Livingstone's name. As Gordon pressed Egyptian claims southward toward Lake Victoria, the missionary field around Lake Malawi, to which Livingstone had attracted the UMCA in the early 1860s, was being reentered through the efforts of Dr. James Stewart. Deeply disillusioned by the prospects of the Shire Highlands twenty years before, Stewart studied medicine and founded an industrial mission, the Lovedale Institution, in South Africa.[4] Home on leave early in 1874, he attended Livingstone's funeral and, one month later, delivered a speech to the General Assembly of the Free Church of Scotland recommending a new mission for the southern end of Lake Malawi, to be called Livingstonia. Stewart predicted that if the mission were, "placed on a carefully selected and commanding spot in Central Africa," it would "grow into a town, and afterwards into a city and become a great centre of commerce, civilisation and Christianity."[5]

To support his proposal, as he later recorded it, Stewart called upon "the Rev. Horace Waller, formerly of the Oxford and Cambridge Mission," to testify to the merits of the Malawi region where Waller had lived as a missionary.[6] Waller's backing was useful; his knowledge of this prospective field was highlighted by his work in Africa with Dr. Livingstone. Waller attended Free Church meetings in Glasgow, Edinburgh, Dundee, and Aberdeen. He called attention to the site's almost continuous water connection to the sea. He recommended its prominence as "the fountain head of the slave trade." He pointed out that E. D. Young had found in 1867 that the local population still harbored "a good feeling" toward the "English," remembered from the days of the Universities' Mission to Central Africa and Livingstone's Zambezi Expedition. "Dr. Livingstone himself," Waller proclaimed, "had always indicated it as the place where of all others a Mission would prove most beneficial and successful."[7]

Central to Stewart's appeal was his emphasis on the Malawi region as a land of "very considerable trade, . . . consisting chiefly of ivory, beeswax, and gum copal." "Trade is certain to follow in the track of the Mission. . . ."[8] The people were of a natural "agricultural" character.[9] In a study of the origins of the Livingstonia Mission, John McCracken deems Stewart's proposal to connect a new mission in East Africa with Livingstone "fortuitous." He discounts the notion that "Livingstone's ideas . . . weighed with the authorities of the Free Church in their decision to found an East African mission." He admits, however, that "for those who were to finance and administer Livingstonia, their influence was of considerable importance."[10]

The men who promised Stewart help in founding the mission (with a pledge of £1,000 each) included James White and James Stevenson, owners of rival Glasgow chemical manufacturing companies; Livingstone's old friend James Young of Kelly, who had also made his fortune from chemical manufacturing; Stewart's father-in-law and brother-in-law, wealthy Glasgow shipbuilders Alexander and John Stephen; and William Mackinnon, founder of the British India Steam Navigation Company. With a few changes, due solely to death, these Glasgow businessmen continued their support until 1914. These were men who had prospered from the application of science to industry and transport. Since they were Scotsmen, a mission to immortalize David Livingstone was a memorial to the beliefs they shared with him about "the spiritual values inherent in Victorian industry." As "firm believers in economic progress," they expected the mission to become a center of economic activity.[11] The inclusion of James Young, the Stephens, and William Mackinnon made it a unique and influential group. Their commitment

Zanzibar Cathedral, c. 1886. Christ Church was built over the site of the old slave market and its first service was Christmas Day, 1877, while the church was still roofless. The tunnel-shaped roof was designed by Bishop Steere and made of local coral mixed with cement. The flooring is paved with black and white marble. Susi was baptized in it in 1886, taking the name David.

to Livingstonia and Lake Malawi made them tenacious of British influence in that part of Africa and powerful enough to ensure that it remained within the British sphere during the European acquisition of empire in Africa in the late 1880s.

The choice of E. D. Young to lead the first party was yet another direct link to Livingstone. He had the distinctive advantage of having visited the area twice. The first group, which left in May 1875, consisted of one ordained minister and five artisans (a sailor, an engineer, a gardener, a blacksmith, and a carpenter). The predominantly nonclerical composition of the mission made clear its emphasis on African economic development. Livingstonia was to be the embodiment of Livingstone's dream of an agricultural and industrial mission to encourage Africans to reshape their society in a British Christian image and to restructure their economy to produce agricultural products for a world market.[12] The presence of the sailor signalled the realization of Livingstone's early hopes of placing a small steamship on Lake Malawi. That first steamer, carried by the pioneer party, was called the *Ilala*, to commemorate the place of Livingstone's death.[13] Waller helped outfit the Livingstonia party, and after they left, he was still busy ordering last minute additions of trading cloth for use as currency.

In December 1875, Waller introduced to the Livingstonia Subcommittee H. B. Cotterill, son of the (Church of England) Bishop of Edinborough. Cotterill wished to join the mission as an ivory trader. It was "a branch of enterprise I have always strongly advocated," Waller wrote to the Mission secretary, "in order that the natives may see that the white man will open up a market for their goods so long as they will give up selling slaves."[14] Waller believed that it was the function of the European trader to persuade Africans that legitimate commerce was a replacement for the slave trade. Livingstone had been convinced that the existence of a European demand for African products would make it obvious to chiefs that it was more profitable to keep their labor force at home. He assumed that once this fact became clear, chiefs would be encouraged to end the practice of selling off their labor supply. Neither Livingstone nor Waller anticipated that the economics of the situation might work the other way. For example, after the 1873 Zanzibar treaty forbidding the seaborne export of slaves, a rubber trade developed on the East Coast. By the 1880s, the Africans involved in this new export trade were using their proceeds to buy slaves to work their plantations.[15] Despite clear evidence to the contrary, therefore, Livingstone's faith that legitimate European trade would encourage free labor remained an attractive doctrine. It persisted in the minds of Europeans who continued to link the end of the slave trade with the increase of their own commerce.

Cotterill obtained financing from James Stevenson, William Mackinnon, and James Young, but soon found that transport costs made his trading efforts totally unprofitable. Dr. Stewart predicted this problem three months after Cotterill arrived in Africa. Late in 1876, Stewart wrote to the Livingstonia Subcommittee to finance, instead, a mission trading store. He argued that it would save the mission the cost of buying imported goods from independent merchants, while selling to local Africans the cloth, axes, and needles they otherwise bought from the Arabs. To mission authorities in Scotland, a trading store run directly by the mission provided the welcome vision of a useful commercial venture. James Stevenson, in particular, was sympathetic. He had already proposed to the Subcommittee, in October 1876, that they consider a scheme for a "Commercial Adventure in Central Africa," a business enterprise to be kept separate from the Livingstonia Mission. After receiving Dr. Stewart's arguments, the Subcommittee voted in 1877 to accept Stevenson's recommendation to establish a separate trading company. The Livingstonia Central Africa Company was officially incorporated in July 1878.[16]

The two men who agreed to manage the Livingstonia Trading Company were John and Fred Moir, whose father, an Edinburgh physician, had joined the Livingstonia Subcommittee. According to a later account by Jane Moir, Fred's wife, in 1876 the brothers "paid a visit to the Rev. Horace Waller" because "the elder [John] had been set aglow by reading Livingstone's Last Journals. . . ." John "had persuaded the younger [Fred] that there was work for both of them to do in Africa."[17] The African Lakes Company had little success in its attempt to realize Livingstone's ideas about legitimate commerce. While trying to dominate the trade of Europeans carrying goods along the route from the Zambezi River to Lake Tanganyika, they simultaneously encouraged cash-crop production in the Shire Highlands. Yet all the ivory the Moirs exported during their first five years was purchased from white hunters or obtained themselves; they could not offer prices high enough to break the Yao-Arab ivory monopoly of the interior. Only in 1883 did they begin buying ivory from the Arabs and Swahili who visited Karonga, at the northwestern end of Lake Malawi. That new connection would have fateful consequences. Despite this introduction of a European market at both ends of the lake, African chiefs and Arab merchants continued to buy, sell, and use slaves. McCracken concludes that what happened was less the "inefficiency of the Moir brothers, their limited resources and Christian scruples," noted by other historians, than the facts of African labor. "The central reason why slaves continued to be sold in Central

Africa was that slave labour was a fundamental feature of most Central African societies."[18]

African chiefs acquired slaves to sell to the export trade and for use in expanding their kinship structures and home economies. The Reverend Duff Macdonald described the process in the early 1880s:

> An old person he [the village chief] obtains for a single [buck] skin, but a young slave costs two; and women cost much more than men. The female slaves thus bought are his junior wives, and he keeps them busy in hoeing the farm, and all such female duties. The male slaves he employs in farming, building, making baskets, sewing garments, and such masculine pursuits. He keeps all these persons strictly at their duties, and at the same time welcomes an opportunity of selling them at a profit. The gain thus realized he lays out in purchasing more people. If his daughters were unmarried, he would give them slave-husbands.[19]

Livingstone's expectations about the interaction of legitimate commerce, the slave trade, and Christianity did not proceed as he and those who implemented his ideas assumed they would. By opening a vigorous market for ivory on Lake Malawi in the 1880s, the Moirs encouraged the expansion of traditional ivory expeditions, which used slave porterage. The larger ivory dealers, such as the Arabs of Karonga and the African chief Mponda at the southern end of the lake, who were also slave traders, benefitted.

Livingstone's hope for a Christian, not an "inferior," Muslim Central Africa proved illusory. The Yao chief Makanjila, at the southeastern end of the lake, converted to Islam in the 1870s. By 1885 his head village had Koran instruction for children; that same year Chief Mponda was buried according to Muslim rites. Islam spread steadily among the Yao. By 1910, a Christian missionary lamented that the Yao of the lake region viewed Islam "as their natural religion. The Yao who does not accept it will soon find himself a stranger among his own people." Livingstone's expectation that export agriculture would engender a free labor system foundered. Because transport costs remained high and land was more plentiful than labor, the market for farm products became primarily a local one. The low levels of water and many sandbanks on the Zambezi-Shire River route—problems Livingstone had encountered during his Zambezi Expedition—meant only small, shallow ships with limited carrying capacity could work regularly. Meanwhile, settlers considered the wages necessary for free labor uneconomically high. With the coming of a British administration in the 1890s, according to McCracken, the African Lakes Company began *"to demand that the colonial government use forms of coercion* in recruiting the porters and labourers whom it wished to employ."[20]

By the mid-1870s, however, the ideas that Livingstone had pioneered for developing Central Africa were common currency. For example, in 1877, after his own journey across Africa, V. Lovett Cameron set his views before the geographical and general educated public. Echoing Livingstone, whether consciously or not, he predicted that "when the chiefs find it more profitable to employ their subjects in their own country than to sell them as slaves, they will lose the most powerful incentive toward complying with the demands of the slave-dealer."[21] Like Livingstone, Cameron sought to "prove the existence of incalculable wealth in tropical Africa," by enumerating the plants, animal products, and minerals he had encountered: sugarcane, cotton, oil-palms, and coffee; tobacco, rice, wheat and corn; soft and hard wood trees, India-rubber trees, copal, and hemp; ivory, iron, coal, copper, gold, silver, and salt. For Cameron, as for Livingstone, these raw materials represented the basis of the economic potential of Central Africa and, by implication, its free labor system: "Missionary efforts . . . will not avail to stop the slave-trade, and open the country to civilization, unless supplemented by commerce."[22]

Cameron recommended that Great Britain acquire a port on the East Coast, such as Mombasa, and build a "light line of railway" to Lake Tanganyika, which could then branch both north and south. He urged placing a steamship on each section of the major rivers of Central Africa and erecting depots at impassable rapids, constructing "small lines of tram-ways" or roads for bullock-carts to carry goods around them. He asked: "Why are not steamers flying the British colors carrying the overglut of our manufactured goods to the naked African, and receiving from him in exchange those choicest gifts of nature by which he is surrounded, and of the value of which he is at present ignorant?" He predicted the solution: "[W]e shall not have to wait long ere the fertile and healthy lands round the Zambesi are colonized by the Anglo-Saxon race."[23]

Like Livingstone, therefore, Cameron linked the fate of the slave trade and slavery in Africa with British policy. "Let us hope that England, which has hitherto occupied the proud position of being foremost among the friends of the unfortunate slave, may still hold that place." During his travels, Cameron acted upon his convictions as Livingstone had only dreamed of doing. He signed a number of treaties with chiefs in the Congo area, proclaiming, December 28, 1874, a British protectorate over the region. But he was a decade too early to benefit from the new sense of competition growing among European nations for territorial claims in Central Africa. The men who directed the Foreign Office quashed his initiatives, just as they had discouraged Livingstone's earlier queries on the same subject; in February 1876, on the advice of the Colonial Office, they disapproved the treaties.[24]

Another significant step toward increased British involvement in East Africa, however, occurred in 1876, when the Church Missionary Society sent out pioneer parties to establish stations in Buganda in response to H. M. Stanley's letter to the *Daily Telegraph* of November 15, 1875. Stanley wrote that Mutesa, the Kabaka of Buganda, would welcome Christian missionaries. Cameron and Grant—whose late companion in exploration, Speke, recommended in 1864 that missionaries be sent to the kingdoms around Lake Victoria—aided the society in their writing of twenty-nine pages of "Instructions." The missionaries were to explain the "true objects of the Mission," which were to bring salvation, to introduce "a knowledge of trades, arts and sciences among his people so that their national prosperity might be increased," to promote peace, and "to substitute lawful trade" for the slave trade. It was Livingstone's formula for African regeneration.[25]

The final Instruction involved the issue of force, and was headed, "Active Interference with the Slave Trade." The CMS followed the general principles specified in the "Instructions to Lake Nyassa [Malawi] Mission Party," issued by the Foreign Missions Committee of the Free Church of Scotland. It advised that use of firearms was justified only "in self-defence when actually attacked." In addition, according to Matson, missionaries were encouraged "to *imitate Livingstone's practice* of trying the effect of conciliation, forbearance and patient endurance and, if needs be, to retire for a time from the scene of a possible conflict." The CMS committee endorsed the "Nyassa" rule; the Instructions warned that it was to be considered "*absolute and to be scrupulously observed by all members of the party, that active interference by force initiated on your side is in no case, and on no account whatever, to be resorted to.*"[26] These "Instructions" did not address what the Church Missionary could not know: the political realities of Mutesa's kingdom, and the fact that he had been led by Stanley to expect that missionaries would supply him with arms. In consequence, despite Stanley's assurances, "the missionaries soon found that the Kabaka was more interested in saving his kingdom than in saving his soul."[27] Under Mutesa's successor, Mwanga, the force of this reality would lead to religious warfare by the early 1890s.

In just over two years after the publication of Livingstone's *Last Jour-*

Bishop Edward Steere. A colleague of the second UMCA missionary bishop Tozer in Africa from 1863, Steere made himself a Swahili scholar. He succeeded Tozer as head of the mission in 1873. By that time he had determined to begin efforts to reopen missionary labor in the interior, a situation to which Waller remained sensitive as he edited the *Last Journals*.

nals, the number of Horace Waller's correspondents in East and Central Africa had grown significantly. He was sought as a consultant by men going out or returning from these fields of action. His bulging mail bag increased his fund of information, continuing to make his opinions valuable. From his quiet rectory in Twywell, Northamptonshire, the benefice he occupied from 1874 to 1895, he maintained contact with the major British efforts to increase missionary, antislavery, and commercial connections with Africa. When Waller spoke, Livingstone's name was sure to be invoked. When he wrote, Livingstone's work was used as a precedent for new labors. Waller linked himself with Kirk's work at Zanzibar, Gordon's antislavery efforts in the Sudan, the reentry of UMCA missions on the mainland, and with the Scottish evangelical and commercial efforts at Lake Malawi. In 1876, he published a pamphlet called "Paths into the Slave Preserves of East Africa, being some Notes on Two Recent Journeys to Nyassa-land, performed by Right Rev. Bishop Steere, of the Universities' Mission, and Mr. E. D. Young, R.N. attached to the Scottish Missions." He edited E. D. Young's *Nyassa: A Journal of Adventures,* which appeared in 1877. He wrote a preface to the posthumous edition of Frederic Elton's *Travels and Researches among the Lakes and Mountains of Eastern & Central Africa,* edited and completed by Cotterill and published by John Murray in 1879.

In March 1875, Waller delivered the opening address at the new African Section of the Society of Arts. He spoke on "Livingstone's Discoveries in Connection with the Resources of East Africa." The text was simple: "Livingstone held firmly to the belief that civilisation and Christianity must be made to operate upon Africa together." In the discussion that followed, Waller's words reflected Livingstone's early views of the slave trade on Lake Malawi. Waller's analysis, as the next decades would reveal, totally misapprehended the structure and strength of the slave trading in East and Central Africa. Nevertheless, his diagnosis became a standard one: the slave trade was carried on by "a few poor miserable, half-caste Arabs, almost too contemptible to talk about. . . . half a dozen Englishmen on the lake, with a good boat, would be sufficient to put down the trade."[28] Waller's language only implied that it would be the threat of resort to arms that would accomplish the desired end. In time, missionaries, traders, and even consuls would be calling specifically for gunboats on the lake to check slave trading.[29]

In his 1876 pamphlet, Waller conjured up a vision of a select group of strong men who would solve the slave trade problem along with issues of peace and order for missionary life in Central Africa. His suggestions, reprinted in the *Anti-Slavery Reporter*, were labelled "practical observations." He called for "forty men, carefully selected, under a competent leader" to induce every village to report the presence of slave caravans in the country. Waller assumed that slaves existed in African societies in the interior only in response to externally created situations, such as raids or demands for slaves by slave merchants. He anticipated the growth of "a large population . . . around the City of Refuge," trading local products in all directions. He also linked his views with the traditional British commitment to stop the export of slaves from Africa. Inland activities of this type, he said, were to be viewed as an extension of the coastal patrols whose official duty was to end the slave trade at sea. "The home Government might well afford to be answerable for the military and naval element . . . as . . . part of the suppressive policy . . . on the coast. . . ." Waller offered no suggestions as to legal or diplomatic implementation of this armed force, but he was sure that private enterprise, in anticipation of increased legitimate trade, would support the remaining costs. He referred to "the deep longing on the part of the natives for the presence of the English," making it possible for twelve Englishmen on Lake Malawi, and forty more stationed between the lake and the East Coast, "as Bishop Steere proposes," within three years, to "make the slave-trade a thing of the past over an enormous tract. . . ."[30]

Waller's "City of Refuge" proposal assumed that individuals could justify their use of force merely by the righteousness of their cause. It was all the myths of Robin Hood and medieval knights on white chargers transmuted into the British Empire heroes later found in George Henty, H. Rider Haggard, and John Buchan stories. It was an uncomplicated idea, oblivious to the realities of the locale on which it was to be imposed. It called for the assertion of civil jurisdiction by Europeans over passive, grateful Africans against unreasoning, barbarous Arab and African forces. It was a stopgap goal until the more desirable imposition of European (British) colonial power. This notion captured Waller's view of his role as a defender of Africa and Africans, and it recurred in his public pronouncements.

Waller was a self-conscious enthusiast. He used his many sources of information to become and remain a polemicist in the antislavery cause. His ideas were well-formed by the time he edited Livingstone's *Last Journals*. They were shaped by contact with Livingstone in the 1860s and advanced by correspondence with him until his death in 1873. His early hero worship of Livingstone and the labor of editing his last journals fixed Waller's views in a rigid pattern resistant to change. He enlarged the scope of his information about Africa; his views were sought because he was perceived as well-informed. His concepts of Africa and the solutions to be found in British intervention in Africa, however, did not seriously change after the early 1870s. For this reason, he later had clashes over policy with his old friend John Kirk, who became equally set in his views, but who had the advantage of twenty additional years in Africa. With the passage of time, Waller's assessment and those of others, drawn from more recent, personal experiences, continued to diverge. As circumstances in Africa changed, the Livingstone legacy, to which Waller had devoted so much of his life, became simpler, more mythic, and primarily useful to justify the British presence in Africa.

The greatest number of pamphlets and articles by Waller would appear after the international competition for African territory quickened in the late 1880s. In the meantime, he frequently wrote letters to the editor of *The Times*, which were very often, but not always, published. Using this access to a wide, highly educated and politically interested readership, he kept his opinions, and Livingstone's memory, before a nationally significant audience. Waller continued to serve on the Committee of the British and Foreign Anti-Slavery Society. By the 1880s, he was an elected member of the new Home Committee of the Universities' Mission to Central Africa. Waller's link with Livingstone and Kirk, his developing connections with William Mackinnon and Colonel Gordon, and—from the late 1880s—his ties with Frederick Lugard kept him active in influential behind-the-scenes activities concerning Central Africa. Between 1869 and 1896, the year of his death, *The Times* published eighty-five letters to the editor, over seventy of them after 1874. In only two years during this quarter century did no Waller letter appear in that newspaper, in 1878 and 1882. The years when an exceptional number appeared included 1884 (7), 1888 (8), 1890 (9), and 1892 (9). In 1884, Gordon in the Sudan and the Berlin Conference accounted for four letters and events in Malawi for three. In 1888, four dealt with the East African slave trade and the remainder with threats to imperial interests posed by Islam, the Portuguese, the French, and Germany. Waller wrote two letters in 1890 on the Portuguese threat to British interests in Malawi and the rest dealt with the Brussels Conference and the continued recruitment of slave labor at Zanzibar by Europeans, including H. M. Stanley. The 1892 letters focused on concern lest the British withdraw from Buganda and the problems of the "pacification" of the new "Nyasaland" Protectorate.[31]

In 1877 the apparently well-informed character of Waller's letters encouraged *The Times* to print them as straight news items rather than as letters of opinion. The first, May 30, was entitled "The Lake Nyassa Mission." It began: "The Rev. Horace Waller writes to us from Twywell Rectory, Thrapston." Waller's letter included extracts from two letters he had received from H. B. Cotterill, dated February and March 1877. From the Livingstonia mission on Lake Malawi, Cotterill portrayed Africans fleeing from slave merchants on the west coast of the lake and seeking refuge at the mission. Cotterill then described a visit Livingstonia missionaries had paid to the slave dealing chief at Makanjila on the southeastern coast of the lake. Waller distilled this news to demonstrate the need for a steamship to patrol Lake Malawi. He presented it as "the presence of some small vessel armed with British authority to lay down the law."[32] The careful phrase "armed with British authority" invited the reader to interpret his meaning.

Waller's second letter appeared October 26, 1877, under the title "Central Africa." Its contents revealed a miscellany of news from Gordon, Kirk, and Cotterill. A letter from Gordon, written in July from Darfur in the Sudan, stated that slave dealers were threatening open revolt. In a letter from Zanzibar in September, Kirk reported on a sudden and unexpected visit he had made to the chief points on the coast, where he found the slave trade "smoldering." Cotterill wrote news from Livingstonia in August, as he was about to embark with Consul Elton on a trip to explore the slave paths to the East Coast.[33]

Waller's letters to *The Times* in 1877 did not reveal the role he was playing in an attempt to establish a major British commercial commitment in East Africa. In January 1877, Colonel Gordon was in England, professing his desire to see no one "geographical or philanthropic." Waller broke through Gordon's reserve, using his ability to listen carefully to other men's concerns, a capacity which lay at the heart of his gift for friendship. He asked the publisher to send Gordon a copy of Livingstone's *Last Journals*. He wrote Gordon of his misgiving that Gordon continued to work for a ruler whose antislavery commitment seemed a farce. These forthright opinions reached the core of Gordon's preoccupation, his ongoing relationship with Khedive Ismail. Waller spent two days in London, listening to Gordon's distress and frustrations at not achieving any permanent suppression of the slave trade in the Sudan. He assured Gordon that he was right to distrust the Khedive. He then suggested that there was another way Gordon might help the equatorial lake region of Central Africa—he could aid the march of civilization and legitimate commerce, the only way the slave trade would truly be eradicated. He need only offer his services to philanthropic businessmen like the Scottish shipping magnate William Mackinnon who, with like-minded friends, had begun discussing ways of opening East Africa to legitimate trade.[34]

When Ismail employed Gordon in 1874, he asked him to bring the Equatorial Province under regular Egyptian administrative control and to put an end to slave trading in the region. Gordon employed Europeans and Americans to aid him, thus associating Egyptian rule in the Sudan with the imposition of European personnel as well as the prohibition against the slave trade. Gordon's dilemma, according to P. M. Holt, was to set up an administration despite the continuing influence of the slave traders, the suspicions of the Africans in the south, whose villages had been raided for slaves, and "the unwilling co-operation of a lethargic [Egyptian] bureaucracy. He could neither conciliate nor coerce his opponents, except within very narrow limits."[35]

Gordon decreed a government monopoly over the ivory trade, forbade the importation of guns, and moved to discourage the formation of private armies. He cordoned off the province of Equatoria, bringing all trade to a halt. He established new provincial headquarters at Lado—disassociating himself from the rule of his predecessor Baker—and a chain of military stations within the province. In January 1875, aware of Ismail's desire to plant his flag in the northern interlacustrine region of East Africa, Gordon directed the Khedive's attention to the East Coast of Africa as an alternate route to Lake Victoria, suggesting that it would be useful to "take Formosa Bay, or rather north of it, where the Dana or Ozy river debouches." Gordon dismissed the Nile route south from Khartoum as a "wretched marsh," while he believed "the only valuable parts of the country are the high lands near Mtesa [Mutesa]. . . ." Gordon's plan accorded with Ismail's expansionist aims in Ethiopia and Somalia. Late in 1875, the Khedive sent McKillop Pasha, a former British officer in his employ, to lead an Egyptian force to the East Coast near the Juba River. He was forced to order him to pull back in 1876 in response to pressure from the British Foreign Office, which informed him that he was invading the territory of the sultan of Zanzibar, whose sovereignty they upheld.[36] Feeling frustrated over the difficulties he had encountered, Gordon left the Sudan for England late in 1876.

At home, Gordon wrote Waller to thank him for having the publisher send him a copy of Livingstone's *Last Journals*, but also to warn him off. The letter, Waller later confessed to Mackinnon "showed me he was in perplexity concerning his future relations with the Khedive."[37] "It was a venture," Waller acknowledged, "but I wrote to tell him in the eyes of his countrymen he was putting himself in a false position by continuing in the service of a man who we knew was as much a slaver at heart as ever." "We" were the antislavery and philanthropic circles with whom Waller identified and whom Gordon did not wish to see. Whatever attracted Gordon to Waller in the brief time they met in January 1874—the fact that he was a clergyman, had had African experience, had known Livingstone, was a fellow of the Royal Geographical Society and might help him obtain the loan of some instruments, was a member of the British antislavery circles, or even that he encouraged him to collect botanical specimens for Kew—Gordon decided to write to him from the Sudan and to use him as a sounding board. In January 1877, three years later, to Waller's delight, his open criticism of Gordon's position actually made Gordon wish to see him, presumably to continue to probe him for his views about these problems.[38] Waller called on him in London at noon, January 11; he left him again the next day. Before leaving London, Waller looked for Mackinnon at his business address; not finding him, he wrote him a long letter.

Waller informed Mackinnon that Gordon was leaving the Khedive's employ. "Up to this time, knowing the peculiarities of the man, I had not dared to approach the subject of further work in Africa." Then

> . . . after dinner a new chapter in the man's heart seemed to open. He told me . . . that his most intense desire was to go back and serve . . . [the African people]. . . . He pointed out to me that the country to the South of the Lakes Albert & Victoria is an enormously rich one; that his resignation will for the moment cause a great hunt for slaves over the territory he has annexed but that no Pasha will follow his work up and that very quickly it will pass back to its original state. One thing he is certain of it can never be held with Egypt as a base.[39]

This last comment was the opening Waller sought. He told Gordon that the way to help the Africans of the northern lake region, about whom he felt such "interest and pity," was to work with Mackinnon, who "had means and influence to gather together the raw materials of a venture which should have for its historical type the East India of old."[40] Waller reported to Mackinnon that this analogy was the key to winning Gordon's interest: "He jumped at the word and said it expressed exactly all he felt. . . . He added—and this is most important—that during his occupation he had realized £140,000 in ivory alone . . . and that the Khedive had a clear £90,000 gain out his work and in hard cash." Gordon was prepared to talk seriously:

> He said if it were possible to raise a sufficient sum that is amongst some 5 or 10 men he would instantly submit a plan for their approval and carry it out and . . . he had no doubt of his entire success. Geographically he would enter at one of the rivers near Juba and work West and North. . . . He believes £5000 . . . would be enough to start with. . . . He would like to see it take the form of a

little Company and he would himself in that case invest a small stake, equal to his means, and he believes as a mere commercial matter it must pay largely.[41]

To the extent that these initial thoughts linked a British venture on the East Coast of Africa with an interest in the lake region where the Nile arose, Gordon was directing Mackinnon's attention—and later would do the same with King Leopold—to an area which would become a preoccupation of both men down to the mid-1890s. In January 1877, it was Waller who chose to alert Mackinnon that he and men like James Young and Donald Currie should "get this in shape."[42] Waller enclosed a letter from Gordon, probably dated January 11 and addressed to Waller, saying, "You are aware that I have left the service of the Khedive and therefore am free. I am however little disposed to let matters rest in Africa in the state they are, and if any opening could be seen, by which I could benefit the people, I am willing to accept the service." Gordon's conditions were discretion; that he receive two years' leave from the army; his reasonable expenses; an annual salary of £150; and "that I should be allowed as far as is compatible with my rank, independence."[43]

Waller's sheer enthusiasm for forwarding British interests in Africa, conviction that Gordon was Livingstone's successor, assumption that legitimate trade was the key to suppressing the slave trade, and prophecy that a new "East India Company" was the solution to the British government's reluctance to act there, all worked to fashion a detailed plan of action. He was able to attract Mackinnon to interest himself in a scheme that, though it failed to materialize in the 1870s, helped crystallize future thoughts about ways of introducing British enterprise into East Africa among men who would, in time, ensure that a British East African Empire became a reality.[44] Waller and Gordon were catalysts to the new, serious consideration of Livingstone's legacy.

Gordon's view of his part in this venture replicated his service for the Khedive. Once concessions were obtained and a headquarters established, he might then "act as I have done in the Province of the Equator, viz, select the best line towards the interior, and establish a post in the same, raise the troops, and command them, and see to the communications, with the head-quarters." Gordon maintained he had no wish for the general command of the project and reserved the right to leave, "*should* they [in charge] act in a spirit contrary to my ideas." In contrast to his first thoughts on the matter, Gordon became adamant that he must not be involved with the venture in any commercial way. His reasoning was clear; he feared the government would not grant him a leave from the army to engage in any business undertaking, especially if he had a

Anti-Slave Trade Decree by Khedive Ismail, 1877. Waller wrote on the side: "Khedive's decree about slavery sent me by Col. Gordon (see his writing)." Waller remained convinced until Gordon's death that he was the man to take up Livingstone's mantle in East Africa. Gordon's decisions seemed to be made out of a combination of mysticism and utter self-confidence that created his special brand of charisma.

personal stake in it. He even contemplated simply asking for a leave to travel in Central Africa, then exploring in the direction of the operations of the intended company. He cited the military leaves for exploration granted Cameron and Grandy, in connection with Livingstone Relief Expeditions, as precedents. It was an extraordinary document, and Waller understood its significance. He later wrote a memorandum on the back of it: "This was really the first step in the development of Brit: [sic] interests in East Coast: Africa."[45]

On January 18, Gordon received a telegram from the Khedive demanding his return. By the next day, he confessed he was "sorely troubled," learning that "my brother and some of my army friends look on my action in thinking of Zanzibar, as *gross treachery* toward H.H." The news travelled fast. Shortly after Gordon handed a telegram to the War Office for cyphering—telling the Khedive he refused to return, he was informed that the Duke of Cambridge required him to go back. The Commander in Chief of the Army would not allow Gordon to break his promise to the Khedive of Egypt. "[A]nd *back I must go*." Gordon was quite clear on this point. He had been given a military order; and "as I cannot afford to break off my military position," he had to obey. He sent a last word for Mackinnon, "There is no reason why he should not carry out his scheme with another man."[46]

Ismail was willing to pay a high price for Gordon's return, the Governor-Generalship of the Sudan, a post no other European had ever held. By mid-1878, Gordon used that authority to adopt harsher and less cautious methods of suppressing the slave trade. He alienated many around him by replacing several Egyptian subordinates with both Europeans and Sudanese. By the time Gordon left Egyptian service, after Ismail was deposed as Khedive in 1879 as a result of pressures from England and France, the Egyptian hold over the administration in the Sudan was "precarious in the extreme." Gordon's Egyptian successor dismissed Gordon's European lieutenants; the slave trade resumed, and the disaffected in the Sudan turned to a new leader, the Mahdi, who by 1882, organized a major revolt against any further imposition of Egyptian government.[47]

In the meantime, in 1877, the enterprise Waller was fostering gathered momentum. Waller offered Mackinnon the services of his younger brother, Gerald; and he advised him how to proceed.[48] "We should have to make it perfectly clear to Lord Derby," he wrote, "that the opportunity was so great, and the convictions of many men so well matured that an effort would be made to lay the foundations on nothing less than those of the old East India Company. If you look closely you will see the spirit of a Clive in this man—let us try, by God's help, to make him a Clive or greater if we can: less he is not, and you will say so when you know him well. . . . Think whether the right end of the stick for us to begin at is not in Downing St."[49]

Waller ventured his opinion on the nature of the commercial company that should be established. He emphasized the need to make clear the philanthropic nature of the enterprise, in principle to simplify obtaining Gordon's services from the army. His recommendation that they obtain a royal charter suggests that he, like Mackinnon, was aware of the activities of Alfred Dent, then seeking a royal charter for a British North Borneo Company. Like Gordon, Waller wished to insure that any commercial activity in East Africa would be seen as a humanitarian effort: "Desirable as it might be from some points of view, it will hardly be wise to make it too much of a *private* venture. An Engineer officer [like Gordon], the service might well say, cannot be chartered by one or even two private individuals. This observation would not hold good if a Charter could be gained by say half a dozen. . . . Six men of well known character (and we should have the six best that could be found), would give it a complexion suited to the object in view and remove it from the general atmosphere of Companies."[50] Trade was an endeavor good in itself, elevated beyond criticism by its dedication to "civilizing" and missionary ends: this was an essential part of Livingstone's legacy.

Waller's East India Company analogy was infectious. Despite the absence of Gordon, the main points of a concession scheme were worked out rapidly. Gerald Waller arrived in Zanzibar April 4, 1877, with a specific set of proposals in hand. In May, Kirk wrote of his hopes to Dr. James Stewart. It was an astonishingly proimperialist statement for a cautious official pledged to carry out his country's, and its Foreign Office's, nonimperialist goals in East Africa. Kirk, in his own way, was as committed to Livingstone's views about the need for British intervention in Africa as was Waller.

> . . . I believe nothing either missionary or industrial can succeed until the country is better governed and this can only be done by us – *I wish we annexed this whole place and gave them a settled government* . . . I am . . . [working] secretly now towards getting the mainland of Africa . . . better ruled and if this scheme succeeds we shall have the country from Nyassa [Malawi] to the Nile under British government. I mean the government of Englishmen who will use the name and the name only of the Sultan. . . . There is £400,000 to begin with and the scheme will be a new East India Company with lots of excitement to draw men out. . . .[51]

At the end of 1878, when the scheme had failed, Kirk wrote privately and regretfully to W. H. Wylde, chief of the Foreign Office Slave Trade Department, who had tried to back Mackinnon there, "I suppose at the present time our Government would not come to take over East Africa. It is a grand chance if they do and we may not always have it."[52] In the midst of a second round of negotiations by Mackinnon's agents in May 1878, Kirk characterized their proposals to the sultan as "a good sound concession and one I should just like to have the financing of myself."[53]

Kirk's concern with linking Britian more closely to East Africa made him wary that other powers, especially France, might wish to interfere in what he considered a British sphere of influence. The longer he stayed in Zanzibar, however, the more fully he identified himself with his duty to uphold the rather shadowy sovereignty the sultan claimed over the East African mainland. In 1884, for example, he hesitated when the Foreign Office asked whether they should take advantage of treaties—signed by H. H. Johnston on a exploring trip—to assert control over the Kilimanjaro region. Kirk's fateful delay led the Foreign Office to take no action. Instead, Johnston offered his treaties to Mackinnon, as a private concession. Meanwhile, Germany—a country Kirk had not anticipated would become a rival in East Africa—established a counter claim to the same region. By 1886, Germany won a sphere of influence over the southern part of the mainland at the European conference tables, including the Kilimanjaro district. When an Imperial British East Africa Company received a royal charter in 1888, Sir John Kirk, no longer consul at Zanzibar, could join Mackinnon openly, as a member of its Board of Directors. As an area ripe for economic investment, however, the East African mainland did not bear out his long-held expectations that any venture would prove profitable to its investors.[54]

❋   ❋   ❋

In 1880, Andrew Chirnside, a Scottish traveller, published a pamphlet accusing the missionaries of the Church of Scotland's Blantyre station, in the Shire Highlands, of cruelty to Africans by punishing them with flogging and, in one instance, ordering the execution of an alleged murderer. The Blantyre mission, named for Livingstone's birthplace, had been founded at the same time as Livingstonia. Dr. John Macrae, convener of the Subcommittee which supervised the mission, was an enthusiastic believer in Livingstone's ideas about establishing a "colony" of British missionaries and artisans to carry on an agricultural and industrial mission. The Reverend Duff Macdonald, sent in 1879 as the new mission supervisor, reported these punishments; he asked for guidance. The Blantyre Subcommittee investigated and found, to their dismay, that British subjects who took the law into their own hands in regions where

Sir John Kirk, c. 1890. Kirk's career in East and Central Africa began on the Zambezi with Livingstone in 1858. He came to embody the British presence there as consul at Zanzibar until Bismarck insisted he be asked to leave. He remained a consultant to the Foreign Office on African matters and represented it at the Brussels Anti-Slavery Conference in 1889. Like Livingstone, he expected East Africa to yield great profits for business enterprise, but he was disappointed in realizing his hopes as a director of the Imperial British East Africa Company.

no recognized government existed were answerable, without time limit, in a British court of justice. Accordingly, early in 1880, the Subcommittee advised the mission "to abandon all civil jurisdiction" and to prohibit "flogging, striking, and all such treatment of adults as would not be lawful in Britain."[55] The Livingstonia Subcommittee, when consulted about these punishments, similarly sent out explicit instructions to the field, indicating that "they did not regard their Mission as the nucleus of a state." It was "inexpedient," they added, "for the Mission to undertake generally the civil adminstration of its territory."[56] The question might have ended here, but for Chirnside's pamphlet, which raised a scandal.

After an official visit of investigation to the field, the Church of Scotland recalled Macdonald and dismissed two artisans involved in what were now deemed unwise and cruel measures.[57] Over the next decade, the offical policies of the two Scottish missions in Malawi appeared to create two different types of missionary work. Yet, by different routes, both missions still insisted they were following Livingstone's tradition. The new head of the Blantyre mission, the Reverend David Clement Scott, emphasized formal education at the expense of teaching the arts of cultivation. He made little attempt to alter the residential nature of the station, which from the beginning had allowed Africans, including runaway slaves, to seek refuge under the mission's protection. According to John McCracken, "Powers of jurisdiction, shorn of the excesses of the earlier period, were also retained." By the late 1880s, "Blantyre was still the 'colony,' the 'nucleus of a state', it had been in earlier days."[58] As another historian of this period has put it, Scott was "an explicit and firm believer in the civilising aspect of mission . . . [He] did not bandy about Livingstone's name . . . , but he built a mission along lines that related to his great forerunner's attitudes to African people, to culture and to the gospel."[59]

Livingstonia, in contrast, made a "dramatic and genuine" change of policy with its move to Bandawe on the western shore of Lake Malawi. Although he conscientiously carried out the new guidelines, refusing to offer the Africans around them any civil jurisdiction, Dr. Laws was a "strong believer in the tradition of Livingstone in the economic role of the mission [and] . . . sought to extend its influence over a wide area through African evangelists. . . ." Despite missionary efforts to remain aloof from local African politics, after the African Lakes Company signed treaties with lakeside chiefs in 1885, resisting involvement in the war at the northern end of the lake proved impossible, since the local people looked to them for protection. This train of events ended in a British Protectorate within a few years.[60]

When missionary societies took seriously Livingstone's recommendations on the need to establish settlements of Christians—whether Europeans, freed slaves, or local converts—the question of civil jurisdiction figured prominently in policy-making. Where no powerful local African authority existed, the issues of missionary jurisdiction—punishment for crime and use of force if attacked—remained unresolved problems before (and in some cases, after) colonial administrations were imposed. The situations that posed this dilemma had their ideological roots in the logic of Livingstone's legacy, namely, the duty to interfere in Africa in the name of the slave trade, African economic development, and Christianity. The uneasiness felt by home mission committees in these matters often led them to favor the direct protection of the British imperial flag. In the years when the rush to empire was at its height, therefore, Livingstone's arguments for an active British role in Africa were used to proclaim a British humanitarian mission there—a powerful call to heed the memory of one who had died in the service of an unrealized goal.

The experiences of the first Universities' Mission to the Shire region—liberating slaves from slave traders, leading a local force into battle, and burning down a village to punish Africans for ill-treating missionaries and their dependents—had been subject to both praise and blame in the mid-1860s in England. The experience of the Scottish missionaries at Blantyre in 1880–1881—in terms of punishments for and battles with local Africans—underlined how little had changed, despite the recognition that missionaries needed precautionary instructions to guide their choice of action. When the Livingstonia Mission and the Church Missionary Society Buganda Mission made formal rules for their agents in the 1870s, they attempted to learn from past missionary experiences. They emphasized noninterference with the slave trade and insisted that African Christian converts, or potential converts, continue to look to their local political authorities for legal protection. Events in the 1880s were to prove that solutions to these problems remained elusive, however, in part because of assumptions about cultural difference and European superiority that missionary societies and their agents brought to the question. According to Roland Oliver, "only three of the missions, the C.M.S., the L.M.S. and the U.M.C.A., made it a matter of policy to keep their temporal authority down to a minimum; and, even so, the exceptions, the freed slave settlements at Freretown [CMS], Mbweni and Masasi [UMCA] were . . . at least as important as the rule."[61]

A Home Committee crisis concerning issues of self-defense arose as a result of an attack on the UMCA freed slave settlement at Masasi, in September 1882. Masasi was established in 1878 by Bishop Steere as a step toward regaining an interior district adjacent to Lake Malawi, which lay seventy miles inland from the East Coast. The attack at Masasi led to a major discussion of defense by a mission subcommittee in London; Bishop Steere had died in Zanzibar shortly before the attack, and no replacement had been named. The UMCA subcommittee appointed to address the Masasi situation included Sir Bartle Frere, chair; Sir John Kirk; and Horace Waller.[62]

Waller took the position that although missionaries must remain "noncombatants," he would not have them relinquish control of the situation when under attack. Instead, he wanted missionaries to instruct their African dependents, as all were viewed, when to act "on the defensive to save themselves" and when it was necessary to take "the offensive to rescue members kidnapped or taken captive." Since these were the very decisions that had led to home criticism of the first UMCA missionaries, including himself, Waller was motivated, at least in part, by a wish to have those earlier actions publicly vindicated. He believed the Gwangwara (Ngoni) attackers of Masasi would interpret the missionaries' subsequent attempt to ransom captives as an invitation to strike again. He therefore recommended abandoning Masasi for Newala, fifty miles away.[63] Kirk agreed with Waller. "If a free civil community is to be raised up on the line of the old slave route, it clearly must be self-defending." Kirk was also conscious that "at Masasi we have . . . freed slaves handed over to the Mission by the British Govt." He considered the continued freedom of these liberated Africans the responsibility of those to whom they were entrusted. In Kirk's opinion, ". . . if the community could have beaten off the enemy by shooting them down the missionary had no right to advise them to stand and see their comrades killed and enslaved."[64]

Calling the Ngoni who attacked the mission "savages," Waller characteristically looked for a strong man, a leader of heroic proportions:

It wants some lay-man, a man of fortune, to go there and institute such a centre; to make himself head chief with consent of the others: then let him construct a strong place, a place of refuge and invite Maples and Porter to come and work there. Then you are clear of all difficulties. Your missionaries appear on the scene as representatives of the Church and need not carry arms. . . . these are no new ideas. They occurred vividly to Livingstone and he laid them before me in the country, but I could not see my way to leave the mission and put myself at the head of the Manganjas [sic] at the time. Nothing would have been easier as far as the natives were concerned. It is important to keep before the public, it seems to me, the fact that this Mission was not raised to carry out Bishop Tozer's plans but Bishop Mackenzie's and Livingstone's.[65]

In a letter to the society's treasurer, Rev. J. W. Festing, which was then printed for private circulation among the various committees of the mission, Waller linked the problem of defense with that of civil jurisdiction. He referred to a problem of assigning punishment that had arisen at Masasi a few months before the raid, which, he said, convinced the missionaries there that a station needed "some code of law such as that which is felt to be necessary in highly civilised communities. . . ." The choices, said Waller, were either send missionaries out to claim the hospitality of powerful chiefs, as Livingstone had done, or "raise up powerful Mission stations, so powerful that no horde of miscreants would ever dream of attacking. . . ." His own solution, again, was to raise up a "City of Refuge," headed by a lay man acting under the authority of the sultan of Zanzibar.[66]

Implicit in this recommendation is the expectation that the sultan would respond to British pressure to recognize an Englishman as his agent to set up a quasi-autonomous state within Zanzibar's domain. The Oxford and Cambridge committees of the Universities' Mission, on February 13 and 19, respectively, seconded Waller's recommendations. They passed resolutions that "defence should be intrusted to the hands of laymen" to act in connection with the sultan of Zanzibar or local chiefs" and that Masasi "should be made sufficiently strong to be capable of resisting a sudden attack." In addition, the Cambridge Committee explicitly expressed "general approval of Mr. Waller's suggestion that the head of 'the establishment' should be a layman invested by competent authority with civil and military jurisdiction." If Waller possessed a rather unrealistic grasp of the situation, his proposals were nonetheless convincing to equally uninformed contemporaries.[67]

Sir Bartle Frere, who understood the implications of Waller's plan, moved swiftly to nip in the bud what he saw as an ill-considered idea. Printed as a confidential circular for UMCA Committees, Frere's letter supplied the reasons why his subcommittee "all agreed that it was impossible to frame [general] instructions which would meet such a [specific] case [as Masasi]." Masasi's position was "untenable"; it had no "Native Civil Government" to defend it and the freed slaves attached to it. General instructions would ". . . risk either prohibiting reasonable measures of self-protection and defence—or appear . . . to sanction acts which might, under the law of England, be punishable as crimes. . . ." Since the situation at Masasi was untenable, it had to be abandoned. Frere stressed that, "[N]o instructions of ours can justify a missionary in setting up a Civil Government in Africa and defending its citizens by force of arms." However, Frere demonstrated his training in diplomacy. He declared that Waller had put forward a good idea, in principle, but he made clear that it was one that lay out of the jurisdiction of the Missionary Society to implement. He wrote as follows:

> I can quite concur in Mr. Waller's suggestion of a "city of refuge," but I would add that the suggestion did not come within the scope of our instructions. . . . For the establishment of such a refuge must depend mainly on secular powers—namely, the Sultan of Zanzibar, the British Consul &c—and could hardly, I think, be effected from funds subscribed for Missionary purposes. . . . Neither the Bishop in Africa, nor the Committee at home would be competent to direct the proceedings of a layman invested with civil authority over any portion of the Continent of Africa.
>
> . . . Meanwhile I would suggest for consideration that at Natal and in many parts of the Cape Colony there is a great demand for civilised native labour at very high wages without the slightest risk to the life or liberty of the labourer—and the Universities' Mission might thus be able to provide for any of the released Slaves who cannot find employment at Zanzibar.[68]

Frere's opinion on the diversion of freed slave labor to Natal is provocative. Frederic Elton, whom Frere recommended for vice-consul at Mozambique in 1874, was deeply concerned in this issue and, three years later, Kirk made an allocation of freed slaves—77 out of 270—to Natal, "where there was a great demand, and where there were proper regulations for their care." Kirk understood that the British government was open to criticism if it regularly shipped the larger number of the slaves liberated by its cruisers to its colonies to engage in labor contracts. Having served as High Commissioner in South Africa in the late 1870s, Frere was aware of the continuing clamor for labor made by European planters in Natal.[69]

As the restraints of British law became clearer to missionaries and their supporters, the pressure increased to seek the patronage of local African authorities for protection—and the exercise of secular power— or to call more loudly for the protection of the British flag. Consider the manner in which Archdeacon Farler described the UMCA coastal settlement of Magila in the spring of 1883. It was made up of freed slaves, Africans educated by the UMCA or the CMS, and an assortment of those "who have cast in their lot with us, who look to us for protection, whom we have adopted, and who are being educated as Readers, Teachers, Masons, and Carpenters." The inhabitants of the station worked "most

UMCA Missionaries, Zanzibar, c. 1884: Charles Alan Smythies (first row center), consecrated Central African Bishop in 1883; the Rev. J. P. Farler (to Smythies' left), Archdeacon of Magila in the Usambara region; the Rev. Chauncy Maples (to Smythies' right) and the Rev. William Porter (sitting front right), of Masasi and Newala.

flourishing plantations of fruit trees." The station was, in a real sense, the embodiment of Livingstone's idea of a small-scale agricultural colony and an industrial mission. As Farler put it, the station was "their only Fatherland, if we abandon them nothing but hopeless misery & slavery can be their lot." He therefore saw a need to defend them from "marauding tribes," in this case the Masai. His answer was to raise buildings of stone around the stations as "strong defensive works" and to sell "good rifles for our people." (Both Waller and Farler took the frugal position that those expected to defend themselves should be asked to purchase their own means of defense.) The missionaries, as ministers of God, were not to engage in actual fighting, but were to be "ready to remain with and give them all the benefit of our superior intelligence and knowledge to assist them in their defence."[70]

Farler's notion was a variant on Waller's concept of a "city of refuge." In this case, the heroes were the missionaries, conceived of as superior men leading a well-disciplined flock of lesser men. Absent is any sense that the local politics and culture of Central Africa might play a role in what actually happened. Even Steere, who insisted that missionaries remember that none of Africa was "No Man's Land," could write: "One method of mission work . . . is to take the natives into tutelage, to make them live by order and work when and as they are bidden. This produces fine plantations, good cultivation, well-kept houses and a most respectful demeanour."[71] If these two perspectives coexisted in Bishop Steere—on one hand, respect for local African authority and autonomy and, on the other, the substitution of the missionary's authority—it is not surprising that other British subjects in Central Africa welcomed the coming of British governmental authority and protection, while wishing to maintain their own immediate powers of control and punishment after the imposition of imperial administrations.[72]

✽   ✽   ✽

As the issue of civil authority symbolized the dilemmas of British missionaries seeking to introduce Christianity into East and Central Africa as part of Livingstone's legacy, so too did the issue assume increasing urgency for those who maintained that the legitimate trade was a strategy for ending the slave trade. The problem played a part in Gordon's efforts to return to East and Central Africa to suppress the slave trade and foster commercial development. He felt keenly that he must rest his use of civil authority and the force needed to uphold it on a recognized national flag. Once he left Egyptian employ, he was left with a narrow range of choices that would enable him to work again in Central Africa.

William Mackinnon, having been frustrated in his plans for a large-scale concession in East Africa in 1877-1878, made a final attempt for a scaled-down version in March 1879. The key to the idea for a concession lay in acquiring control over a port. He therefore asked the sultan of Zanzibar for a long-term lease of territory of the port of Dar es Salaam and the land adjacent to the Mackinnon-Buxton road on the route to Lake Malawi ("houses and land . . . all harbour rights . . . the lease of the customs and taxes").[73] In early May, the sultan informed Mackinnon that he had decided that to allow him to lease this port would make resisting similar demands by others difficult. Mackinnon's failure to obtain even this small concession convinced him that he should turn his efforts to helping King Leopold of the Belgians execute his large-scale schemes for opening the Congo River for trade. Mackinnon's willingness to accommodate the king was already evident in his negotiations for the concession of Dar es Salaam, where he was prepared to "reserve a part of the land near the harbour . . . for the Belgian Committee [of the African International Association] and . . . the necessary lands [for] four or five stations at intervals along the road. . . ."[74]

In October 1879, Leopold instructed General Strauch, secretary-general of the African International Association, to ask Mackinnon to assist in persuading Colonel Gordon to work for the king on the East Coast. His experience with Africanists since the mid-1870s had supplied Leopold with the appropriate rhetoric needed to approach both men. He suggested Mackinnon propose to Gordon that working for the Belgian king was the way to continue a great work of exploration and developing inland communication, to establish agriculture on a large scale and connect the outside world with areas rich in natural resources. Implicit in Leopold's vision was nothing less than the great work that Livingstone had called for as the answer to ending the slave trade and introducing "civilization" and Christianity into Central Africa.[75] Some measure of Leopold's success lay in his sophisticated use of the language that encoded Livingstone's prescription for African development.

From February 1880, after Gordon had resigned as Governor-General of the Sudan and left Egypt, to January 1884, when he formally agreed to serve the king in the Congo, Mackinnon acted on behalf of the Belgian king. Once Gordon had begun negotiations with Leopold, he never wholly pulled back, self-conscious about the turns of "fate" and aware that Mackinnon and Leopold now held out the sole means open to him of returning to work in Central Africa. His objections, until January 1884, rested on his concern that without legitimate civil authority, represented by a national flag, he would find himself powerless to exercise the force required for what he deemed effective governance. Gordon's friendship with Horace Waller provided the continuing link to Mackinnon. Waller hoped Gordon would find a role to play in East Africa, rather than the

Congo, for he viewed him as the direct successor to Livingstone. To this end, Waller saw service under the sultan of Zanzibar as a possible answer; Leopold offered the next best alternative. Gordon, on his side, was aware of Waller's friendship with John Kirk, the embodiment of the British "presence" at Zanzibar. Gordon had already experienced Kirk's enmity—in the shaping of policy if not in person—over the Egyptian attempt to secure a base on the northern Zanzibar coast.[76]

Waller once more acted as intermediary. At Mackinnon's request, Waller agreed to write Gordon, indicating the Belgian king's interest in his career and his desire for "an opportunity of seeing him." By February 2, 1880, Mackinnon informed Strauch that Gordon had arrived in Southampton, noting, too, that Waller promised to keep him informed about the situation. Three days later, Gordon wrote Mackinnon. He was clear about his views; he wanted to revive the East African concession scheme of 1877. Waller had lent him the proposal and "the confidential notes of the interview with the Sultan of Zanzibar." Gordon asked Mackinnon directly, "Are you prepared to carry this out, if so I will be inclined to help as far as I can." Aware of Mackinnon's connection with King Leopold, Gordon spelled out his views in revealing terms. He was used to making his own decisions; royal interference would be intolerable: "I do not like Belgians. I could not dispute with Kings. I must be king of the territory as far as appts [sic] go. Would Kirk get the concession? I think he would never be content with a passive part. Waller thinks otherwise."[77] Gordon wrote to Waller: "I think if Mackinnon got the mouth of the Juba River, given over to him for 20 years, it would be sufficient, if the sultan would give him the use of his troops & flag, in payment. . . . The papers you sent me daze me and require more study than I can devote to them. I hate Companies. Why should not McK get the concession himself."[78]

Once Gordon met with Mackinnon in late February 1880, he was persuaded to visit the king. Their interview was cordial, but the objection Gordon first raised in 1877, regarding not working in Africa unless under a recognized national flag, stalemated their negotiations. Gordon was adamant; he must work under an internationally recognized sovereign power, on which he could base his exercise of civil authority with its implied legitimate resort to force.[79] The African International Association had no such legal status. Waller again pressed him to think about working for the sultan. On a return visit to Brussels, April 6, Gordon suggested to Leopold that he might consider entering the employ of the sultan in order to strike "an effective blow against the slave trade by extending the Sultan's effective authority inland."[80] Leopold objected. He did not want the sultan to strengthen his hold on the East African hinterland. Gordon fatalistically accepted the logic of his position: "The question is whether one would work *with the King, or the Sultan,* there is no choice beyond these two, and I have thrown my lot in *with the King,* or with *neither,* which is more likely to be the case. Had I never come to Brussels, I would have gone with the Sultan, it is now too late."[81]

Just before he left England in early May, Gordon wrote Kirk recommending that the sultan make Captain C. E. Foot, R.N., of the British antislave trade squadron in East Africa, "Governor-General" of his mainland dominions. Rather optimistically, in the light of his own Egyptian experience, but in the tradition of Livingstone's convictions, Gordon insisted that a European Governor would "soon stop the slave trade & increase the revenues of Custom Houses."[82] Gordon, like Waller, had an abiding sense of British superiority in the governance of Arab and African lands. Later that year, Gordon considered a visit to Zanzibar to see what prospects existed on the East Coast. Gordon's connection with the Belgian king was sufficiently known to Kirk that his telegram, asking whether he was welcome at Zanzibar, drew from the British consul a very cautious reply. Mackinnon wrote to urge Gordon to go to Zanzibar; Waller wrote to say he thought it was precipitous (presumably because the ground had not yet been prepared for Gordon's taking employment under the sultan) and urged him to come home first. Kirk telegraphed: "Personally very glad to see you can say no more." Waller's letter "settled it."[83] At the end of the year, still unsure of his next assignment, Gordon spent some weeks with Waller in Twywell, Northamptonshire.[84]

When Mackinnon next wrote to Gordon on behalf of the Belgian king, in July 1882, Gordon had been promoted to Major-General and was serving in Basutoland, South Africa. Mackinnon carefully constructed his letter to win Gordon over to the Livingstonian possibilities in the Congo for effective work developing trade, fostering "civilization," and fighting the slave trade. He led into his subject by first expressing regret that the earlier concession plans for East Africa had failed to become "a practical thing." The suggestion was that, judging by the rate of progress already made on the Congo, their first plans would have been "a long way towards [Lake] Tanganyika and I [would have] made an end of the slave trade throughout the region had you taken the control & management of the affair."[85]

King Leopold had demonstrated how Livingstone's legacy might be fulfilled in Central Africa: "Immense progress has been made in preparing the way for the civilizing influences of good government, the teaching of Christianity and the trading which destroys the slave trade and promotes the well being of . . . the miserable people." Steamers—those symbols of nineteenth-century science and technology—plied the river regularly. All had been accomplished with no "fighting of any kind." Here was an employer "without desire of other reward than is found in the privilege of doing good on a great scale." The problem of civil authority was on its way to solution: African chiefs had signed over their sovereignty with territorial concessions to the great "enterprise," which now had a "special flag." Soon, Mackinnon suggested, it would be possible to "establish and organize a legal government." Stanley wished to step down. The king needed Gordon. "His Majesty is more impressed than ever with the idea that you alone of all the men he knows anything of can control and work out the great problem of African Civilization towards which his aims and efforts have been directed."[86] Mackinnon's words were confirmation of Waller's early judgment that Livingstone's mantle belonged on Gordon's shoulders.

Gordon, on his voyage to England from South Africa, wrote Waller that when this letter arrived, he was "engaged with Cape Govt [sic] and could not get away." Once home, in November 1882, he wrote more fully about his reactions: "As for King Leopold, I told Hill [at the Foreign Office] 3 years ago, that till he [the king] got a charter, he would never hold any jurisdiction over foreigners out in Africa. . . . One would only court failure in going & the more successful one was, the more certain would be the difficulties, so I will not go there." Gordon declared that the rival claims obtained by the French naval explorer Savorgnan de Brazza, competing with Stanley for treaty rights on the Congo, showed all too clearly the importance of working under a recognized national flag.[87] But from whom should the Belgian king get "a charter"? Gordon met with Mackinnon on this visit and reported to Waller that he "was very kind indeed."[88] Before leaving England, at the end of December, Gordon used the UMCA dilemma concerning the Gwangwara raid on Masasi, that had occurred the previous September, to spell out to Waller rather carefully his views concerning civil authority in Central Africa. "Of course," he wrote, "the question is, *do men go as simply ministers of Gospels*, or *do they go as civilizing agents as well.* . . . If they go as civilizing agents, then of course they must have secular power. All setting up of authority or rule by any society unless recognized by the existing Powers is only moral philibustering [sic], and can never succeed in [the] long run."[89] He included Leopold's Congo Association in his strictures.

Despite his deep reservations, however, Gordon finally agreed in October 1883, when Mackinnon raised once more the question of working for the Belgian king. Aware of events in the Sudan, Gordon wrote Waller as if admonishing himself: *he* was not in control, *he* could not be concerned. He was accepting the king's offer to go to the Congo as though it was the only way to divert himself from such concerns. Gordon then visited Brussels, arriving early in January 1884.[90] Having learned in late November that the War Office had refused to sanction his leave for this purpose, Gordon wrote Waller revealing his deeply pessimistic mood, laced with characteristic irony: "I have told Mack: that I will keep my promise to the King, if he will give me 500£ for my life. This he wanted me to take as a retaining fee long ago. I would then leave the Army and go. You say for what? It is not for any idea of great success on the Congo, it is not that I am wrapped up in it, but I have a nice house, with garden & no worries in the horizon, and if by the keeping of my promise, I would get a free & speedy passage to it (not by British India) I would be very glad, and it seems that the Congo is the route which is quickest to it—if, as I think, I am so *called there.*"[91]

Great Britain had occupied Egypt in 1882, in response to an Arab uprising, nationalistic in character, that threatened the Suez Canal. The religious revolt led by the Mahdi in the Sudan, similarly nationalistic in intent, gathered strength as the Egyptian administration in Cairo weakened. In November 1883, as Gordon made his plans to go to the Congo, Mahdist forces annihilated Egyptian troops under the direction of a former Anglo-Indian Army officer, William Hicks, and threatened the Red Sea port of Suakim. Gladstone's Foreign Secretary, Lord Granville, enquired of Sir Evelyn Baring, the British Consul-General in Egypt and its effective ruler under the occupation, whether Gordon should be sent to the Sudan. He received a negative answer. The British cabinet decided to evacuate all Egyptian officials and forces left in the Sudan.[92]

Gordon allowed news of his Congo employment to be leaked to the newspapers by January 5, 1881. Back in Southampton, three days later, he granted an interview to W. T. Stead, editor of the *Pall Mall Gazette.* Stead's lead article the following day informed the country that in Gordon's opinion evacuation meant a massacre. The paper urged the government to send him out "to assume absolute control . . . treat with the Mahdi . . . relieve the garrisons, and . . . save what can be saved from the wreck of the Sudan." *The Times* and other newspapers reprinted part of the interview the next day.[93] A few weeks before, late in December, Baker wrote Gordon, urging him to write a letter to *The Times* against evacuation of the Sudan. After his Stead interview, Gordon visited Baker. Like Leopold, Baker knew what language to employ with Gordon. He warned him, "The slave-trade will re-commence with tenfold vigor. In fact all your work and my own will be absolutely thrown away." He urged him to go to the Sudan if the Government offered him the opportunity.[94]

Wolseley called Gordon to the War Office, January 15, and told him that the Government had reversed its decision of the previous fall; he would not have to resign his commission if he worked for Leopold.[95] He then asked Gordon what he thought about going to Suakim and inquiring into the military affairs in the Sudan. Gordon expressed his willingness to go. Waller, kept apprised of these events, met Gordon for a long talk and accompanied him to Dover. Gordon felt he must inform King Leopold personally that he would have to wait a short while. Leopold, he reported, "is furious at it all." Wolseley telegraphed him to return to London immediately. On January 18, Gordon agreed to go to the Sudan; he left that evening.[96]

By March 1884, Gordon knew he could not evacuate Khartoum without military assistance from Great Britain. When Gladstone's cabinet refused to send relief, he believed it was his duty to remain at Khartoum, in hopes the Government would change its mind. By mid-March communications with the outside world were cut.[97] In the torturous months that followed, tensions built in Great Britain and in the cabinet. The majority of ministers felt they were being manipulated by Gordon into sending a military expedition, and resisted; a minority believed Gordon and Khartoum would fall without immediate aid. Finally, in late July, Gladstone reluctantly asked Parliament to vote the money for a relief expedition.[98] Wolseley was sent to organize it. When he arrived the following February, it was too late. In late November 1884, Gordon wrote bitterly, "I will accept *nothing whatever* from Gladstone's Govt. I will not even let them pay my expenses. I will get the King to pay them. I will never put foot in England again, but will (D.V. if I get out) go to Brussels & so on to Congo. . . ."[99] Khartoum was stormed and Gordon killed January 26, 1885.[100]

In April 1885, at the height of popular outcry over the death of Gordon, Waller vented his opinions in an unsigned book review in the *Contemporary Review*, a monthly journal of some 4,000 circulation with a "decidedly religious tone," whose readers were upper and middle class, "highly educated," and tending to "Evangelicalism." Waller quoted at length from Gordon's unpublished correspondence to himself demonstrate Gordon's antislavery dedication, religious nature, and betrayal by the Liberal Government. Waller expressed a common theme of popular indignation: "Gordon's life was sacrificed by the indecision and procrastination of Her Majesty's Ministers and his blood will, sooner or later, be required at their hands." He proclaimed, as he had in 1874, that "Gordon's place in history will be by Livingstone's side."[101]

A recent study of the mythology surrounding Gordon's death and Britain's attempt to regain the Sudan in 1898 analyzes the continued use of the sentiments Waller voiced in April 1885. ". . . Gordon's death was used in much the same way as his life had been, for many who had urged both his appointment to Khartoum and his relief as a means of extending British power into Central Africa also used his death as a moral justification for the conquest of the Sudan." Gordon, as this analysis points out, "became the symbol of the rightness and righteousness of imperialism. . . . To those of the British public who already believed in the moral superiority of Britain and were inclined to favor the new imperialism, Gordon's mythic moral purity both represented and justified Britain's imperialism." Thus Gordon was used "to embody the ideals of the imperial age."[102] In this sense, Waller was right when he foresaw that Gordon had the potential to be the type of legendary hero of empire that he had discerned and perpetuated as Livingstone's fate.

NOTES

1. Oliver, *Missionary Factor*, 88–89. This "informed" circle in matters concerning tropical Africa between 1860 and 1890 numbered fewer than 150 men, roughly divided into 44 percent connected with the civil or military services, 20 percent businessmen or traders, 16 percent active philanthropists or missionaries, and 20 percent a mixed assembly of geographers, explorers, anthropologists, clergymen, and journalists. Dorothy O. Helly, " 'Informed' Opinion on Tropical Africa in Great Britain, 1860–1890," *African Affairs* 68 (July 1969), 215–16.

2. Waller may have met Gordon for the first time at the Royal Geographical Society, January 17, 1874. On RGS stationary, Waller wrote Hooker at Kew: "I have spent some time today with Col: Gordon (Chinese) known to you as about to take Sir S Baker's place in Africa. I have persuaded him to do some Botany for you tho' alas he is not a Botanist. He leaves London on *Thursday* next for Egypt. . . . He is all we could possibly desire as a noble good fellow, and I look forward to *his* work in Africa being a blessing to all with whom he comes in contact." Waller to Sir Joseph Hooker, January 17, 1874, English Letters, 1857–1900, Royal Botanical Gardens, Kew, Library; *Anti-Slavery Reporter*, July 1, 1874, 78–79.

3. Gordon to Waller, October 4, 1875, Labore, WPRH, 2. Gordon told Waller that Joseph Cooper, one of the honorary secretaries of the Anti-Slavery Society, had sent him his book, *The Lost Continent or Slavery and the Slave-Trade in Africa* (1875; reprint, London, 1968). "His remedy," Gordon complained, "is stop demand & supply will stop of itself. . . . to stop demand you must change the social habits of some

millions of people. . . ." There was comment within the society about the "sharp exchange" between Gordon and Cooper. Bernard M. Allen, *Down the Stream of Life* (London, 1948), 24–25. Waller wrote in his diary, "A long letter from Col: Gordon very bitter against Mr. Cooper and the Lost Continent. Some of his views are mistaken and the whole tenour shows great irritation of mind." Diary of Horace Waller, January 25, 1876, WPYDS. In the same period, Gordon also wrote his sister a rather chary assessment of Waller's offer of friendship: ". . . through Livingstone & slave trade, he worked himself into a good living from a poor one. . . ." Gordon to Mary Augusta Gordon, Labore, October 4, 1875. See also Gordon to his sister, January 13, 1876. Add. MS. 51293, BL. Compare Tom Livingstone's remarks, above, p. 91.

    4. Alexander J. Hanna, *The Beginnings of Nyasaland and North-Eastern Rhodesia, 1859–95* (Oxford, 1956), 10–11. See also, Wallis, *The Zambesi Journal of James Stewart, 1862–1863.*

    5. Quoted in McCracken, *Politics and Christianity in Malawi,* 27. At Sir Bartle Frere's suggestion, early in 1874, the Free Church proposed a mission on the Somali coast "to check the considerable flow of Somali slaves being reported annually from the area around Lamu. . . ." Harris, *African Presence in Asia,* 54. Scottish response was lukewarm and, as Harris notes, so was Dr. John Wilson, the Free Church missionary whom Livingstone had known in Bombay. Wilson declared that Livingstone ". . . himself had suggested the borders of Lake Malawi as the locale for a Free Church Mission." See also, Sheila Brock, "James Stewart and David Livingstone," in Pachai, *Livingstone,* 106. CMS plans for a freed slave settlement to be called Freretown also proceeded slowly until the Reverend W. Salter Price, who had supervised the Nasik Asylum in India, arrived late in 1874. "The death of Livingstone, with the effects this had in Britain, apparently was the main stimulus to this sending of Price with money raised through the renewed interest in missions." Bennett, "Church Missionary Society at Mombasa" (see chap. 2, above, n. 25), 165.

    6. "Memorandum touching the 'Livingstonia' Mission, established on Cape Maclear, Lake Nyassa, E. Africa," Scottish Foreign Mission Records, 1827–1929: Livingstonia Mission Papers (hereafter, Livingstonia Mission Papers, NLS.

    7. *Ibid.*

    8. "Memorandum touching the 'Livingstonia' Mission," Livingstonia Mission Papers, NLS, Young wrote of the southern end of Lake Malawi in 1867, "A little colony here would command a flourishing ivory trade. . . ." Cole-King, "Searching for Livingstone," in Pachai, *Livingstone,* 166. Young settled the first Livingstonia Mission at this site in 1875.

9. "Memorandum touching the 'Livingstonia' Mission," Livingstonia Mission Papers, NLS.

10. McCracken, *Politics and Christianity in Malawi*, 28.

11. *Ibid.*, 29–31.

12. *Ibid.*, 33. To 1900, the skilled artisans sent to Livingstonia greatly outnumbered the ordained clergymen; the explicit strategy was to attract to the mission Africans who wished to learn the technical skills of modern industry. Sheila Brock indicates that Stewart was reluctant to let Young go as leader of the pioneer party, but that he bowed to the mission's committee's judgment that the leader should be familiar with boats. Brock, "James Stewart and David Livingstone," in Pachai, *Livingstone*, 106–7. Stewart's growing misery at the idea that he was not to be the pioneer leader is glimpsed in Waller's diary for 1875. March 30: "Stewart undecided about Young going to Nyassa. In the meantime he runs [the] risk of not starting with a sufficiently high tone in his party if some gentleman does not go with Young and the rest." April 2: Young lost his temper when inspecting the boat being built for him and Waller commented, "I am certain Stewart & he will never do together on the Zambesi." April 23: ". . . Stewart has shown great irritation about Young . . . [and] he . . . said the fact that Young of Kelly [was] corresponding with him showed that he took too much on himself. . . ." May 10: Waller read the minutes of a mission committee meeting in Glasgow and lamented: "They leave it to Young to say whether he [Stewart] shall go!! . . . It is outrageously stupid of Stewart not to have said from the beginning that he wanted to go." May 14: "Had a long talk with Stewart and told him it seemed plainly his duty to go to Lovedale and to let Young go to Nyassa." May 15: Waller had another long talk with Stewart and was still concerned at his "unhappy tone, his cheerlessness, his apprehensiveness being all so many dead logs on such an expedition as this. . . ." Diary of Horace Waller, March 30, April 2 and 23, May 10, 14, and 15, 1875, WPYDS, internal punctuation added.

13. Young first carried a small steamer in sections to Lake Malawi in 1867. Cole-King, "Searching for Livingstone," in Pachai, *Livingstone*, 158–66. Before leaving for Africa, Dr. Robert Laws of the pioneer party spent an evening with Waller, "poring over Dr. Livingstone's maps and papers." On the trip out, he studied a vocabulary compiled by the Universities' Mission "on which Mr. Waller had marked in red ink the most important words to be acquired." On the west coast of Lake Malawi, in November, 1875, Laws saw a "massive, square-shaped bluff, looking . . . 'like a grand old fortress.' " He named it Mount Waller. William P. Livingstone, *Laws of Livingstonia* (London, 1921), 45–46, 78–79. Waller noted in his diary in May 1875, "Got the Manganja [sic] grammars from

Clowes [the printers] and sent 25 off, one specifically noted for Laws."
Diary of Horace Waller, May 21, 1875, WPYDS; Waller to Dr. John Murray Mitchell, May 24, 1875, Livingstonia Mission Papers, MS. 7870, NLS.

14. Waller to Murray Mitchell, Twywell, December 16, 1875. Livingstonia Mission Papers, MS. 7870, NLS. Cotterill's first interest was in joining a new UMCA push toward Lake Malawi. When he was rebuffed by Bishop Steere, he turned his attention to the Livingstonia mission. Diary of Horace Waller, March 11, September 3 and 8, 1875, WPYDS.

15. Norman R. Bennett, ed., *The Zanzibar Letters of Edward Ropes, Jr., 1882–1892* (Boston, 1973), 53 n. 174. Frederick Cooper demonstrates that producing agricultural products for a world market was as compatible with slave-run clove plantations on Zanzibar and Pemba islands and cereal and coconut plantations on the East Coast of Africa as it was on the cotton plantations in the southern United States. Livingstone's thoughts had centered on the development of relatively small-scale African cultivation geared to a world market, with European merchants acting in an entrepreneurial capacity. He assumed that this economic system would dry up the trade in slaves and, once the trade in slaves became unprofitable, that agriculture would depend on free labor. For Livingstone on Arab plantation slavery, see *LJDL*, 1:7. As early as 1873, however, Sir Bartle Frere observed that a slave was a "safe, easy, and profitable investment" for the poorer, landless classes. They could buy one or two, hire them out, give them part of their wages to live on, and pocket the rest. Cooper, *Plantation Slavery on the East Coast of Africa*, 185. For a discussion of this issue, see Miers, *Britain and the Ending of the Slave Trade*, 146–53.

16. Waller helped Cotterill obtain £100 from Mackinnon and £200 from James Young. Diary of Horace Waller, February 2, March 24, and May 20, 1876, WPYDS. On the origins of the Livingstonia trading company, see McCracken, *Politics and Christianity in Malawi*, 42–44. The separation of trading company and mission had an artificial quality about it. The mission's steamship *Ilala* was transferred to the company for three years, and from 1880, the Livingstonia Subcommittee agreed that artisans could be transferred between the trading company and the mission as needed. McCracken, *Politics and Christianity in Malawi*, 161. Alexander L. Bruce, who married Agnes Livingstone in 1875, later became a company director.

17. Jane F. Moir, *A Lady's Letters from Central Africa: A Journey from Mandala, Shire Highlands, to Ujiji, Lake Tanganyika, and Back* (Glasgow, 1891). Waller's diary recorded the visit of one Moir brother, to whom he gave the advice he had received from Archdeacon Mackenzie in 1859. "Young Mr. Moir came to see me about going to Africa. He is

the son of an Edinburgh Doctor. He seems delicate & one eye is damaged. Advised him to wait and fit himself for work." Diary of Horace Waller, December 19, 1876, WPYDS. The Moir brothers volunteered in 1877 to work on building the Mackinnon-Buxton road from Dar es Salaam on the East Coast inland toward Lake Malawi. John Moir to Mackinnon, Edinburgh, January 29, 1877, and Fred L. M. Moir to Mackinnon, March 5, 1877, Mackinnon Papers, Library of the School of Oriental and African Studies, University of London (hereafter MP, SOAS). Mackinnon was considering ways of expanding his interests in East Africa in early 1876. Historians have noted this timing in connection with a letter Waller wrote Mackinnon in January, 1877, saying, "It seemed to me as if some unseen hand was leading him [Gordon] into the presence of four or five men & ladies who sat round a breakfast table in Burlington St about a year ago." MP, IBEA Co., Files 1–2, SOAS. See: Roger Anstey, *Britain and the Congo in the Nineteenth Century* (Oxford, 1962), 70; and John S. Galbraith, *Mackinnon and East Africa, 1878–1895: A Study in the 'New Imperialism'* (Cambridge, 1972), 42 and 42 n. 5. A study of Waller's diary for 1875–76 turns up a number of meetings with Mackinnon, many at breakfast at the Burlington Hotel, where Mackinnon stayed when in London. These meetings dealt with such matters as Livingstonia and Cotterill's trading scheme for Lake Malawi. The breakfast to which Waller referred in his letter of January 1877, judging by Waller's diary, took place early in April 1876: "Breakfasted with Mackinnon who was very nice. He is full of a large trading scheme & w[oul]d like Gordon to undertake that part of Africa. This cannot be: Gordon evidently dislikes the natives." Diary of Horace Waller, April 5, 1875, WPYDS, emphasis added. The last sentence reflected Waller's reaction to the rather caustic letters Gordon had sent him regarding the difficulties he was experiencing in putting down the slave trade and creating an Equatorial Province for Egypt. In the middle of June 1876, Waller learned from Mackinnon that "the King of the Belgians is most enthusiastic on this matter of Central Africa." Diary of Horace Waller, June 13, 1876, WPYDS.

18. McCracken, *Politics and Christianity in Malawi*, 45–46. McCracken bases this assessment of the goals and problems of the African Lakes Company on a 1970 Edinburgh University Ph.D. thesis by Hugh W. Macmillan, "The Origins and Development of the African Lakes Company, 1878–1908."

19. Duff Macdonald, *Africana; or, The Heart of Heathen Africa*, 2 vols. (1882; reprint, New York, 1969), 1:147.

20. McCracken, *Politics and Christianity in Malawi*, 6, 55–56, 46, emphasis added. In 1890, John Moir maintained, "There will always be a

good deal of difficulty about labour . . . [Africans do] not care to do hard work. . . ." He also declared the country was not suitable to "white colonisation. We only want white men to direct." *Anti-Slavery Reporter*, July and August, 1890, 164.

21. Cameron, *Across Africa*, 473.

22. *Ibid.*, 476.

23. *Ibid.* 477–80.

24. *Ibid.*, 480; Anstey, *Britain and the Congo*, 54.

25. A. T. Matson, "The Instructions Issued in 1876 and 1878 to the Pioneer C.M.S. Parties to Karagwe and Uganda," Parts 1, 2, *Journal of Religion in Africa* 12, no. 3–13, no. 1 (1981–82): 192–231; 25–46. See Part 1:199 and 211, and James A. Casada, "James A. Grant and the Introduction of Christianity in Uganda," *Journal of Church and State* 25, no. 3 (1983): 507–22. The Instructions also recommended Waller's pamphlet on African fever. Matson, "Instructions," Part 1:211 and 234, n. 63. When Gordon announced in a letter to *The Times* January 30, 1877, that he was returning to Egypt in the employ of the khedive, Grant wrote a response that was published the next day. He declared that Gordon's "chief object . . . is the annexation of the Victoria Nyanza," and he deplored it. "Indeed, I think honestly it would be a sinful proceeding to allow . . . [Uganda] to be placed under the yoke of Egypt. . . ." He called Mutesa and his officials "in reality more civilised than the Government which is attempting their civilisation, and [Uganda] would derive no benefit whatever from the change." The (incorrect) implication of Grant's plea was that Egypt would introduce slavery and the slave trade into a kingdom where it was absent. Grant called both Mutesa and his "race" "manly," hospitable to English travellers, and altogether "a brave, intelligent people." *The Times*, January 30 and 31, 1877. This public pronouncement served to organize many concerned to aid the CMS attempt to introduce a mission in the area; they sent a protest to the Foreign Office, urging that Egypt be deterred from swallowing up Uganda. For a discussion of Grant's letter and its consequences, see James A. Casada, "James A. Grant: Victorian Africanist," *The Historian* 39 (November 1977), and Casada, "Grant and the Introduction of Christianity in Uganda." Baker wrote Grant: ". . . so very glad to see your letter in the Times today—as I agree cordially with all your views." Baker to Grant, January 31, 1877, Grant Papers, MS. 17909, NLS. According to Grant's diary, he called on Gordon the day his letter appeared in *The Times*: "See [sic] dear little Gordon [sic] in his lodgings . . . he was packed and goes to Paris tonight." Grant Papers, MS. 17917, January 31, 1877, NLS. At this point Grant does not seem to have held Gordon responsible for the policies of his employer. See p. 275.

The matter did not end there. Edward Hutchinson, CMS lay secretary, urged at a meeting of the African Section Committee of the Society of Arts, February 26, 1877, that the society aid the CMS by sending a protest to the Foreign Office deploring Egypt's actions. Both Baker and Grant served on the subcommittee to draw up this resolution, but the project was abandoned March 2, when they learned that the Government had already acted through its consul in Egypt. Minutes, African Section, 1874–1879, General Minute Books, Royal Society of Arts. In fact, this expression of concern, triggered by Gordon's return to Egypt, occurred more than a year after the government had let the khedive know their view that "his financial credit will be seriously impaired by useless and distant wars." Quoted in E. R. Turton, "Kirk and the Egyptian Invasion of East Africa in 1875: A Reassessment," *Journal of African History* 11, no. 3 (1970): 362. See below, n. 36. Sometime toward the end of 1878, from the Sudan, Gordon wrote his former aide, C. M. Watson, who was in England, to "go and see Grant and tell him that in 6 months the whole of our posts will be withdrawn from King M'Tesa's [sic] vicinity. . . ." Watson wrote this message to Grant, adding "he [Gordon] clearly looks on the policy Egypt has pursued in pushing so far as wrong." Watson to Grant, January 14, 1879, Grant Papers, MS. 17909, filed with Gordon letters, NLS. Yet a rift between Grant and Gordon developed, presumably over this issue. Gordon wrote Baker in November 1878, "I never sought Grant's acquaintance, it was forced on me, he is a soured man, why I do not know. Horace W[aller] would introduce me to him, neither he nor his wife have any sense when talking about Africa, and it was wearisome to talk to them." Gordon to Baker, K[h]artoum, November 27, 1878, Papers of Sir Samuel Baker, File 21, Private Collection, courtesy of Valentine Baker, Esq. (hereafter, Baker Papers). Although later, in 1885, Grant wrote in his diary: "Gordon is really dead at Khartoum. . . . What a shame to the Gladstone Government," later still, in 1890, Grant wrote Baker, ". . . what did Gordon ever do? There was no more insubordinate officer in the service than him . . . Gordon was a fanatic." Grant Papers, MS. 17917, February 16, 1885, NLS; Grant to Baker, Nairn, N.B., January 2, 1890, Baker Papers, File 20.

26. Matson, "Instructions," Part 1:214–15, emphasis added only to Matson's words; otherwise as in the original Instructions. Note also: " '*Livingstone's Journals*' will be found to supply some excellent examples of what is here indicated." Emphasis added. "Extracts from the General Directions and Suggestions to the Mission Party Proceeding to the Victorian Nyanza in 1876," Original Letters &c Re *Masasi Raid*, in Papers of A. H. Pike, UMCA, USPGA [hereafter Pike Papers, UMCA,

USPGA]. Compare: "Livingstonia: Instructions to Lake Nyassa Mission Party," Livingstonia Mission Papers, NLS. Alexander Mackay, an engineer, volunteered for the Uganda mission because of his "burning desire to go to the 'region which Livingstone and Stanley had found to be groaning under the curse of the slave-hunter.' " He followed his hero's Shire Highlands example, liberating slaves from an Arab caravan. Matson, "Instructions," Part 1:218. Iain Smith characterizes Mackay as an "imperialist of the most 'forward' school," and comments: "His influence on Emin Pasha [named Governor of Equatoria by Gordon in 1878] was considerable, and his importance in the sequence of events which resulted in the British involvement in the interior of East Africa up to his death in 1890 has perhaps been underrated." Iain R. Smith, *The Emin Pasha Relief Expedition, 1886–1890* (Oxford, 1972), 29.

27. Matson, *Instructions*, Part 2:41

28. *JSA* 23 (1875): 360, 365. For the character of Arab activities in the interior of East Africa see Alison Smith, "The Southern Section of the Interior, 1840–84," in Roland Oliver and Gervase Mathew, eds., *History of East Africa*, vol. 1 (London, 1963), esp. 267–96. A useful overview of the East African slave trade in the nineteenth century, sorting out the elements of European, Arab, and African participation, is Edward A. Alpers, *The East African Slave Trade*, The Historical Association of Tanzania (1967; reprint, Nairobi, 1968). See also above, chap. 7, n. 22.

29. Dr. Laws at Livingstonia recommended to all British consuls who entered the district "the necessity of their having a gunboat on the Lake as the way to suppress the slave trade with the least possible bloodshed." Livingstone, *Laws of Livingstonia*, 242–43. Capt. F. D. Lugard's scheme for pacifying the area in 1889 called for an armed trading steamer on the lake. Four years later, H. H. Johnston, the first British administrator of the region, asked for one armed steamer and received two. He soon conceded there were limitations to their usefulness: they could not be everywhere at once and attacks on slave trading owners of dhows and canoes escalated into retaliation on land against missionaries and traders. Hanna, *The Beginnings of Nyasaland*, 64–65, 78–79, 140, 195–96, 261.

30. *Anti-Slavery Reporter*, July 1, 1876, 92–93. Planning a UMCA freed slave settlement at Masasi, on the slave route between Kilwa and Lake Malawi, Steere was concerned about safety. "If we had the means to hire and feed some hundred or two of men to clear, and plant, and build, and defend themselves if necessary, I think this line of [slave] trade at least might finally be closed, but it would be madness to attempt force unless one had ample means, *and at least the passive support of the English Government.*" *Anti-Slavery Reporter*, May 15, 1876, 62, empha-

sis added. Since Steere did not expect the government's sanction, he emphasized that missionaries should put themselves under a major local African chief. Terence Ranger, "European Attitudes and African Realities: The Rise and Fall of the Matola Chiefs of South-East Tanzania," *Journal of African History* 20, no. 1 (1979): 66–67.

31. Richard Hall writes that in 1872 Waller "had close contacts" at *The Times* and "could get news items to suit his purposes inserted almost at will." *Stanley*, 224. He does not cite a source. Waller had written Livingstone in 1872, ". . . the Editor of the Times at my request in a private note, inserted a letter from me to disprove the almost universal belief that your letters were forgeries—I mean those written to J. G. Bennett." Waller to Livingstone, August 12, 1872, WPRH, 1. Waller noted in his diary in June 1876, "The Editor of the Times sent me back all my MSS. and a very polite note to say he had not room & had the same news in a shorter form." Diary of Horace Waller, June 2, 1876, WPYDS. As years passed, however, Waller's position as a knowledgeable Africanist and the valuable information he could supply were probably reason enough for publishing his letters. For a complete list of Waller's letters to the editor of *The Times*, see Appendix B, pp. 374–76.

32. *The Times*, May 30, 1877. See McCracken, *Politics and Christianity in Malawi*, 42–44. Even though Cotterill was in the Malawi area as a private trader, Elton forwarded to Lord Derby his suggestion for a gunboat "to counter an expected Portuguese incursion," February 3, 1877. Norman Etherington, "Frederic Elton and the South African Factor in the making of Britain's East African Empire," *Journal of Imperial and Commonwealth History* 9, no. 3 (May 1981): 264; 273 n. 59. During Elton's tenure as consul at Mozambique, 1875–1878, the Foreign Office passed on his dispatches to Lord Carnarvon at the Colonial Office. Carnarvon viewed East Africa up to Egypt as South Africa's hinterland and potential labor source. On December 12, 1876, Carnarvon wrote Frere, whom he had just named High Commissioner at the Cape, of how he viewed the proposals by Leopold II to open all Central Africa to European influences: "I should not like anyone to come too near us either on south toward the Transvaal, which *must* be ours; or on the north too near to Egypt and the country which belongs to Egypt. . . . We cannot admit rivals in east or even the central part of Africa: and I do not see why, looking to the experience we now have of English life within the tropics—the Zambezi should be considered to be without our range of colonisation." Quoted in Etherington, "Frederic Elton and the South African Factor," 267; see also Clement F. Goodfellow, *Great Britain and South African Confederation, 1870–1881* (Cape Town, 1966), 177.

33. *The Times*, October 26, 1877.

34. Gordon to Waller, January 4, 9, 16, 17, 18, 19, 21 and 28, 1877, WPRH, 3. In his letter of January 4, Gordon said that Nubar Pasha counseled him in Egypt that he had two choices: "[No.] 1 *going back and breaking out to sea* & [No.] 2 *throwing over H.H. altogether.* Gordon declared: "I cannot agree to No. 2, but I see no reason agst carrying out No. 1, & though *I may have no hand in it*, I feel sure that No. 2 will follow No. 1, this I look on as a certain eventuality." He made a point of telling Waller that the income of his province had been £40,000 a year while its expenses were only £15,000. See Galbraith, *Mackinnon and East Africa*, 51–55.

35. Peter M. Holt, *The Mahdist State in the Sudan, 1881–1898: A Study of Its Origins, Development, and Overthrow*, 2d ed. (Oxford, 1970), 35. The analysis of Gordon's situation in Egypt is taken from chap. 1. Holt portrays Sir Samuel Baker as "deficient in administrative qualities and, a more serious defect in the circumstances, totally blind to his delicate and invidious situation." Holt, *Modern History of the Sudan*, 68. For Baker's concerns about the Sudan in 1884–1885, see below, n. 94.

36. George Birkbeck Hill, ed., *Colonel Gordon in Central Africa, 1874–1879*, 3d ed. (London, 1884), 151, 65; Turton, "Kirk and the Egyptian Invasion of East Africa," 356. Gordon's ready plans for Waller and Mackinnon reflect mature thought about how Buganda might be approached from the East Coast. Turton points out that Gordon was under a misapprehension concerning the distance between the East African Coast and the lakes, believing it to be 258 miles instead of nearly 450. Compare Galbraith, *Mackinnon and East Africa*, 50–53. By the time Mackinnon's concessions were presented to the sultan of Zanzibar, in May 1877, Gordon was back in the Sudan. Kirk, who identified Gordon with the Egyptian threat to the sultan's northern coast, denounced him to Mackinnon as "the Curse of Central Africa." Kirk to Mackinnon, Zanzibar, "Private, Confidential," May 4, 1877, MP, SOAS. Kirk made use of the threat posed by Egyptian invasion of the East Coast near the Juba River late in 1875 to obtain the sultan's agreement to the 1876 proclamation against overland slave caravans. "I had in view getting more," Kirk wrote W. H. Wylde at the Foreign Office, "if we had only been left to turn the Egyptians out by force, in which case I intended asking abolition of all land traffic and *a Settlement on the Juba [River] under British administration.* . . ." Kirk to Wylde, Zanzibar, February 8, 1876, emphasis added. Kirk Papers, Private Collection, courtesy of Mrs. Daphne Foskett. Kirk's expression of territorial aims was in keeping with his secret wish at this time that Great Britain would annex the sultan's mainland territory, see p. 280.

37. Waller to Mackinnon, London, January 12, 1877, MP, SOAS.

38. Gordon telegraphed Waller, January 8, 1877, that he had received his "kind welcome letter" and gave him his London address. The next day, he wrote: "Your letter as to my return embodied the floating ideas I had in very forcible language." Gordon to Waller, January 9, 1877, WPRH, 2.

39. Waller to Mackinnon, London, January 12, 1877, MP, SOAS.

40. Waller was one of the earliest imperialists of the period to use this analogy; by the 1880s it had become commonplace. Edward Hutchinson, lay secretary of the CMS, alluded in March 1877 to "the formation of a company—such as the old Hudson's Bay Company—to be composed of men" ready to accept gradual profits over time. "For such a company," he went on, "I would seek a concession from the sultan of Zanzibar. . . ." How much he knew of Mackinnon's plans is not clear. Edward Hutchinson, "The Best Trade Route to the Lake Regions of Central Africa," *JSA* 25 (March 30, 1877): 438.

41. Waller to Mackinnon, London, January 12, 1877, MP, SOAS. Waller warned Mackinnon that Gordon was unwilling to work with "the King of the Belgians' scheme." Leopold II had founded the African International Association at Brussels in September 1876, bringing together an international group of geographers, explorers, philanthropists, and businessmen. Waller kept abreast of Leopold II's interest in Africa through his friends. Frere told Waller that he had given the king a copy of Waller's recently published "Slave Preserves" pamphlet in June 1876; and in September Sir Rutherford Alcock ordered a copy of the proceedings of the Belgian committee to be sent to Waller. Diary of Horace Waller, June 2 and September 29, 1876, WPYDS. Mackinnon was particularly active in seeking to raise money for the new organization and planned a meeting "of influential merchants in Glasgow" in November for this purpose. Grant to Bates, Househill, November 6, 1876, Correspondence Files, RGSA. On November 9, Waller received a telegram from Young to come to the meeting, which was held the next day. At Glasgow, Waller, Frere, and Mackinnon "arranged the resolutions." Waller thought Frere "spoke feebly and in a rambling way . . . I only spoke for 5 min[ute]s about the breakdown in the slave-trade. Sir James Watson was in the chair." Waller lunched with Young and A. L. Bruce and visited a statue of Livingstone being made. He later wrote at length about the meeting to Kirk. Diary of Horace Waller, November 9, 10, 11, and 16, 1876. See Anstey, *Britain and the Congo*, 70–71, 71 n. 3.

42. Waller suggested James Young's participation. They were working closely on Livingstone family financial investments; Waller and his wife were visitors at Young's home in Scotland; and in August 1876, Young made Waller a personal loan of £500. Diary of Horace Waller,

June 25, 1875; August 11 and 21, 1876. Galbraith mistakes E. D. Young for James Young here. Galbraith, *Mackinnon and East Africa*, 60, 73, 93. Donald Currie, a self-made millionaire from Belfast, owned the Union Castle Steamship Company serving India and South Africa. He was the most wealthy of the men associated in Mackinnon's East African ventures. W. D. Rubinstein, *Men of Property: The Very Wealthy in Britain since the Industrial Revolution* (New Brunswick, 1981), 98. At the Royal Colonial Institute, June 7, 1877, Currie called the "missionary and commercial zeal" of the British who had gone into the Lake Malawi region a "fitting tribute" to Livingstone. He added that it would be "by opening up facilities for commerce" that the problem of civilization would be solved in the interior of Africa. "Thoughts upon the Present and Future in South Africa, and Central and Eastern Africa," *PRCI* 8 (1877): 387, 391–92. Waller also mentioned a "Mr. Denny," whom he had met at a breakfast with Mackinnon at the Burlington Hotel. Diary of Horace Waller, April 15, 1875, WPYDS. Denny may have been the Peter Denny, Esq. of Dumbarton who contributed an initial £1,000 to the Emin Pasha Relief Expedition in 1887. Galbraith, *Mackinnon and East Africa*, 116. Compare Smith, *The Emin Pasha Relief Expedition*, 302, and *The Diary of A. J. Mounteney Jephson: Emin Pasha Relief Expedition, 1887–1889*, edited by Dorothy Middleton (Cambridge, 1969), 427, where the name appears as "Bonny."

43. Waller to Mackinnon, London, January 12, 1877, MP, SOAS, and Gordon to Waller, London, January 11, 1877, WPRH, 2.

44. Waller wrote Mackinnon, "There is your man, and *the* man." He underlined it three times, conscious of playing a part in shaping the future of East Africa; he added, ". . . money must do the rest and here my powers end." Waller to Mackinnon, London, January 12, 1877, MP, SOAS.

45. Waller to Mackinnon, Twywell, January 15, 1876 (corrected by another hand to 1877), MP, SOAS; Gordon to Waller, London, January 16, 1877, Gordon continued to refer to "this Riv: Ozy scheme." Waller to Mackinnon, "Private," Twywell, January 24, 1877, MP, SOAS.

46. Gordon to Waller, London, January 19 and January 28, 1877, WPRH, III. Gordon did not see the Duke of Cambridge; instead, he learned from General Horsford that he would be ordered back preemptorily if he did not reconsider on his own. Waller to Mackinnon, "Private," London, January 22, 1877, MP, SOAS. Galbraith comments, "The manner in which Gordon decided to inform the Khedive of his resignation suggests that he may have wanted to be dissuaded." *Mackinnon and East Africa*, 54. Gordon wrote his friend Mrs. Freese, ". . . it is all for the best, and I even like it. . . . I am destined to that land. . . ." Gor-

don to Mrs. Freese, London, January 25, 1877, Gordon Papers, St. Anthony's College, Oxford.

47. Holt, *The Madhist State in the Sudan*, 39, 40–41. Ironically, it would be the Mahdist revolt in the Sudan that would cut Egypt off from its principal source of slaves. Soon after Gordon returned to the Sudan, on August 4, 1877, Khedive Ismail signed a Convention with Great Britain for the Supression of the Slave Trade. All private sale and purchase of slaves was to come to an end in Egypt in 1884 and in the Sudan by 1889. British vessels were to be allowed to patrol the Red Sea for slaving ships and to free any slaves captured. See illustration, p. 278. By 1879, Gordon believed the Convention inoperable in the Sudan. Baer, "Slavery in Nineteenth Century Egypt," 433, 439, 437.

48. Waller to Mackinnon, Twywell, January 18, 1877, MP, SOAS. In offering to send Gerald, Waller reminded Mackinnon that Gerald was related to Kirk: ". . . you know Dr. Kirk's brother (Alexander Kirk of Elder & Co) married my sister [Ada]. . . ." Making clear that Gerald was also available at short notice, Waller expanded on the subject at the end of his letter: "I had intended to tell you when we met that I am very anxious to get a berth for a younger brother in some business where he may in time get a chance. My brother in law offers to make him an Engineer and he is with him at Elder & Co, but he is almost too old. It has struck me that possibly out of all this some nitch [sic] may be cut out for a young fellow with a head on his shoulders; if so I hope you will not think me very importunate if I speak a word for him. His health up to a certain time in life was his enemy but some two years traveling about in America set him up I trust for life."

49. *Ibid.* On January 20, Waller advised Mackinnon that delay was now necessary; however, he had received a telegram from James Young in Algiers placing £5,000 "at the disposal of our scheme as his part of it." Waller to Mackinnon, "Private," Twywell, January 20, 1877, MP, SOAS.

50. Waller to Mackinnon, Twywell, January 18, 1877, MP, SOAS, with one redundant comma eliminated. On Mackinnon's friendship with Alfred Dent, see Galbraith, *Mackinnon and East Africa*, 37–39. Sir T. Fowell Buxton, who was separately working with Mackinnon on road-building from Dar es Salaam inland, asked advice concerning his participation in the concession scheme of 1877–1878 of his friend and cousin William E. Forster. Forster's reply suggests something of the issues raised: "Dear Fowell. I hardly think I can advise you with regard to this most important proposal. . . . On the one hand this new company may stop the Slave Trade, on the other hand, its working is thickly beset with difficulties not to say dangers. It is in fact an 'East India Company' in East Africa, & *if it succeeds must end in empire*." Forster to

Buxton, December 19, 1877, emphasis added. BFASSP, MSS. Brit. Emp. s22/G2, RH.

51. Kirk to Stewart, Zanzibar, May 7, 1877, emphasis added. Stewart Papers, ST 1/1/1, fol. 687–98, NAZ. Kirk wrote Wylde from Zanzibar, September 19, 1877, "I hope you have enjoyed your trip to Scotland where Mackinnon tells me you are assisting him to . . . consider our grand scheme." Kirk Papers. The willingness of Kirk and Wylde, despite their official capacities, to aid Mackinnon in pursuing his concession, is striking. Mackinnon wrote Kirk that "Wylde had given me privately a copy of your dispatches [to Lord Derby at the Foreign Office] on the subject of the Concession." Mackinnon to Kirk, Glasgow, July 27, 1877, copy, MP, SOAS. Kirk continued to supply Mackinnon with information about Foreign Office matters, as in the case of the Anglo-Portuguese treaty negotiations of 1883–1884. In addition, Mackinnon helped a junior clerk in the Foreign Office, Henry Austin Lee, to get out of a range of bad debts and in return heard news of interest to him between 1878 and 1892. Where the exact line of propriety about such behavior was drawn among Victorians is worthy of closer investigation.

52. Wylde shared the view that Great Britain should be taking a leading role in the region. He minuted on a dispatch from Elton at Mozambique in April 1876, "We are every day assuming a more active Policy on the East Coast of Africa both as regards the suppression of the Slave Traffic and the exploration of Africa and development of its resources, and from this Policy we can scarcely withdraw, even if we wished, considering the interest taken by the Public in African Affairs." Etherington, "Frederic Elton and the South Africa Factor," 260.

53. Kirk to Wylde, Zanzibar, "Private," December 12, 1877, and May 3, 1878, Kirk Papers. In the second letter, Kirk blamed the Arabic translater George Percy Badger for problems arising with the sultan. Later he blamed Mackinnon for not being "hot enough on it. . . ." Kirk to Waller, Zanzibar, November 14, 1878, WPRH, 1. Kirk's first formal reports to the Foreign Office about Mackinnon's concession scheme, in April 1877, were carefully couched in official, impartial terms. He pointed out where the concession breached the treaty rights of other nations at Zanzibar (a matter he had not been clear enough about in his first advice to Mackinnon, perhaps to allow himself to be able to point to some technical flaws when the concession came forward). He then ventured to show how much the British Government would save in its annual expenditure for an antislave trade squadron on the East Coast of Africa should such a British scheme come into existence. As he presented it, this concession, dedicated to law and order and trade, would inevitably "tend to stop the Slave trade. . . ." Kirk to Lord Derby, April 10 and

April 25, 1877, F.O. 84/1485, Public Record Office, London. To Mackinnon, Kirk wrote encouragingly, "The plan has succeeded above all expectations." Kirk to Mackinnon, Zanzibar, Private and Confidential, April 19, 1877, MP, SOAS. The standard theory about why the concession came to nothing, supplied by Marie de Kiewet, is that Badger discouraged it on orders from Lord Salisbury, who took over at the Foreign Office in 1878. Galbraith, *Mackinnon and East Africa*, 66–70. On Kirk's unique relationship to all these parties, see *Mackinnon and East Africa*, 58.

54. Galbraith, *Mackinnon and East Africa*, 105–7; 124–43. Asked by the Foreign Office, in November 1884, whether he would recommend making the Kilimanjaro district a British colony, Kirk wrote the Foreign Secretary, Lord Granville, he could not recommend it, "Nor do I think a colony in the true sense of the term where the white race can permanently exist and perpetuate itself can be founded anywhere in Central Africa." Kirk's reluctance to take advantage of the idea in 1884 has puzzled historians. On the whole, the conclusion has been that Kirk had become convinced that working through the sultan of Zanzibar was the wisest course in East Africa. It has been suggested that by virtue of his role as supporter to the Zanzibar ruling house, he failed to see that the sultan's power, always tenuous, was collapsing under the European scramble for concessions. For an assessment of Kirk's role as British representative at Zanzibar and his slowness in reacting to the German threat in 1884, see Galbraith, *Mackinnon and East Africa*, 85–90, esp. 89 n. 2. Galbraith agrees with Roland Oliver, *Sir Harry Johnston and the Scramble for Africa* (London, 1957), 66–77, esp. 76. In the light of more recent scholarship, there is a need for a new, full-scale look at Kirk's career, reappraising the classic works of Sir Reginald Coupland *The Exploitation of East Africa, 1856–1890: The Slave Trade and the Scramble* and *Livingstone's Last Journey*.

55. *The Blantyre Mission Case*, 4–6. Scottish Foreign Mission Records, Blantyre Papers, NLS (hereafter, Blantyre Papers, NLS). In setting up the Blantyre Mission in 1874, Macrae had consulted Frere, Kirk, and Waller. Andrew C. Ross, "Livingstone and the Aftermath: The Origins and Development of the Blantyre Mission," in Pachai, *Livingstone*, 191. When the question of civil jurisdiction arose in 1879, Macrae consulted Waller, whose reply of December 27, 1879, was privately printed for circulation to the Blantyre Subcommittee, Blantyre Papers, NLS. Macrae told the General Assembly meeting March 2, 1881, that "assumption of civil jurisdiction was essential in the type of Christian colony that Livingstone had visualised and of which Blantyre was meant to be a model." McCracken, *Politics and Christianity in Malawi*, 66 and n. 37.

56. McCracken, *Politics and Christianity in Malawi*, 69.

57. For cases of flogging by Church Missionary Society agents at Frere town, see Bennett, "The Church Missionary Society at Mombasa," 164, 173, 178, and Oliver, *Missionary Factor*, 53–54, n. 4. One of the artisans dismissed from Blantyre in 1881, Andrew Buchanan, became a large-scale coffee planter, and as Acting British Consul, declared a British protectorate over the Shire Highlands, September 21, 1889. McCracken, *Politics and Christianity in Malawi*, 157.

58. McCracken, *Politics and Christianity in Malawi*, 69, 70.

59. Ross, "Livingstone and the Aftermath," in Pachai, *Livingstone*, 207, 214.

60. McCracken, *Politics and Christianity in Malawi*, 70, 75, 77.

61. Oliver, *Missionary Factor*, 51. Oliver notes that "[I]t is unlikely that any mission in East Africa at this time in practice escaped the exercise of some such powers," adding that the LMS still found it necessary as late as 1904 "to pass a resolution that no missionary should be involved either directly or indirectly in the flogging of adult natives for offences of any kind." Oliver, *Missionary Factor*, 59 and 59 n. 2.

62. Sir Bartle Frere, "Provisional Report of SubCommittee on Masasi Station recently attacked by Wagwangwara [sic], November 29, 1882. Pike Papers, fol. 7, UMCA, USPGA.

63. *Ibid.*; "Memorandum upon 'Reasons for abandoning Masasi &c,' " initialled "HW." Pike Papers, fol. 23–24, UMCA, USPGA.

64. Untitled memorandum, in Kirk's handwriting, Pike Papers, fol. 27–32, UMCA , USPGA. Kirk to Penney, December 12, 1882, Pike Papers, ff. 87–91, UMCA, USPGA. Kirk was aware of the problems concerning civil jurisdiction that had checkered the history of Freretown, the CMS freed slave settlement at Mombasa. As British consul at Zanzibar, he had dealt with the missionary assertion of right "to enforce their own concept of the law," despite repeated warnings to conform to the laws of the sultan and his local agents, especially with regard to the return of runaway slaves. Bennett, "The Church Missionary Society at Mombasa," 167 and *passim*.

65. Waller to Penney, Twywell, January 26, 1883, Pike Papers, fol. 129–133, UMCA, USPGA, some internal punctuation added for clarity. Waller even believed, earlier in January, that he had found such a man, a Lt. Smith, who had asked the UMCA if he could help them in any way and about whom the Kirks spoke "in *the highest terms possible.*" Waller sent Penney a letter he proposed to write to Smith, laying out in detail what should be done, including the building "of stone and lime" a 'city of refuge' and arming it with the mission's freed slaves prepared to defend themselves with firearms "under the control of the man who holds the

caps." Waller to Penney, Twywell, January 15, 1883, and a copy of Waller to "My dear Sir," January 15, 1883. It seems likely this letter was never authorized. In 1884, a Lt. Charles Smith took over as vice-consul at Kilwa on the East Coast. Sir John Gray, "Zanzibar and the Coastal Belt," in Oliver and Mathew, *History of East Africa*, vol. 1, 249. I have found no evidence that Livingstone suggested to Waller that he become the leader of the Mang'anjas, but such a proposition momentarily fired his imagination in the fall of 1863, when he was living on Mount Morambala, awaiting Livingstone's return from Lake Malawi. He was visited by Massingire chiefs, made up of the Goan family of Vas dos Anjos and their African supporters, who gave him the impression they were offering him the opportunity to hoist the English flag over them. "In a daydream of his loneliness, he . . . imagined himself . . . carving out a little English principality along the Shire. . . . 'What a chance for an Englishman to step in and say, I will be your leader and ruler, what reins to hold too.' " Chadwick, *Mackenzie's Grave*, 228. For the way this incident represented a possible strategy for the Massingire, see M. D. D. Newitt, "The Massingire Rising of 1884," *Journal of African History* 11, no. 1 (1970): 91–92, and *Portuguese Settlement on the Zambesi: Exploration, Land Tenure and Colonial Rule in East Africa* (London, 1973), 284–85.

66. "A Letter by the Rev. Horace Waller, touching the question, '*How are Missionaries to act when attacked by enemies, such as the Magwangwara of the other day at Masasi?*' " January 25, 1883, Universities' Mission to Central Africa, London, printed for private circulation. Pike Papers, fol. 143–46, UMCA, USPGA. Ranger demonstrates how the need of UMCA missionaries to find a strong local chief, and their misconceptions about Yao and Makua ethnicity, allowed them to believe Chief Matola possessed a "Yao" paramountcy at Newala despite contrary evidence. Ranger, "European Attitudes and African Realities," esp. 86–73.

67. "Resolutions passed by the Oxford Committee of The Universities' Mission to Central Africa," February 13, 1883; "Resolutions passed at a meeting of the Cambridge Committee of The Universities' Mission to Central Africa," February 19, 1833, Pike Papers, fol. 155–56, UMCA, USPGA.

68. "Memorandum, by the Right Hon. Sir H. B. E. Frere, Bart., G.C.B., &c., &c., on a Letter, by the Rev. Horace Waller, F.R.C.S., Touching the Question—'*How are Missionaries to act when attacked by enemies. . . ?*' Confidential—for Use of Committee," Universities' Mission to Central Africa, February 26, 1883, Pike Papers, fol. 151–53, UMCA, USPGA. Archdeacon Farler expressed his concern about find-

ing work for the freed slaves who returned from Masasi. He suggested establishing a freed slave settlement on the East Coast under the authority of the sultan of Zanzibar or the British government. Excerpts copied from a letter from J. P. Farler, November 7, 1882, Pike Papers, fol. 62, UMCA, USPGA; Farler to Kirk, Zanzibar, November 12, 1882, Pike Papers, fol. 64–66, UMCA, USPGA.

69. This "South African factor" in British interest in East Africa has been explored by Norman Etherington. He points out the relationship between Frere's desire to revive a British consulate at Mozambique in 1873 and his recommendation that it be filled by Frederic Elton, experienced in labor recruitment for Natal Colony. Elton, like Livingstone, emphasized that the extinction of slavery and the slave trade depended on the introduction of "commerce and civilization" and "the substitution of free labour for slave labour." Elton saw work on Natal plantations as "accustoming the Native mind to the practicality of earning the goods they covet by their own industry." On the exploratory trip which proved fatal to him that year, Elton was accompanied by Herbert Rhodes, Cecil Rhodes's older brother, who was prospecting for minerals. Etherington, "Frederic Elton and the South African Factor," 258.

70. Farler to Festing, May 26, 1882, Pike Papers, fol. 68–69, UMCA, USPGA. Fearing invasions in the early 1890s, LMS missionaries in Zambia "armed villagers so 'as to inspire them with confidence, without in the least disturbing the prevalent impression respecting us that we will fight only in self-defence. . . .' " Quoted, from a letter of August 1892, by Robert I. Rotberg, "Missionaries as Chiefs and Entrepreneurs: Northern Rhodesia, 1882–1924," in *Boston University Papers in African History*, vol. 1, 202 n. 17.

71. Oliver, *Missionary Factor*, 63.

72. For the continuation of whippings, enforced road work, and heavy fines administered by missionaries in Zambia (Northern Rhodesia) after the coming of chartered company rule, see Rotberg, "Missionaries as Chiefs and Entrepreneurs," 197–209. Despite an LMS ruling by directors in England in 1898, when these activities were brought to their attention, the practice continued and was again brought up in 1905. In punishing Africans who disobeyed them, whatever the "disobedience" involved, missionaries shared the feelings of other white men who saw corporal punishment as the only way of asserting and sustaining the "prestige of his race among a wild community," as one government district officer put it in 1900. Rotberg, "Missionaries and Chiefs and Entrepreneurs," 205, n. 29.

73. Anstey, *Britain and the Congo*, 72–73, 73n. Capt. C. E. Foot, R.N. was engaged, with Vice-Consul Frederick Holmwood (Zanzibar) and

Edward Jenkins, M.P., in the winter of 1878–1879, exploring the possibilities of asking the sultan for a concession of land, beginning at Dar es Salaam, to build a railway, presumably toward Lake Malawi. They appeared before the Manchester Chamber of Commerce, February 21, 1879, to test the interest in their scheme, invited there by James Hutton, whose railway investment interests led him, in April, to become, with Mackinnon, a British investor in Leopold's *Comité d'Etudes du Haut Congo.* William G. Hynes, *The Economics of Empire: Britain, Africa and the New Imperialism, 1870–95* (London, 1979), 29–33; Anstey, *Britain and the Congo,* 66; Galbraith, *Mackinnon and East Africa,* 75. Gerald Waller reported to Mackinnon what little he knew about the rival scheme developing about Foot and Jenkins. Gerald also noted that Foot had written Horace Waller on the subject. Gerald Waller to Mackinnon, London, January 10, 1879, MP, SOAS. Kirk reported to the Foreign Office, February 28, 1881, that 73 miles had been constructed along the Mackinnon-Buxton road from Dar es Salaam, but that after the first forty, ". . . the presence of the tse-tse fly . . . makes it hopeless to attempt the use of horses or bullocks. . . ." Coupland, *Exploitation of East Africa,* 303. Joseph Thomson's exploration of the country between Dar es Salaam and Lake Malawi held out few expectations for this route. Gerald Waller to Mackinnon, London, February 2, 1880. MP, SOAS. The harbor at Dar es Salaam had been discovered in the mid-1860s. Plans by the sultan to build a town were reported by the British consul, Col. Lyon Playfair, in November 1866. *PRGS* 11 (1866–67), 18.

74. Anstey, *Britain and the Congo,* 75–76. Leon Lambert to Mackinnon, London, March 21, 1879, and Mackinnon to Lambert, London, March 22, 1879, copy, MP, SOAS.

75. "His Majesty would like you to let him understand that the king's idea is that this is only the first part of a programme capable of great development. . . ." Strauch to Mackinnon, October 20, 1879, translation, MP, SOAS; compare Anstey, *Britain and the Congo,* 76–77.

76. His relations with Zanzibar and Kirk weighed on Gordon's mind. He wrote Kirk late in November 1879, admitting he had suggested the East Coast expedition to Ismail. He declared that he had meant Egypt's intentions to be accomplished by open diplomacy with Britain and Zanzibar. Not content to leave it at that, Gordon recorded his continuing doubts about the sultan's rights to ports north of the equator, or whether such ports benefited from the sultan's claims. He also questioned the wisdom of the sultan's supplying arms to Mutesa in Buganda, when Egypt "has not the least idea of annexation." Gordon to Kirk, Abyssinia, November 23, 1879, Gordon Papers, Acc. 4983, NLS.

77. Mackinnon to Strauch, Balinakill, February 2, 1880, copy, MP, SOAS; Gordon to Mackinnon, London, February 5, 1880, Gordon Papers, Acc. 4031, NLS. See also, Lord Elton, *Gordon of Khartoum: The Life of General Charles George Gordon* (New York, 1955), 222–23; Gerald Waller to Mackinnon, London, January 5 and February 4, 1880, MP, SOAS; and Anstey, *Britain and the Congo*, 77 and 77 n. 2. A fragment of a draft letter from Mackinnon to Gordon appears to answer Gordon's letter of February 5, 1880: "Waller has shown you the Concession the Sultan was prepared to grant me. . . . I agree with Waller in his estimate of Kirk [crossed out] him. Waller's opinion of him is mine." MP, SOAS.

78. Gordon to Waller, London, February 8, 1880, WPRH, 2. Colonel Strauch wrote Mackinnon authorizing him to invite Gordon to Brussels to see the king, as Mackinnon, in a letter at the end of the previous October, had suggested would be the most effective strategy. Strauch to Mackinnon, Brussels, February 6, 1880, MP, SOAS. See also, Gordon to Waller, Southampton, February 25, 1880, WPRH, 2; Anstey, *Britain and the Congo*, 77 and 77 n. 6. For Gordon's concern to continue to fight both domestic slavery and the slave trade in the Southern Sudan, see Gordon to Waller, London, February 7, 1880, WPRH, 2.

79. Gordon was not sanguine about Leopold's prospects in 1880, and from a letter from Kirk to Waller, which the latter lent him, he understood Kirk felt similarly. Gordon to Waller, London, April 7, 1880, WPRH, 2. Compare n. 81, below.

80. According to Anstey, ". . . the Sultan was, in fact, ready, on conditions, to employ an Englishman for such a purpose." *Britain and the Congo*, 77 and 77 nn. 7–8; 78 n. 2. Waller wanted Gordon and Kirk to be "friends in Council," for without Kirk's backing, Gordon would not get Foreign Office permission "for any Zanzibar scheme." Waller warned Mackinnon before Gordon visited Brussels that his real goal was to finish his antislavery work in the Sudan. Waller to Mackinnon, Twywell, March 2, 1880, MP, SOAS. A draft letter (in two handwriting styles) from Mackinnon to Kirk, Paris, March 12, 1880, raises the question whether Mackinnon had in fact given up on a concession on the East Coast: "I hope by the next mail," he wrote, "to learn whether you think it possible that the Sultan would yet make such a concession as would enable us to avail of Gordon's services." "You know I never met Gordon until quite the other day," he continued, "[and] . . . I was greatly taken by him. . . . both Waller and I think that if you knew him personally you would both become fast and firm friends and if embarked on the same good work you could really accomplish great things." Gordon, he

assured Kirk, had "quitted the Egyptian services for good," and he seconded Waller's idea that Kirk "induce the Sultan to assure him of a kindly and cordial welcome. . . ." Mackinnon Papers, MS. 4031, NLS.

81. Gordon to Waller, Brussels, April 6, 1880, and March 3, 1880, WPRH, 2. Before Gordon saw the king in March 1880, Leopold sounded the British Foreign Office about his interest in obtaining a concession for a "colony" on the East Coast of Africa. Asked for his opinion, Kirk replied, March 8, 1880, that any Belgian bid for territory on the East African coast should be met with "caution." In July 1880, Leopold approached the sultan through the French consulate for a ninety-nine year lease at Malindi on the East African coast, again without success. Coupland, *Exploitation of East Africa*, 346; 346 n. 1; 347–348. Compare Anstey, *Britain and the Congo*, 78–79.

82. The letter began with "Private & confidential *now* and for ever," and ended with "Please tear up this letter." Gordon to Kirk, May 7, 1880, Gordon Papers, Acc. 4083, NLS. From China, later in 1880, Gordon reported to his sister, "I had a nice letter from Kirke [sic] of Zanzibar, he sees the same difficulties, as I did with respect to King of Belgians." Gordon to Mary Augusta Gordon, Tientsin, August 8, 1880 - Singapore, August 30, 1880, Gordon Papers, Add. MS. 51296, BL. Captain Foot, R.N., was well-known in Waller's circles. His comments were recorded in the discussions of presentations by Cameron at the Society of Arts, *JSA*, 25 (January 1877), 161–71, esp, 170; Archdeacon Farler at the Royal Geographical Society, *PRGS* 1, n.s. (November 1878): 81–94, esp. 94; and James Bradshaw, a Manchester cotton merchant, on "Africa; A Paramount Necessity for the Future Prosperity of the leading Industries of England," *JSA*, 27 (March 1879): 368–76, esp. 372. Foot delivered a paper at the Society of Arts in May 1880, on "Transport and Trading Centers for East Equatorial Africa," *JSA* 28 (1880): 362–69. He saw East Africa as "a field . . . for commerce, such as has rarely been excelled. . . ."

83. "When I got to Aden, I got a letter from H. Waller, who spoke as if I could do no good at Zanzibar (read his letter & tear it up)." Gordon to Mary Augusta Gordon, Red Sea, September 25, 1880, Gordon Papers, Add. MS. 51296, BL.

84. While at Twywell in December, 1880, Gordon took High Communion for the first time. It made a deep impression on him. "I am well & have become more quiet, all through the sacrament as a means, which I learnt at your house at Twywell." Gordon to Waller, Mauritius, March 14, 1882, WPRH, 2. Of the Wallers, he wrote his sister Augusta on December 16, 1880, ". . . the female W [sic] is more spiritual than the male who is wrapped up, to some degree, in Church, and other dogmas,

which are adamant." During the last two weeks of his stay, Gordon took lodging in the village. He confessed to Augusta, "There is a *little* wish to show me, & I have escaped with difficulty dinners & long consequent drives." Gordon to Mary Augusta Gordon, Twywell Rectory, December 16; Twywell, December 23 and 30, 1880, Gordon Papers, Add. MS. 51296, BL. Local tradition at Twywell developed this one visit into a legend of a series of them. Later, Gordon did agree to act as godfather for Waller's son. Gordon to Mary Augusta Gordon, Jaf[f]a, September 15, 1883, Gordon Papers, Add. MS. 51298, BL.

85. Mackinnon to Gordon, Balinakill, July 18, 1882, Gordon Papers, Add. MS. 51305, BL.

86. *Ibid.*

87. Gordon to Waller, Near Madiera, October 31, 1882, and Southampton, November 9, 1882, WPRH, 2. Gordon wrote Baker, "The King will do nothing unless he gets a charter from some regular govt [sic] and I told him that two years ago." Gordon to Baker, Off the Isle of Wight, November 7, 1882, Baker Papers, File 21.

88. Gordon to Waller, Southampton, November 18, 1882, WPRH, 2.

89. Gordon to Horace Waller, Southampton, December 16, 1882, WPRH, 2.

90. Mackinnon to Gordon, Dunrobin Castle, n.d. (by context, October 13, 1883) and Balinakill, November 1, 1883, Gordon Papers, Add. MS. 51305, BL. Gordon wrote his sister, "If any one asked me, what is the object, I could not tell them . . . and what I see, is a certain collision with Zanzibar, as soon as the Expedition emerges into the [lake] shore districts." From Brussels, he wrote, "I have seen the King, he wishes me to retire from the army, and go to Congo. I said "yes." . . . Will you kindly tell Waller privately," Gordon to Mary Augusta Gordon, Jaf[f]a, November 20, 1883, and Brussels, January 2, 1884, Gordon Papers, Add. MS. 51298, BL.

91. Gordon to Waller, Jaf[f]a, November 20, 1883, WPRH, 2. Gordon responded to Waller's comments on Egyptian affairs in 1883 that he believed it of no use to be so concerned about events over which he had "*no control.*" Gordon to Waller, Jerusalem, April 8, 1883, WPRH, 2. Compare: "I do not write about Egyptian affairs, for there is a small nest of sleeping devils in me, on *that* subject, and I do not want to awaken them." Gordon to Baker, Jerusalem, March 8, 1883, Baker Papers, File 21.

92. Holt, *Mahdist State in the Sudan*, 84–85, 87–88; Lord Granville wrote Gladstone, November 27, 1883: "He has an immense name in Egypt—he is popular at home—He is a strong but sensible opponent of Slavery. . . ." Agatha Ramm, ed., *The Political Correspondence of Mr.*

Gladstone and Lord Granville, 1876-1886, 2 vols. (Oxford, 1962), 2:116 (hereafter, Ramm, *Gladstone and Granville*).

93. Elton, *Gordon of Khartoum,* 272-73. Gordon's Congo plans were leaked, with his consent, by the journalist Demetrios Boulger. Boulger thought Gordon the right man to send to the Congo, but not for philanthropic reasons: "let me congratulate you on a return to that sphere in which you can do good . . . I am sorry that it is only blacks, poisoning themselves with gin & rum, who will benefit by your efforts." Boulger to Gordon, London, January 4, 1884, Gordon Papers, Add. MS. 51305, BL.

94. "I wish you would write to the Times immediately and discountenance the abandonment of the Soudan-: shewing [sic] also the injustice to Europeans and others who hold property in Khartoum &c, should the country be forsaken." Baker to Gordon, Sandford Orleigh, December 28, 1883, Gordon Papers, Add. MS. 51305, BL; Elton, *Gordon of Khartoum,* 279-80. Baker, frankly concerned about imperialist aims in the Sudan and Central Africa, wrote Gladstone in January, 1885, urging him not to abandon Khartoum. The Treasury advised Gladstone that Baker was not "a disinterested adviser," because he had "considerable investments in the Soudan, rumour says to the extent of £30,000. . . ." Baker sent a second letter, suggesting that selling off the "fertile portions" of the Sudan to companies or individuals and the construction of a Suakim-Berber railroad would open a new field for British enterprise. Capital would be attracted for the "development of Upper Egypt, a British colony would be quickly established. . . ." As for the Sudanese, a "paternal form of Government similar to our administration of India is the form of administration best suited to their natures." Baker seemed totally oblivious to Gladstone's disdain of such views. Baker to Gladstone, Sandford Orleigh, January 6, 1885, and Baker to Edward W. Hamilton [Gladstone's private secretary], Gladstone Papers, Add. MS. 56451, BL. Considering his own plans, there is irony in Baker's despairing words to Gordon, ". . . if we abandon Khartoum the French or the Germans will manage to walk in, by establishing Missions or trading stations, or anti slave hunting safeguards, or upon some pretense or other. . . ." Baker to Gordon, January 12, 1885, Sandford Orleigh, Gordon Papers, Add. MS. 51305, BL. The Anti-Slavery Society endorsed building a railway from Suakim to Berber as a means of fighting the Sudan slave trade. *Anti-Slavery Reporter,* September and October, 1891, 213.

95. Granville had refused leave to Gordon "to act in the K[ing] of the Belgians African Association. I gave an opinion against an officer on full pay being connected with this nondescript association." Ramm, *Gladstone and Granville,* 2:149.

96. Holt, *Mahdist State in the Sudan,* 89-91; Elton, *Gordon of Khar-*

toum, 282; Gordon to Mary Augusta Gordon, Brussels, January 17, 1884, Gordon Papers, Add. MS. 51298, BL. The day before Gordon saw Wolseley, Granville consulted Gladstone: "If he says he believes he could by his personal influence, excite the tribes to escort the Khartoum Garrison, & inhabitants to Suakim, a little pressure on Baring might be advisable." Gladstone telegraphed Granville; he agreed. On January 15, Granville telegraphed Baring for his approval. Granville reported to Gladstone, January 18, that Gordon ". . . perfectly understands that he is to consider the evacuation as a final decision & that his only mission is to see how it can be best carried out. . . . He was very pleasing & childlike in his manner." Ramm, *Gladstone and Granville*, 150; 150 nn, 1, 3; 151. In the Sudan, in early February, Gordon began planning how to add the Equatorial provinces to the Congo: "I want the King of Belgians to let me take the Equator & Bahr Gazelle [sic] Provinces for him, this would save me going back to Cairo, & starting again for Congo, this would also stop the slave trade, and we would soon DV [Domine Volente or God willing] join those Provinces to Congo, at a place called Karuru." Gordon to Mary Augusta Gordon, January 19, 1884, Korosko, February 1, 1884, Gordon Papers, Add. MS. 51298, BL. Gordon made this proposal to King Leopold in Brussels, in January. The idea of extending Congo territory to the Nile became a fixed notion of the king's. Smith, *Emin Pasha Relief Expedition*, 73, 146, 158, 292; Robert O. Collins, "Origins of the Nile Struggle: Anglo-German Negotiations and the Mackinnon Agreement of 1890," in Prosser Gifford and Wm. Roger Louis, eds., *Britain and Germany in Africa: Imperial Rivalry and Colonial Rule* (New Haven and London, 1967), 127.

97. Holt, *Mahdist State in the Sudan*, 99.

98. Wolseley wrote Gordon's brother Henry, July 24, 1884, that he worried about his brother's ammunition giving out at Khartoum. "I think therefore that no time should be lost. . . . At any rate I do not wish to share the responsibility of leaving Charley Gordon to his fate. . . ." Gordon Papers, Add. MS. 56451, BL.

99. Gordon to Watson, Khartoum, November 26, 1884, Gordon Papers, Add. MS. 51305, BL.

100. Julian Symons, *England's Pride: The Story of the Gordon Relief Expedition* (London, 1965); Adrian Preston, ed., *In Relief Of Gordon: Lord Wolseley's Campaign Journal of The Khartoum Relief Expedition, 1884–1885* (London, 1967).

101. Ellegård, "The Readership of the Periodical Press in Mid-Victorian Britain," 13. The circulation figure is for the mid-1870s. [Horace Waller], "General Gordon's *Life* and *Letters*," *Contemporary Review* 159 (April 1885): 475, 479. The review included: Egmont Hake,

The Story of Chinese Gordon, 1884; George Birkbeck Hill, *Colonel Gordon in Central Africa,* 1881; Sir Samuel W. Baker, *Ismailia,* 1874; Reginald H. Barnes and Charles Brown, *Charles George Gordon, a Sketch,* 1885; *Papers Presented to both Houses of Parliament—Egypt,* No. 1, 1885; and *Unpublished Private Correspondence, 1877-85.* The unpublished correspondence quoted is clearly Gordon's to Waller. Knowledgeable contemporary readers would have guessed Waller's authorship. Acceptance of Waller's article by the Liberal-identified journal was itself a sign of party dismay at Gladstone's policy regarding Gordon. Politically active Conservatives, however, were "carefully ambiguous" about criticizing the Liberals over the Sudan issue; once in power they were equally adamant that Egypt must let go of the Sudan. Andrew Jones, *The Politics of Reform, 1884* (Cambridge, 1972), 117; A. B. Cooke and John Vincent, *The Governing Passion: Cabinet Government and Party Politics in Britain, 1885-86* (Brighton, 1974), 63-64.

102. Douglas H. Johnson, "The Death of Gordon: A Victorian Myth," *Journal of Imperial and Commonwealth History* 10, no. 3 (May 1982): 285-310, esp. 301, 302, 307.

§ 9 &

Horace Waller and Livingstone's Legacy: The Second Decade

In the second decade after the publication of Livingstone's *Last Journals*, the European competition for empire in East Africa entered a new, more active phase. Robinson and Gallagher (with Denny) in *Africa and the Victorians* point out the existence within the permanent staff of the Foreign Office of a "forward party," whose views were expressed in a memorandum by Clement Hill for Prime Minister Gladstone in December 1884. Hill's language echoes a Livingstone-inspired rhetoric:

> Is it not worth considering whether in view of the European race for territories on the West Coast . . . we might [seek] . . . compensation on the East Coast . . . where *commerce* is capable of vast extension, and where our influence could be exercised . . . in the extension of *civilisation*, and the consequent extinction of the *Slave Trade* for which we have so long laboured?[1]

These calculations were not a priority for Gladstone. Robinson and Gallagher demonstrate that the prime minister, having found himself more deeply enmeshed in Egyptian affairs than he wanted to be, needed Bismarck's diplomatic friendship more than Great Britain needed new imperial responsibilities in East Africa. Only after Lord Salisbury and Bismarck came to a diplomatic understanding in 1889 were Salisbury and Rosebery, as foreign secretaries in their respective governments, able to pursue the course of action that ended in a British Empire in the East and Africa by 1895.[2]

With treaties by African chiefs offering Germany sovereignty over the Kilimanjaro area, Bismarck was able to arrange a Delimitation

321

Commission in East Africa to establish German, British, and Zanzibar claims. An Anglo-German agreement worked out thereafter in London, in October-November, 1886, divided Zanzibar's hinterland, ten miles beyond the coast, into German and British spheres of influence. Into the German area fell the port of Dar es Salaam, the Mackinnon–Buxton road, and several mainland stations of the Universities' Mission to Central Africa. By December 7, 1886, the sultan of Zanzibar, recognizing he had no other option, agreed.

In the course of these maneuvers, Bismarck dislodged Sir John Kirk, fierce defender of Zanzibar's rights, making him a diplomatic *persona non grata* in Zanzibar after a career there that spanned almost two decades.[3] Both countries assigned their domains to chartered companies for economic development, the Germans leading the way in 1886. The founding of a British East Africa Association in 1887 allowed Mackinnon and his colleagues to obtain a concession from the sultan of Zanzibar granting commercial, judicial, and political authority over the northern portion of his mainland territory for fifty years. From the beginning, Mackinnon projected an expansion of British East African interests into the area Gordon had first brought to his attention in 1877, the region bounded by the southern Sudan and great lakes that fed the Nile. His first step was to send out H. M. Stanley at the head of the Emin Pasha Relief Expedition.

As Governor-General at Khartoum, Gordon had appointed Emin Pasha (Eduard Schnitzer) Governor of the Equatorial Provinces in 1878. After the withdrawal of Egypt from the Sudan in 1885, Emin remained isolated in a province wealthy in ivory. He was in communication with Buganda to the south, where Alexander Mackay, a lay missionary with the CMS mission, urged him to think of taking over ". . . the whole territory of the Nile sources . . . England will no doubt help you if you say so." Leopold II developed an interest in this area from discussions with Gordon in January 1884. He viewed it as strategically and commercially important territory to join to his Congo domain. He was agreeable to having Stanley, whom he still considered in his employ, lead the expedition so long as he took a Congo route. A large part of the finances to send Stanley to this Egyptian outpost cut off by the Mahdists was supplied by Sir Evelyn Baring, using the British financial administration in occupied Egypt. Although Mackinnon had supported the activities of Leopold II in the Congo, his reactivated plans for a British East Africa Association made him Leopold's rival on the Nile. Mackinnon was convinced that the opportunity afforded by this expedition ". . . of extending British influence from the coast up to Wadelai [north of Lakes Victoria and Albert] is one which if . . . not taken advantage of now, will be lost forever."[4] Waller's name was initially linked to this project, and he may at first have viewed the rescue of Emin as a legacy of Gordon's work in the Sudan. As he subsequently made it a point to say, he never was a member of its organizing committee.[5]

The period 1889 to 1895 saw the culmination of British imperial acquisition in East and Central Africa. In August 1889, Acting Consul Buchanan, under orders from Salisbury's agent, H. H. Johnston, H. M. Consul to Mozambique, announced to a Portuguese agent that Great Britain had placed the Kololo district and the Shire Highlands under their protection. Final delimitation of boundaries took place with an Anglo-Portuguese treaty of 1891, when a British Protectorate over "Nyasaland" (Malawi) was formally announced. In 1890, Great Britain declared a Protectorate over Zanzibar, the new formal price of reliance on British influence. In April 1894, when Lord Rosebery became prime minister, the annexation of "Uganda" (including Buganda, Toro, and Bunyoro) was voted in Parliament, followed in 1895 by the creation of an "East Africa" (Kenya) Protectorate. Consonant with the intense international competition that gave rise to these annexations, the Protectorates were administered by the Foreign Office, the official rationale being their continued involvement with "diplomatic negotiations over frontiers."[6] Each new imperial acquisition represented the climax of multiple pressures. From within the nation, the variables included the efforts by antislavery, missionary, and business interests as well as elected officials and civil servants; abroad, they involved layers of diplomatic strategy. Coordination of groups that wished to influence politics on foreign and imperial matters made them more effective; Horace Waller was often at the core of these efforts when the interest of the parties sprang from their connection to areas touched by Livingstone and Gordon.

In January 1887, for example, Waller published a pamphlet entitled *Title-deeds to Nyassa-land*. In his preface, Waller declared he had been asked "to draw up this historical sketch . . . by the Church of Scotland, the Free Church of Scotland, and the Universities' Mission to Central Africa, and also by the African Lakes Company (limited), and Messrs. Buchanan and Co. of Mount Zomba." As a propagandist, he spoke for every British agency in the Malawi region. He took as his text Livingstone's word to Cambridge undergraduates in 1857: "I have opened the door. . . . I leave it to you to see that no one closes it after me." In light of the "scramble for Africa," Waller linked the deeds of Gordon and Livingstone to enable Great Britain to lay out clearly its "title-deeds" to contested areas. The pamphlet told the history of the region from the British perspective, from the time of Livingstone's first discoveries to the existence in the mid-1880s of "a little Colony on the Shire." By way of contrast, Waller pointed to a history in the same area of Portuguese inactivity and worse: the harmful neglect of those possessions by those who had early gained an access to the Southeastern Coast, consigning them to criminal classes of whom they wished to be rid. His conclusion was based on an assumption, shared by most of his contemporaries, that the nation which was prepared to develop the economy of an "undeveloped" region of the earth had the right to insist upon that development for the general good. "Manchester already has a market capable of easy and rapid extension in Nyassa-land. . . . Portugal has neither means, men, nor mercantile power to develop these regions. . . ."[7]

The "logic" of this notion was built on Livingstone's ideas about the duty of European nations like Great Britain to bring about the development of Africa. The impact of those ideas on succeeding generations may be measured by their adoption by one of the greatest critics of imperialism at the turn of the century, John A. Hobson. He expressed this view as follows:

There is nothing unworthy, quite the contrary, in the notion that nations which . . . have advanced further in certain arts of industry, politics, or morals, should communicate these to nations which from their circumstances were more backward, so as to aid them in developing alike the material resources of their land and the human resources of their people. . . . there can be no inherent natural right in a people to refuse that measure of compulsory education which shall raise it from childhood to manhood in the order of nationalities. . . . The real issue is one of safeguards, of motives, and of methods.

For this late Victorian critic of imperialism, therefore, it was not *whether* Africans and African resources should be "developed," but whether it was done with adequate "safeguards" against the "perils of private exploitation" and justified by "acting for the real good of the subject race." Livingstone's legacy helped create this logic; and this presumption, in turn, led to the use of Livingstone's legacy for the acquisition of empire.[8]

In a similar vein, late in June 1888, angry and discouraged at what he viewed as a lack of Government support for the missionaries, merchants, and settlers of Malawi, Waller published an eight-page pamphlet called *On Some African Entanglements*. Since 1887, active warfare had erupted with the Swahili ivory merchants who had settled in the area at the northeast corner of Lake Malawi. "The natives must either believe and be convinced that we are powerful," he warned, "or they will quickly imbibe the contrary notion." He saw a pattern of loss of prestige for the British on the East Coast, and he believed the Arabs and Swahili of the interior saw the same pattern.[9] Waller admitted to being "bellicose," but he insisted it was "more murderously wicked" to

> raise up the hearts and hopes of these unfortunate tribes of Africans, only to dash every aspiration to pieces—to double their darkness by suddenly flashing a lamp and then putting it out. Why send your Livingstones, your Kirks, your Mackenzies? Why subscribe your tens of thousands to fortify your African Lake Company, and your splendid Missions on the lake and shore, and then . . . mismanage them in this way?

Waller brought these laments to a finale with a high resolve to bring about the end he desired:

> We cannot leave Africa alone now; we have gone too far; we must concern ourselves with the civilisation of those natives . . . [for] amongst the many wrongs dealt out to Africa none is more dastardly than to send to her tribes men like Livingstone, with messages concerning Christianity and civilisation—bidding them to lean upon your arm—only to leave them in a slough of despond. . . ."[10]

The rhetoric of these arguments emphasized, increasingly, that Africans were helpless and unable to manage on their own. Only the protection of a European power could defend them against the predatory Arabs of the interior. Any suggestion made in the past, that Africans, or at least their chiefs, were responsible for engaging in the slave trade, was gradually eliminated. In the new algebra of imperialism, Africans were dependent variables. If Africans were not brought within the power of a great nation, they would collapse into anarchy. They needed to be governed for their own good; it was cowardice to deny them this succor. Yet, privately, Waller found the news from Malawi unsettling: "The more I hear of what is going on the less one [sic] likes it. Lord Salisbury has given the greatest license to the Moirs to fight it out with the Arabs. . . . Lord Salisbury's line is very alarming."[11]

    As the events of the next two years moved swiftly toward resolution on the question of British claims to the Lake Malawi region and the Shire Highlands against Portugal, Waller continued to shift the emphases of Livingstone's legacy to undergird the structure of imperial arrangements. In the 1860s and 1870s Livingstone's voice (amplified in 1874 by

Capt. Frederick J. D. Lugard, c. 1890. On leave from India, Lugard became involved in the Arab war on Lake Malawi in 1888. Waller and Kirk recommended him for work for the Imperial British East Africa Company, which led him to Uganda. He later became a major exponent of "indirect rule" in Nigeria. Waller saw him as the next hero after Livingstone and Gordon who would change the life of the African continent.

his *Last Journals*) raised the humanitarian conscience in Great Britain to the facts of the interior slave trade in Central Africa. He called for European (British) intervention in Africa to put down the slave trade and introduce Christianity by means of fostering agriculture and introducing international commerce (accompanied by nineteenth-century science and technology). Waller used his seemingly inexhaustible energy and considerable influence to publicize Livingstone's legacy as a call for greater intervention in Africa. To him the first sign of success—defined as channeling others' aims to be expressed in this way—was Sir Bartle Frere's mission to Zanzibar in 1873 to obtain a new treaty suppressing the seaborne slave trade from the East Coast. The second solid building block was the creation of enduring missionary and antislavery interest in East and Central Africa. At the end of the 1880s, achievement lay in renewed and widespread public interest in the issues of slavery, first in a European antislave trade crusade preached by Cardinal Lavigerie, the Archbishop of Algiers and Carthage, then in the calling of a European Anti-Slavery Conference at Brussels in 1889.

Cardinal Lavigerie founded the White Fathers' missions around Lakes Victoria and Tanganyika. In response to local Arab hostility, his missions withdrew into Leopold's Congo State. Their territory grew to include six thousand inhabitants. They "appointed and deposed African rulers, collected tribute, including slaves, settled disputes and dispensed justice. They gave flags to their adherents and sent out levies to fight those who attacked their proteges."[12] In 1887, Lavigerie sent to care for these secular affairs a lay agent whose forceful policies provoked further attacks on the missions, until they became "armed camps, [and] centres of refuge, rather than of evangelism."[13] The Catholic White Fathers experienced the same problems of the exercise of temporal powers in the name of missionary labors familiar to the British Protestant missionaries in East and Central Africa.

With a papal blessing, Cardinal Lavigerie set out to raise the conscience of Christian Europe. He preached a sermon July 1, 1888, at the church of St. Sulpice in Paris, appealing to public opinion to stir government action. He announced that nearly half a million Africans died yearly as a result of Arab slaving depredations; Christian Europe must rise up and once again send crusaders to fight the infidel. It needed only five or six hundred volunteers, financed by public subscription, to end this terrible evil. As Suzanne Miers notes, "His picture of a handful of Arabs devastating Africa was inaccurate. Much of the slaving was conducted by Africans and much of the raiding was unconnected with the slave traffic."[14] The reality did not matter; Cardinal Lavigerie successfully caught the public attention. His rhetoric fired the imagination; it placed all the blame for the slave trade in Central Africa on the Arabs and suggested a "simple," but forceful, solution to stop this depopulation of the African continent.

The Cardinal issued a challenge: "Christians of Europe, cross the sea which separates us, and come to our aid! . . . Pass . . . towards the country of the negroes; pass over, some by your acts of charity, others by the strength of your arms, and rescue these people, laying [sic] under the shadow of death, and under the still sadder darkness of Slavery."[15] The cardinal's message was doubly significant for British humanitarians. Not only did he insist that the slave trade in Africa was a major problem for European governments to solve, but he portrayed Central Africa as a land in which helpless Africans were prey to evil, marauding Arabs, hence in need of European protection. He invested willingness to engage in armed retaliation, on a relatively small scale, with the character of a Christian crusade. This set of images precisely met the needs of the proimperialist British humanitarian interests at Lake Malawi.[16]

Lavigerie quoted "the courageous and noble LIVINGSTONE, who had himself been an eye-witness for many years of these inhuman undertakings. . . ." He knew well how to employ the Livingstone legend. He quoted Livingstone, in the heart of Africa, confessing:

> The scenes which I have witnessed, the every-day events of this traffic, are so horrible that I try continually to chase them from my thoughts, but in vain. The most painful recollections are effaced by time, but the fearful scenes which I have seen keep reappearing, and at night I wake up startled and horrified at the vividness of the picture."[17]

The British and Foreign Anti-Slavery Society reacted quickly to this new antislavery force in Europe. Its Committee invited Cardinal Lavigerie to come to England for a great meeting at the end of July. Implicit in the decision were two issues. First, it was important that the British, who prided themselves as leaders in the antislavery movement in Africa, should not be left behind in this new cry for a Christian crusade. Secondly, since it was an organization largely financed and led by British Quakers, its Committee had reservations about the Cardinal's call for a solution based on arms. They wished to make sure they had a hand in shaping coming events. Lord Granville, long connected in his public career with missionary and antislavery efforts in Africa, presided over the meeting held July 31, 1888. Since his Liberal Party was out of power, Granville could lend lustre and distinction to the gathering without compromising any political position. The resolutions that resulted would then be sent to the Conservative foreign secretary in power, Lord Salisbury. On the platform with Lavigerie and Granville were an array of high-level British philanthropists. Cardinal Manning, a leading British Roman Catholic and a recent member of the Committee of the Anti-Slavery Society, sat alongside such prominent stalwarts in British (Protestant) humanitarian circles as Bishop Smythies of the UMCA, Sir John Kennaway, M.P., lay head of the CMS, Sir John and Lady Kirk, Commander V. L. Cameron, Rev. Laurence Scott "late of Nyassa," William Ewing of the African Lakes Company, W. H. Wylde, the Reverend Horace Waller "companion of LIVINGSTONE," and other leading members of the Anti-Slavery Society.[18]

To Waller fell the honor of proposing the second substantive resolution of the meeting. He placed the proposed actions of the distinguished people assembled in the line of precedents that marked the great European Congresses of Vienna (1815) and Verona (1822), at which strong resolutions had been announced against the slave trade. He said, "[T]he time has now fully arrived when the several nations of Europe . . . should take the needful steps for giving them a full and practical effect. And inasmuch as the Arab marauders (whose murderous devastations are now depopulating Africa) are subject to no law, and under no responsible rule, it devolves on the Powers of Europe to secure their suppression throughout all territories over which they have any control." His resolution called upon Her Majesty's Government to work in concert with the Powers to adopt "appropriate" measures. No mention was made of armed force. Waller, however, had something characteristic to add: "He hoped young men, instead of going to Africa to shoot big game, would join the ANTI-SLAVERY SOCIETY, and help put down the Slave-trade." "The true heart of Africa," he reminded his audience, ". . . was LIVINGSTONE'S heart buried there."[19]

Cardinal Lavigerie's appeal "fell on fertile ground because Britain wished to remain at the head of the antislavery movement. Lord Salisbury and Foreign Office officials believed that the public expected them to take the initiative." That such expectations existed is noteworthy, but their motives were not unmixed. They wanted to make sure that whatever forces the Cardinal mustered were channeled into lines that were not inimical to British interests . . . [and] that others did not profit from a traffic they had outlawed." The fact that the British public remained willing to spend public monies to sustain an antislavery effort, the fact that governments knew that the cause of antislavery had strong public backing, ultimately made a difference, in both the decisions of government and the way those decisions were presented. In addition, it was a tenet of popular belief, unshaken by events, "that Britain would

gain from the growth of legitimate trade which was confidently expected to replace the slave traffic." Livingstone had taught them to expect it. Similarly, maintaining the leadership in the antislavery movement became an imperial talisman; as Miers sums it up succinctly, a high
antislavery stance "enhanced their belief in the civilising agency of British rule."[20] That too was Livingstone's legacy.

Clement Hill and T. V. Lister at the Foreign Office, and Sir James
Fergusson, the parliamentary undersecretary, pressed Salisbury in August, 1888, about a response to Lavigerie's call for a crusade. Cameron
proposed his own plan to raise money to station armed men along the
slave route from the mouth of the Shire River to the northern end of Lake
Tanganyika. Alarmed, the Anti-Slavery Society's secretary announced in
The Times and the *Anti-Slavery Reporter* that they disassociated themselves from his fund-raising efforts. The idea of a conference of the European powers on the subject of the slave trade in Africa became both
evidence of doing something about it and the " 'safest' course of action."
Hill and Kirk began to work on the proposal, but implementation had to
wait for the end of the East African blockade. By that time, October
1889, the kinds of international agreements they wanted had become
clear to the governments of several nations; in particular, they wanted
international agreements restricting trade in munitions. An antislavery
conference would allow colonial powers the opportunity to bring up the
embargo of arms and ammunition among African peoples in the process
of being "pacified" by imperialist powers "as a humanitarian question."[21] The international Anti-Slavery Conference was held at Brussels
beginning late in 1889; the General Act for the Repression of African
Slave trade was signed July 2, 1890. Before that time, the climax of
events leading to empire in the Malawi region had been played out.

Between September 1888 and July 1890, *The Times* published nineteen "Letters to the Editor" from Horace Waller. A major motif running
through a majority of these letters was the "fanaticism" of the Arabs,
especially but not exclusively in terms of those engaged in the slave trade
in the interior of Africa. This heightened stereotype grew out of a ner-
vous reaction to the message of Khartoum and the Mahdists' takeover of
the Sudan. European observers in Africa or, like Waller, in Britain, were
suspicious of Arab actions throughout East and Central Africa as strands
of an anti-European conspiracy. Waller handled this "Arab peril" image
by quoting repeatedly from Livingstone and by sending his readers to
the *Last Journals*, vol. 2, chap. 6, to read his vivid description of Arab
slaving and the bloody Nyangwe massacre of Manyema market women.

The corollary—and underlying purpose—of this emphasis upon the
Arabs as the prime movers of the slave trade was a sharper emphasis on

the only "sure" solution to that "illicit" trade: European rule and settlement. An editorial in *The Times*, October 19, 1888, agreed with this explanation; it was reprinted in the *Anti-Slavery Reporter*. Lugard's reportage on the Arab-Swahili War in Malawi demonstrated the way this growing conviction operated there: all the Europeans he met were adamant—and made him believe—that fighting and defeating the Arabs at the northern end of Lake Malawi "was absolutely necessary to save the missions on Nyasa from annihilation." If the African Lakes Company station at Karonga were abandoned, it would be a signal to the hostile Arabs to combine "to kill all Europeans and open a new great slave route."[22] Whatever the merits of the idea that there was a new resistance to Europeans among the Arab and Swahili of the interior of Africa, this new, more ominous image about the consequences of their unleashed power also represented a projection of what those Europeans wished to accomplish: a complete removal, even annihilation, of the "enemy."

During this same twenty-two month period, Waller published a review article (unsigned) in the *Quarterly Review* of January 1889; a presentation of Lugard's scheme for ending the slave trade at Lake Malawi in the *Contemporary Review* of April 1889; and a fifty-nine-page booklet on *Nyassaland: Great Britain's Case against Portugal*, early in 1890. In addition, he prepared a paper for an Anti-Slavery Congress called by Cardinal Lavigerie at Lucerne for August 4, 1889. The paper was then printed in the *Anti-Slavery Reporter* when the Congress was cancelled.[23]

The *Quarterly Review* article, combining recent and older publications about Livingstone and the missionary efforts in Malawi over the previous thirty years, gave Waller an opportunity to connect current affairs in East and Central Africa with their history, and especially to Livingstone and pioneer missionary efforts in the Malawi area.[24] Describing the Portuguese slaving that Livingstone had discovered in the early 1860s, Waller emphasized a relatively recent interpretation of land ownership in Malawi. In this region, African societies were small-scale and not organized in terms of hierarchical leadership. The new interpretation of what those societies were like and how the land was occupied accommodated the desire of all who had settled in the country since the mid-1870s—for missionary labor, legitimate trade, or large-scale agriculture—to bring the area under the British flag. In Waller's words: "This was a 'no man's land' in particular, and quite outside and behind Portuguese territory."[25]

Waller retold the tale of the past in a manner that underscored what he wished it to say about the present. For example, in describing the release of a gang of eighty-four slaves, he said they were told they were free to

Rev. Horace Waller, c. 1890, standing with paper in hand. Waller seems utterly at ease in this pose, ready to speak from or about the letter, speech, or other document that he has in his hand. We can imagine him standing thus at a meeting of the Committee British and Foreign Anti-Slavery Society, or the Home Committee of the Universities' Mission to Central Africa, or the Royal Geographical Society. He believed that his experiences in Africa and among the humanitarian circles in England let him speak with authority about his nation's imperial duties.

return to their homes, and that they responded they could not because their homes had been destroyed during their capture. Since those homes were as easily built as destroyed, the underlying issue, not mentioned by Waller, was that since many Africans had been sold into slavery by chiefs or kin, going back was merely putting themselves again at risk. By emphasizing *their choice to become the dependents* of "the English," Waller was suggesting that Africans, then and in the late 1880s, were defenseless against enslavement by predatory Arabs and Portuguese *except under protection by the British*. Waller did not resist spelling out the moral of the story, though ostensibly simply recounting the facts of the past: "[I]t was agreed to lead them to a place of safety, in order to begin life afresh under the white man's auspices."[26]

Another example of how Waller turned "history" into precedent for present needs involved Livingstone's role in dealing with the "slave-dealers," a term which, to his contemporary audience, implied the Portuguese or the Arabs. In fact it included, in the events described, the fighting undertaken by Livingstone and the UMCA missionaries of the 1860s with the slave-trading Yao, who were overrunning the Shire Highlands at that time, and the Mang'anja who lived there. "Livingstone," wrote Waller, "has been rather reticent on what ensued. A 'special reporter' [Waller was an eye witness to these events] would have told a story of *slave-dealers* being put into their own yokes and marched about the country, and of a *hard fought tussle* as a wind-up, which led to the complete discomfiture of a horde of some 800 men."[27] Waller was accurate; Livingstone was reticent and never mentioned in his published works the extent of that fighting; he was dismayed when he learned that Bishop Mackenzie had advertised his "wars" in his letters home. Livingstone understood better than Mackenzie, in the early 1860s, that missionaries must not be exposed as warriors, even in a "good cause." In telling this much, Waller's careful euphemism, "hard fought tussle," conveys his attempt, in 1889, to identify Livingstone with the fighting currently going on at Lake Malawi, just as Rowley—to Livingstone's anger—had attempted to identify him with the use of arms by the missionaries in the 1860s.

As Livingstone's editor, and a man continually labeled "companion of Livingstone" in his platform appearances, Waller felt free to link together the actions of Britains' great missionary hero with the current fighting by elements of the British missionary and commercial community at Lake Malawi. He had been very much a participant in the fighting of the UMCA in the 1860s—Bishop Mackenzie had assigned him a leadership role because he was a *lay* missionary. Raising the issue again in 1889, Waller was making another effort to obtain, even in retrospect, the sanction he felt had been erroneously denied his little band of missionaries a quarter century before. Focusing on this question also allowed Waller to turn that precedent to good use in the current conflict with the Swahili chiefs at Lake Malawi. Of the continued need faced by the UMCA missionaries once they were established at Magomero, in the Shire Highlands, to fight in local skirmishes to defend themselves and their camp of African dependents, Waller wrote, "At times the advance of the Ajawas [Yao] was repelled; for *the offensive is inseparable from a plan of defence*,"[28]

Waller found a particularly apposite reflection of Livingstone's, based on his reaction to his recall by the government in 1863, to offer the reader "because the same might be almost written to-day by the missionaries and trading companies of Nyassa-land!" Waller was drawing upon a letter from Livingstone to himself, dated July 6, 1863, and he simply cited it as "Personal Correspondence" in the review. The words captured just what Waller would have wanted Livingstone to say about the current crisis:

> In my recall . . . we see that this country is to be given up as a slave-preserve to the Portuguese, but it would have been impolitic to have said so. I have put it so pointedly to our Government that, unless some check were given to the Portuguese following on our footsteps with this slaving, and the restrictions taken off rivers which they never use, the objects of our expedition could not be attained.

Waller ended the review article by returning to the subject he knew how to use best, Livingstone: "We are told that no tomb is visited so often as that of Livingstone in Westminster Abbey. Men of all nations stand and spell out the words . . . . : 'All I can say in my solitude is, may Heaven's rich blessing come down on every one, American, English, Turk, who will help to heal the open sore of the world.' "[29]

In the last years of his life, Horace Waller concentrated on embarrassing the Government in every way he knew to dramatize the continuation of the status of legal slavery and domestic slaves within their Protectorates, and on Zanzibar and Pemba in particular. He produced a fifty-one-page pamphlet, *Heligoland for Zanzibar*, in January 1893, making the point that Anglo-German agreement of 1890 had exchanged an island of "free men" for two islands of slaves.[30] Involved in this crusade was the issue of the employment of slaves as porters, and he did not hesitate to denounce loudly from the platform, in *The Times*, in his pamphlets, and wherever he went all who engaged in this activity—from the Imperial British East Africa Company to the King of the Belgians, from H. M. Stanley to H. H. Johnston, now the Commissioner in Nyasaland, and on one occasion even Frederick Lugard.[31]

He wrote two other broadsides on this subject, *Slaving and Slavery in our British Protectorates*, eight pages in length, published December 1, 1894—making two in one year on the subject—and *The Case of Our Zanzibar Slaves: Why Not Liberate Them?* dated January 27, 1896, less than a month before his unexpected death from influenza and acute pneumonia.[32] As always, whenever Waller wrote, and whatever he wrote about, he managed to frame the information and exhortation in terms of Livingstone, the African experiences he shared with him, and with some reference to Gordon. By the time Waller wrote the last of these pamphlets, he had retired from his rectory at Twywell and was living at East Liss in Hampshire.[33]

In his last years he took an independent line at the Anti-Slavery Society whenever he felt impelled to do so. This was particularly true over his concerns to dramatize the status of slavery within the British African Protectorates. On one notable occasion, at the height of the Uganda retention campaign in October 1892, he was the second man to take the floor among a deputation of over a hundred prominent gentlemen to address the foreign secretary, Lord Rosebery. His assigned task was to suggest all the reasons why a government subsidy which helped the Imperial British East Africa Company to build a railway from Mombasa to Buganda would, in one stroke, end the East African slave trade. The premise was that the slave trade owed its existence primarily to the need to supply the porterage required for this route. Waller deviated from his "script." He questioned whether a railroad would indeed work such miracles. He took advantage of his distinguished and captive audience to castigate everyone, including the Company, for using slaves as porters in the first place. Most newspaper reports of the occasion, the next day, mentioned his conduct with surprise and dismay. Sir T. Fowell Buxton was outraged, as a Company director and a member of the society. Arthur Pease, the president, and Edmund Sturge, the elder statesman of the society, attempted to get him to resign. Waller held fast. He mentioned the fracas in later letters with a sense of pride. He explained his views at some length to Frederick Lugard at the end of 1895, as follows:

. . . with a hearty desire to explain to you why I have never deemed it right to leave the "Anti Slavery Society." . . . As a

Slaves rescued by *HMS Philomel*, April 1893. The British East African naval patrol picked up such groups regularly after the 1873 treaty prohibiting the shipment of slaves from Zanzibar. Need for slaves to work plantations and supply porterage continued unabated, however, as did their occasional rescue. The British consulate assigned freed slaves to missionary and freed-slaves settlements willing to take them.

piece of machinery, useful for collecting facts, the Society is most useful. Left to itself, and allowed to ride its Quaker hobby [horse], it is also capable of infinite harm.

It is the only organization of the kind, and public opinion requires some such instrumentality. I belong to it, because I hope to make it useful & to correct some of it tendencies. Having done this fearlessly, as at Lord Rosebery's meeting, I was asked to resign! I refused to, quite against my own liking, but in order that I might continue to try and keep its head straight: no easy task, although one or two others are quite with me in the effort.

Of course one rather loses caste by such an association. But remember we can't always have things just as we like, jump up, shove on our hats, and slam the door, if we are to turn means to an end. Take Kirk for instance, part and parcel of several African enterprises more compromising to a man of self respect than anything [doubtful] which can be laid to charge of the Anti Slavery Society. When Stanley had to ship Tippoo tippoo [sic] off in a British ship from Zanzibar with a cargo of slaves and white men of sorts, did he resign his seat upon the 'Emin Relief Com[mi]tee'? Or, again, take the precious I.B.E.A. Company, an undertaking about which he had the gravest doubts from the first, would it have done for him to turn round and say, 'I put on my hat'? Once more, knowing what the King of the Belgians['] enterprise was doing in Africa as a civilizing agency (!) did he abstain from being taken into the councils of the King and his crew (for I suppose I am correct in believing that his counsel has been sought)? Lastly, he is employed voluntarily by the Foreign Office and I think you and he have your own opinion about its honesty of purpose. He is your paragon of wisdom, your master at whose feet you sit; but he has been associated, we must admit, with three projects, each and every one of them guilty every bit as much as the Anti-Slavery Society of exceedingly equivocal conduct if we are first to place *their history opposite to the intention of this country to destroy the African slave trade*, & then calculate how far their existence, as projects, has militated for or against that evil.[34]

This excerpt is a long one, but as it was written less than two months before Waller died, and does much to explain his views to a younger man about whom he obviously cared, it makes a fitting centerpiece for bringing this chapter and this book to a close. All his adult life, Horace Waller found his identity by aligning himself to the antislavery cause. He was not a brilliant thinker, nor a particularly astute analyst of the politics of the situation in which he found himself and his countrymen. He did, however, remain faithful to the cause he had learned at Livingstone's side, and though he increasingly sounded like a confirmed racist when he explained his views about the role Africans might play in their own world, so—we have discovered—could a man like David Livingstone. Judging these men by the standards of their own day, and not by ours, we find them less crude than many who held the predominant opinions of their world, and ever steadfastly committed (for all the complex personal and professional reasons any person brings to passionately held opinions) to ending not only the slave trade but the institution of slavery in Africa. The meanings of that institution for them might be widely different from those which attached to African realities, as suggested in the introduction to this book, but insofar as slavery and the slave trade meant an oppressive system of limited choices and constrained lives, Livingstone and Waller, Gordon and Kirk all understood what they were seeking to end. How they worked out their need to deal with this great question is the stuff of history.

NOTES

1. Quoted in Ronald Robinson and John Gallagher with Alice Denny, *Africa and the Victorians: The Official Mind of Imperialism* (London, 1961), 191. For critiques of their thesis about the overriding importance of Egypt in decision making south of the Sahara, see George Shepperson, "Africa, the Victorians and Imperialism," in Wm. Roger Louis, ed., *Imperialism: The Robinson and Gallagher Controversy* (New York and London, 1976), 162–72, and Eric Stokes, "Imperialism and the Scramble for Africa: The New View," in Louis, *Imperialism*, 173–95. Shepperson notes in particular that Robinson and Gallagher consistently underplayed "the role of Leopold II in the partition of Africa" and that nowhere "do they examine the factor of nineteenth-century European racialism in this imperialism." Shepperson, "Africa, the Victorians and Imperialism," in Louis, *Imperialism*, 166–67. Other critics note the need to look also at the effect of Anglo-French rivalry in West Africa and the Congo in 1884 and the Berlin Conference that year. Colin W. Newbury, "Victorians, Republicans, and the Partition of West Africa," *Journal of African History* 3 (1962): 493–501, and Wm. Roger Louis, "The Berlin Congo Conference," in Prosser Gifford and Wm. Roger Louis, eds., *France and Britain in Africa: Imperial Rivalry and Colonial Rule* (New Haven and London), 1971, 167–220, esp. 168–70.

2. Robinson and Gallagher, *Africa and the Victorians*, chaps. 6–11, esp. 189–98, 290–91, 305. Salisbury wrote his foreign secretary in August, 1885: "I have been using the credit I have got with Bismarck in the Caroline Islands and Zanzibar to get help in Russia and Turkey and Egypt. He is rather a Jew, but on the whole I have as yet got my money's worth." Quoted in Coupland, *Exploitation of East Africa*, 440. On Salisbury's use of *Jew* as a term of opprobrium, compare Iain Smith: "The assertion that Emin [Pasha] was a Jew [though he was not] was made most vociferously by Englishmen after 1890 when Emin took service with the Germans in Africa. In the context of the 1890s it served as a common and useful [sic] term of abuse." Smith, *Emin Pasha Relief Expedition*, 13, n. 1. For example, Kirk wrote in January 1892: "Uganda and the Nile Valley is aimed at by those who work for the King [Leopold] and I think that Emin Pasha, who after all is a Jew, has been secured." Kirk to Eric Barrington, Sevenoaks, January 15, 1892, Private. The Private Papers of Robert, Third Marquess of Salisbury, Class E (E. 107), Hatfield House, Hatfield, Herts. (hereafter, Salisbury Papers). In 1892, Barrington was in the Foreign Office; he had been private secretary to Lord Salisbury.

3. The Germans made clear that they wished a British representative other than Kirk to serve on the Delimitation Commission. Salisbury Papers, Class A, vol. 40 (12), October 13, 1885: minutes by Barrington. On April 1, 1887, Kirk wrote a friend, "my return is disliked by Bismarck and he had quite as much to say in our political appointments as our own Government." Quoted in Coupland, *Exploitation of East Africa*, 481. Compare Galbraith, *Mackinnon and East Africa*, 105–6. In March 1887, Bismarck demanded the withdrawal of Acting Consul Holmwood on the grounds that he was acting against German interests. Coupland, *Exploitation of East Africa*, 481 n. 2. Kirk, who served on the UMCA Home Committee when in England, feared he might be blamed for not defending them from being placed by the Delimitation Commission within the German sphere. He wrote W. H. Penney, the UMCA secretary, "I believe a reply is being sent to our [UMCA] letter & that the F.O. therein put the blame on me for Magila being left outside the British sphere. . . . It was a deal agreed between Germany & our Government. We sacrificed our integrity and joined in ignoring the Sultan's interests in return for help against France. The basis of the arrangement was agreed to before the German delegate left Berlin. . . ." Kirk to Penney, Sevenoaks, Sunday, n.d., UMCA, A 1 (V), USPGA. The UMCA and CMS missionaries who found themselves within the German sphere of influence were indignant. Farler expressed this sentiment to Penney, May 7, 1888: "I think the action of the English Government, to sacrifice its own children in this way, is unnatural and monstrous." Quoted in Åke

340   LIVINGSTONE'S LEGACY

Holmberg, *African Tribes and European Agencies: Colonialism and Humanitarianism in British South and East Africa, 1870– 1895* (Goteborg, 1966), 342.

4. Mackay to Emin Pasha (in German), June 2, 1886, translation quoted in Smith, *Emin Pasha Relief Expedition*, 33; Mackinnon to Henry Sandford, September 29, 1887, quoted in Smith, *Emin Pasha Relief Expedition*, 55. Letters from Emin, dating to August 1887 and expressing his appreciation of Mackay's help, appeared in the *Anti-Slavery Reporter*, March and April, 1888, 39–45. Excerpts were reprinted in the *Anti-Slavery Reporter*, July and August, 1890, 165–69.

5. Smith, *Emin Pasha Relief Expedition*, 66. On October 29, 1886, Charles Allen, the secretary of the British and Foreign Anti-Slavery Society, sent to *The Times* the letter just received from Emin, giving the public the impression that ". . . 'a second Gordon' was in danger of being left to the same fate." Smith, *Emin Pasha Relief Expedition*, 45. On November 20, 1886, in trying to rouse support for rescuing Emin, his friend the CMS missionary Dr. Robert W. Felkin wrote Charles Allen, "Could you not get [W. H.] Wylde or Horace Waller to write to the *Standard* or *Daily Telegraph?* Smith, *Emin Pasha Relief Expedition*, 47. The Committee of the Anti-Slavery Society, which had counted Waller a member since 1870, sent a resolution November 8, 1886, on the claims Emin had on the British Government to rescue him. Smith, *Emin Pasha Relief Expedition*, 46; *Anti-Slavery Reporter*, October and November, 1886, 108–9.

The names of the Emin Pasha Relief Committee forwarded by Col. Sir Francis de Winton to the Foreign Office December 30, 1886, included: William Mackinnon, the Hon. Guy Dawney, H. M. Stanley, Sir Lewis Pelly, A. F. Kinnaird, Col. J. A. Grant, and the Reverend Horace Waller. "Further Correspondence respecting the Relief of Emin Pasha at Uganda," Part 2, no. 1, Confidential Prints 5617 (May 1888), F. O. 403/79, Public Record Office. To H. R. Fox-Bourne, secretary of the Aborigines Protection Society (from 1889) and author of *The Other Side of the Emin Pasha Relief Expedition* (London, 1891), Waller wrote that he was aware that in several accounts written by "Mr Stanley's followers my name appears as one of the committee. This is an error for which Sir F. de Winton is responsible. Most of the members are old friends and acquaintances it is true – men utterly above suspicion of harshness or duplicity in any walk of life." Waller to Fox Bourne, St. Leonards, January 18, 1891, BFASSP, MS. Brit. Emp. s18, typescript, C153/25, RH. Waller denied participation more publicly, in a letter dated September 23, 1892, and published in *The Times* three days later. In a letter to Mackinnon in March 1885, however, Waller suggests that he had an early interest in Emin's fate: "Curiously enough I met Mr Malcolm Lupton at . . . [your] office today. He points to a telegram on p. 5 of the "Times" yesterday showing that the Austrians are going to send an exploring expedition via the Congo to try to reach Lupton Bey and Emin Bey. I had not seen this. He is anxious to ascertain particulars with a view to joining the party: he himself knows Egypt well. *I have not said anything either to Bates [at the RGS] or to Mr Lupton concerning our conversation.*" Emphasis added. Waller to Mackinnon, written on RGS notepaper, March 19, 1885, MP, SOAS. This may be one of the earliest allusions to an interest on Mackinnon's part to the fate of Emin Pasha. Compare Smith, *The Emin Pasha Relief Expedition*, 50 and chap. 3, *passim*.

    6. Ray Jones, *The Nineteenth-Century Foreign Office: An Administrative History* (London, 1971), 81. A Memorandum by the Earl of Selborne, the lord chancellor, January 3, 1885, prepared for the Foreign Office, gave his view on the difference between *annexation* and *protectorate*. The former he described as "the direct assumption of territorial Sovereignty." The latter, "is the recognition of the right of the aboriginal or other actual inhabitants to their country, with no further assumption of territorial rights than is necessary to maintain paramount authority & to discharge the duties of the Protecting Power." Louis, "The Berlin Congo Conference," in Gifford and Louis, *France and Britain in Africa*, 209. Three years later, Waller commented on the new terms that came into use with the "scramble" for empire: "I had 1/2 an hour with Sir P. Anderson & Sir C. Hill over the big map. Germany's Protectorate is not yet clearly defined. Bismarck drew a line round a small patch and said 'that would do to go on with' or words to that effect, but one thing is clear viz that our Magila district is right *out* of the [British] Protectorate and right *in* the sphere of influence accorded to Germany. . . . They [the Germans] cannot be called upon to interfere on behalf of any Englishman who is in peril or maltreated within their 'sphere of influence.' " Waller to Penney, Twywell, April 25, 1888, UMCA, USPGA.

    7. Rev. Horace Waller, F.R.G.S., *The Title-Deeds to Nyassa-Land* (London, 1887), 3–4, 5, 7, 12, 36–37. The Portuguese published a pamphlet that attempted to "answer" Waller: *Os Caes Britannicos ou A Nyassaland do Rev. Horace Waller*, Commentada por Henrique A. D. de Carvalho (Lisbon, 1890), 71pp. It appeared as part of a protest against the Ultimatum of January 11, 1890, by which Great Britain ordered Portugal to withdraw from parts of Malawi. The Portuguese pamphlet contested the claims made by Waller's *Title-deeds* in an effort to counter what the Portuguese considered as the British propaganda campaign that led to the Ultimatum of January 11. The writer

protested Livingstone's assertion that he was the first European to explore the Shire River and Lake Malawi and equally denied the claims of British settlers since that time that they were occupying territory that was *not* within Portuguese jurisdiction.

8. Hobson, "Imperialism and the Lower Races," *Imperialism*, 228–29, 231, 235.

9. Horace Waller, *On Some African Entanglements* (n.p., June 26, 1888), 1–5. For an early interpretation of the outbreak of Arab hostility in the interior of Central Africa, including the Arab-Swahili War at the northern end of Lake Malawi, see Oliver, *Missionary Factor*, 101–16; for Arab reactions to the Belgian incursions, see Hanna, *Beginnings of Nyasaland*, 98; for a reevaluation in connection with the Swahili War at Lake Malawi, see H. W. Macmillan, "Notes on the origins of the Arab war," in Pachai, *History of Malawi*, 263–82. Turton makes yet another argument, citing McKillop's expedition on the East Coast in 1876 as being responsible for changed Arab attitudes toward Christian missionaries, see Turton, "Kirk and the Egyptian Invasion of East Africa," *Journal of Africa History*, II, no. 3 (1970):369. The most recent assessment concludes that "the theory that there was a Muslim conspiracy against Christians at the end of the 1880s cannot be confirmed. The supposed conspiracy was deduced from coincidence. . . . There can be no doubt [however] that a sense of confrontation and rivalry rippled through the rumour-prone Swahili system, to the particular consternation of those committed to the illicit sector." Wright, "East Africa, 1870–1905," in Oliver and Sanderson, *The Cambridge History of Africa*, vol. 6, 566.

10. Waller, *On Some African Entanglements* 6, 8. James Stevenson published a twenty-six-page pamphlet, *The Arabs in Central Africa and at Lake Nyassa*, Glasgow, 1888, which painted a melodramatic and sexually-charged picture of the Swahili threat at the northern end of Lake Malawi. Reports spoke of: "Arabs of the sort with whom we have dealt in the Soudan, who combine the grossest cruelty with a species of fanaticism." Men on the spot emphasized the helplessness—and sexual vulnerability—of women and children at the hands of Arab slavers. For example, Fred Moir: "And the women! . . . fastened to chains or thick barks," carrying "little brown babies, dear to their hearts as a white man's child to his [sic]"; or the Reverend Mr. Scott of Manchester: "the fate [of women] was not one of slavery only we have too much reason to fear," referring to comments of a Swahili leader who threatened "what would be done with the 'young Wa-Ngonde girls,' accompanying his atrocious statement with the foulest language." Stevenson, *Arabs in Central Africa*, 24, 10–11. Although the pamphlet was dated December 3, 1888, its first appearance was as an address by James Stevenson at the

conference on "The Nyassa Question," held as a meeting of the Manchester Geographical Society, May 18, 1888. It was then published as "The Arabs in Central Africa," *Manchester Geographical Journal* 4 (1888): 72–86. The Reverend Laurence Scott was the brother of C. P. Scott, editor of the *Manchester Guardian*, and the brother-in-law of Henry E. O'Neill, consul at Mozambique through the mid-1880s. He was a participant in one of the first skirmishes with the Swahili at Lake Malawi, delivering a paper on "a Holiday in Central Africa" at the Manchester Geographical Society, December 5, 1888. He asked: "Is English influence, with its foresight, its sympathy with the best elements of native character, its capacity for orderly progressive government, to be the guiding and ruling force there, or are we to forget our trust and leave these young peoples [sic], before they are able to stand alone, to be devastated and broken by the Arab slave-hunters?" Quoted in the *Anti-Slavery Reporter*, November and December, 1888, 237. In addition to his emphasis on female sexual peril in need of strong champions, therefore, he assigned all Africans to the status of children or young people needing the protection of 'more mature' caretakers.

11. Waller to Penney, Twywell, July 10, 1888, UMCA, A 1 (VI), USPGA.

12. Miers, *Britain and the Ending of the Slave Trade*, 201.

13. *Ibid.*, 202.

14. *Ibid.*, 202–3 n. 77.

15. *Anti-Slavery Reporter*, July and August, 1888, 90. These words were part of a translation of excerpts from the sermon provided by the *Anti-Slavery Reporter* for its readers.

16. In particular, the emphasis that those connected with the Malawi region placed in 1888 upon the need for Christian Europeans to protect Africans against Arab power and Arab slave traders grew out of a controversy that developed in October 1887, at the Church Congress held at Wolverhampton. The Reverend Isaac Taylor, Canon of York, read a paper on "Mohammedanism in Africa" which pointed out that "The faith of Islam . . . is spreading across Africa with giant strides. It stretches with an almost unbroken front from the Mediterranean nearly to the Equator, and is swiftly advancing southwards." Its success, according to Canon Taylor, must indicate that it satisfies "the religious needs and aspirations of the Indian and African races, or it could not thus succeed." He called Islam "eminently adapted to a civilising and elevating religion for barbarous tribes." He asked, "Can we expect the Negro, with a low moral and cerebral development, with centuries of fetishism and savagery behind him, to receive at once that lofty Christian morality . . . ?" He painted a picture of Islamized Africans: "The natives

begin to dress, filth is replaced by cleanliness, and they acquire personal dignity and self-respect. . . . Industry replaces idleness, license gives place to law, order and sobriety prevail. A feeling of humanity, benevolence, and brotherhood is inculcated." Islam was attractive to Africans because it offered them social equality, while "a Christian convert is not regarded as a social equal. . . ." Isaac Taylor, "The Church in Africa: Mohammedanism," in Reverend C. Dunkley, ed. *The Official Report of the Church Congress held at Wolverhampton* (London, 1887), 326–29, 331. Taylor was undismayed by the outraged comment stirred by his remarks. See, for example: *Church Congress . . . Wolverhampton*, 347–51; and "K" [Rev. George Knox], "A Rejoinder," *Church Missionary Intelligencer and Record* 12, n.s. (December 1887): 713–38.

In the fall of 1888, Taylor published two more provocative articles. Just as missionary societies and their supporters were calling upon government protection in light of the great sums they had expended on evangelical work in Central Africa, and just as Cardinal Lavigerie preached the need for Christian Europe to raise money and men to move against the Arabs of Central Africa, Taylor took on the issues of "The Great Missionary Failure," *Fortnightly Review* 44, n.s. (October 1888): 488–500, and "Missionary Finance," *Fortnightly Review* 44, n.s. (November 1888): 581–92. He focused on the lack of success of Christian evangelization in India as well as Africa, despite nearly a million pounds sterling raised by Protestant missions in the United Kingdom each year. He attacked the low social status of most missionary recruits, representing, in his word "an inferior education at cheap colleges," sent out to work under inferior bishops. He exempted the Universities' Mission to Central Africa from these strictures, but concluded "It is plain that these futile missions [among Muslims] should be given up." Taylor, "The Great Missionary Failure," 491. Taylor, it should be noted, was not alone or even original in these criticisms. Livingstone and Burton had clashed over this issue in the 1860s. R. Bosworth Smith delivered a series of lectures in London in 1874, calling Islam the "nearest approach" to Christianity, "which the unprogressive part of humanity can ever attain in masses. . . ." R. Bosworth Smith, *Mohammed and Mohammedism* (New York, 1875), 236. Bosworth Smith pointed out the similarity between his lectures and Canon Taylor's address in "Mohammedanism in Africa," *Nineteenth Century* 22 (December 1887): 792. In addition, the explorer Joseph Thomson said essentially the same things about the progress of Islam in Africa in 1886: "Sketch of a trip to Sokoto by the River Niger," *Journal of the Manchester Geographical Society* 2 (January 1886): 1–18; "Note on the African Tribes of the British Empire," *JAI* 16

(June 1886): 182–86; "Niger and Central Sudan Sketches," *SGM* 2 (September 1886): 577–96; and "Mohammedanism in Central Africa," *Contemporary Review* 50 (December 1886): 876–83. The difference between all these champions of Islam and critics of Christianity and Canon Taylor was that Taylor spoke from within the Church of England.

17. *Anti-Slavery Reporter*, July and August, 1888, 88.

18. *Ibid.*, 91; *The Christian World*, August 2, 1888, 609; Miers, *Britain and the Ending of the Slave Trade*, 203. As Miers notes, "Lavigerie had not said anything that explorers, missionaries and consuls had not already reported but his fiery oratory had made a deep impression on all who heard him and the press relayed his appeal forcibly to a wider public. Miers, *Britain and the Ending of the Slave Trade*, 203–4. Lavigerie had a superb sense of the dramatic, as well as knowledge of how to please his audience. According to the *Daily News*, Lavigerie pointedly told this English meeting of his visit to Livingstone's "modest tomb" at Westminster Abbey, where he "was reminded once more of the touching last words of that noblest of England's illustrious band of African explorers." The *Daily News* wrote of his "final stirring appeal to the English people to take heart and believe that it is possible—nay, not very difficult to destroy the traffic once and for all. . . ." The cardinal referred to his "crusade" as a "little war," and he appealed not only to the men listening to him, but also "to all women present to bring their influence to bear on husbands, fathers, and brothers to exert themselves in the great cause of 'liberty, humanity, and justice.' " Quoted in *Anti-Slavery Reporter*, July and August, 1888, 92–93.

19. *Anti-Slavery Reporter*, 108–9. As Miers put it, "Horace Waller called on young Christians to go to Africa and shoot slavers rather than big game." *Britain and the Ending of the Slave Trade*, 204. After printing the society's letter to Lord Salisbury, conveying the resolution put by Waller, the *Anti-Slavery Reporter* printed comments on the meeting from *The Times, Birmingham Daily Post, Sussex Daily News, The Baptist, Yorkshire Post, Standard, Weekly Bulletin, Stock Exchange, Glasgow Herald*, and *Pall Mall Gazette* of July 30. *Anti-Slavery Reporter*, July and August, 110–17. The *Stock Exchange* noted that "The papers all make much of the meeting," but as the cardinal spoke in French, only *The Times* gave a verbatim report of his speech, and the *Daily Telegraph* and *Daily News* "each make a longer report of Lord Granville's few introductory remarks . . . than they do of the Cardinal's speech." The *Glasgow Herald*, however, as the chief organ of a city closely tied to the Scottish missionary efforts in Malawi, pointedly commented: "It is the Mohammedan Arab who has taken possession of Africa, and in the im-

mediate future the contest will be between him and the Christian civi-
liser as to the question with whom the final mastery is to remain." *Anti-
Slavery Reporter*, July and August, 1888, 115.

20. Miers, *Britain the Ending of the Slave Trade*, 315.

21. *Ibid.*, 206–8, 219, 229. Cameron set out to raise funds for an organization he proposed to call the "Gordon-Livingstone Association,"
Anti-Slavery Reporter, September and October, 1888, 168–69. In *Good
Words*, a weekly journal, the circulation of which had reached 80,000 in
1870 and the price of which (one pence) made it available to the lower
reaches of the middle classes, Cameron wrote, ". . . I think that it
would be right, advisable, and proper to use all the resources of modern
warfare in order to rescue the native of Africa from Slavery, rapine,
murder, and sudden death." Quoted in *Anti-Slavery Reporter*, September and October, 1888, 192. On *Good Words*, see Ellegard, "Readership of the Periodical Press in Mid-Victorian Britain," 20, 21–22. When
the Anti-Slavery Society secretary Charles Allen sent letters to the editors of *The Times* and *Daily News*, stating explicitly that Cameron's
"military" campaign was not linked to the society, Cameron replied to
The Times that he believed moral force alone ineffectual against the
slave trade in Africa. *Anti-Slavery Reporter*, November and December,
1888, 231–33. Although Cameron attended a meeting of the Committee
of the society January 4, 1889, to explain his views, the Committee
formally approved of their secretary's course of action. *Anti-Slavery
Reporter*, January and February, 1889, 37. Waller—who was not a
pacifist—advised Allen to consider the Cameron episode "at an end."
Nonetheless, he could not resist adding, "If Cardinal Lavigerie meant
anything he meant – and means resort to arms. We, with a light heart,
received his large gift, and the world may well dig us in the ribs and say
'Why then do you come down so heavily on Cameron. . . .' " Waller to
Allen, January 26, 1889, BFASSP, MS. Brit. Emp. s18, C69/46, RH.

22. Lugard, *Rise of Our East African Empire*, 1:42; compare, Lugard,
Rise of Our East African Empire, 1:27, 46, and Perham, *Lugard*, 98, 111.
More recently, scholars have commented on the lack of clarity in a situation that seemed so straightforward to Europeans in the nineteenth century: "The European participants and their supporters in Britain found it
useful, for propaganda purposes, to think of the war as a crusade in
which one side was the representative of good, and the other of evil, but
there was nothing so clear-cut about the background. . . . Mlozi received very little overt diplomatic or practical help from the other Arab
powers in the area . . . he never mounted a serious offensive after his
initial successes in the latter months of 1887. . . . It is probable that
Mlozi was making a deliberate effort to assert his supremacy over the

Ngonde, and even over the Company itself, which cannot have appeared a very formidable opponent, represented as it was by never more than two agents. The extent to which his action was concerted with other Arabs in the area, may never be known." Macmillan, "Notes on the origins of the Arab war," in Pachai, *History of Malawi*, 263, 275, 276. See also n. 9, above.

23. "The Universities' Mission to Central Africa," *Quarterly Review* 168 (January 1889): 229–48 (author identification: *Wellesley Index to Victorian Periodicals*, vol. 1); "The Two Ends of the Slave-Stick," *Contemporary Review* 55 (April 1889): 528–38; *Nyassaland: Great Britain's Case Against Portugal* (London, 1890), 59pp.; "The Immediate Extinction of the Legal Status of Slavery in the Dominions of the Sultan of Zanzibar," *Anti-Slavery Reporter*, July and August, 1889, 170–75. Cardinal Lavigerie wrote July 24, 1889, calling off the August 4 conference because the French delegation were detained at home as a result of the calling of General Elections. *Anti-Slavery Reporter*, July and August, 1889, 160–61.

24. Only four items reviewed were recently published: R. M. Heanley's *Memoir of Bishop Steere* (1888); Henry Drummonds's *Tropical Africa* (1888); Parliamentary *Reports on Slave Trade on the East Coast of Africa, 1887–1888*, and *Central Africa, a Monthly Record of the Universities Mission*, 1888. The older works were: E. D. Young's *Mission to Nyassa* (1877); Harvey Goodwin's *Memoir of Bishop Mackenzie* (1864); Henry Rowley's *Story of the Universities' Mission to Central Africa* (1866); and Livingstone's *Zambesi and Its Tributaries* (1865) and *Last Journals* (1874). Thus Waller was reviewing, anonymously, his edited work!

25. [Waller], "Universities' Mission to Central Africa," 231.

26. *Ibid.*,

27. *Ibid.*, 231–32, emphasis added. In his paper for the Lucerne Antislavery Congress, Waller was even more forthright about the UMCA fighting of the early 1860s: "My companions and I felt that any means—all means—battles, surprises, the interception of Slave gangs, the forcible liberation of captives, were legitimate. . . ." Waller, "Immediate Extinction of the Legal Status of Slavery," *Anti-Slavery Reporter*, July and August, 1889, 174. That the editor of this journal did not add any disclaimer to these views is surprising, considering the pacifist outlook of the leaders of the organization.

28. [Waller], "Universities' Mission to Central Africa," 234, 248, emphasis added. Waller's desire to justify deeds condemned a quarter of a century before may be compared to Livingstones' brooding over the past on his last journey. See chap. 4 above.

29. Waller's essay on the "Immediate Extinction of the Legal Status of

Slavery in the Dominions of the Sultan of Zanzibar" was presented as one of several additional papers by Anti-Slavery Society members to the Brussels Anti-Slavery Conference. *Anti-Slavery Reporter*, November and December, 1889, 245–46, 250. Waller had written Allen, September 17, 1889, "I confess that for some months I have naturally supposed that our society . . . [was] very much on the qui vive [sic] respecting this Brussels conference which is of greater importance than any which any Cardinal can call together and on which a great deal depends." Waller's insider tone here, as often was the case, came from information he received from Kirk, who was Britain's major representative at the conference. BFASSP, MS. Brit. Emp. s18, C69/69, RH.

30. Horace Waller, *Heligoland for Zanzibar* (London, January 24, 1894), 51 pp. In this pamphlet, Waller continued to retaliate against Stanley's accusations concerning Kirk's hiring of slaves for Livingstone in 1872. He referred to "Mr. Stanley's horror at the use of slaves (when he 'found Livingstone')" compared to his hiring of 623 men at Zanzibar for his Emin Pasha Relief Expedition, out of whom 450 perished en route. Waller then quoted one of Stanley's officers, Major Barttelot, before he died, "Three-quarters of our men our slaves; when they get to Zanzibar, poor fellows, they only receive one-fourth of their money, the rest goes to their master." Waller, *Heligoland for Zanzibar*, 10–11.

31. These accusations did not impair Waller's relations with Kirk or Lugard, though Kirk sometimes sounded rather annoyed by Waller and may have become more circumspect about what he reported to him. See, for example, Kirk to Lugard, Private, Sevenoaks, October, 1892, Lugard Papers, MS. Brit. Emp. s69, RH. Waller was a constant correspondent of both, and throughout 1893 he aided Lugard in making arrangements with Blackwood to publish his two-volume work, including reading proofs and writing the unsigned review of the book when it was published. [Horace Waller], "The Rise of our East African Empire," *Blackwood's Magazine* 154 (December 1893): 875–91. The correspondence between Waller and William Blackwood concerning Lugard's publication is at the National Library of Scotland. Waller also contributed "Sidelights on Uganda," for *Blackwood's Magazine* 152 (July 1892): 127–37. Waller ended this article with a dire warning: "A train of circumstances is already laid [in Uganda], which, with one touch of vexatious folly, might instantly lead to a disaster—not so very different to that which occurred in Khartoum."

32. Horace Waller, *Slaving and Slavery in our British Protectorates* (London, December 1, 1894), 8 pp., and *The Case of our Zanzibar Slaves: Why Not Liberate Them?* (London, January 27, 1896). In 1897, the year after Waller's death, and as the result of concentrated pressure

from the antislavery lobby, the legal status of slavery was abolished for Zanzibar and Pemba and compensation was paid slave masters. According to Miers, "Concubines were not included in this emancipation for fear of disrupting domestic life." Miers, *Britain and the Ending of the Slave Trade*, 299. Only in 1907 was slavery legally abolished in Great Britain's Kenya Protectorate, and with the same proviso. Miers, *Britain and the Ending of the Slave Trade*, 301.

33. Kirk commented to Lugard on Waller's decision to retire from his active clerical life. "Waller was here yesterday. He is to leave Twywell and seek a house nearer London. He will retire. I fancy he is very well off indeed. His wife came in for a fortune & his Nyassa estate is just becoming of value. His is an enormous district. I don't know how many thousand acres & is valued now I believe at 5/ an acre but land has been sold at twice that for planting." Kirk to Lugard, Sevenoaks, June 29, 1894, Lugard Papers, MS. Brit. Emp. s69, RH. For details on the claims by Waller (5,441 acres) and other Europeans, see Bridglal Pachai, *Land and Politics in Malawi, 1875-1975* (Kingston, Ont., 1978), chap. 3, esp. 37–40. For comment on the ill-treatment of Africans on the Bruce Estates, see George Shepperson, "The Place of John Chilembwe in Malawi historiography," in Pachai, *History of Malawi*, 419.

34. Waller to Lugard, East Liss, December 27, 1895, Lugard Papers, MS. Brit. Emp. s71, RH. For the speeches of the deputation to Lord Rosebery, October 20, 1892, including Waller's, Rosebery's reply, a large selection of newspaper comment, Waller's subsequent letters to *The Times*, and finally, his letter to Arthur Pease, the president of the Anti-Slavery Society, see *Anti-Slavery Reporter*, November and December, 1892, 257–76, 286–311, 313–18. Waller publicly commented on this behavior: "Personally, I had the temerity to state before Lord Rosebery, on a rather notable occasion, that if a downright well-trodden slave route had to be identified in the British sphere of influence, I could commend his Lordship to the caravan route between Mombasa and Uganda." Waller, *Heligoland for Zanzibar*, 13. The secretary of the Anti-Slavery Society, Charles Allen, agreed with Waller's assessment that his presence had been critical to bringing non-Quaker views into its policies. Allen wrote within a week of Waller's death, "Probably the Society will now be mainly under the direction of the 'Friend' element on the Committee, for Mr. Wylde & Dr. Cust will probably not attend regularly now that Mr. Waller is gone. *We shall often miss him for he was a strong man.*" Allen to C. R. Kemp, February 28, 1896, BFASSP, MS. Brit. Emp. s20 3/8, RH, emphasis added.

EPILOGUE

Livingstone believed that Africa and Africans would prosper if brought into contact with Europeans of good hearts and minds. Impressed by the promise of science in industry, the healthy human exchanges that would be fostered by free trade, and deeply believing in the inevitable shape of social reform, Livingstone could not but wish to bring material and spiritual enlightenment to the societies he found in the heart of Africa. To pursue the tale as it meshes with the beginnings of the colonial period in Africa would merely pile irony upon irony. The crux of Livingstone's faith that good trade would drive out bad, agriculture would nourish free labor, and English and Scottish settlers would serve as brave and pure models of enlightened behavior for the Africans with whom they lived, worked, and prayed was a backward-looking vision for all its attempt to break with the past.

The agricultural model Livingstone had in mind was already disappearing at home at the turn of the nineteenth century. The belief in ranks of men who acknowledged duties and obligations to one another was a vision of a golden age that lived more in Livingstone's imagination than in the history from which he emerged. His grandfather had left the hard highlands where a living could no longer simply be scratched from the soil and landless cottagers faced being turned out by improving landlords. His father had resisted a service profession that spelled out closely the need to tailor one's way as well as one's cloth. His boasted days in the mill as darting piecer and solid spinner, Latin book poised at the edge of his machine, were also days of being taunted by other boys and developing his strengths as a loner. Livingstone's world, despite the cotton mill, gave him much in common with the small-scale societies he met inside Africa. For that very reason, his ideas seemed feasible. His notions of settlement colonies ended before he embarked on his last journey.

Livingstone came to believe that white men could bring to Africa those management skills he thought were lacking among the societies he passed through, but of course white men were skilled at organizing what they were quick learning at home: capital invested in relatively large-scale production or food processing to supply a world demand nurtured by the cheapness of prices that followed abundant supply. Except for the gold, diamond, and copper mines and the rubber plantations, Africa's economic development did not promise to fit so readily into the Procrustean bed of Western industrialization. In Africa, domestic slavery still functioned in the warp and woof of indigenous institutions and structures, mores and manners. We return full circle to where we began: the question of cross-cultural misunderstandings; the culture-bound definitions of social norms that Europeans like Livingstone and Waller, Gordon and Lugard, Cameron and Baker, brought with them when observing nineteenth-century Africa.

Some facts of life were easier to absorb than others. When Waller wrote yet another pamphlet in early 1891, called by him '*Ivory, Apes, and Peacocks;' An African Contemplation*, he promised his reader "to look upon African matters more from the *natives' point of view* than is usual." The word *natives* should remind us that it was the European colonization of "other races" throughout the world that gave a special, implicitly denigrating, meaning to this otherwise neutral word. "Natives" could be adults in chronological time only; they were dependents, viewed as "children," and called "boys" and "girls" (Lugard mentioned the "station boys" at Karonga already in 1888). "Natives" were those born in the country, and thus they were better able than the newcomers to "work" in the country. That, in fact, was the warning that Waller wished to impart to his countrymen in his *African Contemplation.* "Africa will be for the Africans for many a day yet," he explained, because "traditional" colonization was "altogether beside the question in Africa."

The moral Waller drew from his realization was that "the man born of her soil is the one who must inevitably develop her riches . . . it comes to this—the African must do the European's work. . . ." For several years he had been loud in the denunciation of the use of contract labor to build railways in the Congo or slave labor to act as porters for goods on white men's expeditions through Africa. Yet he apparently felt no sense of the contradictions he raised in drawing a picture of Livingstone and himself lying on the banks of the Shire River in 1861, contemplating the "cowardly tribes" on the northern side of the Zambezi, and calling them victims "fit for the slave-traders' purposes, and disintegrated by the presence of firearms, without power of cohesion, and not given to discipline of any sort." Having established the blameworthy character of these victims, he then suggested how easily the problem could be solved: "Give your African the slightest advantage—afford him just the lick-and-promise of *law and authority at the white man's hand,* [and] at once his tribe increases. . . ." It was clear to Waller, as it would be clear to his contemporary readers, that from the "African point of view" European rule was essential, that "the native" needed "that high-principled, gentlemanlike element . . . the frank and joking Englishman" who would help him find work on his own soil and teach him how to prosper.[1]

Implicit from the very beginning of Livingstone's vision of Africa, though not original to him, was the conviction that Africans must be taken by the hand and guided to a better way. From the first, too, Livingstone interpreted the core of the relationship between Africans and Europeans as that of dependents/subordinates to masters/superiors. It seemed reasonable to him, awed as he was by the possibilities of applying science to industry, of reforming old systems into new efficient, effective, and ultimately *better* ones. He believed in linear progress as completely as did any nineteenth-century evolutionist, even as he dismissed Darwin's threat to biblical teachings of divine origins of the earth and its inhabitants.

As we have seen, Livingstone aligned himself with the "sanitary reformers . . . inventors of telegraphs and steam engines, promoters of emigration and of prison reform" of his generation. He saw his goal of African "regeneration" as both possible to achieve and inevitable if only he found the right formula to trigger the momentum. This fundamental optimism lay at the base of Livingstone's strategies; it gave him the determination to ignore obstacles, to look again for solutions in the face of them, and to predict with confidence eventual success once his prescription for material and spiritual change took hold and the logic of its development followed. He finally fixed on the combination of forces that would effect the looked-for social changes in Africa: the introduction of European civilization, Christianity, and commerce. At the heart of his vision lay the ultimate implications of his thinking, though the nearest he came to seeing them was his concession that the Europeans would have to come to Africa as managers and organizers, not tillers of the soil in their own right. The logic implicit within Livingstone's formulation, however, allowed Waller to call it forth when he needed it, to provide the ultimate rationale for imperialism.

Livingstone's first legacy was to Horace Waller. The younger man set forth to Africa uncertain of his future, in search of a firm identity to supplant his rejected past. Livingstone provided him with that new sense of self and gave him a cause that could sustain him in a transition from City stockbroker to lay missionary to clergyman and antislave-trade crusader. In 1867, the news that Livingstone had been killed in Africa acted as the catalyst that triggered Waller's final decision to commit himself to a new life. As he busied himself at the Royal Geographical Society, talking endlessly of Livingstone and his own experiences in Africa, as he began to share Kirk's Zanzibar news of the slave trade with Fowell Buxton, his resolve took shape. By August, he spoke in Paris at an Antislavery Convention, describing at length Livingstone's (and his own) experiences with the horrors of the slave trade in Central Africa, and he was overwhelmed by the excitement of the reactions of the audience. By the end of the year, he was ordained a clergyman. Livingstone's legacy to Waller was palpable, and it lasted through his lifetime.

Livingstone's legacy to the British Empire was equally direct. His formulation of the European need to intervene in Africa for the Africans' sake, sharpened into a challenge to his country by means of Waller's editing of his *Last Journals*, became the justification for British interference there on an ever-increasing scale. Explorers, missionaries, commercial companies, and consular agents, all marching under the twin banners of "LIVINGSTONE" and "CIVILIZATION, CHRISTIANITY, AND COMMERCE," ventured into the African interior, as Livingstone hoped they would, and brought in their train the British Empire, as Livingstone always believed they should. What we learn from this is that all generalizations about the course of late nineteenth-century European imperialism must be tested against the circumstances of specific acquisitions. When this is done, we see the multiple strands represented by particular participants and the specific motivations they carried with them, and we begin to understand that individual personalities as well as types of persons, mixed personal motives as well as larger-scale forces, were interwoven into the phenomenon called "imperialism."

We have been engaged in such an exercise, examining individual motivation as well as the broader trends in society that impelled them to act. We have looked minutely at the warts on the skins of the living, breathing people like Livingstone and Waller who inhabited this imperialist era. We have seen their passionate good intentions, gauged by their standards; and we have become aware of their blindspots, their tunnel vision, the singular preoccupations that gave rise to these blinkers, and what followed from them. We have been able to observe these facts of history the more clearly to the extent that they differ from our own perceptions of the past. In addition to this different angle of vision, we enjoy the perspective of time, distance, and in many cases, greater knowledge about how it all fit together, and how it all worked out.

We have been tracing the theme of mythmaking, the creation of a legend out of a public hero to serve the purpose of a humanitarian cause and imperialist ends. The hero did exist, the cause was a real one, and the ends were served. Inventing a legend out of human clay was necessary to meet the need for enduring propaganda for the cause of antislavery.

The editor of Livingstone's *Last Journals* brought himself, his ideas, the needs of the moment, and his hopes for the future to that creative process. To understand is not to applaud. We can see information lost, perspective cheated, and a loss to history of the real human being about whom the myth was shaped. The act of discovery in this book makes evident the need for further investigation. David Livingstone *was* an extraordinary man. We need to learn more intimately about his life and work and his unvarnished observations of his world. What we have learned in the process of peeling back the layers of the editing process that Waller—and Tom Livingstone and John Murray—engaged in is exciting in itself and provocative for understanding the particular mixture of motivations that made the antislavery cause a peculiarly English obsession, to use H. A. C. Cairns's phrase.

This study shows the need to consider psychological dimensions as well as economic ones when assessing the course of imperialism. It is critical to our understanding of the imperialist era to deal with the underlying structures and assumptions of British society in an industrial age. Africa, unexplored Africa, appealed to particular kinds of Britons, but at base because of their vision of themselves and their own society. Just as Livingstone's vision of the future encompassed his imagination of a past that never was, a patriarchal paradise, so those who clamored for British intervention in Africa by the early 1890s echoed the chords of a Livingstone legacy whose full implications were unexamined.

D. A. Low tells us that in the fall of 1892, from hamlets and villages, Rural Deanery Chapters and town halls, nonconformist meetings and Church of England associations, Mutual Improvement Societies and (mainly but not solely Conservative) political organizations, 147 sets of Resolutions, 11 memorials, and 16 petitions flooded into the Foreign Office. With one voice they called upon the government not to withdraw British influence from Uganda, a place the reality of which few who raised their voices could possibly have imagined. He concludes that "the preachings of Wilberforce, Buxton, and Livingstone had sunk deep into the national mind, and any reverse in Africa instantly recalled the horror of slavery which was the one thing that most of them knew about Africa."[2] This outpouring was unplanned and unsolicited. It resonated with memories of Gordon and Khartoum, "*and confidence that the keys to progress had been found and could easily be transferred to Africa.*"[3] Low was surprised at what he found. He called this preoccupation with "legitimate" trade, slavery and the slave trade, the need for peace, order, and good government in Africa, fears for Christian missions already there, and a sense of national duty and "moral" influence "strange bedfellows." From what we have now found to be the history of these ideas in nineteenth-century Britain, we are not surprised at their juxtaposition; they are Livingstone's legacy.

The logic of these beliefs played itself out in new colonial administrations which imposed law and order, saw the need to discipline "natives" by enlightening them with Christian education and insisting that they offer their labor services in a regular way to their white rulers. Colonization, even where Europeans were settlers in very small numbers, entailed the creation of a new Africa that may have been beyond the dreams of Livingstone and Waller, but it was certainly a logical development of those dreams. On April 6, 1896, shortly after Waller's death, a young medical officer in the administration of British Central Africa wrote home to his mother that when Africans refused to pay the newly imposed hut tax, "we kill their men and burn their houses and collar their cattle and ivory and cloth and beads and their women whom we call slaves and to whom we give papers of manumission, which papers are found afterwards thrown away in heaps. . . . But Exeter Hall and the old ladies and the missionaries at home think a lot of it. . . . It is with many winks and digs in the ribs and chuckles that we read the effusions of the Rev. Horace Waller and others in the papers from home."[4] The new British colonial generation had taken control; European intervention under the banner of civilization, Christianity, and commerce had arrived.

NOTES

1. Horace Waller, *'Ivory, Apes, and Peacocks;' An African Contemplation*, London, 1891, *vii*, 1, 14–15, 23, 24–35. In reviewing the book, the *Anti-Slavery Reporter* remarked that it was "filled with the vigorous and outspoken sympathy for the *children of Africa* which always characterizes his writings. . . ." *Anti-Slavery Reporter*, 1891 (March and April), 73, emphasis added. The reviewer agreed that since the "manual strength of the patient negro will always have to be depended upon by those who wish to win fortunes from the hidden riches of the vast continent," they would have to keep that labor from being kidnapped or expatriated.

2. D. Anthony Low, "British Public Opinion and 'The Uganda Question': October-December 1892," chap. 2 in *Buganda in Modern History* (Berkeley and Los Angeles, 1971), 76–77.

3. *Ibid.*, 78, emphasis added.

4. Cited in Cairns, *Prelude to Imperialism*, 237, 299 n. 21.

BIBLIOGRAPHY

[For a list of the abbreviations used, see p. x. For books and articles by Horace Waller, see Appendix A, p. 372. For a list of his letters to the editor of *The Times*, see Appendix B, p. 374.]

MANUSCRIPT SOURCES
Royal Society of Arts
   General Minute Books, African Section, 1874–1879
Baker, Valentine, Esq., Private Collection
   Baker Papers
Royal Botanical Gardens, Kew
   English Letters, 1857–1900
The British Library
   Gladstone Papers
   Gordon Papers
Foskett, Mrs. Daphne, Private Collection
   Kirk Papers
Royal Geographical Society Archives
   Cameron Papers
   Correspondence Files
   Council Minute Books, 1867–1896
   Newspaper Clippings, 1872–1875
Hatfield House, Hatfield, Herts.
   Salisbury Papers
Institute of Royal Engineers, Chatham, Kent
   Gordon Papers
John Murray, Publisher, Archives
   Copybook, Outgoing Letters
   Correspondence, Incoming Letters
   Ledger Journals
Public Record Office
   Foreign Office, Series F.O. 84, 403
Rhodes House Library
   British and Foreign Anti-Slavery Papers
   Lugard Papers
   Waller Papers

St. Anthony's College,
   Oxford Gordon Papers
School of Oriental and African Studies, University of London
   Mackinnon Papers
National Library of Scotland
   Blackwood Papers
   Cameron Papers
   Church of Scotland, Foreign Mission Papers
      Livingstonia Mission Papers
      Blantyre Mission Papers
   Grant Papers
   Gordon Papers
   Livingstone Papers
   Mackinnon Papers
   Stanley Papers
National Museum of Zambia, at Livingstone
   Livingstone Papers
National Archives of Zimbabwe
   Livingstone Papers
   Stewart Papers
United Society for the Propagation of the Gospel Archives
(Now located at Rhodes House, Oxford)
   Universities' Mission to Central Africa Papers
   Pike Papers
University of Witwatersrand, Library
   Livingstone Papers

UNPUBLISHED THESES
De Kiewet, Marie. "History of the Imperial British East Africa Company, 1876–1895." Ph.D. diss., University of London, 1955.
Visram, Rozina. "David Livingstone and India." Master's thesis, University of Edinburgh, 1973.

SERIALS
Anti-Slavery Reporter, 1865–1896
Journal of the Society of Arts, 1874–1896
Church Missionary Intelligencer, 1865–1895
Proceedings of the Royal Colonial Institute, 1879–1896
Transactions of the Ethnological Society of London, 1864–1870
Proceedings of the Royal Geographical Society, 1860–1896
Illustrated London News, 1874

Men of the Time, A Dictionary of Contemporaries. Edited by G. Washington Moon. 13th ed. London, 1891.
Mission Life (variously subtitled), 1866–1890
The Times, 1864–1896

BOOKS AND PAMPHLETS

Acton, William. *Prostitution, Considered in Its Moral, Social, and Sanitary Aspects.* . . . 1857. 2d ed. London, 1870.

Alderson, Frederick. *Bicycling: A History.* Newton Abbot, England, 1972.

Allen, Bernard M. *Down the Stream of Life.* London, 1948.

Alpers, Edward A. *The East African Slave Trade.* The Historical Association of Tanzania. 1967. Reprint. Nairobi, 1968.

―――. *Ivory and Slaves. Changing Patterns of International Trade in East Central Africa to the Later Nineteenth Century.* Berkeley and London, 1975.

Anstey, Roger. *Britain and the Congo in the Nineteenth Century.* Oxford, 1962.

Beachey, R. W. *The Slave Trade in Eastern Africa.* London, 1976.

Bennett, Norman, R. *Mirambo of Tanzania, 1840(?)–1884.* London and Toronto, 1971.

―――, ed. *The Zanzibar Letters of Edward Ropes, Jr., 1882–1892.* Boston, 1973.

Bennett, Norman R., and Marguerite Ylvisaker, eds. *The Central African Journal of Lovell J. Proctor.* African Studies Center. Boston University. Boston, 1976.

Berg, Maxine. *The Machinery Question and the Making of Political Economy, 1815–1848.* 1980. Reprint. Cambridge, 1982.

Berger, Peter L., and Thomas Luckmann. *The Social Construction of Reality: A Treatise on the Sociology of Knowledge.* New York, 1967.

Blaikie, William Garden. *The Personal Life of David Livingstone, LL.D., D.C.L., Chiefly from His Unpublished Journals and Correspondence in the Possession of His Family.* New York, 1881.

Bolt, Christine. *Victorian Attitudes to Race.* London, 1971.

Buffon, Georges Louis Leclerc, comte de. *Histoire naturelle generale et particuliere, avec la description du Cabinet du roy.* . . .Paris, 1747–1789.

Burrow, John W. *Evolution and Society. A Study in Victorian Social Theory.* Cambridge, 1966.

Burton, Richard. *The Lake Regions of Central Africa.* 2 vols. London, 1860.

Cairns, H. Alan C. *Prelude to Imperialism: British Reactions to Central African Society, 1840-1890.* London, 1965.

Cameron, V. Lovett. *Across Africa.* New York, 1877.

Campbell, Reginald J. *Livingstone.* 1930. Reprint. Westport, Conn., 1972.

Casada, James A. *Dr. David Livingstone and Sir Henry Morton Stanley: An Annotated Bibliography.* New York and London, 1976.

Chadwick, Owen. *Mackenzie's Grave.* London, 1959.

―――. *The Victorian Church. Part 2.* New York, 1970.

Cooke, A. B., and John Vincent. *The Governing Passion: Cabinet Government and Party Politics in Britain, 1885-86.* Brighton, England, 1974.

Cooley, W. D. *Dr. Livingstone and the Royal Geographical Society.* London, 1874.

Cooper, Frederick. *Plantation Slavery on the East Coast of Africa.* New Haven and London, 1977.

Cooper, Joseph. *The Lost Continent or Slavery and the Slave-Trade in Africa.* 1875. Reprint. London, 1968.

Coupland, Reginald. *The Exploitation of East Africa, 1856-1890: The Slave Trade and the Scramble.* London, 1939.

―――. *Livingstone's Last Journey.* London, 1945.

Curtin, Philip. *The Image of Africa: British Ideas and Action, 1780-1850.* New York, 1964.

De Carvalho, Henrique A. D. *Os Caes Britannicos ou A Nyassaland do Rev. Horace Waller.* Lisbon, 1891.

Eldridge, Colin C. *England's Mission: The Imperial Idea in the Age of Gladstone and Disraeli, 1868-1880.* London and Basingstoke, 1973.

Elton, Lord. *Gordon of Khartoum: The Life of General Charles George Gordon.* New York, 1955.

Flandrin, Jean-Louis. *Families in Former Times: Kinship, Household and Sexuality.* Translated by Richard Southern. Cambridge, 1979.

Fox-Bourne, Henry R. *The Other Side of the Emin Pasha Relief Expedition.* London, 1891.

Fraser, Augusta Z. *Livingstone and Newstead.* London, 1913.

Frere, Sir [Henry] Bartle [Edward]. *Eastern Africa as a Field for Missionary Labour: Four Letters to the Archbishop of Canterbury.* London, 1874.

Galbraith, John S. *Mackinnon and East Africa, 1878-1895: A Study in the 'New Imperialism'.* Cambridge, 1972.

Gelfand, Michael. *Livingstone the Doctor: His Life and Travels.* 2d ed. Oxford, 1957.

Goetzmann, William H. *Exploration and Empire: The Explorer and the Scientist in the Winning of the West*. New York, 1966.

Goodfellow, Clement F. *Great Britain and South African Confederation, 1870–1881*. Cape Town, 1966.

Gray, Richard, and David Birmingham, eds. *Pre-Colonial African Trade. Essays on Trade in Central and Eastern Africa before 1900*. London, New York, and Nairobi, 1970.

Greenberg, Dolores. *Financiers and Railroads*. Newark, Del., London, and Toronto, 1980.

Hall, Richard. *Lovers on the Nile: The Incredible African Journeys of Sam and Florence Baker*. New York, 1980.

————. *Stanley: An Adventurer Explored*. Boston, 1975.

Hammerton, A. James. *Emigrant Gentlewomen: Genteel Poverty and Female Emigration, 1830–1919*. London, 1979.

Hanna, Alexander J. *The Beginnings of Nyasaland and North-Eastern Rhodesia , 1859–95*. Oxford, 1956.

Harris, Joseph E. *The African Presence in Asia: Consequences of the East African Slave Trade*. Evanston, Ill., 1971.

Healey, Edna. *Lady Unknown: The Life of Angela Burdett-Coutts*. London, 1978.

Hill, George Birkbeck, ed. *Colonel Gordon in Central Africa, 1874–1879*. 3d ed. London, 1884.

Hobson, John A. *Imperialism: A Study*. 1902. Reprint. Introduction by Philip Siegelman. Ann Arbor, 1965.

Holmberg, Åke. *African Tribes and European Agencies: Colonialism and humanitarianism in British South and East Africa, 1870–1895*. Goteborg, 1966.

Holt, Peter M., *The Mahdist State in the Sudan, 1881–1898: A Study of Its Origins, Development, and Overthrow*. 2d ed. Oxford, 1970.

————, *A Modern History of the Sudan: From the Funj Sultanate to the Present Day*. London, 1961.

Hynes, William G. *The Economics of Empire: Britain, Africa and the New Imperialism, 1870–95*. London, 1979.

Jeal, Tim. *Livingstone*. New York, 1973.

Johnston, Harry H. *Livingstone and the Exploration of Central Africa*. London, 1891.

Jones, Andrew. *The Politics of Reform, 1884*. Cambridge, 1972.

Jones, Ray. *The Nineteenth-Century Foreign Office: An Administrative History*. London, 1971.

Kiddle, Margaret. *Caroline Chisholm*. Melbourne, 1950.

Kirk, John. *The Zambesi Journal and Letters of Dr. John Kirk, 1858–*

1863. 2 vols. Edited by Reginald Foskett. Edinburgh, 1965.

Knorr, Klaus E. *British Colonial Theories, 1570-1850*. 1944. Reprint. London, 1963.

Koebner, Richard, and Helmut Dan Schmidt. *Imperialism: The Story and Significance of a Political Word, 1840-1960*. Cambridge, 1964.

Lee, Susan Previant, and Peter Passell. *A New Economic View of American History*. New York and London, 1979.

David Livingstone and Africa. Proceedings of a Seminar held on the occasion of the Centenary of the Death of David Livingstone, Centre of African Studies, University of Edinburgh. May 4 and 5, 1973.

David Livingstone: A Catalogue of Documents. Compiled by G. W. Clendennen, assisted by I. C. Cunningham. National Library of Scotland for the David Livingstone Documentation Project. Edinburgh, 1979.

_____. *A Supplement*. Comp. by I. C. Cunningham. Edinburgh, 1985.

David Livingstone: Family Letters, 1841-1856. 2 vols. Edited by Isaac Shapera. London, 1959.

Livingstone, David. *The Last Journals of David Livingstone*. 2 vols. Edited by Horace Waller. London, 1874.

_____. *Livingstone's African Journal, 1853-1856*. 2 vols. Edited by Isaac Shapera. London, 1963.

_____. *Livingstone's "Private Journals," 1851-1853*. Edited by Isaac Shapera. London, 1960.

_____. *Missionary Travels and Researches in South Africa: Including a Sketch of Sixteen Years' Residence in the Interior of Africa, and a Journey from the Cape of Good Hope to Loanda on the West Coast, Thence Across the Continent, Down the River Zambesi, to the Eastern Ocean*. London, 1857.

_____. *The Zambesi Doctors. David Livingstone's Letters to John Kirk, 1858-1872*. Edited by Reginald Foskett. Edinburgh, 1964.

_____. *The Zambesi Expedition of David Livingstone, 1858-1863*. 2 vols. Edited by John P. R. Wallis. Oppenheimer Series of the Central African Archives, no. 9. London, 1956.

Livingstone, David, and Charles Livingstone. *Narrative of an Expedition to the Zambesi and Its Tributaries; and of the Discovery of the Lakes Shirwa and Nyassa, 1858-1864*. New York, 1866.

Livingstone, William P. *Laws of Livingstonia*. London, 1921.

Lorimer, Douglas A. *Colour, Class and the Victorians: English Attitudes to the Negro in the Mid-Nineteenth Century*. New York, 1978.

Lovejoy, Paul E. ed. *The Ideology of Slavery in Africa*. Beverly Hills and London, 1981.

Lyons, Charles H., *To Wash an Aethiop White: British Ideas About Black African Educability, 1530-1960*. New York, 1975.

Maine, Henry Sumner. *Ancient Law*. New York, 1864.

Maitland, Alexander. *Speke*. London, 1971.

Malan, A. G., ed. *Eagle House, 1820-1908: A Register of the School*. London, 1909.

McCracken, John. *Politics and Christianity in Malawi, 1875-1940*. Cambridge, 1977.

McLaren, Angus. *Birth Control in Nineteenth-Century England*. New York, 1978.

Miers, Suzanne. *Britain and the Ending of the Slave Trade*. London, 1975.

Miers, Suzanne and Igor Kopytoff, eds. *Slavery in Africa. Historical and Anthropological Perspectives*. Madison, 1977.

Moir, Jane F. *A Lady's Letters from Central Africa: A Journey from Mandala, Shire Highlands, to Ujiji, Lake Tanganyika, and Back*. Glasgow, 1891.

Monk, William, ed. *Dr. Livingstone's Cambridge Lectures*. 2d ed. Cambridge, 1860.

Newitt, M. D. D., *Portuguese Settlement on the Zambesi: Exploration, Land Tenure and Colonial Rule in East Africa*. London, 1973.

Northcott, Cecil. *David Livingstone: His Triumph, Decline and Fall*. Philadelphia, 1973.

Oliver, Roland. *The Missionary Factor in East Africa*. 2d ed. London, 1965.

————. *Sir Harry Johnston and the Scramble for Africa*. London, 1957.

Oliver, Roland, and Gervase Mathew, eds. *History of East Africa*. vol. 1. Oxford, 1963.

Oswell, E. Edward, ed. *William Cotton Oswell: Hunter and Explorer*. 2 vols. New York, 1900.

Ozment, Steven. *When Fathers Ruled: Family Life in Reformation Europe*. Cambridge, 1983.

Pachai, Bridglal. *Land and Politics in Malawi, 1875-1975*. Kingston, Ont., 1978.

————, ed. *The Early History of Malawi*. London, 1972.

————, ed. *Livingstone: Man of Africa. Memorial Essays, 1873-1973*. London, 1973.

Perham, Margery. *Lugard: The Years of Adventure, 1858-1898*. London, 1956.

Perham, Margery, and Mary Bull, eds. *The Diaries of Lord Lugard*. 3 vols. London, 1959.

Preston, Adrian, ed. *In Relief Of Gordon: Lord Wolseley's Campaign*

Journal of the Khartoum Relief Expedition, 1884-1885. London, 1967.
Ragg, Lonsdale. *A Memoir of Charles Edward Wickham,* London, 1911.
Ramm, Agatha, ed. *The Political Correspondence of Mr. Gladstone and Lord Granville, 1876-1886.* 2 vols. Oxford, 1962.
Ransford, Oliver. *David Livingstone: The Dark Interior.* London, 1978.
Reade, Winwoode. *Savage Africa.* London, 1864.
Roberts, Andrew. *A History of the Zambia.* London, 1976.
Robertson, Claire C., and Martin A. Klein, eds. *Women and Slavery in Africa.* Madison and London, 1983.
Robinson, Ronald, and John Gallagher, with Alice Denny. *Africa and the Victorians: The Official Mind of Imperialism.* London, 1961.
Rotberg, Robert I. *Joseph Thomson and the Exploration of Africa.* London, 1971.
————, ed. *Africa and Its Explorers: Motives, Methods, and Impact.* Cambridge, Mass., 1970.
Rubinstein, W. D., *Men of Property: The Very Wealthy in Britain since the Industrial Revolution.* New Brunswick, 1981.
Runciman, Steven. *The White Rajahs.* Cambridge, 1860.
Shostak, Marjorie. *Nisa: The Life and Words of a !Kung Woman.* 1981. Reprint. New York, 1983.
Simpson, Donald H., *Dark Companions: The African contribution to the European exploration of East Africa.* London, 1975.
Skultans, Vieda. *Madness and Morals: Ideas on Insanity in the Nineteenth Century.* London, 1975.
Smith, Iain R. *The Emin Pasha Relief Expedition, 1886-1890.* Oxford, 1972.
Smith, R. Bosworth. *Mohammed and Mohammedism.* New York, 1875.
Southgate, Donald. *"The Most English Minister . . .": The Policies and Politics of Palmerston.* London, 1966.
Stanley, Henry M. *How I Found Livingstone. Travels, Adventures, and Discoveries in Central Africa; including four months' residence with Dr. Livingstone.* 1st ed., 1872. 2d ed. 1874. London, 1890.
————. *Stanley's Despatches to the "New York Herald," 1871-1872, 1874-1877.* Edited by Norman R. Bennett. Boston, 1970.
————. *Through the Dark Continent, or the Sources of the Nile around the Great Lakes of Equatorial Africa and Down the Livingstone River to the Atlantic Ocean.* 2 vols. 1878. Reprint. New York, 1969.
Stewart, James. *The Zambesi Journal of James Stewart, 1862-1863.* Edited by John P. R. Wallis. Oppenheimer Series of the Central African Archives, no. 6. London, 1952.
Stevenson, James. *The Arabs in Central Africa and at Lake Nyassa.* Glasgow, 1888, 26pp.

Stock, Eugene. *The History of the Church Missionary Society.* 3 vols. London, 1899.

Strayer, Robert W. *The Making of Mission Communities in East Africa.* Albany, 1978.

Sullivan, G. L. *Dhow Chasing in Zanzibar Waters and on the East Coast of Africa.* 1873. Reprint. London, 1968.

Symons, Julian. *England's Pride: The Story of the Gordon Relief Expedition.* London, 1965.

Temperley, Howard. *British Antislavery 1833-1870.* London, 1972.

Temu, A. J. *British Protestant Missions.* London, 1972.

Thomson, Joseph. *To the Central African Lakes and Back: The Narrative of the R.G.S.'s Central African Expedition, 1879-80.* 2 vols. London, 1881.

Thornton, Richard. *The Zambezi Papers of Richard Thornton.* 2 vols. Robins Series, no. 4. Edited by Edward C. Tabler. London, 1963.

Ure, Andrew. *The Philosophy of Manufactures.* London, 1835.

Van Orman, Richard A. *The Explorers: Nineteenth Century Expeditions in Africa and the American West.* Albuquerque, 1984.

Walkowitz, Judith R. *Prostitution and Victorian Society: Women, Class, and the State.* New York, 1980.

Wallis, John P. R. *Thomas Baines of King's Lynn.* London, 1941.

Webb, Sidney, and Beatrice Webb. *English Poor Law Policy.* 1910. English Local Government series, vol. 10. Reprint. London, 1963.

Wohl, Anthony S., ed. *The Victorian Family: Structure and Stresses.* London, 1978.

Young, Edward D. *Nyassa: A Journal of Adventures.* London, 1877.

―――――. *The Search after Livingstone.* Revised by the Reverend Horace Waller. London, 1868.

ARTICLES AND CHAPTERS

Atmore, A. E. "Africa on the Eve of Partition." In *The Cambridge History of Africa*, edited by Roland Oliver and G. N. Sanderson, vol. 6, 10–95. Cambridge, 1985.

Baer, Gabriel. "Slavery in Nineteenth Century Egypt." *Journal of African History* 8, no. 3 (1967): 417–41.

Baker, Sam[uel] W. "The Last Journals of David Livingstone." *Macmillan's Magazine* 31 (1874–1875): 281–92. Also appeared in *Littell's Living Age* 124 (1875): 617–27, and *Eclectic Magazine* 53 (1875): 181ff.

Bennett, Norman R. "The Church Missionary Society at Mombasa, 1873–1894." In *Boston University Papers in African History*, vol. 1, edited by Jeffrey Butler, 157–94. Boston, 1964.

Berger, Iris. "Rebels or Status-Seekers? Women as Spirit Mediums in

East Africa." *Women in Africa: Studies in Social and Economic Change*, edited by Nancy J. Hafkin and Edna G. Bay, 157–81. Stanford, 1976.

Birdwood, George. "Last Journals of David Livingstone." *Academy* 7, no. 145, n.s. (February 13, 1875), 159–61.

Bontinck, François. "Le Diaire de Jacob Wainwright (4 Mai 1873 - 18 Fevrier 1874)." *Africa: Revista trimestrale di studi e documentazione dell' Ististuto Italo-Africano*, 32–33 (Settembre 1977–Dicembre 1978): 399–435; 603–4.

———. "La Mort de Livingstone Réexaminée." *Africa: Revista trimestrale di studi e documentazione dell' Ististuto Italo-Africano*. 33 (Dicembre 1978): 579–603.

Bradshaw, James. "Africa; A Paramount Necessity for the Future Prosperity of the leading Industries of England." *Journal of the Society of Arts* 27 (March 1879): 368–76.

Bridges, Roy C. "The Problem of Livingstone's Last Journey." In *David Livingstone and Africa*, 163–77. University of Edinburgh, 1973.

———. "The Sponsorship and Financing of Livingstone's Last Journey." *African Historical Studies* 1, no. 1 (1968): 79–104.

———. "W. D. Cooley, The RGS and African Geography in the Nineteenth Century." *Geographical Journal* 142 (March and July 1976): 27–47, 274–86.

British and Foreign Anti-Slavery Society. *Special Report of the Anti-Slavery Convention held in Paris . . . 26–27 August 1867*. London, 1869.

Brock, Sheila. "James Stewart and David Livingstone." In *Livingstone: Man of Africa*, edited by Bridglal Pachai, 86–110. London, 1973.

Burr-Litchfield, R. "The Family and the Mill: Cotton Mill Work, Family Work Patterns and Fertility in Mid-Victorian Stockport." In *The Victorian Family: Structure and Stresses*, edited by Anthony S. Wohl, 180–96. London, 1978.

Casada, James A. "British Exploration in East Africa: A Bibliography with commentary." *Africana Journal* 5, no. 3 (1974): 195–239.

———. "James A. Grant and the Introduction of Christianity in Uganda." *Journal of Church and State* 25, no. 3. (1983): 507–22.

———. "James A. Grant: Victorian Africanist." *The Historian* 39 (November 1977): 77–94.

———. "Verney Lovett Cameron: A Centenary Appreciation." *Geographical Journal* 141 no. 2 (July 1975): 203–15.

Cole-King, P. A. "Searching for Livingstone: E. D. Young and Others." In *Livingstone: Man of Africa*, edited by Bridglal Pachai, 152–74. London, 1973.

Collins, Robert O. "Origins of the Nile Struggle: Anglo-German Negotiations and the Mackinnon Agreement of 1890." In *Britain and Germany in Africa: Imperial Rivalry and Colonial Rule*, edited by Prosser
Gifford and Wm. Roger Louis, 119–52. New Haven and London,
1967.

———. "Samuel White Baker: Prospero in Purgatory." In *Africa and Its
Explorers*, edited by Robert I. Rotberg, 139–74. Cambridge, Mass.,
1970.

Cooper, Frederick. "The Problem of Slavery in African Studies." *Journal of African History* 20, no. 1 (1979): 103–25.

"Correspondence respecting Sir Bartle Frere's Mission to the East Coast
of Africa, 1872–1873." *Slave Trade 91: British Parliamentary Papers,
Reports, Correspondence, and Papers relating to Slavery and the
Abolition of the Slave Trade, 1861–74*. Shannon, 1971, 293–449.

Crawford, T. W. W. "Account of the Life of Matthew Wellington in His
Own Words, and of the Death of David Livingstone and the Journey
to the Coast." Part 2 of "David Livingstone: Two Accounts of His
Death and Transportation of His Body to the Coast." *Zambia Journal*
(formerly *Northern Rhodesia Journal*) 6 (1965): 99–102.

Currie, Donald. "Thoughts upon the Present and Future in South Africa,
and Central and Eastern Africa." *Proceedings of the Royal Commonwealth Institute* 8 (1877): 380–414.

[Dasent, G. W.] "The Heart of Africa and the Slave Trade." *Edinburgh
Review* 141 (January 1875): 209–42.

Ellegård, Alvar. "The Readership of the Periodical Press in Mid-
Victorian Britain: 2. Directory." *Victorian Periodicals Newsletter*, no.
13 (September 1971): 3–22.

Elston, Philip. "Livingstone and the Anglican Church." In *Livingstone:
Man of Africa*, edited by Bridglal Pachai, 61–85. London, 1973.

———. "A Note on the Universities' Mission to Central Africa:
1859–1914." In *The Early History of Malawi*, edited by Bridglal Pachai, 344–64. London, 1972.

Etherington, Norman. "Frederic Elton and the South African Factor in
the making of Britain's East African Empire." *Journal of Imperial and
Commonwealth History* 9, no. 3 (May 1981): 255–74.

Foot, C. E. "Transport and Trading Centers for East Equatorial Africa."
Journal of the Society of Arts 28 (1880): 362–69.

Gallagher, John. "Fowell Buxton and the New African Policy, 1838–
1842." *Cambridge Historical Journal* 10, no. 1 (1950): 36–58.

Gavin, R. J. "The Bartle Frere Mission to Zanzibar, 1873." *The Historical
Journal* 5, no. 2 (1962): 122–48.

Ghosh, R. N. "The Colonization Controversy: R. J. Wilmot-Horton and the Classical Economists." In *Great Britain and the Colonies 1815–1865*, edited by A. G. L. Shaw, 110–31. London, 1970.

Gluckman, Max. "As Men are Everywhere Else." *African Social Research: Journal of the Institute for Social Research, University of Zambia* (formerly *Rhodes-Livingstone Journal*) 20 (1956): 68–73.

Gorham, Deborah. "Victorian Reform as a Family Business: the Hill Family." In *The Victorian Family: Structure and Stresses*, edited by Anthony S. Wohl, 119–47. London, 1978.

Gray, Sir John. "Zanzibar and the Coastal Belt." In *History of East Africa*, vol. 1, edited by Roland Oliver and Gervase Mathew, 212–54. Oxford, 1963.

Gross, John. "Editor's Introduction." In John R. Seeley, *The Expansion of England*, xi–xxvii. Chicago and London, 1971.

Hammerton, A. James. "Feminism and Female Emigration, 1861–1886." In *A Widening Sphere*, edited by Martha Vicinus, 52–71. Bloomington and London, 1977.

Heanley, R. M. "In Memoriam. Horace Waller, Fell Asleep February 22, 1896, Aged 63." *Central Africa: A Monthly Record of the Work of the Universities' Mission to Central Africa* 14 (April 1896): 53–58.

Helly, Dorothy O. " 'Informed' Opinion on Tropical Africa in Great Britain, 1860–1890." *African Affairs* 68 (July 1969): 195–217.

Hunt, James. "On the Negro's Place in Nature." *Memoirs of the Anthropological Society of London* 1 (1863–1864): 1–64.

Hutchinson, Edward. "The Best Trade Route to the Lake Regions of Central Africa." *Journal of the Society of Arts* 25 (March 30, 1877): 430–504.

Jephson, A. J. Mounteney. *The Diary of A. J. Mounteney Jephson: Emin Pasha Relief Expedition, 1887–1889*, edited by Dorothy Middleton, in collaboration with Maurice Denham Jephson. Hakluyt Society, Extra Series, no. 40. Cambridge, 1969.

Johnson, Douglas H. "The Death of Gordon: A Victorian Myth." *Journal of Imperial and Commonwealth History* 10, no. 3 (May 1982): 285–310.

Klein, Martin A. "The Study of Slavery in Africa." *Journal of African History* 19, no. 4 (1978): 599–609.

"K." [Knox, George.] "A Rejoinder." *Church Missionary Intelligencer and Record* 12, n.s. (December 1887): 713–38.

Kopytoff, Igor, and Suzanne Miers. "African 'Slavery' as an Institution of Marginality." In *Slavery in Africa. Historical and Anthropological Perspectives*, edited by Suzanne Miers and Igor Kopytoff, 3–81. Madison, 1977.

"*The Last Journals of David Livingstone.*" *London Quarterly Review* 44 (April and July 1875): 34–61.

"Letter from a Native Lad." *Mission Life: A Magazine of Information about Church Missions and the Countries in Which They are Being Carried On* 1 (February 1, 1866): 26–30.

"Livingstone's 'Last Journals.' " *British Quarterly Review* 61 (January and April 1875): 395–420.

"Livingstone's *Last Journals.*" *Canadian Monthly and National Review* 7 (1875): 254–63.

"Livingstone's Last Journals." *Mission Life: An Illustrated Magazine of Home and Foreign Church Work* 6 n.s. (1875):241–85.

"Livingstone's Last Journals." *The Saturday Review*, vol. 38, no. 999 (December 19, 1874): 801–2.

"Livingstone's Last Journey." *Appleton's Journal* 13 (1875): 97–102, 129–34, 161–65, 193–97.

Louis, Wm. Roger. "The Berlin Congo Conference." In *France and Britain in Africa: Imperial Rivalry and Colonial Rule*, edited by Prosser Gifford and Wm. Roger Louis, 167–220. New Haven and London, 1971.

Low, D. Anthony, "British Public Opinion and 'The Uganda Question': October-December 1892." Chap. 2 in *Buganda in Modern History*. Berkeley and Los Angeles, 1971.

McMartin, A. "Sekeletu's Sugar Mill." *Geographical Journal* 139, no. 1 (February 1973): 96–103.

Macmillan, H. W. "Notes on the Origins of the Arab War." In *The Early History of Malawi*, edited by Bridglal Pachai, 263–82. London, 1972.

MacQueen, James. "Notes on the Geography of Central Africa from the Researches of Livingstone, Monteiro, Graça and Others." *Journal of the Royal Geographical Society* 26 (1856): 109–30.

Martel, Gordon. "Cabinet Politics and the African Partition: The Uganda Debate Reconsidered." *Journal of Imperial and Commonwealth History* 13, no. 1 (October 1984): 5–24.

Matson, A. T. "The Instructions Issued in 1876 and 1878 to the Pioneer C.M.S. Parties to Karagwe and Uganda." Parts 1–2. *Journal of Religion in Africa* 12–13 (1981–82): 192–237; 25–46.

Newbury, Colin W. "Victorians, Republicans, and the Partition of West Africa." *Journal of African History* 3 (1962): 493–501.

Newitt, M. D. D. "The Massingire Rising of 1884." *Journal of African History* 11, no. 1 (1970): 87–106.

Oliphant, Laurence. "African Explorers." *North American Review* 124 (1877): 383–403.

Oliver, Caroline. "Richard Burton: The African Years." In *Africa and Its Explorers*, edited by Robert I. Rotberg, 65–93. Cambridge, Mass., 1970.

[Owen, Richard.] "Last Journals of David Livingstone." *Quarterly Review* 138 (1875): 498–528.

Pachai, Bridglal. "The Zambesi Expedition 1858–1864: New Highways for Old." In *Livingstone: Man of Africa*, edited by Bridglal Pachai, 29–60. London, 1973.

Pridmore, Isobel, and Donald H. Simpson. "Faithful to the End." *Numismatic Circular* 78 (1970): 192–96.

Ranger, Terence. "European Attitudes and African Realities: The Rise and Fall of the Matola Chiefs of South-East Tanzania." *Journal of African History* 20, no. 1 (1979): 63–82.

Roberts, Andrew D. "Livingstone's Value to the Historians of African Societies." In *David Livingstone and Africa*, 49–67. University of Edinburgh, 1973.

Roberts, David. "The Paterfamilias of the Victorian Governing Classes." In *The Victorian Family: Structure and Stresses*, edited by Anthony S. Wohl, 59–81. London, 1978.

Robertson, Claire C., and Martin A. Klein. "Women's Importance in African Slave Systems." In *Women and Slavery in Africa*, edited by Claire C. Robertson and Martin A. Klein, 3–28. Madison and London, 1983.

Ross, Andrew C. "Livingstone and the Aftermath: The Origins and Development of the Blantyre Mission." In *Livingstone: Man of Africa* edited by Bridglal Pachai, 332–51. London, 1973.

Rotberg, Robert I. "Introduction." In *Africa and Its Explorers: Motives, Methods, and Impact*, edited by Robert I. Rotberg, 1–11. Cambridge, Mass., 1970.

———. "Joseph Thomson: Energy, Humanism, and Imperialism." In *Africa and Its Explorers: Motives, Methods, and Impact*, edited by Robert I. Rotberg, 295–320. Cambridge, Mass., 1970.

———. "Missionaries as Chiefs and Entrepreneurs: Northern Rhodesia, 1882–1924." In *Boston University Papers in African History*, vol. 1, edited by Jeffrey Butler, 195–216. Boston, 1964.

Shepperson, George. "Africa, the Victorians and Imperialism." In *Imperialism: The Robinson and Gallagher Controversy*, edited by Wm. Roger Louis, 162–72. New York and London, 1976.

———. "The Case of John Chilembwe in Malawi historiography." In *The Early History of Malawi*, edited by Bridglal Pachai, 405–28. London, 1972.

――――. "Livingstone and the Years of Preparation, 1813-1857." In *Livingstone: Man of Africa*, edited by Bridglal Pachai, 7-28. London, 1973.

Siddle, D. J. "David Livingstone: Mid-Victorian Field Scientist." In *David Livingstone and Africa*, 87-99. University of Edinburgh, 1973.

Simmons, Jack. "A Suppressed Passage in Livingstone's Last Journals Relating to the Death of Baron von der Decken." *Journal of the Royal African Society* 40, no. 161 (October 1941): 335-46.

Simpson, Donald H. "The Part taken by Africans in the European Exploration of East and Central Africa." In *The Exploration of Africa in the Eighteenth and Nineteenth Centuries*, 87-112. Proceedings of a Seminar held on the occasion of the Mungo Park Bi-Centenary Celebration at the Centre of African Studies, University of Edinburgh, December 3 and 4, 1971.

Smith, Alison. "The Southern Section of the Interior, 1840-84." In *History of East Africa*, vol. 1, edited by Roland Oliver and Gervase Mathew, 253-96. London, 1963.

Smith, F. Barry. "Sexuality in Britain, 1800-1900: Some Suggested Revisions." In *A Widening Sphere: Changing Roles of Victorian Women*, edited by Martha Vicinus, 182-98. Bloomington, 1977.

Smith, R. Bosworth. "Mohammedanism in Africa." *Nineteenth Century* 22 (December 1887): 791-816.

Stevenson, James. "The Arabs in Central Africa." *Manchester Geographical Journal* 4 (1888): 72-86.

Stokes, Eric "Imperialism and the Scramble for Africa: The New View." In *Imperialism: The Robinson and Gallagher Controversy*, edited by Wm. Roger Louis, 173-95. New York and London, 1976.

Taylor, Isaac. "The Church in Africa: Mohammedanism." In *The Official Report of the Church Congress held at Wolverhampton*, edited by the Reverend C. Dunkley, 326-29, 331. London, 1887.

――――. "The Great Missionary Failure." *Fortnightly Review* 44, n.s. (October 1888): 488-500.

――――. "Missionary Finance." *Fortnightly Review* 44, n.s. (November 1888): 581-92.

Thomas, H. B. "The Death of Dr Livingstone: Carus Farrar's Narrative." *Uganda Journal* 14 (1950): 115-28.

Thompson, Leonard. "Co-Operation and Conflict: The Zulu Kingdom and Natal." Chap. 8 in *The Oxford History of South Africa*, vol. 1: *South Africa to 1870*, edited by Monica Wilson and Leonard Thompson, 334-90. Oxford, 1969.

Thomson, Joseph. "Downing Street *versus* Chartered Companies in Africa." *Fortnightly Review* 46, n.s. (August 1889): 173-85.

———. "East Central Africa, and Its Commercial Outlook." *Scottish Geographical Magazine* 2 (1886): 65–78.

———. "Mohammedanism in Central Africa." *Contemporary Review* 50 (December 1886): 876–83.

———. "Niger and Central Sudan Sketches." *Scottish Geographical Magazine* 2 (September 1886): 577–96.

———. "Note on the African Tribes of the British Empire." *Journal of the Anthropological Institute* 16 (June 1886): 182–86.

———. "Sketch of a trip to Sokoto by the River Niger." *Journal of the Manchester Geographical Society* 2 (January 1886): 1–18.

Turton, E. R. "Kirk and the Egyptian Invasion of East Africa in 1875: A Reassessment." *Journal of African History* 11, no. 3 (1970): 355–70.

Visram, Rozina. "Livingstone and India." In *David Livingstone and Africa*, 143–58. University of Edinburgh, 1973.

Whymper, Edward, "Livingstone's Last Journals." *Leisure Hour: A Family Journal of Instruction and Recreation*, nos. 1208–9 (February 20 and 27, 1875): 124–28, 134–40.

Wright, Marcia. "Bwanikwa: Consciousness and Protest among Slave Women in Central Africa, 1886–1911." In *Women and Slavery in Africa*, edited by Claire C. Robertson and Martin A. Klein, 246–67. Madison and London, 1983.

———. "East Africa, 1870–1905." In *The Cambridge History of Africa*, edited by Roland Oliver and G. N. Sanderson, vol. 6, 539–91. Cambridge, 1985.

APPENDIX A

Articles, Papers, and Pamphlets by Horace Waller (1833-1896)

All works were published in London; unsigned articles are noted.

[The *Anti-Slavery Reporter* from 1867 to 1896 also regularly carried excerpts of remarks Waller made at special antislavery meetings, regular annual meetings (from 1870), and deputations to the Foreign Office, as well as short articles, reprints of his letters to *The Times* on antislavery subjects, reviews of his published pamphlets, and information supplied by him on British activities in East and Central Africa, including excerpts of letters written to him by travellers, missionaries, and Chuma and Susi.]

1865. "Scenes in an African slave preserve." *Macmillan's Magazine* 11 (April 1865): 426-435 (signed with F.R.G.S.).

1873. *Remarks on the Bilious Remittant Fever of Africa: Its Treatment and Precautions to Be Used in Dangerous Localities.* [4th ed. (1888)], 16 pp.

1875. "Livingstone's Discoveries in Connection with the Resources of East Africa." *Journal of the Society of Arts* 23:360-67

1876. *Paths into the Slave Preserves of East Africa: Being Some Notes on Two Recent Journeys to Nyassa-Land, Performed by Right Rev. Bishop Steere, of the Universities' Mission, and Mr. E. D. Young, R.N., Attached to the Scotch Missions.* One shilling.

1881. "Some Results of Fifty Years' Exploration in Africa." Delivered at the British Association for the Advancement of Science. *Proceedings of the Royal Geographical Society*, n.s., 3:687-91.

1885. "General Gordon's *Life* and *Letters*." *Contemporary Review* 159 (April): 450-79 (unsigned).

1887. *Trafficking in Liquor with Natives of Africa*, 35 pp.

1887. *The Title-Deeds to Nyassa-Land*, 37 pp.

1888. *On Some African Entanglements* (June 26), 8 pp.

1889. "The Universities' Mission to Central Africa." *Quarterly Review* 168 (January): 229-48 (unsigned).

1889. "The Two Ends of the Slave Stick." *The Contemporary Review* 55 (April): 528–38.

1890. *Nyassaland: Great Britain's Case Against Portugal*, 58 pp.

1891. *Ivory, Apes, and Peacocks: An African Contemplation*, 90 pp.

1892. "Side-Lights on Uganda." *Blackwood's Magazine* (July): 127–37.

1893. *Health Hints for Central Africa*, 57 pp.

1893. *Heligoland for Zanzibar*, 51 pp.

1893. "The Rise of Our East African Empire." *Blackwood's Magazine* 154 (December): 875–91 (unsigned).

1894. *Slaving and Slavery in our British Protectorates*, 8 pp.

1894. "The Slave Trade and Grievances of Native Races." Read before the Conference on Church Missions, London, May 30.

1896. *The Case of our Zanzibar Slaves: Why Not Liberate Them?* (January 27), 19 pp.

APPENDIX B

Letters to the Editor of *The Times* by Horace Waller, 1869–1896

[For their help in compiling and checking this list, I wish to acknowledge with gratitude the initial efforts of Rita Christopher and the more recent work of Daniel Grzywacz.]

DATE SIGNED	PLACE WRITTEN	DATE PUBLISHED	PAGE(S)
1. Jan. 19, 1869	St. John's Chatham [Kent]	Jan. 20, 1869	10
2. Feb. 2, 1870	Chatham	Feb. 3, 1870	5
3. Mar. 14, 1870	Chatham	Mar. 15, 1870	12
4. Dec. 4, 1871	The Vicarage, Leytonstone [Essex]	Dec. 7, 1871	4
5. May 20, 1872	Leytonstone	May 21, 1872	12
6. July 31, 1872	Leytonstone	Aug. 2, 1872	5
7. Christmas Day	Leytonstone	Dec. 27, 1872	5
8. n.d.	Leytonstone	Sept. 25, 1873	8
9. Feb. 11, 1874	Leytonstone	Feb. 12, 1874	5
10. Mar. 30, 1874	Leytonstone	Mar. 31, 1874	10
11. Apr. 9, 1874	Leytonstone	Apr. 10, 1874	10
12. Dec. 5, 1874	Savile-row	Dec. 7, 1874	6
13. Dec. 14, 1875	Twywell Rectory, near Thrapston [Northants]	Dec. 16, 1875	11
14. n.d.	Twywell	Nov. 18, 1876	10
15. n.d.	Twywell	May 30, 1877	10
16. n.d.	Twywell	Oct. 26, 1877	5
17. Feb. 11, 1879	Twywell	Feb. 13, 1879	10
18. Aug. 30, 1879	Twywell	Sept. 3, 1879	6
19. n.d.	Twywell	Mar. 27, 1880	7
20. July 3, 1880	Twywell	July 8, 1880	5
21. July 10, 1880	Twywell	July 15, 1880	5
22. Oct. 17, 1881	Twywell	Oct. 20, 1881	11

DATE SIGNED	PLACE WRITTEN	DATE PUBLISHED	PAGE(S)
23. n.d.	Twywell	Dec. 24, 1881	4
24. May 15, 1883	Twywell	May 17, 1883	17
25. n.d.	Twywell	Oct. 30, 1883	3–4
26. Nov. 14, 1883	Twywell	Nov. 15, 1883	8
27. n.d.	————	Feb. 2, 1884	8
28. Feb. 7, 1884	Twywell	Feb. 8, 1884	4
29. Mar. 18, 1884	Twywell	Mar. 20, 1884	6
30. May 24, 1884	Twywell	May 26, 1884	9
31. Sept. 12, 1884	Twywell	Sept. 15, 1884	6
32. Sept. 17, 1884	Twywell	Sept. 20, 1884	7
33. Nov. 26, 1884	Twywell	Nov. 28, 1884	3
34. May 22, 1885	Twywell	May 26, 1885	10
35. June 4, 1885	Twywell	June 11, 1885	8
36. Sept. 11, 1886	Twywell	Sept. 15, 1886	13
37. Jan. 4, 1887	Twywell	Jan. 7, 1887	7
38. Nov. 2, 1887	Twywell	Nov. 7, 1887	13
39. Mar. 29, 1888	Twywell	Apr. 4, 1888	3–4
40. Sept. 1, 1888	Twywell	Sept. 4, 1888	4
41. Sept. 15, 1888	Twywell	Sept. 17, 1888	8
42. Oct. 22, 1888	Twywell	Oct. 25, 1888	13
43. Nov. 1, 1888	Twywell	Nov. 5, 1888	10
44. Nov. 7, 1888	Twywell	Nov. 12, 1888	13
45. Nov. 20, 1888	Twywell	Nov. 27, 1888	11
46. Dec. 6, 1888	Twywell	Dec. 10, 1888	8
47. Feb. 14, 1889	Twywell	Feb. 19, 1889	14
48. n.d.	Twywell	Aug. 13, 1889	13–14
49. Oct. 7, 1889	Twywell	Oct. 10, 1889	3
50. Oct. 21, 1889	Twywell	Oct. 23, 1889	13
51. New Year's Day 1890	Twywell	Jan. 3, 1890	4
52. Jan. 9, 1890	Twywell	Jan. 10, 1890	10
53. Jan. 22, 1890	Twywell	Jan. 25, 1890	11
54. Apr. 11, 1890	————	Apr. 12, 1890	13
55. Apr. 14, 1890	Twywell	Apr. 16, 1890	6
56. May 17, 1890	Twywell	May 28, 1890	3
57. n.d.	Twywell	May 29, 1890	6
58. July 26, 1890	Twywell	July 29, 1890	13
59. Sept. 18, 1890	Twywell	Sept. 20, 1890	7
60. Sept. 20, 1891	Twywell	Sept. 22, 1891	5
61. Dec. 4, 1891	Twywell	Dec. 8, 1891	7
62. Dec. 26, 1891	Twywell	Jan. 2, 1892	14

DATE SIGNED	PLACE WRITTEN	DATE PUBLISHED	PAGE(S)
63. Jan. 30, 1892	Twywell	Feb. 1, 1892	7
64. n.d.	Twywell	Apr. 15, 1892	8
65. Apr. 20, 1892	Twywell	Apr. 25, 1892	10
66. Whit Monday	Twywell	June 8, 1892	5
67. Aug. 11, 1892	Twywell	Aug. 13, 1892	8
68. Aug. 26, 1892	Twywell	Aug. 29, 1892	8
69. Sept. 29, 1892	Twywell	Oct. 1, 1892	8
70. Nov. 12, 1892	Twywell	Nov. 14, 1892	10
71. Sept. 23, 1893	Twywell	Sept. 26, 1893	3
72. Sept. 30, 1893	Twywell	Oct. 3, 1893	5
73. Oct. 21, 1893	Twywell	Oct. 25, 1893	13
74. Dec. 9, 1893	Twywell	Dec. 26, 1893	12
75. Feb. 22, 1894	Twywell	Mar. 2, 1894	14
76. Mar. 8, 1894	Twywell	Mar. 9, 1894	4
77. July 30, 1894	Twywell	July 31, 1894	11
78. Aug. 21, 1894	Twywell	Aug. 23, 1894	6
79. Oct. 24, 1894	Twywell	Oct. 26, 1894	10
80. n.d.	Twywell	Feb. 22, 1895	3
81. Apr. 22, 1895	Twywell	Apr. 25, 1895	4
82. Sept. 28, 1895	East Liss [Hants.]	Sept. 30, 1895	7
83. Oct. 16, 1895	East Liss	Oct. 18, 1895	7
84. n.d.	East Liss	Jan. 4, 1896	13
85. Jan. 13, 1896	East Liss	Jan. 20, 1896	13

INDEX

(References to illustrations are *italicized*; relationships to central figures, based on family names, are noted in parentheses.)

and Livingstonia Mission (Malawi),
262–63
and Livingstonia Subcommittee,
229n.16, 269
and James Stewart, 259n.55, 262–63,
298n.12.
Mentioned: 9, 49, 297n.5, 323. *See also*
Wilson, Rev. John
Frere, Sir Henry Bartle Edward, *46*
and British antislavery, 45, 46, 151,
160n.35
and Zanzibar Treaty, 1873, 26,
46–47, 52, 55n.6, 62n.42,
100n.39, 151–52, 208, 327
and domestic slave labor, 299n.15
and freed slave settlements, 46, 151–52,
208–9, 251n.4
and UMCA Subcommittee on
Masasi, 285–87
as High Commissioner in South Africa,
287, 304n.32
and Leopold II, 306n.41
and David Livingstone, 45–46, 69, 113,
145, 151–52, 169
as president, RGS, 122, 131n.3
Freretown, 208–9, 284, 297n.5, 311n.57,
311n.64

Gallagher, John, 321
Gardner, Edward (Nasik man), 118, 165,
173–74, 178
Germans, in Africa: and Delimitation
Commission, 339n.3, 341n.6
East African sphere of influence, 322,
341n.6
Mentioned: 1, 273, 281, 310n.54,
318n.94, 321
Gladstone, William, 294, 321
and Gordon, 295, 302n.25, 318n.94,
319n.96, 320n.101
Glasgow, 8, 64, 235–36, 251n.8, 306n.41
Glasgow Herald, 345n.19
Gluckman, Max, 196–97
Gondokoro, Sudan, 21
Good Words, 346n.21
Gordon, Col. (later Gen.) Charles George:
and Baker, 275, 294, 296n.2, 302n.25,
317n.87, 318n.94
and East African commercial conces-
sion, 277, 291, 305n.36

insistence on a national flag, 289–91,
293
and John Kirk, 291–92, 314n.76,
316n.82
and Leopold II, 291–95, 315nn.78–80,
316n.82, 317nn.87, 90, 318n.93,
322
and William Mackinnon, 277, 279,
290–93
and Horace Waller, 91, 106n.69, 262,
273–80, 290–96, 296n.2, 316n.83,
317n.90
attraction to, nature of, 275–76,
306n.38
early chary opinion of, 297n.3
gave him Ismail's 1877 Anti-Slave
Trade Decree, 278, 308n.47
learned to take High Communion
from, 316–17n.84
made point to him of profits of
Equatoria, 305n.34
and Sudan, 279, 296, 301n.25, 302n.25,
307n.46
access from Zanzibar Coast, 275–76,
305n.36, 314n.76
evacuation of Khartoum, 294–96,
318n.94, 319n.96
as Governor General, 1877–79, 279,
290, 322
ivory trade and profits of, 275,
305n.34
and slave trade, 271, 274–75, 279,
294–95, 296–97n.3, 300n.17,
308n.47, 315n.78, 338
and sultan of Zanzibar, 291, 314n.76,
317n.90.
Mentioned: 261, 280, 316n.81, 319n.96,
323, 326, 338, 351, 354
Gordon, Henry (brother), 319n.98
Gordon, Mary Augusta (sister),
316–17n.84
Grandy, Lt. W. J., 85, 279
Grant, James A.: and Emin Pasha Relief
Expedition, 340n.5
and Uganda, 269, 301–2n.25.
Mentioned: 21, 59n.23, 67, 69, 145, 180,
213
Granville, 2d Earl of, 328–29. *See also*
Foreign Office, British, under Lord
Granville

INDEX

253n.19, 263
and freed slave settlements, 46, 70–71,
    98n.25, 151–52, 208–9,
    220–21n.31, 251n.4, 260n.56,
    284–89, *336*
and imperialism, 15, 29, 223, 271, 284
and Islam, 343–44n.16
and Livingstone's legacy, 223, 271, 281,
    283–87
in terms of the slave trade, 269, 284,
    345n.18
in terms of steamers on inland water-
    ways, 45, 244–45, 271–72, 274,
    253–54n.19, 298n.13, 303n.29,
    331
and Niger Expedition (1841–42), 229–30
and social reformers, 233, 254n.23.
Mentioned: 1, 12–13, 32, 152, 200, 232,
    250n.2, 331
*Missionary Travels and Researches in
    South Africa*, by David Livingstone
editorial review by Murray, 135–36n.30,
    149, 160n.31
sales record of, 55n.7, 195, 216–17n.2
cheap edition, with *Zambesi* book,
    195, 216–17n.2.
Mentioned: 2, 9, 28, 32, 45, 55n.7,
    103n.52, 132n.10, 142, 156n.11,
    158n.17, 161, 233–34, 248n.1
Mlozi, Chief, 346–47n.22
Moffat, Bessie (Roger Price's second
    wife), 139
Moffat, John S. (Livingstone's brother-in-
    law), 138–39, 155n.7
Moffat, Dr. Robert (Livingstone's father-
    in-law), 67, 68, 91, 98n.27, 139,
    221–22n.40
Moffat, Mrs. Robert (Livingstone's
    mother-in-law), 257n.42
Mohammed Malim, 65
Moir, Fred L., 266–67, 300n.17, 325,
    342n.10
Moir, Jane (wife of Fred), 266
Moir, John, 266–67, 299–300n.17,
    300–301n.20, 325
Morambala, Mount, 312n.65
Morrell, J. Conyers, 249n.2
Mombasa, 208–9, 231, 268, 335, 349n.34
Mozambique. *See* Portuguese in Africa: at
    Mozambique
Mponda, Chief, 149, 165

Mpundu tree (also "Mvula" tree), 115–18,
    134n.20
Mudie's lending library, 200, 202, 211
Muhammad bin Gharib ("Mohamad
    Bogharib"), 173, 178–79, 191n.40
Murchison, Sir Roderick, 22, 23, 182,
    159n.22, 192n.47, 218n.6, 234, 237,
    243–44
Murchison, Cataracts, Shire River, 240,
    244
Murphy, Lt. Cecil, 65, 67, 94n.6, 102n.48,
    115, 119, 121–22, 132n.13,
    134–35n.24, 199
Murray, John, III, 82, 271
and British geographical and humani-
    tarian circles,
and Sir Bartle Frere, 72, 152
and Edward Hutchinson (CMS),
    71–72, 98n.25, 98n.27
and Jacob Wainwright's diary,
    71–72
and William F. Webb, 72, 78
and James Young, 85
and *Last Journals*,
editorial decisions, 86–89, 91,
    104–5n.61, 107, 123
initial instructions to printer, 138,
    147
and Livingstone family,
    Agnes, 66, 79, 81, 79
    Janet, 90, 133n.15
    Tom, 69, 71–91
and related correspondents,
    W. Cotton Oswell, 81, 101n.44
    Henry M. Stanley, 72, 78, 100n.38
    and Horace Waller, 79–81, 83, 86–90
    and remarks concerning Camer-
        on, 104–5n.64
    and review in *Quarterly Review*, 199
Mutesa ("M'tesa"), Kabaka of Buganda,
    210, 269, 275, 301n.25
    and Gordon, 302n.25, 314n.76
Musa, 42, 102n.48, 187n.21
Mwanga, Kabaka of Buganda, 369
Mweru, Lake, 188n.24, 213

Napoleon III (Emperor of France), 2
Nasik ("Nassick") Asylum, near Bombay,
    190n.29
achievements, 97n.19
an issue in editing *Last Journals*, 152,

396 INDEX

188n.23, 234, 275, 296n.2,
316n.82, 332, 352n.53
Rutton, James (Nasik man), "a Nindi,"
136n.36, 165, 172, 190n.31

Sampson, Low, Marston & Co., 71,
97n.22, 100n.38
Salisbury, 3rd Marquess of, 339n.2. *See
also* Foreign Office, British, under
Lord Salisbury
Saturday Review, 198, 203
Scotland, 8-9, 37, 230, 242-43, 266,
298n.12, 306n.42, 309n.51.
Scott, Rev. David Clement, 283
Scott, Rev. Laurence, 329, 343n.10
Sedgwick, Adam, 240
Seeley, John R., 251n.4
Selborne, Earl of, lord chancellor, 341n.6
Sekeletu, Chief of the Kololo, 155n.8, 162,
234-35, 255n.34
Sewji, Jairam, 179-80, 192n.43
Sexual relations, African, 142-44, 242
and "Arab peril," 343n.10
passage on, changed by Tom Living-
stone, 143
and *purity*, concept of, 142-43,
157-58n.16.
See also Women: African
Sharanpur Christian Village, 208-9. *See
also* Nasik Asylum
Shire Highlands, 25, 31, 34-36, 38-39,
57n.15, 61n.25, 62n.41, 87, 102n.47,
118, 128, 133n.15, 149, 173, 181,
240-41, 243-44, 262, 266, 281, 284,
303n.26, 311n.57, 323, 325, 333-34
Shire River, 31, 37, 108, 240, 267, 342n.7
Simon. *See* Price, Simon
Slave Trade:
and African chiefs, 229, 231, 265, 274,
325, 327
and Yao, 35, 266-67, 274, 333-34
Atlantic, and British role in its suppression, 14, 227
British attitudes concerning, 8, 13-16,
26, 204, 212, 228, 231-32, 234,
241, 243, 249n.2, 261, 269, 271,
274, 313n.69, 321, 325, 328-31
and Thomas Fowell Buxton, 228-31
in the Congo, 292
and demand for human resources, 5, 6,

25, 265
predominance of women as slaves,
5, 6, 18n.11,
in East Africa, 1, 3-4, 13-16, 25-26, 31,
36, 42, 53, 148, 150, 179,
220-21n.31, 228, 231-32, 234,
241, 243, 271, 273-74, 306n.41,
309n.53, 321, 325, 331, 333-35
and Gordon's solution, 291
in Egypt and Sudan, 4, 18n.7
Anti-Slave Trade Decree of 1877,
278, 308n.47
and efforts of Gordon in Sudan, 271,
274-75, 279, 294-95,
296-97n.3, 300n.17, 308n.47,
315n.78, 338
Mahdist revolt and end of slave
supply to Egypt, 308n.47
and interference in,
by missionaries, 284, 269, 303n.26,
303n.29, 325
by an external power, 210, 265,
271-72, 274, 292, 308n.50, 321,
325, 328-31
and introduction of railways, 249n.2
and Cardinal Lavigerie, 327-29,
345nn.18-19
and David Livingstone, 26-27, 42, 44,
48, 52, 109, 112, 128-29, 239, 244,
247-48, 290, 313n.69
his colonization ideas, 233-35, 237,
239-45, 247-48
his record of, in words and drawings, 149, 212
his "open sore" metaphor, 28, 199,
211, 248, 334.
See also Antislavery; Arabs, and the
slave trade; British and Foreign
Anti-Slavery Society; Livingstone, David, and exposure of
the Central African slave trade;
Waller, Horace, an antislave
trade crusader; Zanzibar, and
slave trade
Slavery:
in Africa, 3-5, 16, 231, 234, 241, 243,
267
and free labor, 16, 231, 234, 241,
257n.40, 265-67, 299n.15,
313n.69

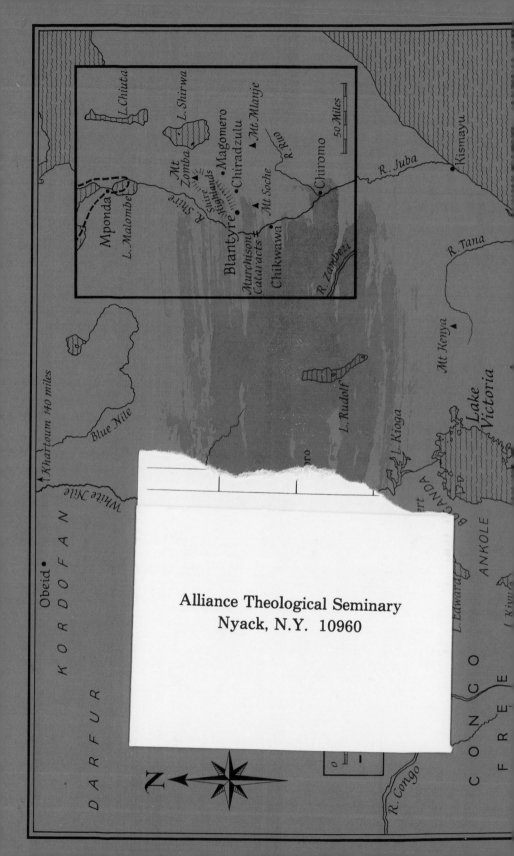